Engaging College Men:
Discovering What Works and Why

EDITED BY
GAR KELLOM AND MILES GROTH

MEN'S STUDIES PRESS
HARRIMAN, TENNESSEE
2010

Engaging College Men: Discovering What Works and Why
Edited by Gar Kellom and Miles Groth

All rights reserved. No part of this book may be reproduced or utilized in any form or by any means, electronic or mechanical, including photocopying, recording, or by any information or retrieval system without written permission from the publisher. For information, contact Men's Studies Press, PO Box 32, Harriman, Tennessee, 37748 USA.

Published by the Men's Studies Press, LLC, Harriman, Tennessee 37748 USA

Copyright © 2010 by Gar Kellom and Miles Groth.

James A. Doyle, Acquisitions editor
Ethan Wang, Cover photo
Diederik Janssen, Cover design and interior design editor

First Edition
ISBN: 978-1-931342-28-5 (paperback)
ISBN: 978-1-931342-29-2 (cloth)
ISBN: 978-1-931342-30-8 (e-book)

Library of Congress Cataloging-in-Publication Data

Engaging college men : discovering what works and why / edited by Gar Kellom and Miles Groth.
   p. cm.
 Includes bibliographical references and index.
  ISBN 978-1-931342-28-5 (pbk. : alk. paper) -- ISBN 978-1-931342-29-2 (cloth : alk. paper) -- ISBN 978-1-931342-30-8 (electronic)
 1. Male college students--Counseling of--United States. 2. Male college students--United States--Conduct of life. 3. Male college students--Vocational guidance--United States. I. Kellom, Gar E. II. Groth, Miles.
 LB2343.E57 2010
 378.1'9821--dc22
                        2010020195

CONTENTS

ACKNOWLEDGMENTS   5

PART I. INTRODUCTION

Chapter 1. INVOLVING MORE MEN IN VOCATIONAL DISCERNMENT ACTIVITIES: IDENTIFYING AND IMPLEMENTING BEST PRACTICES — *Gar Kellom*   8

Chapter 2. GENDER DISPARITY IN COLLEGE AND UNIVERSITY VOCATIONAL EXPLORATION PROGRAMS: THE EFFECT OF PROGRAMS TO ADDRESS THE DISPARITY — *Catherine Brooks*   24

PART II. REPORTS OF PROJECTS

Section A. Connecting to the Curriculum

Chapter 3. ADDRESSING MALE PARTICIPATION THROUGH THE ACADEMIC PROGRAM: THE HOPE COLLEGE EXPERIENCE — *David S. Cunningham*   39

Chapter 4. THE MOREHOUSE MALE INITIATIVE SEMINAR: PROVIDING A PATH TO VULNERABLE EXPRESSION, LEADERSHIP, AND CALLING — *Bryant T. Marks* and *Marquan Jones*   61

Chapter 5. ENGAGING MEN IN SERVICE: LESSONS FROM HASTINGS COLLEGE — *Ronald D. Chesbrough* and *Daniel G. Deffenbaugh*   74

Section B. Involving Men in Athletics and Fraternities

Chapter 6. MENTORING LUTHER COLLEGE MALE ATHLETES FOR REFLECTION AND DISCERNMENT — *Stu Johnston, Peter Wehr,* and *Jordan Grimm*   85

Chapter 7. BRINGING FRATERNITY BROTHERS AND ALUMNI TOGETHER AT AUGUSTANA COLLEGE — *Rebecca A. Poock*   98

Section C. Building New Programs

Chapter 8. ENGAGING SAINT JOHN'S COLLEGE MEN THROUGH INTERNATIONAL SERVICE AND RESEARCH — *Gar Kellom, Corbin Cleary, Alvin Thomas, Jessica Nelson, Ashleigh Leitch, Michael Wallace,* and *John Van Rooy*   107

Chapter 9. DEEP M-PACT: MENTORING GUSTAVUS MEN FOR MASCULINITIES OF MEANING AND MAKING A DIFFERENCE — *Christopher Johnson* and *Benjamin Hilding*   134

CONTENTS

Chapter 10. COLLEGE MEN AND THE HEROIC IMAGINATION: REFLECTIONS ON THE GUSTAVUS ADOLPHUS DEEP M-PACT PROJECT— *L.A. Parks Daloz*   146

Chapter 11. VOCATION AND THE PTEV INITIATIVE AT WABASH COLLEGE — *Anne Bost* and *Sonia Ninon*   158

Chapter 12. MICRO-GRANTS AND ADVENTURE TRAVEL: ENGAGING COLLEGE MEN IN VOCATIONAL DISCERNMENT AT GEORGETOWN COLLEGE — *Bryan Langlands* and *Coran Stewart*   170

Chapter 13. ROAD-TRIPPING: THE MALE INITIATIVE PROJECT AT DAVIDSON COLLEGE — *Karen Martin*   183

Section D. Forming Men's Groups

Chapter 14. THE LEAGUE OF EXTRAORDINARY GENTLEMEN AT THE UNIVERSITY OF PORTLAND — *Josh Noem, Thomas Bruketta,* and *Jamie Grimm*   195

Chapter 15. THE SIENA COLLEGE MEN'S SPIRITUALITY GROUPS — *Merle Longwood*   208

Chapter 16. MEN TALKING: THE "CORE FOUR" AND MORE. THE WAGNER COLLEGE PROJECT — *Miles Groth, William Jock, Andrew Hager,* and *Kyle Glover*   217

Chapter 17. WHAT MEN WANT AT DUKE UNIVERSITY: AN ADVENTURE TO SHARE – AN ACCOMPLISHMENT TO ENJOY — *Keith Daniel* and *Jesse Huddleston*   227

Chapter 18. MALE COMMITMENT TO GENDER EQUITY AND ANTIVIOLENCE: A NATIONAL COLLEGE STUDY — *Ed Heisler* and *Michael Firmin*   236

PART III. FINDING NEW DIRECTIONS

Chapter 19. VOCATION, GENDER AND YOUTH MINISTRY: THE YOUTH TRACK — *Jeff Kaster*   251

PART IV. BEST PRACTICES FOR WORKING WITH COLLEGE MEN

Chapter 20. SOME FINAL THOUGHTS — *Gar Kellom*   266

PARTICIPATING SCHOOLS   283

FURTHER READINGS   284

APPENDICES   285

INDEX   290-294

Acknowledgements

There is no more important person for this project, especially in the development of international service trips, than my partner for 35 years, Kolleen Kellom. Her collaboration in the understanding of gender and her role as a leader of women at the College of Saint Benedict provides inspiration and insight daily. This project was originally developed in careful consultation with Chris Coble of the Lilly Endowment (and a graduate of a men's college) who suggested many of the early participants and how to approach the topic. In many ways this was his vision. Brother Dietrich Reinhart also saw the importance of this project and the contribution it could make through the Center for Men's Leadership and Service we developed together. It still grieves me that he did not live to carry out the plans we had for Saint John's to make to men's education in America.

The real inspiration and ground breaking work has been done by the pilot project leaders who have guided over a dozen experiments to increase men's involvement and author the chapters that are the heart of this volume. Together with the key student leaders many of them helped design the original proposal, shared their work and insights at the national conferences and synthesized what we were learning into the final chapter. Those collaborations continue as a network of colleges working together to understand how to enhance the learning of college men.

Key insights through the research and theory team were also provided by Bill Mathias (one of my first colleagues) and many colleagues in the American Men's Studies Association (Steve Boyd, Mark Justad, Robert Heasley, Jim Doyle, Whitney Harris, and Steve Hoover, to mention a few). Tonya Miller was tremendous in her logistical support of the conferences, the Men's Center and the grant administration as well as coordinating so many student contributors like Ghaith Hijazin, Meera Mansingh, Brett Saladin, Grant Wollenhaupt, Ethan Wang, Mike Wallace, Corbin Cleary, and many others. Original conceptualization of the project in Tibet and India and initial interviews in 2008 were done by Meagan Kellom and Kolleen Kellom. Interviews in 2009 were done by Michael Arnold, Jay Ranfranz, Patrick Sitzer, Nicholas Smith, Jacob Hvidson, Ethan Wang, Benjamin Hansberry, Kevin Crane, Ryan Crane, Ryan Millis, Michael Radtke, John Van Rooy (in the cover photo), Matthew C. Johnson and Benjamin Briese. Father Mark Thamert, a Saint John's University professor and monk from the Saint John's Abbey was invaluable in organizing this group. Brother Aaron Raverty consulted on the project and very special assistance came from Iris Cornelius and her granddaughter Kayla. Iris was instrumental in the AMES volunteer project, supporting the men's center and helped organize the Caribbean Project with student leaders

ACKNOWLEDGMENTS

Cheval Morrison, Kevin May, Mark Osborne and Corbin Cleary. Other researchers and contributors were Sarah Skolte and Father Asante Jude. Terry Franke, Rich Agness, Bob Metcalf, Tom Vyskocil and the men of Lawrence University's Delta Tau Delta have proven that what we have learned here can be successfully applied in fraternities.

Miles Groth, my steady editorial colleague and Jim Doyle, have kept this project on track and, if it were not for them, this would not be in print.

PART I.
INTRODUCTION

1

INVOLVING MORE MEN IN VOCATIONAL DISCERNMENT ACTIVITIES:
IDENTIFYING AND IMPLEMENTING BEST PRACTICES

GAR KELLOM

THE NEED

At a conference in Indianapolis in 2006, sponsored by the Lilly Endowment for 88 colleges and universities participating in its Programs for the Theological Exploration of Vocation (PTEV), schools reported on their activities to foster college students' examination of the relationship between their faith and their vocational choice. Many creative and successful programs were described, and successes were celebrated. During the meeting, one haunting question emerged that did not seem to get a satisfactory answer: Was there a significant gender imbalance between the participation of college men and women in the PTEV activities?

Preliminary investigation of a small group of PTEV schools indicated that there were consistently more women than men involved, a fact that could not be explained by the official gender balance of each school. For example, Davidson College, which maintains a 50/50 gender balance in its student body, had an imbalance in its programs, ranging from a high of 40% to only 10% men participating in some of its programs. Duke University reported that it had more of a challenge attracting men into its Pathways Program despite an overall gender balance of 50/50 each year at the university. Their vocational discernment groups have a history of involving more women than men: 45% women and 15% men in 2005–2006 and 32% women and 18% men in 2006–2007.

Luther College reported "a pattern of disproportionate male enrollment" in its vocational discernment programs, ranging from 23–35% men despite a college gender balance of 58% women and 42% men. Furman University had participation in their discernment grant program of only 20% men with an institutional gender balance of 55% women and 45% men. Hope College's student body was 40% male, but enrollment in their pre-seminary program was 30%. Their multicultural ministry program had no men at all, and most of the other programs included no more than 20% men. The Georgetown College gender balance was 61% women and 39% men, but the male participation in their programs was even more imbalanced, with the percentage of men taking part in retreats falling in the last 2 years from 22 to 12%.

Our suspicion was that this was not an anomaly in PTEV programs but part of a larger pattern of lagging male enrollment in many types of programs in higher education. For example, a recent Corporation for National and Community Service study says that 32% of women volunteer compared to 25% of men, and in all

50 states, women volunteer more than men in each state. According to Campus Compact Annual Service Statistics, of the students who participate in service-learning on college campuses, 35% are men. The latest Higher Education Research Institute study (Astin & Astin, 2003) on college student spirituality indicates strong interest among students but greater interest among women than men. We also looked briefly at younger age groups and the involvement of boys in the high school programs sponsored by the Lilly Endowment. We did not have conclusive data, but preliminary conversations indicated there were more girls than boys involved in those programs as well.

We proposed to the Lilly Endowment that this may be one of the pieces of unfinished business left for PTEV schools: how to involve more boys and men in theological exploration of vocation both inside and outside the classroom. While there is growing awareness of this trend in higher education, there were no coordinated programs to look at the issue of men's involvement in these programs or attempts to address it. The preliminary talks we held also revealed that several schools were keenly interested in addressing this topic if a coordinated effort could be organized. What was needed was a broader examination of participation rates by gender to include the youth programs and an exploration of how these participation patterns might be having an impact on college programs in general.

What to Do About It

We proposed a program to help us better understand the ratio of women and men in PTEV programs and how to address the imbalance of males. The program would also have a track to help better understand the trends in boys' involvement in high school programs that might be contributing to college men's participation rates. We sought to identify the best practices to get more boys and men involved in these programs, both broadly in activities such as volunteerism or service learning and specifically in programs of preparation for pastoral leadership. Finally, we hoped to develop a conceptual model that would help explain what was happening with men's involvement and how to increase it and to provide that model to all interested PTEV schools and any other schools that wanted to design programs for enrolling more men.

We wanted first to cast a wide net by studying the participation data of the 88 PTEV programs to identify what patterns existed and to ask the schools to identify any best practices for involving more men. In February 2008 we convened those schools that had already realized there was a problem, had begun to describe it, and were considering how to address it. By gathering those schools together to look at the data, we expected that a clearer picture would emerge of what the patterns were. A clearer picture of the highs and lows of male participation would set the context for designing pilot projects to identify some best practices for improving men's participation.

We identified a core group of colleges and universities and began talking with them about their experiences. In some cases there had been specific attempts to address the imbalance and some encouraging successes that might be replicable on other campuses. However, one of the first steps in the proposed program was an identification of other PTEV schools that we were not aware of that were working on the issue of gender imbalance. We also began talks with leaders of some of the high school programs and found a keen interest in getting together for a think tank on gender and vocation among high school programs.

With emerging interest nationally in the general topic of men's enrollment (especially in liberal arts colleges and religiously affiliated colleges) and their academic success and retention as well as their engagement in experiential learning activities and programs (such as alternative spring break trips, volunteering, study abroad, internships, campus ministry programs, health education, and campaigns to end violence), the Men's Studies Press offered to publish the results of this program. The press recognized the value of the program as a contribution to understanding the larger pattern of gender imbalance in student engagement. We also planned to get some of this information out in key publications available to higher education and church leaders as soon as it was conclusive.

THE SAINT JOHN'S CENTER FOR MEN'S LEADERSHIP AND SERVICE AND INVOLVING MEN'S COLLEGES

The Center for Men's Leadership and Service (the Center) at Saint John's University was the ideal place to begin the program because it had been established to enhance the leadership preparation of college men and involve them in leadership activities that help them discover who they are as men, what their gifts and talents are, and how best to use those gifts for the common good. As the first men's center on a liberal arts campus, its conferences and programs were already providing a focal point for convening those interested in discussions about college men. The Center's work has been described by men's studies scholars, such as Chris Kilmartin of Mary Washington University, as "doing more programs for college men and doing them better."

One example of the Center's work was an ongoing project called Men's Spirituality Groups. For the past 10 years, over 200 college men and 30 adult mentors have participated in theological exploration of vocation in groups that meet every few weeks for the entire 4 years that students are enrolled. The groups have been highly successful and have been studied by experts in religious studies with the results published in a chapter entitled "Men, Spirituality and the College Experience" (Longwood, Muesse, & Schipper, 2004). This concept, which was unique in its involvement of college men, inspired women's spirituality groups called Companions on a Journey that are now funded in a PTEV grant at the College of Saint Benedict.

Another successful initiative of the Center has been exploring ways to increase the number of men involved in service projects. By initiating projects with male students and staff leaders to travel to sites such as Uganda, Trinidad and Tobago, the Bahamas, Peru, Israel, India, Tibet, and many states of the United States, the number of men enrolled in service projects has increased dramatically while the programs are still made available to women at the College of Saint Benedict. In many cases a gender balance has been achieved. A student-faculty research project was also underway to determine how best to involve men in service projects. This pilot project was presented at the Fourth Annual Conference on the College Male and at the American Men's Studies Association annual meeting in 2009 at Concordia University in Montréal and was preparing for a new phase of data collection. The Center at Saint John's has thus served as a home for these discussions through its annual conferences and use of its resources to connect interested schools.

The Center also provided a unique opportunity to convene three of the men's colleges (Wabash, Morehouse, and Saint John's) in a program to examine different ways that they encouraged college men to identify their calling. Men's colleges are a very interesting laboratory to help us understand what is going on with college men in general and what works in their vocational discernment activities. Although only a handful of men's colleges remain in the country (a topic itself worth further elaborating), three of them are actively involved in articulating what the ideal educational environment is for college men. Wabash College, has consistently shown great success in the preparation of men for the ministry. High numbers of men volunteer in service projects there. Preliminary discussions with William Placher (Chair of the College's Religion Department) indicated that the environment at Wabash may have established norms for its male students to participate in these activities.

Morehouse College was also engaged in the process of articulating the uniqueness of its all-male college environment for its students. Having received a $1 million grant from the Mellon Foundation to address the issues of African-American men in higher education, Morehouse is eager to pursue research to articulate what it means to be a "Morehouse Man." The college was identifying 20 indicators (including leadership, service, spirituality, and character development) that it hoped would clearly explain how men develop while on campus. The new president of Morehouse, Dr. Robert Michael Franklin, is a minister who has said he wants to intentionally enhance the moral development and spiritual life of the Morehouse Man.

We speculated that getting Morehouse together with Wabash and Saint John's to explore how the three schools intentionally enhance men's moral and spiritual development might make a valuable contribution to the grant process and certainly stimulate thinking on the part of other schools.

Men's colleges can be examined for the environment they have fostered that makes spiritual reflection, vocational discernment, and religious practice more normative. Preliminary studies done at three campuses indicated that a special social norm has been established that encourages spiritual reflection, participation in religious activities, and discernment opportunities. In an age when women's roles are changing so rapidly and women have more and more opportunities to undertake roles that have not been traditionally available to them, college men may need to redefine what it means for them to be men. Kilmartin (2000) says that a redefinition of the one traditional masculinity into multiple masculinities more attuned to the uniqueness of each young man is needed.

Taking an Interdisciplinary Approach

At its core, involving more males of any age in examining the relationship between their faith development and their choice of what to do with their lives is a theological matter. To better understand males' involvement in this process and what to do to improve it, we proposed to first look at the issue through the lens of theology. To see it more clearly also required other perspectives, such as those of psychology, myth and ritual, modern church history, sociology, and gender theory. Our goal was to identify scholars from these diverse disciplines who had knowledge of men's religious and spiritual development in order to help us better understand the issues.

One key outcome was to construct a conceptual model of what we thought was going on with male involvement in discernment programs and how to understand it. This understanding would lead us to predict with more certainty the types of activities that will be successful in attracting more male participation, increasing retention in these programs, and ultimately seeing men take leadership roles in the church and society. The goal may be to help each boy or college man to find his true self and to answer the questions: Who am I? What is my core purpose? What is my passion? What do I do about it? What does the world need from me?

The study of spirituality groups (funded by PTEV) showed that they enhance the ability of participants to understand who they are as men through a process of telling their confidential stories in safe places. Such enhanced self-understanding is reflected in deeper and satisfying relationships within the groups ("I am closer to the group members than to my friends") and enhanced relationships with significant others outside the groups. Members developed a greater sense of spirituality and connection to God, the universe, and others. In the later years of our 4-year program, there emerged a more sophisticated understanding of what vocation means to the participants in terms of improved life skills of listening, sharing, reflection, and confidence. Even though not all men had decided on their true calling, their vocational priorities had been refined in the process.

Involving theologians, sociologists, and psychologists helped us construct a more durable conceptual model and framework for understanding the reality of what might be going on with college men, but it also helped us explain what is working to increase men's involvement and why and what is not working and why. A pool of scholarly resources already existed on many PTEV campuses that contributed to addressing this issue. These schools shared their insights into better understanding college men's decision-making processes in general.

To enrich the discussion of theological reflection and the men's college perspective, we added the dimensions of men's socialization and psychological development. From a psychological perspective, for example, some critical clarity has been emerging on the importance of college men achieving a deeper emotional connection with each other. This clarity may be one component of a successful discernment program because it meets a deeper need that these men have in their maturation process. It can perhaps be facilitated by activities where men have safe places to open up with each other—activities including participating in gender-specific discernment groups where safety, confidentiality, and trust develop.

Also important psychologically to college men is the affirmation from adult men who are role models for them and can verify that spiritual activities have worth and that young men themselves have worth, skills, and abilities (that are needed in our time) to contribute to the church and society. The inclusion of mentors and skilled leaders and the need of young men for the affirmation from adult men cannot be ignored in the design of successful programs. As the reader will find in the following chapters, the critical role that student leaders play in the involvement of young men in these activities has been another consistent theme in the reports of schools that participated in the program.

Psychologists who have been studying college men's physical and mental health consistently find that men's life expectancy is seven years less in the United States (14 years less in Eastern Europe) and that three out of four college-age suicides in the United States are men. Courtenay (2002) has written extensively about college men's physical and mental health from a gender and ethnic perspective. In a very real sense, the study of college men and their participation in programs and services designed for them is about saving men's lives. Stuart Johnston at Luther College (among others) is passionate about how to successfully counsel boys and men and explored this approach in a project that would be more intentional about connecting men to counseling centers, academic advising, career centers, and their PTEV project (see Chapter 6, page 85).

ESTABLISHING A RESEARCH AND THEORY TEAM

To take an interdisciplinary approach and gain access to some of the best thinking on the topic as well as to guide the program's first steps, a research and theory team was formed and included the following:

- Melissa Wiginton, from the Fund for Theological Education, Atlanta, Georgia. She had been seriously interested in this topic because the schools she works with consistently reported an underrepresentation of men in their programs and fellowships.
- Bryant T. Marks, from Morehouse College, Atlanta, Georgia, the leader of the Morehouse Male Initiative project.

- Gary Phillips, Dean of the College, and Charles Blaich, Director of Inquiries at the Center for Inquiry, at Wabash College. As noted above, an added benefit of their membership on the team was that it brought together Wabash College, Saint John's, and Morehouse College for a comparison of what all-men's colleges do to enhance the education of their students.
- Mark Justad, Guilford College, was a former president of the American Men's Studies Association and served as a consultant for this study and helped devise a conceptual model to help explain current patterns and suggest why some solutions might work better than others.
- Merle Longwood, Professor of Religious Studies at Siena College. He specializes in men and religion and offered his school as a potential pilot project site to replicate men's spirituality and discernment groups. His research has also led to a forthcoming publication (Longwood & Schipper).
- David S. Cunningham, Professor of Religion at Hope College, Director of the CrossRoads Project, and Chair of the Christianity and Academia Consultation for the American Academy of Religion. In his work as a Christian theologian and ethicist exploring a number of questions of gender, sex, and sexuality, he contributed to the team concerning these issues.
- Gar Kellom, Program Director and Chair of the Center for Men's Leadership and Service at Saint John's College in Collegeville, Minnesota.

The responsibilities of the Research and Theory Team were to:

- design a survey or work with a firm to design a survey;
- collect data on male participation in PTEV schools;
- analyze the data and prepare presentations of the data for the annual conferences at Saint John's;
- develop a research agenda and award research grants to continue research;
- invite experts to the annual conferences;
- provide publication incentives and make offers to authors;
- create a theoretical model and present and publish it;
- identify and communicate best practices;
- analyze data for evaluation and ongoing assessment of the program's work; and
- determine future directions of the program.

Faculty-Student-Expert Partnerships and Pilot Schools

To bring about change in male participation, we proposed a three-way partnership among students, faculty and administration, and outside experts. This was considered to be a combination of a top-down, bottom-up, and outside-in approach, where all worked together to increase male engagement in vocational discernment, leading to greater male involvement in leadership roles in the church and in volunteer activities.

A metaphor for this process was that of a hothouse where many seeds are planted in fertile soil, germinate, and begin the growth process. The environment is carefully nurtured by the gardener who provides ample water, sunlight, and the conditions deemed to be most conducive to growth gleaned from experience. The three-way partnership of male student involvement (the seeds we seek to nurture), faculty and staff experts from the current PTEV programs, and the expertise and resources from the Endowment joined with higher education expertise from all disciplines (all sources of energy and leadership) to enhance the success of our program.

We proposed from the outset that there would be significant student involvement in each college's project, including the hiring of at least one student from each school to be involved in the project throughout. An influential student who knows the campus culture and has the relationships and respect of fellow students can often have the greatest impact on involvement. We also proposed including a motivated faculty or staff member (often the current director of the PTEV program and the lead person on the campus) as a second partner focused on the college's project. These two members would form a team on each campus. The teams were brought into contact with the third partners, experts in the field—including the Religion Division of the Lilly Endowment—who added insights, expertise, resources, and inspiration to involve college men.

Faculty-student pairs from 14 PTEV colleges and universities formed a research community where best ideas and practices were identified and tried out in conditions designed to enhance the success of the projects. At the annual conferences we attracted some of the best minds on male involvement and asked them to focus their expertise on the issue of PTEV involvement and share in dialogue with all other teams to design pilot projects that would germinate on each campus. After the first joint conference, participants tried their projects and returned to a second gathering to share the results midway through the projects with each other and with outside experts to allow for any adjustments in the growth process by making changes and improvements in the projects.

The following pilot schools and their leaders volunteered to participate in this program and agreed to become actively engaged in collecting data, understanding and using the data to plan pilot projects, and initiating new approaches on their campuses to increase men's participation:

- Davidson College: Tim Beach-Verhey, PTEV Program Director;
- Duke University: Reverend Keith Daniel, Campus Ministry Office;
- Luther College: Stuart Johnston, Licensed Mental Health Counselor;
- Hope College: Professor David S. Cunningham;
- Georgetown College: Roger Ward, Coordinator of the Meetinghouse Project, who turned it over to Bryan Langlands of Campus Ministry;
- Wabash College: Charles Blaich, who turned it over to Anne Bost and Sonia Ninon, research fellows at the Center for Inquiry in the Liberal Arts;

- Morehouse College: Professor Bryant T. Marks, Psychology Department;
- Saint John's University: Gar Kellom, Director, the Center for Men's Leadership and Service;
- Hastings College: Professor Daniel Deffenbaugh, Department of Religion, and Ronald Chesbrough, Vice President for Student Affairs;
- Siena College: Professor Merle Longwood, Religion Department;
- University of Portland: Josh Noem, Assistant Director for Faith Formation in the Office of Campus Ministry;
- Wagner College: Professor Miles Groth, Psychology Department;
- Augustana College: Professor Robert Haak, who turned it over to Rebecca A. Poock, Community Engagement Coordinator; and
- Gustavus Adolphus College: Chris Johnson, Director of the Center for Vocational Reflection.

PROGRAM ACTIVITY

PHASE ONE—RESEARCHING CURRENT MALE INVOLVEMENT

The first step in this phase of the program was to get a more accurate picture of the involvement of women and men in the 88 programs funded by the Lilly Endowment. We developed and administered an online survey with the help of Brooks Research and sent it to project directors and key staff people on the campuses. This was to give us a more accurate picture of involvement in PTEV programs by gender and establish if indeed there were more women than men involved and if there were consistent patterns to that involvement.

The survey was also to discover successful approaches for working with men that had been tried on any of the campuses and identify possible characteristics of their campuses that might have contributed to increased participation. We also sought to discover other thinking that might be going on to help explain participation imbalances or best practices.

These data were analyzed for patterns of what had been successful in attracting men to these programs, what inhibited their participation, and what could be done differently to increase their participation in vocational discernment programs and in the actual process of theological reflection on vocation as a continuing part of campus life.

As a further step in the data-collection process, a formal presentation of the data was prepared for the initial meeting of the schools and pilot project leaders at Saint John's University so that schools could participate in the analysis and interpretation of the preliminary findings. This provided an opportunity not only to look at the results of the survey and the focus groups but also to get responses from the participating schools that might enrich the interpretation of the data.

Data collection for the Youth Track, a part of our study to be devoted to high school male involvement, also began in advance of the first meeting as the facilitator, Jeffrey Kaster, contacted schools that were interested and invited them to a separate conference. He asked leaders to bring data they had on the participation of boys in their high school programs. We were especially interested in what might be working as well as what some obstacles might be with that age group of males.

PHASE TWO: SHARING DATA WITH PILOT SCHOOLS AND CHOOSING PILOT PROJECTS

The second phase of the program was to convene the pilot schools for the first time and share with them the data about male participation rates, the good ideas already underway, and preliminary thinking about what was working and why. We knew schools had tried various approaches that had achieved success. Men's spirituality groups, international service projects, and the use of key male student paraprofessionals in leadership roles in the grants are examples of approaches that were already working. While some of these ideas still needed refining on the campuses where they had been initiated, they could be tried on other campuses to see if they would work in those environments.

A pair of participants was invited from each of the schools already chosen for the program due to their initial interest. So one faculty or staff person and one student participant were invited to the February 2008 Conference on the College Male at Saint John's University, where the Center for Men's Leadership and Service made the program the focus of its annual meeting. Any other schools who participated in the data collection were also invited to participate and apply to join the program. The last three schools named above (i.e., Wagner, Augustana, and Gustavus Adolphus) were chosen from the competition at the conference.

The 2008 conference was an opportunity to share the results of the data collection phase with participants. Formal presentation of the data by Brooks Research and the Research Team (see Chapter 2 for the Brooks data) showed the full picture of PTEV participation by gender in the 88 programs and any patterns that might have emerged. The first day was dedicated to understanding the data and the patterns that seemed to be occurring with respect to men's participation in vocational discernment activities, and the second day was dedicated to planning and preparation of the schools for their pilot projects.

Speakers were invited to address both the data and the patterns that had emerged as well as the specific programs that had been successful involving boys and men. Student participants were asked to share their experiences and perceptions of the programs that worked to increase male involvement. Melissa Wiginton of the Fund for Theological Education, who strongly encouraged the student-centered approach, organized a panel of pastors to reflect on their own youth and college experiences and what had affected them positively in their decisions to enter the ministry.

The sessions stimulated further brainstorming. Ultimately, each of the 14 participating schools chose a pilot project and committed to pursue it in the coming year. Before leaving the conference, each school created a work plan for the next phase. This was the beginning of interactions and relationships we hoped to sustain for the coming years.

This phase was designed for schools to share possible projects with each other and determine which project was to be attempted at each campus. Discussions focused on what was working to enhance men's participation and on what the students were learning. It was essential that each project include ways for participants to reflect on their faith formation and how it might be having an impact on their vocational choices.

The method we used to establish pilot projects on each college campus created a process of continuous feedback and conversations among the participating schools to share what worked (and what did not work) to engage men. As projects were improved and refined, best practices that were the most successful began to emerge, allowing for replication and transference to the other schools to affect their participation rates.

The Youth Track: Convening a Think Tank

Meanwhile, another track of investigation was forming. What do the directors of Lilly-funded Theological Programs for High School Youth know about the impact of gender on their efforts to promote vocations? Why are the registration and participation of males typically lower than those of females? What gender disparities exist in the recruitment and outcomes associated with these programs? What particular assumptions about teenage males are shared among youth program directors? What, if anything, has been written about this? What can be learned about the impact of gender on vocation formation when evaluation data from these programs are analyzed through the lens of gender? What interventions might program directors design to address male program participation?

These questions not only intrigued Jeffrey Kaster, Director of the Youth in Theology and Ministry Program of Saint John's University's School of Theology, and Fred Edie, faculty director, and Katherine Hande of the Duke Youth Academy, Duke Divinity School but also motivated them to agree to collaboratively coordinate a think tank on the impact of gender on vocation, spirituality, and theological inquiry among high school age youth. These three people also readily admitted to a lack of familiarity with literature associated with gender as it relates to teen spirituality and vocation. They thought that if the three of them were interested in this, then it was likely that other directors of Lilly-funded theological programs for high school youth would be interested too. The think tank on adolescent gender, vocation, and spirituality sought to gather 10 directors of theological programs for high school youth to discuss these questions as they relate to teenage males.

The goals of the think tank on vocation and gender were to:

- become knowledgeable about gender theory and its impact on vocation among males;
- share assumptions and hunches about gender's impact on vocation, spirituality, and theological inquiry in high school youth;
- analyze and compile program data through the lens of gender;
- articulate common assumptions and understand the basis of the impact of gender on vocation among high school youth;
- sponsor interventions by program directors that were designed to address male program participation, with the results to be reported at the final gathering; and
- sponsor the publication of case studies or articles associated with the goals listed above.

All the directors or key leaders of Lilly Endowment-funded Theological Programs for High School Youth were invited to participate. Funding for travel and a stipend for participation were provided for 10 directors or key leaders. Their strategy was to gather in November 2007 for a meeting to set the agenda, choose the pre-reading, and develop homework for the think tank meeting to be held in February 2008. For the think tank's initial gathering at the 2008 Conference on the College Male, the agenda included discussing of the literature on boys and youth that might serve as background for the project, sharing assumptions and hypotheses about what might be happening with gender patterns of participation in youth programs, exchanging program data, working out common assumptions and a common foundation for affecting gender balance in vocational discernment programs for high school youth, and outlining the parameters for papers to be commissioned.

The think tank's second gathering was in February 2009 at the conference for the pilot schools. Results of male participation interventions by program directors were shared and the commissioned papers were presented and discussed. An agenda for further research was proposed. With some college pilot schools such as Duke University and Saint John's also having high school programs, the Youth Track added a richness and breadth of age range to the discussions and exploration. To have the dialogues between the two programs—both at the individual schools and conference levels—improved our understanding of the broader issue of male involvement in vocational and ministerial discernment. Readings of key authors, such as Smith and Denton (2005), on youth topics added to the breadth of investigation.

The conference meetings were also an attempt to come together to try to understand the roots of the issues of college men's participation at the high school level. What emerged in addition to reports from the projects was a broader conceptual model for boys and college men from two different perspectives on what some of the issues might be, how to understand them, and what best practices had emerged. Jeffrey Kaster's chapter on the Youth Track is a more detailed report of this part of the program (see Chapter 19, page 251). The work was of such keen interest at the Lilly Endowment that it led to another grant to continue the work, starting in 2010.

Phase Three: Conferences in 2009 and the Present Publication

All participating schools were invited to the Saint John's University Conference on the College Male in 2009, where they presented on how far they had come in implementing their pilot projects. All participants still had the opportunity to take what they learned from the conference and return to their campuses to finish their pilot projects. Relationships and contacts were enhanced and ongoing discussions encouraged as the group worked toward the common goal of this publication and presentations at other national conferences.

Each school was asked to author a chapter, telling the story of its approach to involving men in programs on its campus and how the story was related to its particular campus culture. Authors were to reflect on what approach worked the best at their schools to involve their colleges' men and how it had enhanced the men's choices about their careers. The unique mission and purpose of each campus have no doubt added to the richness and variety of the findings. The bulk of the offerings in the following chapters are case studies that show the large variety of best practices for getting college men involved.

The Research and Theory Team met at one of the most extraordinary sessions of the conference to develop a more advanced version of a conceptual model to help explain what works and why. The model included a more comprehensive theological account of the issue, providing some suggestions for church-related colleges. The discussion of this model and what pilot project leaders thought was going on conceptually was the highlight of the conference.

A capstone chapter is included, following the chapters on individual school projects (see Chapter 20, page 266). It includes an analysis of the themes from each of the case studies. This theoretical analysis together with a list of best practices is offered to any schools interested in how to improve educational environments to enhance men's awareness of who they are as men, what they believe, and how to live lives of integrity and authenticity informed by those beliefs.

One of the most interesting conclusions of the program was the general interest that developed in many of the schools for men's groups. How that emerged as one of the best practices is detailed in the capstone chapter. Merle Longwood designed the Siena College pilot project to study the development of men's spirituality groups on several of the campuses and will publish his findings in an additional publication (Longwood & Schipper, in press). Longwood and Schipper's study is one of the exciting and unexpected outcomes of this program. As this volume goes to press, the Lilly grant has ended, but research continues on campuses, on spirituality and masculinity, to further analyze what attracts college men into discussions of spirituality and how that relates to their perceptions of masculinity.

Our hypothesis is that there is widespread misperception of the interest college men have in spirituality. Providing these kinds of opportunities for them to discuss their spiritual lives in a confidential intergenerational setting with skilled facilitators begins to correct this misperception and better meet students' needs on this level. The underestimation of the interest in spirituality and men's spirituality groups may be related to an overestimation of college men's commitment to traditional masculinity. Participation in traditional masculine behaviors (even if misperceived to be valid) leads to poor men's health and well-being.

A third conference on the college male was held in November 2009 to convene college men's groups working to end gender-based violence. At the suggestion of Michael Kimmel, Michael Kaufman, and Harry Brod, the Center for Men's Leadership and Service was asked to serve as the convener of the many groups that have started spontaneously on college campuses in the United States to involve more men in stopping violence. A remarkable turnout of schools occurred and provided another opportunity for some pilot project leaders and some of the research team to meet and refine their thinking on best practices and theory.

Edward Heisler, a Saint John's alumnus working in a women's shelter in Duluth, Minnesota, developed a research project to interview these men about their vocational discernment process to become involved in this social justice work. Michael Firmin, a skilled researcher in this field, joined Heisler to produce an additional chapter for this book (see Chapter 18, page 236). Heisler's project will also, no doubt, outlive the grant. It is another unanticipated but exciting outcome of the project.

OTHER PRESENTATIONS OF PROGRAM FINDINGS

The participating schools were also invited to submit articles for publications in current journals or magazines and disseminate their findings on best practices to a broad-based audience of colleges and congregations. Following is a list of some of the related publications and presentations:

- The Academic Impressions Web Seminar for 20 Schools in February and March 2009: "Strategies for Improving Men's Campus Engagement Through Programming" sponsored by Academic Impressions (Webcast, March 23 and 27, 2009) at www.academicimpressions.com. Participating schools included South Dakota School of Mines and Technology, Rapid City, South Dakota; Bemidji State University, Bemidji, Minnesota; Olivet Nazarene University, Bourbonnais, Illinois; Immaculata University, Immaculata, Pennsylvania; College of Sisiyous, Weed, California; Randolph College, Lynchburg, Virginia; University of North Carolina, Greensboro; University of Wisconsin, Milwaukee; Voorhees College, Denmark, South Carolina; and University of San Diego, California.
- "Calling College Men: Men's Spirituality Groups at Saint John's" in *Calling: A Journal for Leaders Who Nurture Vocation*, 3(2), Spring 2008.

- National Association of Student Personnel Administrators conference in Chicago, cosponsored by the Knowledge Community for Men (March 2009).
- American Men's Studies Association presentation in Montréal (March 2009).
- Longwood and Schipper's (forthcoming) book on men's spirituality groups.
- Kellom's introduction (2006) to a special issue of *The Journal of Men's Studies* relating to the Center for Men's Leadership and Service at Saint John's University.

PROGRAM DIRECTOR

Gar Kellom led the program. Kellom was Vice President for Student Development and Executive Director of the Center for Men's Leadership and Service at Saint John's University, Collegeville, Minnesota. He holds a MA and MDiv from the Pacific School of Religion and a PhD in theology from the Graduate Theological Union and the University of California, Berkeley. He is the author of several articles (Kellom, 1999, 2000, 2008) on college student spirituality, the editor of a Jossey-Bass monograph on designing effective programs and services for college men (Kellom, 2004), and the editor of the fall 2006 issue of *The Journal of Men's Studies* (see Kellom, 2006), which published the most recent research of the Center for Men's Leadership and Service (CMLS) at Saint John's. As the founder of the CMLS and the Conference on the College Male and the designer of several successful service projects for college men, his interest in the topic of the program was central to its success. His advanced degrees and teaching experience in both the Theology Department and Gender and Women's Studies Program at Saint John's University were also assets to the program.

REFERENCES

Astin, A., & Astin, H. (2003). Spirituality in higher education, a national study of college students' search for meaning and purpose. *Higher Education Research Institute* (HERI), http://www.gseis.ucla.edu/heri/spirituality.html

Courtenay, W. (2002). A global perspective on the field of men's health. *International Journal of Men's Health, 1*(1), 1–13.

Kellom, G. (1999). Improving the recruitment, education and retention of men in residential colleges and universities. In C. Huick, S. Horwood, & D. Robertson (Eds.), *Collaboration in higher education: Residential programs* (pp. 122–130). Louisville, KY: Oxford Roundtable.

Kellom, G. (2000). Serving men effectively in residential colleges. In C. Huick, S. Horwood, & D. Robertson (Eds.), *Collaboration in higher education: Residential programs* (pp. 12–24). Louisville, KY: Oxford Roundtable.

Kellom, G. (2004). *Developing effective programs and services for college men*. New Directions for Student Services series (Monograph). San Francisco: Jossey-Bass.

Kellom, G. (2006). Introduction: The Center for Men's Leadership and Service at Saint John's University. *The Journal of Men's Studies, 14*(3), 265–268.

Kellom, G. (2008). "Calling college men: Spirituality groups at Saint John's. *Calling,* 3(2). http://www.thefund.org/ejournal/item.php?issueid=13&itemid=76

Kilmartin, C. (2000). *The masculine self* (2nd ed.). New York: McGraw Hill.

Longwood, M., Muesse M., & Schipper, W. (2004). Men, spirituality and the college experience. In G. Kellom (Ed.), *Developing effective programs and services for college men* (pp. 87–95). San Francisco: Jossey-Bass.

Longwood, M., & Schipper, W. (in press). *Forging the male spirit: The spiritual lives of college men.* Eugene, OR: Wipf and Stock.

Smith, C., & Denton, M. (2005). *Soul searching: The religious and spiritual lives of American teenagers.* New York: Oxford University Press.

2

Gender Disparity in College and University Vocational Exploration Programs: The Effect of Programs to Address the Disparity

Catherine Brooks

Is there a gender disparity in participation in vocational exploration programs at the college and university level? This chapter will explore a study of this question at colleges and universities around the country. The chapter will also summarize the results of efforts to address this disparity over the 2008–2009 academic year.

From 2000–2007, the Fund for Theological Education and Lilly Endowment Inc. supported the Programs for the Theological Exploration of Vocation (PTEV) at 88 colleges and universities around the country. These institutions received implementation grants and ongoing technical support to establish or strengthen programs that assist students in examining the relationship between faith and vocational choices, provide opportunities for gifted young people to explore Christian ministry, and enhance the capacity of a school's faculty and staff to teach and mentor students effectively in this arena.[1]

Gar Kellom, Director of the Center for Men's Leadership and Service at St. John's University and also a PTEV program director, noted that PTEV colleagues had often remarked that men are underrepresented in vocational exploration programs. Kellom proposed to Lilly Endowment Inc. an examination of gender balance in PTEV programs and a focus on ways to increase men's participation in these programs. Although anecdotal evidence indicated that male participation was often lower than overall campus enrollments would suggest, Kellom was in search of concrete information to use as a basis for moving forward.

Kellom worked with me (I am an independent consultant who had done previous work with PTEV program directors) and with an advisory panel to design and implement an Internet survey of program directors. The advisory panel suggested that compiling exact enrollment numbers by gender for each PTEV program at each institution would be an overwhelming task for most program directors and that most would not participate in the survey at all if this was asked of them. Instead, the survey asked for the directors' general impressions of enrollment by gender, overall as well as relative to campus enrollment. The survey also asked which types of PTEV programs tended to attract more men or more women and whether PTEV program directors perceived gender imbalance as a problem and if they were addressing it.

The advisory team also noted that it was important to view these questions in the context of overall campus culture as well as the culture of the PTEV programs.

---

[1] Source: http://www.ptev.org/history.aspx?iid=48

To that end, the survey asked program directors whether student leadership in the PTEV programs was more heavily male, more heavily female, or balanced and also asked the same question about adult leadership. This information was augmented by statistics from the Integrated Postsecondary Education Data System (IPEDS), including the size of the campus, percent male/female, percent full-time/part-time, percent undergraduate/graduate/first professional, distribution of students by race, and percent of male/female faculty.

The survey was administered over the Internet in the fall of 2007. Program directors at 87 of the 88 PTEV institutions were invited to take the survey (at one institution, the program director position was vacant), and representatives from 58 institutions responded (a 67% response rate).

Is There a Gender Imbalance in PTEV Program Participation?

Figure 1, based on responses from the 57 survey respondents who answered the question, shows that survey respondents do indeed perceive a gender imbalance in PTEV program participation. When reporting overall participation in PTEV programs, none reported that men were more likely than women to participate. Only 15 reported balanced enrollment, and 42 reported that PTEV participation is more heavily female.

In many institutions of higher learning, women outnumber men overall, and so their participation would be expected to be higher in any activity. We asked respondents to compare PTEV participation with the overall gender distribution of the campus and found that only four respondents reported that men participated in excess of what their enrollment numbers would indicate. All four of these respondents said that their PTEV participation was about equally distributed

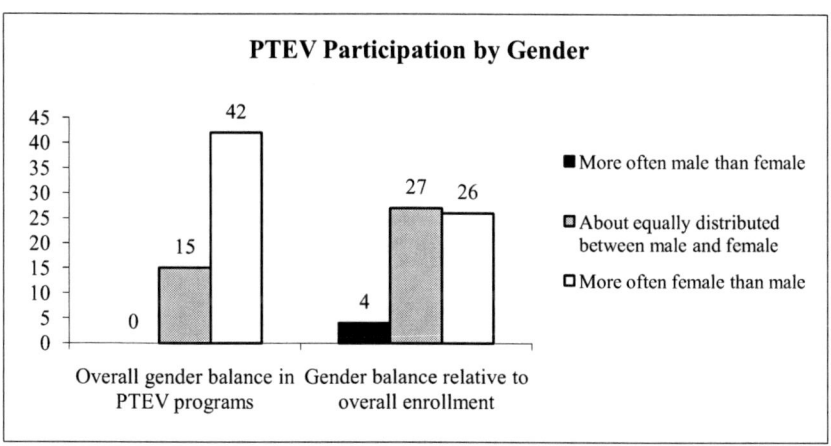

Figure 1. PTEV participation by gender.

TABLE 1
INTERSECTION OF ANSWERS TO GENDER BALANCE QUESTIONS

PTEV participation	Reflects overall enrollment	More heavily female than enrollment	More heavily male than enrollment	Total
Predominantly female	16	26	0	42
Balanced by gender	11	0	4	15
Total	27	26	4	57

between men and women but that their overall enrollment was more heavily female (ranging from 59 to 67% female) and so men were more involved in PTEV than their enrollment would indicate.

The remaining respondents were divided between having programs that were balanced by gender relative to overall enrollment and having programs in which women outnumbered men in even higher proportions than their overall enrollment would indicate.

Table 1 shows how the answers to the above two questions of overall gender balance and gender balance relative to enrollment intersect.

How Do Campus Demographics Affect PTEV Participation?

Gender Balance of Adult Leaders

The next stage of survey analysis examined whether the gender of adult program leaders correlated with male participation in PTEV. Survey respondents were asked for the gender balance of adult leaders in the PTEV program. Most institutions (35, or 60%) reported gender-balanced adult leadership in the PTEV program. Thirteen institutions (22%) reported that PTEV adult leaders are more heavily male than female. Nine (16%) reported that PTEV adult leaders are more heavily female than male.

Figure 2 shows PTEV participation by gender relative to campus enrollment for institutions according to the gender balance of their PTEV adult leadership. Three respondents did not answer both questions and are omitted here.

Gender Balance of Student Leaders

Survey respondents were asked to indicate whether student leaders in the PTEV program (if they exist; not all institutions operate on this model) are more heavily male or female. Fifty-three respondents answered the question. Only one respondent indicated that student leaders are more often male than female; this person represents an institution that is only 36% male overall and reported that

2 / GENDER DISPARITY IN COLLEGE

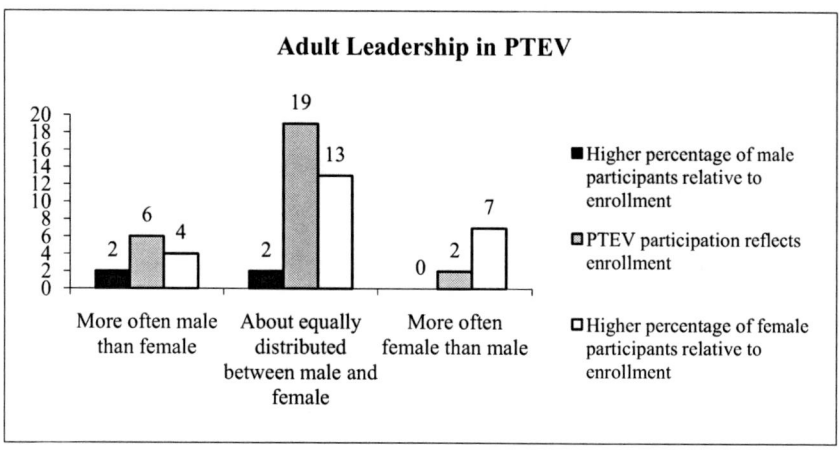

Figure 2. Adult leadership in PTEV.

PTEV participation is roughly equal between men and women and reflects the gender balance of the campus. Twenty-eight respondents (48%) reported that student leaders are more often female, and 24 (45%) reported that student leadership is balanced by gender.

Figure 3 shows PTEV participation by gender relative to campus enrollment for institutions according to the gender balance of their PTEV student leadership. One respondent did not indicate PTEV participation by gender and is omitted here.

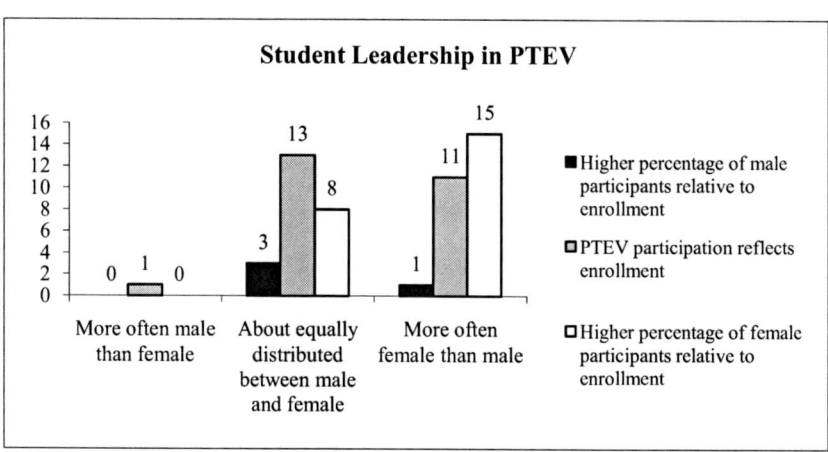

Figure 3. Student leadership in PTEV.

IPEDS data was used to determine the following for each institution:

- overall enrollment;
- student breakdown by gender;
- student breakdown by race;
- percent of students who are full-time or part-time;
- percent of students who are undergraduate, graduate, or first professional; and
- faculty breakdown by gender.

ENROLLMENT

Of the seven respondents representing larger institutions (10,000 students or more), only one reported that PTEV enrollment was about equally distributed between male and female students (this campus is 49% male). The remainder reported that female enrollment was higher. However, comparing the size of the campus to participation by gender relative to enrollment by gender showed no obvious differences by size. Figure 4 graphs these results.

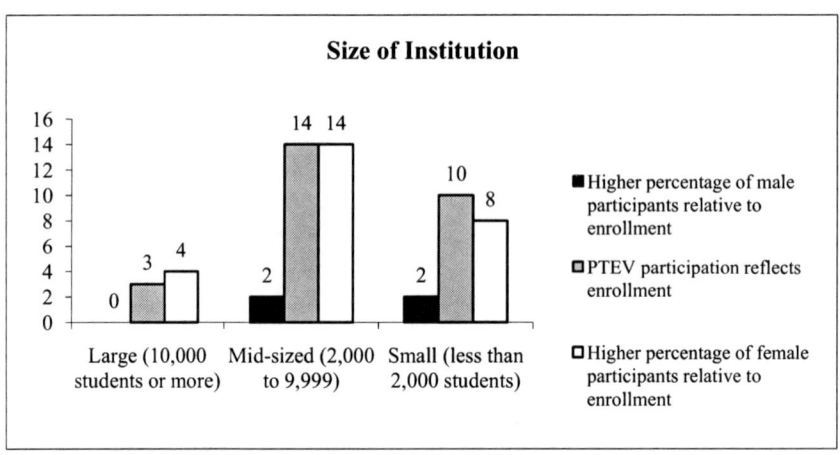

Figure 4. Size of institution.

STUDENT BREAKDOWN BY GENDER

In the section entitled, "Is There a Gender Imbalance in PTEV Program Participation?", we learned that the PTEV institutions often have majority female enrollment. Of the 58 campuses that responded to the survey, all are coeducational,[2]

---

[2] One respondent answered for two institutions that are each officially single-sex institutions that work closely together; this person reported a balanced gender participation for PTEV that reflects overall enrollment.

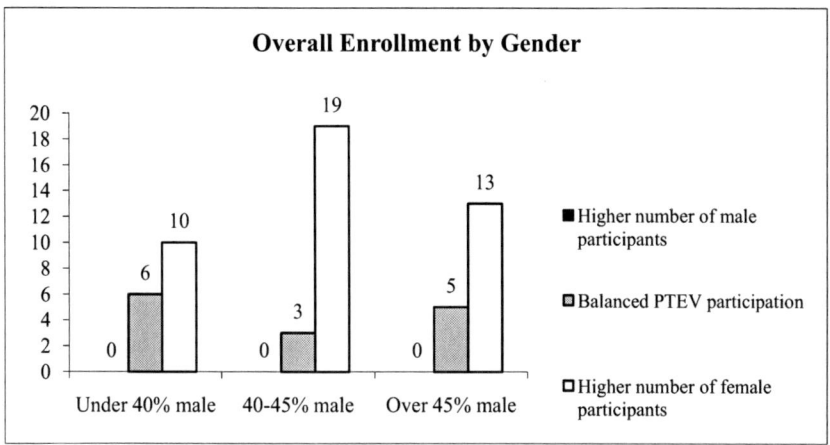

Figure 5. Overall enrollment by gender.

but sixteen are less than 40% male and 37 are less than 45% male. Do institutions that are more gender balanced overall have an easier time attracting males to their PTEV programs?

An analysis of overall participation by gender showed—unexpectedly—that a higher percent of respondents reported balanced PTEV participation at campuses that were less than 40% male than at campuses that were 40% or more male (see Figure 5).

Analyzing PTEV participation relative to overall enrollment showed that campuses that were less than 40% male were far more likely to report participation that reflects enrollment than were campuses that were 40% or more male (see Figure 6). None of the campuses that were over 45% male reported a higher percentage of males in PTEV programs than their enrollment would predict.

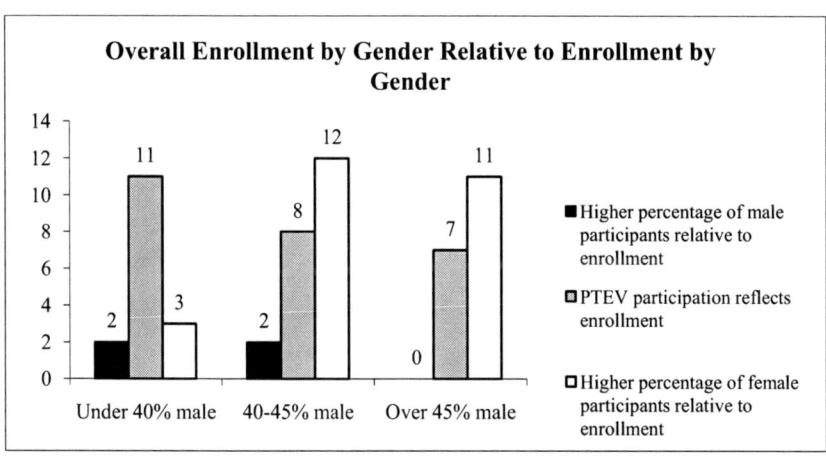

Figure 6. Overall enrollment by gender relative to enrollment by gender.

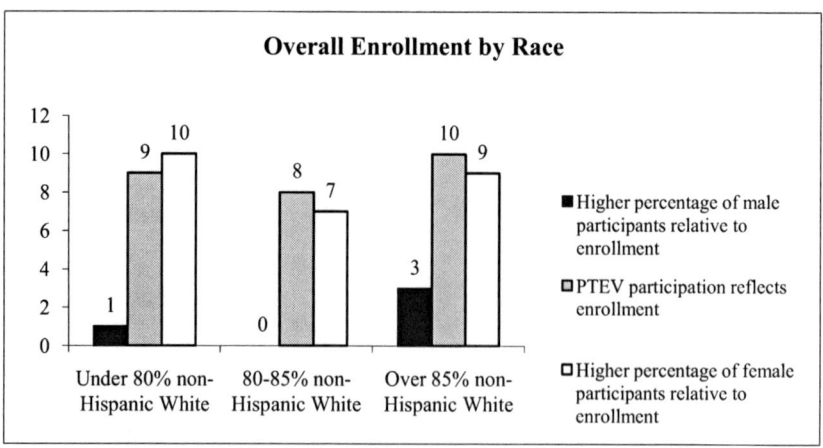

Figure 7. Overall enrollment by race.

STUDENT BREAKDOWN BY RACE

Most PTEV campuses are predominantly white; at only one institution that responded to the survey were non-Hispanic whites a minority (this campus is 61% Hispanic). Thirty-eight of the 58 institutions that responded to the survey were at least 80% non-Hispanic white, and 14 were at least 90% non-Hispanic white.

An examination of PTEV participation relative to enrollment for campuses with differing racial compositions showed that there were no dramatic differences, except that most of the campuses reporting that males participate in PTEV in excess of the numbers that their enrollment would predict are at campuses that are at least 85% non-Hispanic white (see Figure 7).

FULL-TIME AND PART-TIME STUDENTS

Most PTEV campuses primarily enroll full-time students; at 47 of the 58 institutions that responded to the survey, at least 75% of students were full-time, and at 26 of them, at least 95% of the students were full-time.

Campuses that are at least 95% full-time were more likely to have female participation in PTEV exceeding the overall enrollment of women at the campus (see Figure 8).

PERCENT OF STUDENTS WHO ARE UNDERGRADUATE, GRADUATE, OR FIRST PROFESSIONAL

Although graduate and first professional students do not usually participate in PTEV programs, their presence or absence on a campus has an effect on campus culture. Most PTEV campuses primarily enroll undergraduate students; at 41

2 / GENDER DISPARITY IN COLLEGE

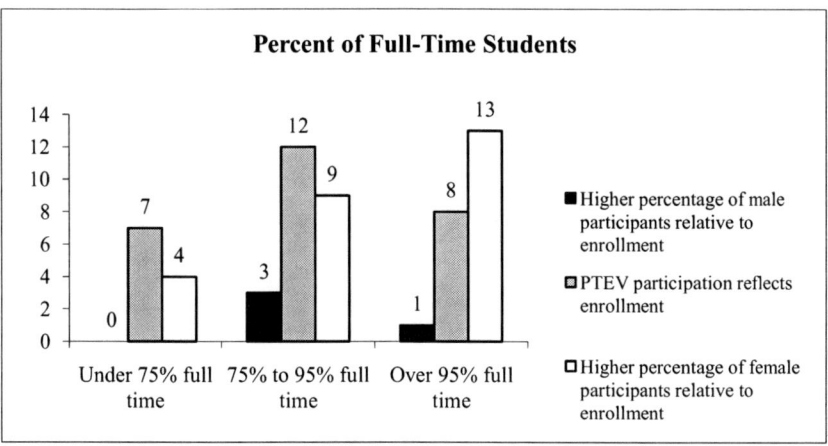

Figure 8. Percent of full-time students.

of the 58 institutions that responded to the survey, at least 75% of students were undergraduates, and at 27 of them, at least 95% of the students were undergraduates.

Campuses with lower numbers of undergraduates were more likely to report balanced PTEV participation than were campuses with higher numbers of undergraduates (see Figure 9).

FACULTY BREAKDOWN BY GENDER

PTEV institutions generally have majority-male faculty; at only six of the 58 institutions that responded to the survey were men a minority among the faculty

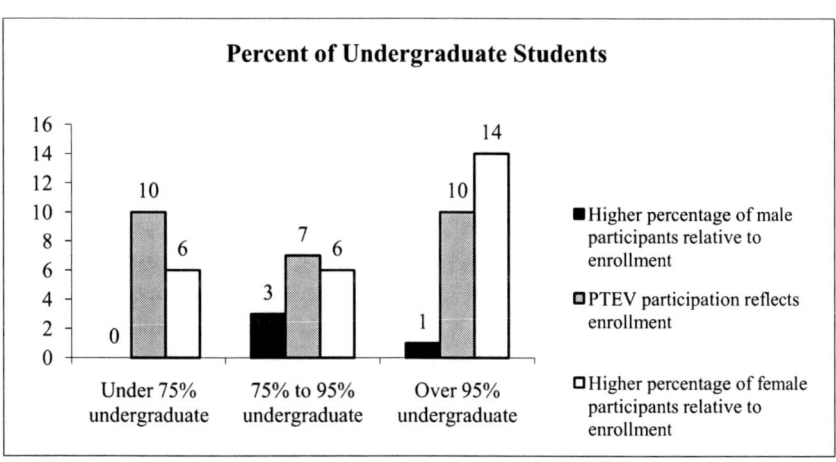

Figure 9. Percent of undergraduate students.

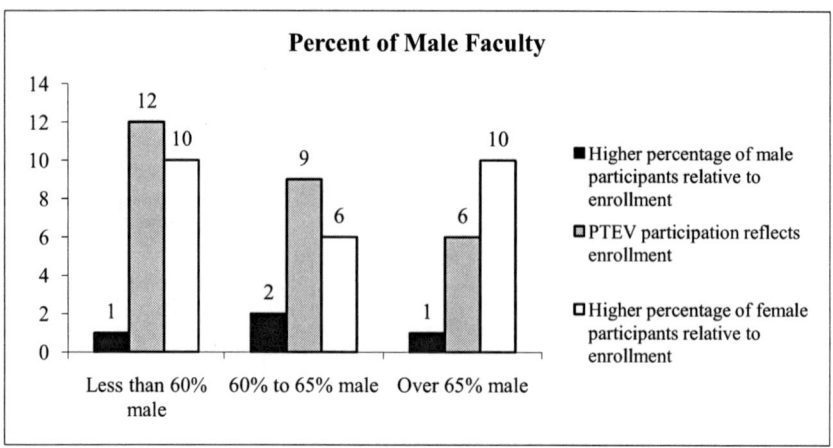

Figure 10. Percent of male faculty.

(and at 3 of them men comprised 48 or 49% of the faculty). At 35 institutions, 60% or more of faculty members were men.

Campuses with the highest numbers of male faculty were the most likely to have heavier female participation in PTEV programs that would be predicted by enrollment. Balanced participation was most likely at the campuses with the lowest percentages of male faculty (see Figure 10).

PTEV PROGRAMS MORE LIKELY TO ATTRACT MEN OR WOMEN

Survey respondents were asked to indicate which types of programs, if any, on their campus attract substantially higher numbers of one gender over the other. Their responses are summarized in Appendix A (see page 286).

The types of programs most frequently cited as attracting more women, with nine responses each, were service learning programs and retreats. No one noted that these events were more likely to attract men; one respondent said that men and women participated in retreats in proportion to their enrollment at the campus. Other programs that were cited as more likely to attract women were discussion groups (5), ministry preparation (5), and internships (4).

Ministry preparation programs were most frequently cited as attracting men, although only five people noted this at their institutions, the same number who reported that these programs were more likely to attract women. Four people cited different types of activities, such as sports or camping, as being more likely to attract men. As one respondent said, "[Men] want to 'do' together much more than 'be' together."

Other programs cited as attracting men were seminary/divinity school preparation (3) and internships (2). Both of these were also cited by other respondents as attracting women and as attracting similar numbers of men and women.

Respondents' Perception of Gender Imbalance as a Problem

Twenty respondents (34%) perceived gender imbalance in their campus's PTEV programs as a problem. Twenty-eight (48%) did not perceive it as a problem, and 10 (17%) were not sure.

Table 2 compares reported PTEV participation by gender relative to enrollment with the respondent's perception of gender imbalance as a problem.

TABLE 2

Perception of Gender Imbalance (GI) as a Problem Relative to PTEV Participation by Gender

	PTEV participation reflects overall enrollment	PTEV participation is more heavily female than enrollment	PTEV participation is more heavily male than enrollment
GI is a problem	3	16	1
GI is not a problem	20	4	3
Not sure whether GI is a problem	4	6	0

Addressing Gender Imbalance

At the time of the survey (fall 2007), 26 (45%) of the survey respondents reported that their institutions were addressing gender imbalance; 32 (55%) reported that they were not. Table 3 compares respondents reporting that their institutions were addressing the problem with their belief that the problem exists.

Of the 26 respondents whose institutions were addressing gender imbalance, 9 were either pilot schools for the Lilly grant (described above) or made presentations about their institutions' efforts at a conference held in February 2008. Telephone and e-mail contact with representatives from the remaining 17 institutions resulted in responses from 12 of them with further information.

Responses had similar themes, summarized in Appendix B (see page 288). Many PTEV program directors had found that men were not interested in the traditional vocational exploration programs of service and reflection (this was less the case at campuses that have a strong evangelical student body and/or a long history of service). They found that they needed to help men become comfortable with programs that were sometimes dismissed as "women's work" or not something that "regular guys" did. This might involve recruiting groups of men together, so that they have the assurance of being with their friends during these activities. It might also involve gaining the support and involvement of strong men on the campus, either in faculty or staff positions (particularly sports coaches) in order to give a sense of maleness to the PTEV activities.

Table 3

Belief that Gender Imbalance (GI) Is a Problem Relative to Belief that Institution Is Addressing the Problem

	Institution is addressing GI	Institution is not addressing GI
GI is a problem	14	6
GI is not a problem	9	19
Not sure whether GI is a problem	3	7

PTEV leaders also recognized the need to do focused outreach, often in different ways than they were used to, in order to draw men in. The outreach needs to come from leaders who are well integrated in the campus life, so they are more aware of the activities that engage men and can use them to make personal connections that can lead to relationships. Personal invitations are often needed to draw in men who might not respond to flyers and e-mail, and faculty nominations can help achieve gender balance in programs.

Many PTEV directors are conflicted and may have experienced divisions within their PTEV program staff over the need to target men and sometimes exclude more qualified women from selective programs in order to achieve something close to parity. This is particularly the case within religious traditions that exclude women from liturgical ministry or on campuses where the culture does not support women as church ministers. The need to affirm women's spirituality and provide outlets for their spiritual gifts is an important goal for many PTEV programs. Some directors have addressed this by supporting women-oriented programs within PTEV at the same time they are actively recruiting men for other programs.

Moving Forward: Pilot Programs to Address Gender Imbalance

The results of this study showed that the gender imbalance in vocational exploration programs was real, at least in the minds of PTEV program directors, and that many program directors were willing to address it. Lilly Endowment Inc. funded pilot programs at 15 institutions (most of which had participated in PTEV) that were designed to address gender imbalance in vocational reflection activities. Each of the pilot programs included information about the programs and the individual assessments in this book.

Kellom and I also worked together to devise an assessment that would show results for the program overall and provide a comparison point from institution to institution. This assessment consisted of a pre- and posttest, administered in the fall of 2008 and the spring of 2009, to students who had participated in the pilot programs. The instrument was an Internet survey, asking to what extent students agreed with the following 10 rating-scale statements:

1. I consider myself a person of faith.
2. I enjoy spending time thinking about and trying to understand how my faith can be a part of shaping my adult life (vocational exploration).
3. I have previously participated in vocational exploration activities and/or classes.
4. I would like to participate in additional vocational exploration opportunities in college and beyond.
5. I sometimes feel embarrassed about my faith or my participation in vocational exploration activities when I'm with my friends.
6. Many of my friends have participated in vocational exploration activities and/or classes.
7. I enjoy vocational exploration activities that involve a lot of activity and teamwork (outdoor retreats, volunteer work involving physical exertion).
8. I enjoy quiet, reflective vocational activities (classes, discussion groups, indoor retreats).
9. The vocational exploration activities and classes at this college are well suited to my interests.
10. My understanding of vocation and its place in my life has been strengthened by my participation in classes and vocational exploration activities.

The questionnaire was deliberately kept simple and brief to encourage participation; pilot programs were expected to do more in-depth assessments on their own. Twelve institutions provided e-mail addresses for their program participants; the number of participants and survey respondents at each institution is summarized in Appendix C (see page 289).

The surveys sought to determine attitudinal changes about vocation in program participants. At all institutions except for Hope College, participants were men. At Hope College, the pilot program consisted of vocational exploration being interwoven into the curriculum, and therefore both men and women were participants (and participation numbers were much higher than for other institutions, whose programs were extracurricular).

Overall results do not show attitudinal changes in participants between the fall of 2008 and the spring of 2009. Participants responded on a scale of 1 to 5 when answering each question, with 1 being *strongly disagree* and 5 being *strongly agree*. The average response to each question (omitting responses of N/A or blank responses) is shown in Table 4.

The responses show little strengthening of vocational purpose from the first round to the second round. Students were more likely to report having participated in vocational exploration activities and to have friends who have participated in vocational exploration activities. But no other averages increased over the academic year, other than the statement of feeling embarrassed about faith when around friends (a result that goes counter to pilot programs' goals). Students reported high levels of personal faith and enjoying vocational exploration activities at the start of the academic year, and it may not be realistic to expect these levels to increase further. However, the survey results show a decrease in students' level of agreement with these statements.

The responses below represent all of the students who responded to each of the surveys, even though some only responded to the first survey or only to the second survey. While this shows a snapshot of participants at the time of each survey, an analysis of responses only from students who responded to both surveys is useful as well in order to reflect changes in individual attitudes. The same averages, calculated only for students who responded to both surveys, are shown in Table 5.

As is also demonstrated in Table 4, increases in Table 5 are shown only for previous participation in vocational exploration activities, embarrassment over faith, and friends' participation in vocational exploration activities.

TABLE 4

RESPONSES TO QUESTIONS CONCERNING ATTITUDES TOWARD VOCATION

	First round average	Second round average
I consider myself a person of faith.	4.33	4.30
I enjoy spending time thinking about and trying to understand how my faith can be a part of shaping my adult life (vocational exploration).	4.06	3.97
I have previously participated in vocational exploration activities and/or classes.	3.74	3.86
I would like to participate in additional vocational exploration opportunities in college and beyond.	3.90	3.77
I sometimes feel embarrassed about my faith or my participation in vocational exploration activities when I'm with my friends.	1.98	2.10
Many of my friends have participated in vocational exploration activities and/or classes.	3.50	3.57
I enjoy vocational exploration activities that involve a lot of activity and teamwork (outdoor retreats, volunteer work involving physical exertion).	3.92	3.75
I enjoy quiet, reflective vocational activities (classes, discussion groups, indoor retreats).	3.77	3.65
The vocational exploration activities and classes at this college are well suited to my interests.	3.56	3.47
My understanding of vocation and its place in my life has been strengthened by my participation in classes and vocational exploration activities.	3.75	3.64

TABLE 5

Responses to Questions Concerning Attitudes Toward Vocation From Students Who Responded to Both Surveys

	First round average	Second round average
I consider myself a person of faith.	4.25	4.03
I enjoy spending time thinking about and trying to understand how my faith can be a part of shaping my adult life (vocational exploration).	4.00	3.83
I have previously participated in vocational exploration activities and/or classes.	3.69	3.95
I would like to participate in additional vocational exploration opportunities in college and beyond.	3.91	3.60
I sometimes feel embarrassed about my faith or my participation in vocational exploration activities when I'm with my friends.	1.95	2.23
Many of my friends have participated in vocational exploration activities and/or classes.	3.51	3.62
I enjoy vocational exploration activities that involve a lot of activity and teamwork (outdoor retreats, volunteer work involving physical exertion).	3.80	3.78
I enjoy quiet, reflective vocational activities (classes, discussion groups, indoor retreats).	3.75	3.51
The vocational exploration activities and classes at this college are well suited to my interests.	3.59	3.44
My understanding of vocation and its place in my life has been strengthened by my participation in classes and vocational exploration activities.	3.81	3.56

What should be made of these results? It is difficult to draw conclusions only from this survey. It was limited in scope, and participation was not high. In some cases, there was only a 5-month window between the initial survey and the second survey, because some programs started later in the academic year and some institutions finish their academic year in early May. And students may not have completed the survey in a way that reflects a thoughtful analysis of their feelings. Each institution's more thorough analysis of its program's effectiveness will provide more relevant data.

However, the results are consistent and cannot be completely dismissed. There is additional work to do toward the goals of supporting and nurturing positive attitudes toward vocational reflection. Activities over the past year have not been enough to move student attitudes in the right direction. Some retooling and rethinking is in order before the pilot programs are expanded to more institutions.

PART II.
REPORTS OF PROJECTS

Section A.
Connecting to the Curriculum

3

Addressing Male Participation Through the Academic Program: The Hope College Experience

David S. Cunningham

Hope College was happy to accept the offer from St. John's University to become a pilot school for its project on increasing male participation in the Programs for the Theological Exploration of Vocation (PTEV), funded by the Lilly Endowment Inc. Over the past eight years, the college has developed a highly successful PTEV program; however, like many schools, it has found that a disproportionately small number of male students participate in these programs. Moreover, because Hope's PTEV program is deeply rooted in the academic division of the institution, questions about male participation in its various initiatives can be examined alongside questions about broader issues of academic engagement and achievement among male students. Since this issue was already part of an ongoing discussion at the college, the offer to participate in the new grant administered at St. John's was a timely and relevant one. This chapter seeks to describe the college and its PTEV program and to demonstrate what it learned from the implementation of an academically focused approach to improving engagement and achievement—both in its PTEV programs and in the curriculum as a whole.

The Setting

Hope College is a 4-year liberal arts college located in Holland, Michigan. The city is on the coast of Lake Michigan, on the far western edge of the state; hence, its landscape, socioeconomic climate, and overall ambience are not necessarily those that come immediately to mind when the word *Michigan* is heard by those who are less familiar with its diversity. The western part of the state bears a much greater similarity to parts of the upper Midwest (particularly Wisconsin and Minnesota) than it does to the urban concentrations typical of its southeastern corner. In addition, Western Michigan is marked by a very specific religious climate: here, 19th-century Dutch immigrants established settlements, bringing with them a strong commitment to the Reformed traditions of their homeland. The nearby city of Grand Rapids is home to the national headquarters of two major protestant denominations, The Christian Reformed Church and the Reformed Church in America; the latter is the founding denomination of Hope College. The area has a very high concentration of churches, church-related colleges, religious publishing houses, and related organizations.

Among liberal arts colleges, as strictly defined (i.e., with no graduate-level programs of any kind), Hope College is fairly large: slightly over 3,000 students are enrolled, with the overwhelming majority of those living on campus. In some fields of study, the college has a national reputation and recruits widely; this is particularly the case in the natural sciences and the arts. But its academic programs are very solid across the entire disciplinary spectrum, making it a good choice for students (particularly in the immediate region) who are seeking a solid liberal arts education coupled with strong preparation for a particular career (including further study—33% of its graduates go on to graduate or professional school).

Like most academic institutions in the United States, Hope College enrolls a majority of female students. Although the numbers fluctuate slightly from year to year, the typical proportion is approximately 60% female and 40% male. Among the academic divisions, only in the natural and applied sciences does the gender ratio approach 1:1, with the result that male-female proportions in the arts, humanities, and social sciences are even more strongly majority female.

Hope College is recognized (particularly within Michigan and in the upper Midwest) as an institution that has sought to maintain its Christian character, yet without the use of significant regulatory requirements. For example, the college does not mandate chapel attendance, and although its broader codes of conduct certainly grow from Christian convictions, these are not significantly different from those at more secular institutions.[3] Neither students nor faculty are required to sign a faith statement nor to demonstrate membership in (or attend) a church. The general curriculum includes a requirement in religion, but these courses are largely investigatory and academic rather than didactic or catechetical in the narrow sense. For some observers, the mark of a Christian college is its membership in the Council of Christian Colleges and Universities; thus, it is relevant to note that Hope College is not a member of this consortium.

And yet, Hope College flourishes precisely as an institution with a thoroughly and deeply Christian character. In spite of the absence of church-membership requirements, nearly every faculty member is an active participant in a local congregation. The college's four-times-per-week services regularly fill its 1,150-seat chapel to capacity; elective courses in religion are extremely popular; and Bible studies and other informal religious activities are a highly visible feature of its undergraduate life. The college intentionally seeks to bring students into conversation with a broad range of Christian traditions, while at the same time allowing them the freedom to explore, embrace, reject, or tolerate various forms of religious faith. Although this middle ground can sometimes be difficult to maintain, Hope College's history is marked by valiant efforts in this regard and by a reasonable modicum of success. As a recent detailed historical case study (Kennedy & Simon, 2005) demonstrates, Hope College is an institution that has sought to steer a mid-

---

[3] A possible exception: the college does enforce restrictions on visitation hours for men in its all-female residence halls, though this is also the case at some secular institutions. Hope also forbids all alcohol on campus; this applies to everyone, not just to students.

dle course between the secularizing tendencies of most mainline American protestant institutions, on the one hand, and the highly defined and narrowly specified character of institutions that self-identify as Christian colleges.

Two other characteristics of Hope College should be noted as offering helpful background for this case study. Both of these elements are clearly identified in the college's recently revised mission statement:

> The mission of Hope College is to educate students for lives of leadership and service in a global society through academic and co-curricular programs of recognized excellence in the liberal arts and in the context of the historic Christian faith.

The two additional elements are the college's emphasis on both leadership and service, which makes programs on vocational discernment particularly central to its mission, and an emphasis on academic excellence, which requires that such programs be thoroughly integrated with its students' academic pursuits.

Needless to say, giving equal emphasis to these goals requires considerable vigilance. Evidence from our National Survey of Student Engagement data suggests that, on average, our students arrive somewhat less academically prepared than is the case at some of our comparable institutions; this finding has been confirmed through our participation in the current Wabash Study of Liberal Arts Education. In order to fulfill the central elements of its mission, Hope College is currently seeking ways of sharpening its curricular focus. New programs that build on this emphasis can make a particularly strong contribution to the college's mission.

In addition to providing a general sense of the character of Hope College, the elements of its setting are important for understanding the nature of its Program for the Theological Exploration of Vocation, which was established in 2003 with funding from the Lilly Endowment Inc. The grant-writing committee recognized that Hope College's specific location on the spectrum of church-related institutions would call for a very particular instantiation of the PTEV vision. While more secularized institutions might locate such a project in its (relatively marginal) chapel or campus ministry programs and while more self-designated Christian colleges might successfully place it as a major focus within their student life divisions, neither of these strategies would be quite right at Hope College. Instead, Hope's grant proposal specified the creation of a program that would work closely with a wide range of campus offices—and particularly with the college's academic departments—in order to integrate its programming more fully into Hope's academic life. To this end, it called for the hiring of an established scholar as its director (preferably at the associate or full professor level); this person would report directly to the provost, who serves as the college's chief academic officer. The committee was convinced that Hope's PTEV program would be most likely to succeed and that its impact on the lives of students would be maximized if it could be integrated into the institution's broader academic program. The next section of this chapter explores the degree to which these convictions were validated by the actual program that came into being.

The Program

Hope College's PTEV program was inaugurated in 2003 and given the name The CrossRoads Project. The name was chosen in recognition of the fact that, for most students, college is a time when many paths of life intersect with one another. Moreover, what students encounter at college is not simply four-way stops or forks, where "two roads diverged in a yellow wood" (in spite of the vocational appropriateness of Frost's poem). Rather, the roads come from all directions and lead out in all directions. The program's logo represents this complexity with a picture of a typical urban "spaghetti junction," with a myriad of entrance and exit ramps. During their college years, students merge into the rest of the traffic, travel for a while, turn onto a different road, change lanes, and avoid collisions. Eventually (one hopes), they will exit the junction altogether and head off in the right direction.

The program is therefore designed to encourage the entire college community to explore significant questions: the purpose of their lives, gifts, and abilities, as well as their directions for the future. The program's understanding of vocation is rooted in the Reformation insight that God calls *all human beings* to a particular way of life, making it a key element, not just for *certain* professions, but for *all* of them. In addition, these callings concern more than just career choices; they are also lived out through service, friendship, church life, parenting, and many other walks of life. Hence, alongside the spaghetti junction logo, a phrase appears that might be considered the program's miniature mission statement: "Thinking Theologically About Career, Calling, and Life."

The program's initiatives (which are many and various) were all designed to help students explore faith, learning, work, and vocation. These initiatives have included the development of new first-year seminars and senior seminars with a special focus on vocation; alternative placement internships that take students to areas of special need; preprofessional programs in business, education, and the health professions; faculty seminars and workshops for theological conversation on vocation; a variety of forms of support for students exploring graduate work in theology or ministry; a new Studies in Ministry minor for students called to other forms of ministry; and collaborative research grants for students and faculty engaging in joint research.

True to its original vision, Hope College's PTEV program focuses most of its energies on the academic division of the institution. Its director is a full member of the faculty who reports directly to the provost; its associate director, who also serves as director of the ministry minor, is also a faculty member. Both hold PhD degrees in religion and are published scholars. Moreover, most of The CrossRoads Project's initiatives are related to specific courses, academic for-credit internships, faculty development opportunities, and other extensions of the academic program. In this respect it differs from a number of PTEV programs nationwide that operate primarily through offices such as campus ministry, volunteer services, or student development.

The decision to place The CrossRoads Project squarely within the academic division of the institution was a crucial one; indeed, it has turned out to be decisive for the program's success. In the college's general education program and within many of its academic majors, the language of vocation has established a truly pervasive presence. Particularly important in this regard have been the college's first-year seminar and senior seminar programs, where CrossRoads has been able to make a particularly strong impact, given the fact that all Hope students must take both of these courses and also given structures that already exist for creating commonalities across the many sections of these courses. In addition, the college's Office of Career Services has been a very willing and highly interested conversation-partner throughout the program's existence; because this office was already accustomed to working closely with the curricular program, the academic orientation of CrossRoads made these two college offices natural conversation partners. This has helped to integrate the more theoretical and academic elements of the language of vocation with the practical elements of skills assessment and career planning. Finally, the nature of the Hope College faculty has had a tremendous impact on the success of The CrossRoads Project. Most of the faculty bring to their work a strong religious commitment and a real interest in nurturing the lives of their students in ways that include, but also go beyond, the academic aspects of their programs. As a result, the majority of Hope faculty members have been eager and enthusiastic participants in the various strands of The CrossRoads Project's work. They have developed new internship programs, allowing more students to carry out part of their vocational discernment process in real-life settings; they have organized panel discussions and taken students on course-related field trips, retreats, and weeklong seminars; and, perhaps most importantly, they have integrated the language of vocation into the curricular structure of their courses.

Like almost all PTEV institutions, Hope College has observed that its various vocational discernment programs seem to attract a disproportionately high number of female participants—even more skewed than enrollment ratios would warrant. By the very nature of The CrossRoads Project's offerings, it is difficult to get good quantitative data on this point. While a few of its programs are discrete entities (such as internships, retreats, and various programs that support students considering ministry), most of the CrossRoads' efforts have been directed at integrating the language of vocation into the academic program. Thus, the number of female and male students who have some degree of contact with the program will depend largely on the numbers of female and male students enrolled in those courses in which the instructor brings the language of vocation (and/or other resources of The CrossRoads Project) to bear within the structure of the course. And, even then, it would be difficult to analyze this question in terms of impact;

it may be known that 13 women and 8 men went on a particular vocation-related field trip, but it is very difficult to assess the degree to which it might have affected the shape of their overall understanding of vocation or the particular pattern of their own vocational discernment process. (Although these programs were typically evaluated by means of post-event surveys, the program had not anticipated the disproportionate male-female ratios over the long run and so had usually made no effort to control these surveys for gender.) In those initiatives in which quantitative measures of male and female participation are possible, the ratios hover around 75% female to 25% male—well above the proportion of female to male students at the college.

It should also be noted that the decision to locate The CrossRoads Project within the academic division of the institution and to channel most of its programming through courses and other curricular elements has probably exacerbated this problem. As has been widely noted in the relevant literature, gender-based differences in emotional maturity and other areas of psychological development may play a very significant role in leading men to be less thoroughly engaged in the specifically academic elements of the higher education experience. Needless to say, these issues are beyond the scope of this study, and addressing them is well beyond the reach of one specific program. However, when coupled with (for example) the disproportionate energy that male students sometimes give to sports and other cocurricular activities—as well as quasi-addictive, free-time activities such as online gaming—these circumstances present a serious challenge to any program seeking to involve a higher proportion of male students in its activities.

A final point should be noted. As observed above, the one academic division of the institution in which the number of male students nearly equals that of female students is the Division of Natural and Applied Sciences. Unfortunately, this is also the division where The CrossRoads Project has made the fewest inroads. (The one exception to this is in the Nursing Department, which, interestingly enough, consists of female students almost exclusively.) On the one hand, the relative scarcity of vocational discernment programs within the natural sciences is due partly to the nature of the subject matter (highly technical fields in which the impartation of information and development of specific skills is primary and difficult to integrate with larger questions of meaning) and partly to the faculty in these fields (whose fields often demand a great deal of time in the laboratory and leave little room for integrating optional elements into their courses). On the other hand, these issues are not insuperable, and, indeed, Hope College can boast a relatively high percentage of natural sciences faculty who take an active interest in larger questions of meaning and are willing to integrate these into their courses. In retrospect, The CrossRoads Project has probably not done enough to reach these faculty and to supply them with additional ideas and resources for including conversations about vocation in their courses.

In spite of this caveat, however, the decision to locate The CrossRoads Project within the academic division of the institution was instrumental for its overall

3 / ADDRESSING MALE PARTICIPATION

success and particularly for its ability to achieve a thoroughgoing integration of the language of vocation into the academic life of the college. At the same time, this academic focus has probably made it more difficult for the program to achieve proportionate levels of participation among the college's male student population. I wonder, at times, whether the circumstances that currently dominate the landscape of higher education have put these two goals into fundamental opposition with one another—that is, the goal of integrating the theory and practice of vocational discernment into an institution's academic program and doing so in ways that reach male students as successfully as they reach female students. Must the college simply settle for reduced male participation in these programs? The college would very much like to avoid having to choose between two highly desirable goals; this is why it gladly accepted the invitation to serve as one of the charter institutions for the present study. It also seemed prudent for Hope's pilot project to focus on the academic aspects of the institution, and—to whatever extent possible—on the classroom.

The appropriateness of this approach is reinforced by three additional facts. First, those students who participate in CrossRoads programs tend to be highly engaged and high-achieving students. This suggests that increasing the overall level of academic engagement and achievement among our students—particularly among the male students—may well result in a higher level of participation in vocational discernment activities sponsored by Hope's PTEV program. Second, as noted above, Hope College is currently engaged in a long-term conversation about increasing academic engagement and involvement among its students. The college is actively seeking ways to further this conversation and to experiment with programs and processes that can address this question. And third, through its participation in the Wabash Study of Liberal Arts Education, Hope College is the fortunate recipient of a wealth of data suggesting that, at least among first-year students, positive change is most likely to be brought about through curricular rather than extracurricular channels. This last point is a significant one and will be explored in further detail before turning to the specific nature of Hope College's project.

THE WABASH STUDY

The Wabash Study of Liberal Arts Education[4] is a detailed longitudinal study of how students are affected (and the degree to which various desirable outcomes are or are not achieved) by an institution's liberal-arts curriculum. While not focusing particularly on male/female issues, this study has turned out to be highly relevant to the questions that are explored in this chapter. Although Hope's par-

---

[4] Particular thanks are due to Dr. Caroline Simon of the Hope College Department of Philosophy, who has taken the lead in coordinating Hope's participation in the Wabash Study and who supplied me with considerable written material summarizing the results thus far.

ticipation in this study is still in an early stage, the college has been able to use some of its preliminary results in shaping the approach to the problem of male participation in the PTEV programs.

The Wabash Study is being conducted by a research team that includes members from the Center for Inquiry in the Liberal Arts, ACT, and researchers from Miami University, the University of Iowa, and the University of Michigan. It studies the institutional conditions, practices, programs, and structures that foster the development and integration of the various positive outcomes among students, including an inclination to inquire and to pursue lifelong learning, leadership skills, well-being, moral reasoning, the integration of learning, effective reasoning and problem solving, and intercultural effectiveness. Eighteen original institutions were selected from among 60 applicants; a few more institutions were added later. The study will gather data on approximately 5,500 students at the beginning of their college careers (both at the beginning and the end of their first year) and during their final year. Original institutions included 10 liberal arts colleges, three regional universities, three research universities, and two community colleges. Data collection for 270 first-year Hope students was done in mid-September 2006 and was repeated in mid-April 2007; it will be collected again in March 2010.

The results of the first phase of the study revealed that Hope College lags behind other liberal arts colleges in providing first-year students with a genuine academic challenge. More specifically, compared with Hope College's counterparts at other liberal colleges, the educational experience of Hope College first-year students is rated lower on three dimensions: (1) higher-order exams and assignments, (2) challenging classes and high faculty expectations, and (3) opportunities for integrating ideas, information, and experiences. The results of the Wabash Study suggest that improving these experiences could result in concomitant improvements in positive personal and educational outcomes.

In order to identify ways in which faculty can facilitate and enhance the behaviors and experiences related to the three dimensions of the academic challenge, the college conducted six focus groups with sophomore and junior Hope College students.[5] These focus groups suggested that Hope College students find the following areas to be significant challenges:

- Participating actively in significant and high-level discussions, particularly if they do not feel sufficiently comfortable with their professors and/or their classmates and thereby worry that their point of view may be rejected out-of-hand or simply not taken seriously.

---

[5] My thanks to Dr. Pat Roehling of the Hope College Department of Psychology, who coordinated the focus groups and wrote a detailed report and executive summary of the findings. The executive summary, in particular, was the basis for my further reduction and summary, which appear in this essay.

- Arguing a point of view or challenging others, particularly if they perceive their own view to be divergent from that of their professors, believe that they do not have adequate background in an area, or worry that they have not had time to prepare their thoughts.
- Integrating concepts across courses, particularly within the broader general education curriculum.
- Applying, discussing, and pursuing material learned in courses outside of the classrooms, unless they find this material either directly relevant to their lives or highly interesting, novel, or counterintuitive.
- Having assignments that do not seem to make them responsible for their own learning (i.e., when work is assigned that allows little freedom for them to choose topics that interest them or asks them merely to summarize research). They tend to respond better to assignments in which they must answer a question, propose a point of view, or solve a problem—particularly when they know such assignments will be graded.
- Finding the time and motivation to make an extra effort in a particular class—unless they perceive that their professors care about their progress and are willing to help them succeed, in which case they will rise to the challenge.

As is indicated by the "unless" clauses that are present in several of these findings, most of them already contain the seeds of their own resolution. Hope College students are more likely to participate in the kinds of activity that foster academic engagement and achievement when they perceive that the classroom environment, particularly as constructed and maintained by the instructor, is receptive to their input, attentive to their interests, and challenging in ways that encourage them to rise to those challenges. Our general sense is that the majority of Hope faculty already work to create precisely this kind of classroom environment but that their efforts are not always perceived this way by students.

The results of the Wabash Study have also suggested two other features of a student's college experience that can have a significant impact on the positive outcomes that the college seeks: increased student contact with faculty, particularly in settings outside the classroom, and diversity experiences (i.e., encounters with people unlike oneself). These are obviously not unique to the academic program; students can come into contact with faculty and/or with other people significantly different from themselves in cocurricular, residential, and informal settings of all kinds. But these experiences may be most valuable when they are initiated within the context of the classroom and/or are integrated back into the classroom in some way. When this occurs, students develop a greater sense of the importance of these experiences and of their relationship to the college's larger academic enterprise. So, for example, while a random encounter with a professor in a coffee shop may be valuable in itself, additional integration might be achieved through a professor's scheduled availability at the same coffee shop, during a particular time frame, for the purpose of discussing topics related to the course (but perhaps not of its essence). Moreover, only within the classroom can these two elements (additional faculty contact and diversity experiences) be programmed as a key element of a student's college experience, as opposed to leaving such encounters to random chance.

Needless to say, the results of the Wabash Study focus on the undergraduate population as a whole; they do not focus specifically on the male students. Nevertheless, given the specific context of Hope College and the faculty's general sense of the challenges (mentioned above) of helping male students take the academic elements of the college more seriously, a natural synergy is at work. At least in Hope College's experience, the greatest impact on positive outcomes related to a student's liberal arts experience seems likely to come from within the academic program of the institution rather than through student development activities, residential life programs, athletics, or other cocurricular pursuits. And yet, it often seems to be the case that a significant number of the male students focus much of their attention on these latter areas rather than on the academic program. Thus, it seems likely that additional efforts to increase academic achievement and engagement will have an especially strong impact on male students, because part of its outcome will be simply to draw these students' attention to the importance of the curricular elements of their education. This general sense was confirmed by Dr. Charles Blaich in his presentation of the initial Wabash Study findings at the Conference on the College Male (held in Collegeville, Minnesota, in February 2008). In this presentation, Blaich emphasized the importance of the three elements mentioned here—academic rigor, faculty contact, and diversity experiences—in improving outcomes. In addition, he and a student assistant presented some initial findings from focus groups consisting entirely of male students, indicating that there may be reason to believe that these three elements are even more important in increasing positive outcomes among male students than in the student population at large. Although these findings are still quite preliminary, informal conversations with Blaich have strongly confirmed the likelihood that these initial suppositions will eventually be borne out in practice.

Thus, a convergence of sorts has been taking place. From the very outset, Hope College located its PTEV program solidly within the academic division of the institution. Thus far, The CrossRoads Project's efforts seem to have had the most success, and to have achieved the greatest degree of integration into the life of the college, when they have concentrated on activities that take place within the structure of a particular course or on activities directly related to a course (field trips, class retreats, and similar events). At the same time, the academic program (and especially the classroom) seems to be the place where the college can expect to achieve the most progress in obtaining other positive liberal-arts-related outcomes, including (but not limited to) a higher level of academic engagement and achievement. Thus, with respect to Hope College's participation in the program to improve male participation in PTEV programs, it seemed possible to create an approach that would not only address the presenting question but also create synergies within the institution with regard to some of its other current goals and pursuits. A program was thus designed that focused on improving engagement and achievement within the college's academic programs, with a special focus on its male students.

THE PROPOSAL

Hope College's proposal consisted of two major parts. The first of these took place in summer 2008 and was grafted on to The CrossRoads Project's current offerings; it was funded internally. The second part took place during the 2008–2009 academic year and was funded by a pilot project grant.

PART I: SUMMER SEMINAR

The CrossRoads Project sponsored a faculty summer seminar during the week of July 14–18, 2008. It was entitled "From 'Losers, Loners, and Rebels' to Readers, Writers, and Thinkers: Empirical, Theological, and Practical Perspectives on Engaging Our Students (Especially the Men)." In this seminar, 14 college faculty members met for five consecutive days for six hours each day in order to read and discuss some significant literature on academic and theological engagement among students, with a particular focus on male participation.

The seminar made a particularly strong effort to weave together theory and practice. Its goals were, first, to advance the college's ongoing effort to improve academic engagement and achievement among its students, with a special focus on the challenges and opportunities that this presents for male students; second, to bring some theological light to bear on this endeavor; and third, to help faculty participants to produce concrete outcomes that would contribute to these larger goals. The seminar sought to provide faculty with opportunities (a) to examine some of the barriers (including theological ones) that tend to impede high levels of academic engagement for students in general and for male students in particular; (b) to consider ways of addressing these problems; and (c) to consider revising or refurbishing one of their current courses—preferably one in their own discipline that they teach on a regular basis—with attention to these issues. Readings for the seminar included general assessments of the academic strengths and weaknesses of today's students, examinations of the challenges faced by male college students in particular, theological accounts of the current shape of academic inquiry, social-scientific studies of the obstacles to achievement, and accounts of best practices in improving the level of student engagement. Mornings were to be spent in discussion of the readings; in the afternoons, a workshop format was employed in which members of the seminar were encouraged to provide one another with feedback as they began work on the practical task of developing appropriate revisions for a course in ways that might address at least some of these questions.

Hope College's proposed pilot project also had a specifically theological component: it included some reflection on the question of what it means to be male or female within the context of a church-related college in general and in the Hope College context in particular. Thus, the reading for the faculty seminar included recent work on the spiritual lives of young men (Dykstra, Cole, & Capps, 2007) and on the larger phenomenon of emerging adulthood (Arnett, 2004). The seminar also sought to investigate the degree to which a generally increased level of academic engagement and challenge might increase students' ability to address and wrestle with complex theological questions. This last point required particular attentiveness to Hope College's specific context within the larger family of Christian churches and church perspectives. Its students frequently come from broadly evangelical backgrounds, and they are not always comfortable with traditional theological claims about the importance of synthesizing faith and reason. Some of the seminar readings (e.g., Noll, 1995) were designed to increase understanding of the history and ongoing nature of this problem.

As part of the seminar, each faculty participant was encouraged to redevelop a single course that she or he had previously taught (perhaps on a regular basis) and planned to teach during the 2008–2009 academic year. During the week, faculty did additional reading on course development and academic engagement, considered the implications of the more theoretical readings on these questions, and identified a specific course for revision (if they had not already done so). Faculty members also exchanged ideas on how to make changes in their selected course in at least two of the three areas identified in the Wabash Study: (a) increasing academic rigor of the course; (b) developing more opportunities for quality faculty-student interaction outside the classroom; and/or (c) increasing student engagement with issues of diversity.

PART II: PILOT PROJECTS IN THE CLASSROOM

At the end of the seminar, faculty who were interested in continuing with the project submitted a proposal for substantially altering a course, along with a revised syllabus. A total of 10 faculty members (five each semester) were chosen to participate in this part of this project.

Faculty members who taught these revised courses were asked to submit a detailed summary report after the conclusion of the course, reflecting on the differences between their experiences of teaching the revised course *vis-à-vis* the course in its previous form. They were asked to offer some specific reflections on the level of engagement among the male students in the course.

Initially, the evaluation of this second phase of the program was intended to include focus groups consisting of students in the revised courses—both those who had taken it previously (in its unrevised form) and those who took the revised version. Although a few focus groups were held, we found it extremely difficult to persuade students to get involved in this project. Part of this had to do with the timeline; for example, it was difficult to gather feedback from students who had taken a particular course in the past, since they had afterwards dispersed into various other academic tracks (and some had graduated). Mostly, though, our difficulties seemed to relate to the fact that our students were feeling somewhat "over-studied"—both with respect to our particular academic culture (the Wabash Study, for example, demands a large pool of students, and this is not the only study in progress) and the culture at large (all of us know how often we receive well-intentioned pleas for responses to surveys). We therefore made a conscious decision not to try to assemble focus groups for each course but instead to rely more heavily on the faculty member's own evaluation of the differences between the pre- and post-revision versions of the course in question. Each instructor wrote two written reports (one while the course was in progress and another when it concluded) and also met with the project director for a summary discussion; this took place one to two months after the course ended in order to allow more time for reflection and analysis.

The Results: Part 1—Faculty Seminar

The summer seminar was tremendously successful.[6] It filled quite quickly to capacity (14 participants); it also generated considerable interest from faculty who were unavailable during the scheduled week but wanted to receive bibliographies and other materials in order to follow up on their own. Attendance during the event was excellent, and the faculty members participated actively in the discussion of the readings each morning. The afternoon workshop sessions were particularly lively, focusing as they did on some of the classroom-oriented ramifications of each morning's discussion. During these afternoon sessions, the participants generated a substantial list of practical suggestions as to how they might alter their own teaching based on the findings of the various texts that we read and discussed.

Needless to say, the faculty was not in uniform agreement about these suggestions nor about their own evaluations of the readings that were chosen. In particular, the book on the spiritual struggles of boys (Dykstra, Cole, & Capps, 2007) was considered by many participants to be too heavily vested in the authors' own experiential assessment of their own childhood and adolescence and that of those with whom they were acquainted. At the same time, this book led the participants to undertake some of their own analyses of the spiritual struggles of the boys and young men with whom they themselves were most closely acquainted

---

[6] I would like to express my gratitude to the 14 Hope faculty members who participated so actively in the Faculty Summer Seminar and who thereby not only contributed significantly to this project but also helped to make my own work a true joy. Thanks also to Dr. Joanne Stewart of the Hope Chemistry Department for offering a helpful presentation during the seminar.

and to consider the implications of these struggles for the way that our male students tend to process their experience of college. Mark Noll's *The Scandal of the Evangelical Mind* (1995) was particularly relevant to the Hope College context and led the group to consider how the author's description of the perceived divorce between faith and reason within many evangelical subcultures may be contributing to the anxiety felt among some of our students to engage their academic subjects as energetically as the faculty might hope they would. Additional help on this issue was discovered among some of the essays in a new collection on the "postsecular" academy (Jacobsen & Jacobsen, 2008); Hope faculty were interested to learn about the degree to which some of the issues that we face are related to national trends about the reemergence of questions concerning faith and theology in some of the country's more secularized institutions of higher learning.

Some of the best seminar discussion was generated by a collection of essays on the enterprise of teaching (Dunaway, 2005). Although this book might not have been considered as central to the theme of the seminar as were some of the other texts, its very specific focus on particular academic contexts (several of which bore certain similarities to those of Hope College) allowed participants to focus in on concrete examples and to offer their own experiences of similar cases. In addition, this book's focus on the genuine rewards and significance of teaching and learning in an academic community helped to provide additional inspiration for the participants in their own explorations of the concerns that the seminar was designed to address.

As noted above, afternoons were devoted to the generation of concrete suggestions. The seminar did not try to develop consensus around particular ideas; instead, recognizing the diversity of academic disciplines and teaching styles that were represented within the group, the participants simply offered descriptions of how they might put a particular idea into action in their own classrooms. Among the concrete practical suggestions that generated the most interest and discussion were the following:

- Helping students to take on a persona in order to discuss or debate a question, thereby alleviating some of the pressure they feel concerning the expression of their own views;
- Encouraging student engagement by creating a more comfortable atmosphere in the classroom, through the use of humor, popular music, Internet resources, or other elements with which students tend to be more familiar;
- Increasing the range of formats through which students can demonstrate mastery of the material, including formats with a greater degree of visual content than is typically the case for many text-based assignments;
- Increasing oral/aural engagement in the classroom by asking students to read aloud or listen carefully to something read by the instructor or by asking certain students to transcribe and/or summarize discussions;

- Finding ways of giving explicit permission for certain topics to be addressed, perhaps through the instructor's willingness to postpone or forgo disclosing his or her own view and/or frequently playing devil's advocate and/or encouraging or even provoking student reaction;
- Paying attention to the physical setup of the room, particularly with respect to the signals it gives about the validity of student input;
- Confounding student expectations about class format by inserting guest speakers, field trips, role playing, or similar elements—and sometimes without warning, so that students are genuinely interested to find out "what's going to happen today";
- Organizing debates, mock trials, and other forms of delegated advocacy (perhaps with the proviso that students be assigned certain roles, thereby alleviating the anxiety that the validity of their point of view will be heavily scrutinized by the onlookers and/or damaged by a poor performance); and
- Setting good discussion standards very early in the course (e.g., requiring students to learn and use one another's names, asking them to summarize another's point of view before they make an opposing claim, and requiring rather than merely allowing students to ask clarifying questions).

Obviously, the applicability of these approaches will vary greatly from one classroom to the next. Nevertheless, faculty expressed a great deal of appreciation for the opportunity to share strategies and approaches—something that they felt is done too seldom in the various settings of higher education.

In summary, Hope College's experience with the faculty summer seminar on this topic was very positive and may be appropriate in other institutions that are facing similar issues and questions on their campuses. In particular, much was gained from the decision to couple the more specific question of *male* participation with the broader issue of student academic achievement and engagement in general—and not only because it capitalized on synergies already present within the college's ongoing conversations (as noted above). In addition, this approach helped to blunt the potential criticism that an excessive focus on the male students might amount to a reversal of gains made over the last several decades with regard to female participation in the academic program; it was less a matter of attending to the men at the expense of the women and more a matter of thinking first about a widespread, general issue and then—within that framework—thinking about how the male students might be impacted by it differently than are female students.

The Results: Part 2—Specific Courses

As noted above, ten faculty members took advantage of the opportunity to restructure a course with the goal of increasing academic engagement, particularly among their male students. While space does not allow a summary of every faculty member's efforts, a few examples are listed here.[7] They are broadly representative of the kinds of course changes that all faculty members undertook as part of this project.

SEXUAL ETHICS. Dr. Carol Simon, Professor of Philosophy, made three adjustments to her Sexual Ethics course. First, she created a point system to evaluate in-class participation. (While this aspect of her course had always been graded, she had been less specific about exactly what one had to do to achieve a certain grade and what kinds of behaviors would count against a student.) Second, she created some flexibility in the way students were evaluated for the course, allowing them to make choices and assign their own relative weights to assignments, such as electronic discussion boards, thesis-driven papers, and a final exam. Third, she used a fishbowl discussion method for some topics, asking male students to speak while the female students observed and vice versa.

All three strategies were relatively successful. Providing more specificity for class participation resulted in livelier discussions; only one student lost points more than once for coming to class unprepared. Creating flexibility among evaluation methods allowed students to do what interested them (although Dr. Simon discovered that creating staggered deadlines is important in such an approach, because otherwise students tend to elect an approach that allows them to turn in the majority of their out-of-class work very late in the term). The use of a fishbowl discussion approach created good conversation, particularly on the question of how the students see themselves as fitting (or not fitting) particular cultural stereotypes. Grades for the male students (at least those who were not taking the course pass/fail) seemed to be stronger when compared with those of the female students. Although the instructor had no hard data with which to compare this performance, her overall sense was that the men engaged in the course material more energetically than had been the case in the past.

This example corroborates two suggestions that developed within the faculty seminar. The first of these was that some male students are particularly appreciative of detailed descriptions of what they must do to achieve a certain result in a course. The point scale was very specific in this regard; one male student (the only one who lost points more than once) scheduled a meeting with the instructor to see how he could improve his level of engagement with the course. The second seminar observation was that the men, more than the women, were likely to bristle against assignments that were perceived as make-work or as insufficiently

---

[7] Many thanks are due to all the faculty members who participated in this project for their diligent efforts in revising their courses and in providing detailed analyses concerning the results. The summaries that follow are my own; I have sought to accurately reflect each instructor's experience, but I recognize that no summary can convey every nuance, and I apologize to my colleagues if I have misrepresented their experiences in any way.

related to their own interests in electing the course. The opportunity to choose the weighting of various assignments allowed students to address this concern.

The question of all-male and/or all-female discussion groups received a mixed reaction in the seminar. Some felt that this would improve the willingness of men to contribute to the conversation with less grandstanding, but others questioned whether this could be achieved with the fishbowl technique. Clearly, Simon's experience was a positive one, but it can still be difficult to determine whether classroom discussion among males is improved simply by temporarily excluding women from the conversation or whether more extreme measures need to be taken. Our next example investigated this question.

Senior Seminar. Dr. Jesus Montaño of the Department of English offers a very popular course in Hope College's Senior Seminar program. Indeed, registration for spring 2009 was so strong that the course quickly developed a waiting list that was almost long enough to offer an additional section of the course. Unfortunately, this could not be justified, given the total number of faculty who were already teaching (i.e., the wait-listed students would simply have to elect a different topic for their Senior Seminar). However, Montaño noticed that every single person on the waiting list was male. Since he was already involved in the project (see the next section), he immediately recognized that this situation provided a perfect opportunity for comparing classroom discussions between an all-male and a mixed environment. With support from the Lilly grant, Montaño was able to offer both sections of the course and to compare their classroom dynamics.

Montaño did discover that the all-male group was often more willing to engage in discussion and that a higher percentage of the course's male registrants actually participated in these discussions. At the same time, the all-male class also produced a certain amount of groupthink, particularly with respect to classroom attitudes toward particular readings. The all-male group was more likely to decide, more or less as a group, that a particular reading did not really capture their interest and to skim sections rather than reading in depth. This, of course, made discussions very difficult.

Montaño considered instituting some kind of stronger check on the reading (quizzes, for example), which is what he probably would have done in an ordinary class. Instead, however, he chose to restructure his teaching approach in the all-male section, assigning smaller sections of the reading but making it clear to students that these would be discussed in detail during class. The students responded positively to this change, reading in greater depth when the length of the assignment was shortened. This allowed Montaño to lead the students through close readings of texts, thereby achieving several of his classroom goals in a way that was different from what he originally planned. This approach led several students to develop a greater interest in the text than they had originally experienced and to go back and read the entire book with care at a later date, even though it was not assigned. (One student did so after the class ended, in fact, after he had graduated, and wrote a letter to Montaño expressing appreciation for the professor's willingness to show him why the reading mattered.)

Montaño's experience strongly confirmed an element that arose during the summer seminar, to the effect that male students are more likely to feel overwhelmed by long reading assignments. Broadly speaking, they have generally not read as many books cover-to-cover as the female students; more than one faculty participant in the summer seminar recalled a male student having commented that a book assigned in a course was actually the first adult-level book that he had ever read in its entirety. Male students often need a great deal of help—carrots, sticks, or both—to complete reading assignments. Because both classroom discussion and overall performance in a course are often related to the ability to complete the require reading, this is an area worthy of further in-depth study. Issues such as time management and general interest level may certainly play a role, but if fewer male students have actually had the experience of finishing a book, this suggests the need to adopt alternative strategies (such as close readings of shorter passages) in order for male students to develop the skills needed in approaching longer assignments.

NATIVE AMERICAN LITERATURE. Montaño also taught a regular (mixed male/female) course in which he developed new strategies that were designed to improve male engagement and achievement. He employed two specific approaches. First, he sought to provide a more in-depth focus on some particular male figures in Native American history, thereby providing more possible routes for his male students to identify with (or contrast themselves with) these figures. Second, he tried to bring more of his own direct research into the classroom—particularly his experiences of traveling to Native American communities, engaging their citizens in dialogue, and using these communities as a basis for some of his own creative work (photography and writing).

Montaño discovered that the male students responded well to these changes, though perhaps in a somewhat different way than he had expected. He did find, for example, that historical figures (rather than fictional characters) were more likely to attract the interest of the male students in their reading and in classroom discussion. However, it was not so much the major figures (Sitting Bull and Crazy Horse) who attracted attention in this way but rather the less well-known historical figures—unsung heroes and ordinary men who had to face difficult circumstances or make complicated moral judgments. By examining more closely some of the issues that arose within classroom discussion, Montaño discovered that the most prominent male historical figures can actually be somewhat off-putting. In other words, with respect to helping male students identify with the figures discussed in Montaño's course, historical prominence was more likely to be an obstacle than a help. Although students seemed to find these figures too distant from their own experiences, other historical figures could serve the purpose well.

With respect to Montaño's second strategy, male students were particularly interested in his own experiences of travel to historical sites and conversations with

Native American communities. He felt that, by focusing on these experiences, he was providing the male students with a different kind of professorial role model than they usually experienced. Because many faculty members focus their research within the university settings (libraries, laboratories, archives, and so forth), many students develop a perspective of the professor as interested in questions that are very different from their own (at least at this stage of their lives). By demonstrating to students that scholarly research takes place outside of these typical environments and that it often involves travel, site visits, and person-to-person contact, he provided them with a very different picture of research in general and of a vocational possibility for an adult male that the male students themselves had never considered.

INTRODUCTION TO RELIGION. Dr. Wayne Brouwer of the Department of Religion adopted two new strategies for his introductory course. The first was to make use of PowerPoint to provide visual data in the classroom—something that he had previously done only on a very limited basis. He kept the number of slides to a minimum—perhaps seven to twelve per class session—and focused their content on major bullet points rather than intricate details. His goal was not so much to provide more visual material— previously he had written these bullet points on the board—but rather to allow him to be more engaged in providing examples and other supporting information within the classroom (he could spend less time writing on the board through use of the prestructured PowerPoint slides). His second strategy was to change the assignment of a major paper, which previously had been based primarily on personal experiences of others that the students were asked to gather through interviews. He felt that the interviewing process had been a good experience for most students but that they were less motivated to write the actual papers, which they saw primarily as summaries of the information they gathered rather than thesis-driven writing assignments. The change was to add a significant element of cultural reflection to the paper, in which students were asked to connect their interviewees' experiences to larger events in politics, the arts, or other areas of reportage in the media.

Brouwer felt that both strategies were successful and that they confirmed two issues that arose during the faculty seminar. First, students (and perhaps especially male students, though the data on this point are mixed) often need visual written cues as to the organization of course material. For a variety of reasons, they often find themselves unable to abstract major points from a lecture, particularly when the lecture is lively and uses a great many examples and narrative illustrations. An outline of some sort is helpful; however, when the professor uses class time and energy to write this out on the board, students sometimes lose the narrative thread of the whole. Visual data that has been prepared in advance (whether PowerPoint slides, handouts, or some other approach) can achieve a balance between the need for visual data and the importance of classroom continuity. Brouwer's second change had similar results to Dr. Simon's decision to allow more breadth in the range of assignments that students could undertake: they were able to pursue topics of interest to them, and they recognized its relevance both to the course material and to their lives.

Expository Writing. This course is an introduction to college-level writing required of all students unless they demonstrate competence through a placement test (in which case they can elect an upper-level course in English instead). A significant number of students do indeed test out of the course, with the result that its sections can sometimes be filled with students who find the work difficult and/or unengaging. This made it an especially promising candidate for attention to questions of academic achievement engagement—especially so in Dr. Jennifer Young's particular approach to the course (subtitled "The Hip Hop Globe" and focusing on rap music), which tends to attract relatively proportionate numbers of male and female students.

Young made three major revisions to her course. First, she sought to increase student accountability for doing the reading by assigning discussion roles in class and by requiring all students to attend a conference with the instructor every other week. Second, she assigned peer reviews in such a way that most students in the class worked with someone of the same gender. Finally, she reconstructed the wording of the assignments and general expectations for the class, breaking them down into specific sections (purpose, evidence, assessment) and used these same categories when providing follow-up and feedback.

All three of these strategies were highly successful. The mandatory individual conferences required a great deal of instructor time; however, in a second offering of the same course, Young was able to obtain funds for a teaching assistant who could help to shoulder this burden. Young indicated that, whether the students met with her or with her assistant, they responded uniformly well to the increased individual attention and the concomitant expectation that they would stay current in their assignments. The gender-specific peer review process also worked well, with some of the more capable and engaged male students providing positive modeling to some of those who were less well engaged and with less of the posturing (sometimes in an anti-intellectual direction) that often seemed to be evoked by male-female interactions within peer review groups.

Finally, the more detailed written assignments and expectations led to higher levels of engagement, particularly among the male students. Although Young had always provided the same information orally in class, many students (and particularly a number of the males) seemed to take written guidelines more seriously. But she also stressed that follow-up was an essential part of this process; male students, in particular, seemed quickly to relapse into undesirable behaviors (tardiness, late papers, missed conference appointments) and needed to be reminded of the standards that they were expected to meet. All the same, when these reminders were given, they tended to respond more positively than had been the case when the assignments and expectations had only been delivered orally in class rather than provided in written form. Young observed that, for the male students in particular, some form of written proof about classroom expectations seemed to make a great deal of difference—a difference that she did not observe among female students.

Envoi

At Hope College, efforts to achieve greater male participation in vocational discernment activities are closely related to efforts to achieve higher levels of academic achievement and engagement among these same students. The nature of the college's PTEV program makes it somewhat difficult to separate these elements from one another; this poses a difficulty for assessment. In spite of the positive results achieved within the classroom setting (at least according to the instructors' own assessments), no one can be certain that these students are necessarily engaging more actively in the vocation-related elements of these courses. Nevertheless, given the high degree to which the college has sought to integrate elements of vocational discernment into its academic program, increased levels of academic engagement seem likely to result in an increased level of attention to questions about vocation.

Since these changes have been made so recently, it is too early to tell whether they will have any discernible effect on the number of male students who participate in The CrossRoads Project initiatives in which such participation can be more directly measured. However, numerical accounts may not be the best measure of success in this regard. More useful will be broader measures of the degree to which the language of vocation and calling, along with active attention to matters of vocational discernment, continue to permeate campus life. In this respect, hopeful signs are definitely on the horizon.

If funding and time allow, the logical next step would be to return to the original plan of creating focus groups and designing other means of assessment to examine how seriously students (particularly male students) are attending to questions of vocational discernment. While a complex longitudinal assessment (like that of the Wabash Study) is not really an option, additional means of assessment may help to corroborate the general impression of individual instructors, to the effect that certain kinds of classroom practice can have a significant effect on academic achievement and engagement and that this can carry over into the specific efforts of vocational discernment programs.

References

Arnett, J.J. (2004). *Emerging adulthood: The winding road from the late teens through the twenties.* Oxford: Oxford University Press.

Dunaway, J.M. (Ed.). (2005). *Gladly learn, gladly teach: Living out one's calling in the twenty-first century academy.* Macon, GA: Mercer University Press.

Dykstra, R.C., Cole, A.H. Jr., & Capps, D. (2007). *Losers, loners, and rebels: The spiritual struggles of boys*. Louisville, KY: Westminster/John Knox Press.

Jacobsen, D., & Jacobsen, R.H. (Eds.). (2008). *The American university in a postsecular age*. Oxford: Oxford University Press.

Kennedy, J.C., & Simon, C.J. (2005). *Can Hope endure? A historical case study in Christian higher education*. Grand Rapids, MI: William B. Eerdmans.

Noll, M. (1995). *The scandal of the evangelical mind*. Grand Rapids, MI: William B. Eerdmans.

4

THE MOREHOUSE MALE INITIATIVE SEMINAR: PROVIDING A PATH TO VULNERABLE EXPRESSION, LEADERSHIP, AND CALLING

BRYANT T. MARKS AND MARQUAN JONES

The Morehouse Male Initiative (MMI) is a research-based program, located at Morehouse College, that is designed to identify the factors that contribute to the psycho-social, leadership, and academic development of African American Male college students. Identifying these factors includes the implementation of various activities (best practices). In order to most clearly describe our approach to what we hope can be called a best practice, we will first provide our rationale for designing the project. After several discussions, presentations, and readings with and by members of other Lilly project teams, we took time to process the specific purpose of our activity and how it worked toward the goals of the overall project. We first began with a definition of terms. *Vocational discernment* is derived from the Latin word *vocare*, which means to call; *vocation* is defined by *The American Heritage Dictionary* as "1. A regular occupation, especially one for which a person is particularly suited or qualified; 2. An inclination, as if in response to a summons, to undertake a certain kind of work, especially a religious career; a calling." *Discernment* is defined as "keenness of insight and judgment." Consequently, we viewed vocational discernment as the ability to clearly and accurately identify the specific work that one is called to do.

This work may be an occupation itself, or more likely an occupation is the vehicle through which one's calling is manifested. For example, a man may be called to be a mortgage banker in that he is particularly suited or qualified to originate and process home loans. His calling, however, may actually be the virtuous work of helping others become homeowners, which typically enhances their financial stability, family dynamic, and overall quality of life. Although he works on the finance side of the home buying process, if he were particularly qualified as a developer, homebuilder, realtor, appraiser, credit counselor, or closing attorney, his calling would remain the same. These occupations are merely various vessels through which he could engage in the work he was summoned to do—to help people become homeowners.

The use of the word *called* connotes the existence of an external entity as one does not usually call oneself literally or figuratively, to do something. Those who are theologically oriented may use the name of the deity associated with their belief system (e.g., God, Yahweh, Buddha, Allah) to describe this entity. For others, the universe, fate, or destiny best captures their perspective. Regardless of the source, the all-too-prevalent tragedy is that many can neither hear nor adhere to their calling because they are overly distracted (even by good things), out of order, scared, unable to envision themselves engaged in the call, chasing money, or conforming to norms and expectations of society, friends, family, or other loved ones. Many have so much going on in their lives that their callings are often muted by the overwhelming amount of noise that saturates their existence to the point where their calling cannot be heard, felt, or given proper attention.

Also worth noting is timing. We have heard several Christian preachers and pastors describe the circumstances surrounding their calling and how they knew what they were being called to do. The vast majority of them did not predict being called to the ministry and many of them resisted the calling for several years. Some were called in their youth, others in adulthood, and the process varied from messages in dreams to hearing God's voice to a persistent yet unexplainable gnawing. The lesson is that one's calling can become evident early or later in life and may occur in a direct or indirect manner. For those called later in life, the questions become 1) What do I do in the meantime? and 2) How do I live my life in a manner that allows my ears, head, and heart to remain sensitive enough to acknowledge the calling when it occurs?

Consequently, the goals of our project were threefold: first, to create and facilitate a process by which our students, specifically African-American males, could clearly and accurately identify the work they are called to do; second, to foster in them the courage to pursue and explore said calling; and third, in cases where a calling has not yet occurred, to assist them in determining in-the-meantime activities and lifestyles that will allow them to hear and walk in their calling when it is manifested.

A Word on African-American Males

Endangered species, at risk, disenfranchised, irresponsible, and *thugs* are just a few of the extant labels used to describe young African-American males. Although these descriptors are often erroneously applied to the majority of African-American males, the statistics paint an unfortunate picture relative to their counterparts of other ethnic groups. African-American males do indeed disproportionately experience negative outcomes in many important domains (e.g., infant mortality rates, academic achievement, health, incarceration, negative stereotypes, and employment). While we can debate the reasons for this state of affairs, the bottom line is that a significant proportion of African-American male children have to use considerable energy and attention to manage many of the factors that lead to negative outcomes throughout their childhood and adolescence. Dealing with these factors, along with the noise of life that comes with just being human, is likely to reduce the probability that young African-American males will detect their calling when it occurs.

Males in general, and African-American males in particular, have been found to be less willing and/or able to engage in *vulnerable expression*—sharing their innermost thoughts, feelings, insecurities, fears, dreams, experiences, and concerns—with others, especially their male peers. We believe that vulnerable expression is critical to hearing and walking in one's calling for it allows individuals to openly and authentically express themselves. The challenge for many African-American males is finding a nonjudgmental space where vulnerable expression can occur and be validated. American norms of manhood include mantras such as "big boys don't cry" and "man up" as well as male emotional expression being seen as feminine or sometimes associated with homosexuality. Also, African-American males have less contact with their biological fathers relative to males of other American ethnic/racial groups. Consequently, some (but not all) African-American male children and adolescents do not have the opportunity to witness or engage in vulnerable expression with other Black males, rendering them unsure of when, how, and with whom sensitive expression should occur. This is not to say that all Black fathers have mastered vulnerable expression or that their mere presence will develop mastery in their sons. Many fathers, regardless of race, are not good parents. Further, many Black male children have uncles, grandfathers, or other Black males in their lives who provide constructive models of vulnerable expression. Yet, it is our belief that the likelihood of an African-American male child witnessing vulnerable expression is increased, however small, by a father's presence (biological or stepfather). At some point in the life of a Black boy whose father is present, he will likely have a tender word or moment with his father, see his father cry, share his dreams, respond to setbacks and failures, and hear stories of "when I was your age."

In short, it is difficult for Black males to model behavior that they have not seen or practiced. Vulnerable expression is no exception. The lack of exposure to and socialization by a Black father leaves the Black male child open to the influence of peers and popular media that often present a hyper-masculine caricature of Black maleness/manhood, a caricature that is very difficult to deconstruct during adulthood, which has led us to the questions that drove the secondary goals of our project: (a) How can we undo the negative messaging and years of hyper-masculine behavior that is deeply entrenched in the minds of young Black males? (b) How do we replace this mentality with a more constructive and productive model of manhood that includes vulnerable expression? and (c) How can Black males utilize vulnerable expression to quiet the noise of life so that their calling can be heard?

THE PROJECT

THE INSTITUTIONAL SETTING: MOREHOUSE COLLEGE

It is very important to understand the institutional context of Morehouse College because it aligns very well with theological exploration of vocation and has an extensive and strong history of producing theologically oriented leaders, such as Martin Luther King, Jr., Howard Thurman, Calvin Butts, and Otis Moss, Jr. Morehouse has also produced leaders in many other fields, including politics (e.g.,

Maynard Jackson and Julian Bond), the arts (e.g., Spike Lee and Samuel Jackson), and medicine (e.g., David Satcher and Louis Sullivan). While attending Morehouse, students are "Men of Morehouse;" upon graduation they become "Morehouse Men." The current president, Robert Michael Franklin ('75), describes Morehouse Men as "renaissance men with social conscience and global perspective."[8] Furthermore, he expects Morehouse Men to exemplify five "wells": well read, well spoken, well traveled, well dressed, and well balanced (mentally, physically, and spiritually). The Morehouse mission statement provides further insight and history.

> The mission of Morehouse College is to develop men with disciplined minds who will lead lives of leadership and service. A private historically black liberal arts college for men, Morehouse realizes this mission by emphasizing the intellectual and character development of its students. In addition, the College assumes special responsibility for teaching the history and culture of black people. Founded in 1867 and located in Atlanta, Georgia, Morehouse is an academic community dedicated to teaching, scholarship, and service, and the continuing search for truth as a liberating force.... The College seeks students who are willing to carry the torch of excellence and who are willing to pay the price of gaining strength and confidence by confronting adversity, mastering their fears, and achieving success by earning it. In pursuit of its mission, Morehouse challenges itself to be among the very finest liberal arts institutions in the world.

Morehouse enrolls approximately 2,800 students from over 40 states and 27 countries, has the highest African-American male graduation rate of all historically black colleges, and is a top producer of African-American males who obtain graduate and professional degrees. Given its mission, history, and institutional characteristics, Morehouse is fertile ground for vocational exploration.

THE COURSE

After much deliberation, we decided to create a course that comprised the elements we believe are necessary to achieve our three primary goals (i.e., minimizing the noise of life, identifying one's calling, and pursuing one's calling) and address the three aforementioned questions regarding our secondary goals.

COURSE DESCRIPTION

The class was a 3-credit, 300-level, open enrollment, special topics psychology elective course entitled "African American Male Identity and Spirituality," taught

---

[8] Quote taken from a speech entitled, "The Soul of Morehouse and the Future of the Mystique" given on 4/21/09 at a townhall meeting at Morehouse College.

by by the first author of this chapter. At the time of this writing, the course has been taught for three semesters. The class met once a week between 5 and 8 p.m. (first semester) and 4 and 7 p.m. (second and third semesters) in a medium-sized conference room that sat 12 students in comfortable mesh or leather conference chairs around a large conference table. Although most of the students were sophomore through senior psychology majors, there were several attendees from other disciplines and two freshmen across the three semesters. The class, like the Morehouse student body in general, consisted of students from various states, hometown profiles (e.g., urban, suburban, rural), and socioeconomic backgrounds. I (Marks) referred to the students and they referred to each other as "Brother (last name)" in order to verbally prime a positive connection to one another. Grades were based on attendance, submission of weekly discussion questions, facilitation of class discussion of readings, participation in class discussions, and a short essay. Each class meeting was divided into three 1-hour sections: (a) guest speaker and dinner, (b) discussion of readings, and (c) testimonials.

First Hour: Guest Speakers and Dinner

Dinner, which was provided at the beginning of class, was offered for practical and psychological purposes. On the practical side, I do not know how or why, but students seem to have insatiable appetites and are typically excited by the notion of free, non-cafeteria food. Thus, having the food warm and waiting at the beginning of class increased the probability of them arriving on time if not early (there is actually consideration of not allowing students that are more than 5 minutes late to eat until the end of the first hour). Also, the class meets for 3 hours that encompass dinnertime for most students. Many of them eat lunch between noon and 1 p.m., which could result in growling stomachs by 5:30 p.m. that would likely lead to bathroom/snacking breaks, attention loss, negative association with the class, and resentment toward the professor! The food included pizza, wraps, subs, fried chicken, burgers, and catered selections by a student chef not enrolled in the course (whenever possible, healthy versions of all food were chosen). The psychological rationale for the food was that eating in groups is something in which families, friends, and other social networks engage and it also has a festive, celebratory feel to it. Because people often eat with loved ones who they trust, many personal and meaningful issues are discussed over a meal. That is, it is a space where many people are vulnerably expressive.

A critical prerequisite to hearing and pursuing one's calling is self-knowledge. What one is called to do should be consistent with who one is. Actually, one's calling can be seen as an extension of one's identity that incorporates the talents and strengths of the individual. There are many paths to self-knowledge, one of which is social learning—learning from the experiences of others. An individual is likely to accelerate his development if he can observe, process, and draw lessons from the experiences of others, such as the guest speakers in the course, who faced and overcame challenges. It is a very efficient strategy in that it allows multiple lessons to be learned simultaneously and the individual receives the benefit without the cost. The purpose of the guest speakers, all of whom were African-American men, was to expose young African-American males to elders who walked in their shoes a few or many years ago.

The goal in selecting African-American male guest speakers was not to discriminate but to present students with someone with whom they were most likely to identify demographically, physically, academically, and culturally. We (Marks and Jones) fully recognize that one can learn from a diverse array of human beings. It is our position, however, that these speakers could be viewed and could engage the students as would older brothers, uncles, fathers, or grandfathers, a connection that can foster bonding and learning at a deep, emotional level. The speakers' professions varied (e.g., college staff and professors, community activists, clinical psychologist, Christian and Muslim clergy, business men, politicians, deans, and the Morehouse College president), but all were college educated and about 70% were Morehouse Men (who were very excited about the opportunity to come back to campus and speak to students). Upon acceptance of the invitation to speak, each guest received a syllabus and description via e-mail of what was expected. Their task was to tell their life stories (20–30 minutes) followed by a question-and-answer session (20–30 minutes). We asked them to use the following identity/calling questions to guide the narrative of their life stories.

1. WHO AM I? This question was asked to directly assess speakers' self-knowledge. We did not provide any frame of reference, which resulted in very rich, diverse, unique, and unexpected responses. This question allowed speakers to describe idiosyncrasies and experiences that some students may have considered weird (e.g., not watching TV), atypical of African-American males (e.g., being Jewish), or nonproductive (e.g., procrastinating). It vividly displayed the multiple identities and characteristics that Black males possess and sent a clear message that African-American manhood is personified in many forms. Speakers were also quite clear in describing their development as a process and indicated that they have changed in subtle and significant ways throughout their lives. Most speakers engaged in vulnerable expression quite easily while answering this question. Several of them described their professions as a significant part of their identities, and others literally referred to their professions as callings (i.e., vocations).

2. WHAT DO I BELIEVE? This question was designed to convey the speakers' worldview, philosophy of life, or any other macro-level belief system that guided their existence. This question allowed students to realize that everyone has a particular perspective or way that he sees and approaches life. Like question 1, the open-ended nature of this question elicited varied responses, including the basic nature of human beings, how the world works, the challenges faced by African Americans and potential solutions, and the significance of historical events. The vast majority of the time, however, responses included a direct reference to religion and/or spirituality. Guests described their religious lives growing up (e.g., church attendance, prayer, church-related activities) and the extent to which it changed over time. They also described their spiritual beliefs—the extent to which they believed in a nonphysical entity (e.g., God, the universe) and the degree of influence that entity had on their lives—and how these beliefs changed over time. The students were quite intrigued by the religious/spiritual comments and somewhat relieved to hear successful, older men say that they went through periods of exploration, ambivalence, and confusion during their religious and spiritual development. Vulnerable expression was a common occurrence as this question was addressed, leading to deep introspection by students.

3. *WHY DO I BELIEVE WHAT I BELIEVE?* This question, a direct follow-up to question 2, was intended to extract specific life experiences that had significant developmental impact on the guest speakers. The responses referenced father-son relationships, significant failures and achievements, dysfunctional family life, betrayal, insecurities, peer pressure, family expectations, and events that can only be described as miraculous. The depth of the responses was not lost on the students, evidenced by the apprehensive and tentative tone of their questions and comments. The speakers were typically very warm and invited questions regarding common and very sensitive experiences. Their answers to this question, like those to questions 1 and 2, provided acute descriptions and details of their lives that would rarely arise in typical conversation among strangers or adult and adolescent males; vulnerable expression was present once more. Their responses also contained direct and indirect references to the callings they would describe while addressing question 4.

4. *WHAT DO I BELIEVE I AM CALLED/MEANT TO DO?* We asked this question to ensure that we provided guests with the opportunity to directly describe their respective calling. We intentionally used the word calling and not vocation due to the potential of losing the weight of the question, given the parochial connotation usually associated with vocation. We wanted the question to invoke thoughts of life purpose, the bigger picture, legacy, and significant impact. The answers indicated that the question was processed as intended. The magnificent depth and breadth of the responses were inspirational, motivational, practical, and challenging. After hearing guests describe being called to save lives figuratively and spiritually, write the consummate history of Morehouse College, heal the minds and souls of others, start companies and organizations from the ground up, raise the next generation of leaders, and serve others in a self-sacrificing manner, the students were humbled, yet their vision of what is possible expanded significantly for some and exponentially for others. The speakers usually described the context and events before, during, and after the revelation of their calling/purpose. As previously mentioned, the preachers and pastors recounted varying levels of hesitation to heeding their call. Also, none of the guest speakers mentioned a calling

that involved wealth or success at a purely individual level. The consistent theme of the responses was service—engaging in activities that improved the lives of others—even if it was by way of a traditional occupation, profession, or career.

Notably, while speakers were positioned at varying points on the hearing, accepting, and pursuing their calling continuum, they all felt confident regarding the type of work they were called to do, albeit a minority of them not clearly knowing how they would do it. The lack of specificity regarding the "how" actually seemed refreshing to the students in that it became acceptable to be unaware of how everything in life is going to turn out and that it is possible, although not always preferable, to recover from what several speakers described as a slow start—not fully realizing or functioning in their calling or potential until later in life. The involvement of guest speakers provided several additional benefits. Although the speakers were only present for one hour, students were able to network, meet potential personal and professional role models and mentors, engage in social learning that would allow them to navigate college and career, and build a pool of examples of achievement in the face of adversity.

Second Hour: Discussion of Assigned Readings

The selected weekly readings were loosely based on aspects of the four aforementioned questions. The intent was to identify writings that would engage the students while pushing them to employ critical introspection, wherein they not only became more self-aware but questioned why they are who they are and assessed the costs and benefits of changing. The expectation was that such introspection might also cause them to live better lives, serve others, and reveal the area of their callings if not the specific callings themselves. The readings also provided another opportunity to bear witness to vulnerable expression by male authors (predominantly, but not all African American) of national and international repute. The reading list comprised one to two chapters from recent and classic books that dealt with African-American male identity (e.g., Akbar's [1992] *Visions for Black Men*, the only book students read in its entirety), church experiences (e.g., Kunjufu's [1997] *Adam, Where Are You? Why Black Men Don't Go to Church*), philosophical/spiritual perspectives (e.g., Peck's [1998] *The Road Less Traveled*), Morehouse itself (e.g., Benjamin E. Mays' last commencement address as Morehouse College's president [1940–1967]), and autobiographies of prominent African-American men (e.g., Obama's *The Audacity of Hope* [2006]).

On the first day of class, the professor provided the ground rules for class discussion of the readings that included respect for others' opinions, disagreeing without being disagreeable, allowing others to finish their comments before speaking, addressing each other by Brother (last name), raising a hand to be called on by the facilitator before speaking, and deferring to the facilitators' directions. The facilitators (comprised of two students) sat side-by-side at one end of the conference table with the professor at the other end. This seating arrangement allowed students to physically focus on the facilitators without concern for the professor's reaction or approval and would possibly have worked better if the professor had been removed from the table altogether. The professor rarely spoke during the discussion but he informed the facilitators of when 10 and 2 minutes remained in the hour.

A team of two students assigned at the beginning of the semester facilitated the discussion of the reading on two occasions. Students (except those who were facilitators) were required to e-mail two discussion questions to the facilitators and the professor by noon the day before class. These questions, which were graded, had to refer to specific passages in the reading and served as the basis for meaningful discussion rather than a quick retort or factual, closed-ended response. The facilitators' job was to guide the discussion in an orderly, fair, and diplomatic fashion. Students were graded on their ability to manage a discussion of various aspects of the readings and solicit at least one comment or incorporate at least one question from all of the other students. The facilitators began the second hour with a 10-minute summary (five minutes for each facilitator) of the key points of the reading and offered their general impressions. They then used the discussion questions to guide the conversation. They referred to the student who submitted the question, read it aloud, and then asked the author to describe what led him to asking the question and to provide clarification if he felt it was necessary. Multiple questions were grouped together when there was significant overlap in the perspectives or there were references to the same passage of the reading. The professor did not recall a time when a question posed was met with silence. Because the readings were typically engaging and thought-provoking, many students had thoughts or questions similar to those of the author and their hands shot up with enthusiasm coupled with a "call on me please" energy that made life easy for the facilitators. Discussion, while spirited, was rarely contentious. But, on the infrequent occasion that comments became personal and unable to be handled by the facilitators, the professor would intervene, clarify the students' positions, attempt to find common ground, and remind the students of the ground rules.

Although the primary rationale for student facilitation was to stimulate conversations among peers, there were several beneficial by-products. Group facilitation is actually a skill that develops with practice but can be applied to various situations throughout one's life. Many of these students, however, had no formal facilitation experience. A comparison of their performances at the beginning of their first facilitation with those at the end of their second revealed considerable development. They learned when and how to intervene in a passionate exchange or, when someone was long-winded, to systematically call on students in the order in which they raised their hands so that none felt dismissed or ignored. They learned that good facilitation often means very little speaking on their part, how to cover multiple topics in a limited amount of time, how to find agreement among speakers while still validating differing opinions, when to let a conversation continue or end, and when and how to effectively transition from one topic to another. In addition, the facilitation experience provided all students, including those who were shy or introverted, with a leadership opportunity that was complex and challenging and that required preparation and analytical skills.

Third Hour: Testimonials

Like the first hour, the third hour entailed the telling of life stories. The students, however, were the tellers of these stories, referred to as testimonials. The rationale for student testimonials mirrored that of the guest speakers, with the expectation of less conclusive commentary regarding students' callings. Students had to answer the four identity/calling questions, but I usually asked them to also describe their Morehouse experience (i.e., provide reasons for choosing Morehouse and give a description of their satisfaction and overall experiences to date). They were encouraged to be creative in their presentation (e.g., incorporating pictures, video, poetry, or music) and to reveal as much or as little information as was comfortable. Like the guest speakers, they also had up to 30 minutes for the testimonial, followed by a 20–30 minute question/answer session. As in the discussion of the readings, I also set ground rules for testimonials on the first day of class, reminding them that this was a nonjudgmental and affirming activity. Thus, there was to be no snickering, side conversations, personal attacks, or disapproving facial expressions/nonverbal behavior. I also stated that what was shared in class stayed in the class during the semester and after the course was over.

The student testimonials, by far, were the most insightful and impactful part of the course. The activity provided the opportunity for students to openly and authentically express themselves in a nonjudgmental space, a space designed to validate them as human beings, provide constructive feedback, and convey that they were not alone. Although varying from question to question, vulnerable expression was consistently displayed during the testimonials. Answers to the "Who am I?" question included physical descriptions, childhood trauma and achievements, racial identity, vices, insecurities, challenges they were in the midst of managing or overcoming, and their plans, hopes, and dreams for the future. All students provided background regarding their socioeconomic situations while growing up as well as a description of several members of their family and the developmental impact of specific family members.

The conclusion drawn from this question of identity was radiantly clear: males, and in this case African-American male college students, are very much alike in a limited number of domains (e.g., recognition of how Black males are perceived and the consequential challenges; being Christian; an appreciation for formal education; and an acknowledgment of the impact of others, especially their present or absentee fathers, on their self-concept). These students, however, were also intriguingly diverse. Whether it was their hobbies, interests, political views, musical preferences, views of women, or (somewhat surprisingly) the significance and meaning of their religious and spiritual identities, these young men displayed a level of variance that one would expect from a multiracial sample. Vulnerable expression was consistently displayed, although to varying degrees, with the students who presented later in the semester tending to be more expressive than those who presented early on.

The question "What do I believe?" prompted responses that tended to be complex, insightful, and, for lack of a better word, deep. This question challenged students to introspect with the purpose of teaching/presenting their thoughts. Thinking about personal beliefs is one thing but sharing them in a clear enough manner that others will receive it exactly as intended can be a challenging task. Interestingly, this challenge was intensified when the speaker, in the spirit of political correctness, attempted to sanitize his commentary as not to offend others, an attempt that sometimes resulted in the unintended consequence of reduced authenticity. Comments regarding religion and spirituality were common. What varied was the extent to which their religious/spiritual beliefs were actually reflected in their daily behavior. Many students described themselves as Christian, believing in Jesus and the Bible. However, by their own reports and by my observation, it was clear that several of them had not fully internalized the teachings to which they were exposed. Other responses to this question included general beliefs about how the world works, how to treat other people, factors that facilitate success, the history and culture of African Americans, solutions to challenges experienced by African Americans (especially African-American males), and students' priorities in life that usually included family, education, close friends, and personal development.

In response to "Why do I believe what I believe?" the students shared personal, sometimes very personal, experiences that served as the basis for the beliefs mentioned in response to the "What do I believe?" question. Many of the responses referred to specific family events during childhood, overcoming or failing to overcome challenges that fostered their development, moments of recognition for achievement (often academic), and specific messages received from parents and guardians. It is worth noting that this question illuminated the tender distinction between parental/guardian messages included in their childhood socialization and the students' independent thoughts and experiences. Students were challenged to critically analyze their beliefs. Consequently, they sometimes expressed discomfort or frustration when attempting to incorporate new knowledge and experiences that were not easily assimilated into their existing belief system. Conversely, other students felt that responding to this question strengthened their existing beliefs due the ease of incorporating new knowledge and experiences. Either way, many of them were transitioning from a solely parent/guardian-based belief system to one that was also influenced by their independent thoughts and experiences. This was very much the case regarding religious and spiritual beliefs.

Finally, the question of "What do I believe I am called/meant to do?" resulted in predictable variation. Given their stage in life and class standing (freshmen, sophomore, etc.), some students had only vague notions of their calling or purpose because they were still struggling with selecting a major. Others, usually upper classmen, were very clear regarding their calling/purpose. The overwhelming theme throughout the responses, regardless of class standing, was service. Although the areas of expertise and occupation included but were not limited to medical doctors, politicians (including president of the United States), elementary through high school teachers, professors, therapists, ministers, pastors, entrepreneurs, and attorneys, the vast majority of students explicitly described how their jobs would be a means for helping others. Returning to our definition of vocational discernment—the ability to clearly and accurately identify the specific work that one is called to do—the responses make sense. The work that students described was the work of helping others. Consequently, their jobs/occupations were merely the vehicle through which such work would occur. Some students spoke of their calling as divinely inspired, others did not. What was clear, however, was that the theme of service was supported by an undercurrent of integrity, empathy, and civility; qualities that may have existed prior to college but are at the very core of the Morehouse College socialization.

Student Bonding and Trust Building Activity

As mentioned, vulnerable expression among students requires trust, trust that others will be nonjudgmental, that what is said in the class stays in class, that the benefit of the doubt would be given when comments could be taken negatively or constructively, and that the goal is to assist in the affirmative development of each other. To this end, the students in the class participated in an activity designed to foster bonding and trust. Each class carpooled to Stone Mountain Park, just outside of Atlanta, on a Saturday. The facilitator, a Morehouse alumnus, guided the students through two activities: (a) the human knot, which required 9–12 students to stand in a circle shoulder-to-shoulder, clasp hands with 2 other people across the circle, and then untangle themselves to form one continuous circle where each person with whom they held hands was standing next to them; and (b) to hike up Stone Mountain itself, which required students to work as a team to find the best paths, physically assist each other over obstacles, and encourage each other when they were tempted to quit. The singing of songs, sharing of childhood experiences in the outdoors, and discussions of various topics were a common occurrence during the hike. When the students completed the climb, there was a mountaintop discussion of life in general and the day's events. The vast majority of the students thoroughly enjoyed this event and wished it was longer or overnight, and according to the professor, bonding and trust were enhanced.

Conclusions

To recap, the goals of our project were to (a) create and facilitate a process by which our students, specifically African-American males, could clearly and accurately identify the work they are called to do; (b) foster in them the courage to pursue and explore said calling; and (c) in cases where a calling had not yet occurred, assist them in determining what to do in the meantime and lifestyles that would allow them to hear and walk in their callings when they were revealed. Student evaluations of the course that included open and closed-ended items indicated that all of these goals were achieved. Regarding two of the complementary questions of interest—how to reverse negative messages/hyper-masculine behavior and construct positive models of African-American manhood—the readings, class discussions, guest speakers, and, very interestingly, student testimonials were very effective strategies. The third question, How can Black males utilize vulnerable expression to quiet the noise of life so that their calling can be heard? was a question of focus—defined in this context as spending more time on fewer things. The students consistently indicated that the class forced them to stop and think, ignore distractions, evaluate their priorities, assess how they spend their time, become self-aware, and make tough decisions about people they should and should not allow to influence them. Although the course was effective in its own right, the history and ethos of Morehouse College that emphasizes leadership and service coupled with the clear model of the Morehouse Man were fertile ground within which the seeds of calling/purpose could be planted. Students and guest speakers consistently referred to Morehouse throughout their commentary. Thus, it is recommended that the positive aspects of the institution, including desired character traits, serve as a factor in the implementation of this model by others. Students' vocations/callings are not something to be taken lightly, yet with genuine concern and sincere motives, colleges cannot only engage in exposing students to the liberal arts but also in the art of liberating.

References

Akbar, N. (1992). *Visions for Black men*. Tallahassee, FL: Mind Productions & Associates.
Kunjufu, J. (1997). *Adam, where are you? Why Black men don't go to church*. Chicago: African American Images.
Obama, B. (2006). *The audacity of hope*. New York: Crown.
Peck, M.S. (1998). *The road less traveled*. New York: Touchstone.

5

Engaging Men in Service:
Lessons from Hastings College

Ronald D. Chesbrough and Daniel G. Deffenbaugh

In the spring of 2003, Hastings College implemented its Vocation and Values Program—part of the Programs for the Theological Exploration of Vocation funded by a generous grant from the Lilly Endowment Inc.—with the expressed purpose of giving students on our campus the opportunity to develop talents and skills that could be used to enrich their lives and serve others. Our initiative had three primary foci. First, our Christian Ministry minor was designed to prepare interested students for lifelong, bi-vocational service to the church as lay pastors, Christian educators, youth directors, and ministers of music. Second, our service learning initiative was developed to provide the broader student community with occasions to explore their calling through service to others, whether locally, nationally, or globally. A concerted effort was made in this instance to incorporate service learning into as many courses in the liberal arts curriculum as possible. Finally, the general Vocation and Values Program provided students with a host of opportunities to explore their vocation through specially designed courses, workshops, and presentations offered by nationally renowned speakers and authors. This aspect of the initiative also resulted in an exclusive collection of essays—written by faculty, alumni, and a variety of celebrated authors—on various themes in vocational exploration, including the meaning of work, service and the self, moral leadership, and the liberal arts and the life of the spirit. These essays are now available to all visitors to the Hastings College Vocation and Values Web site (www.hastings.edu).

With respect to men's and women's participation in our various curricular and cocurricular offerings, a clear pattern seemed to emerge several years into the initiative. If, for purposes of illustration, one can imagine the Christian ministry program as the center of three concentric circles, with service learning occupying the second ring and the academic exploration of vocation circumscribing the first two circles, then we can express how students responded to these three initiatives along gender lines. Very simply, as one moves closer to the center of this configuration, one encounters more women than men participating on a sustained basis. Indeed, in the first 3 years in which the Vocation and Values Program was offering full and partial scholarships for students interested in Christian ministry, only 4 of the 18 recipients (22%) were men, and these were chosen from among a very small number of male applicants. Clearly more women were interested in the theological exploration of vocation because it was offered in conjunction with service learning in the church and in the mission field. This is also reflective of male and female participation among our general student body.

In the second concentric circle—service learning—our gender numbers moved slightly closer to parity, but again more women were interested in service opportunities than were their male peers. This could be due to the fact that most of the professors who enthusiastically supported our service learning initiative were women, and among these all of the instructors teaching in our women's studies program were participating from the inception of our program. Over the last 7 years, Hastings College students have maintained a vital presence among the primary and secondary schools in our community as a result of service learning initiatives that were encouraged and supported by the Vocation and Values Program. Among the many worthwhile projects that have been sustained over this period of time is a program called Food 4 Thought in which Hastings College education majors—again, the majority being women—identify at-risk students in local elementary and middle schools and provide backpacks filled with nonperishable meals to sustain these children over the weekends. This and a variety of other creative programs have helped to place Hastings College on the President's Higher Education Community Service Honor Roll every year since 2006.

Finally, our outermost circle—courses developed primarily for first-year students to reflect critically on the notion of call in the classroom—is the place where we have seen the greatest success in moving toward gender parity. These classes were offered primarily during our January term in which faculty tend to develop courses that are unique to their own interests (for example, Psychology and Film, Food and Faith). Faculty members were chosen to be Lilly Mentors, who would shepherd their first-year students not only through the academic study of the topic at hand but also through exercises in reflecting theologically on how the material was relevant to each student's sense of vocation. Evaluations of these courses were mixed but generally positive. However, there was one class that invariably attracted a majority of male students, roughly 75–90% of enrollment.

Business as Calling has been taught by business administration Professor Roger Doerr every January since 2005 and stands as a clear success story in terms of the number of male students it has been able to serve and with respect to its sustained effectiveness in encouraging men to reflect critically on their callings as future business leaders. The course is designed to cover a variety of business ethics issues, but its scope extends beyond this to include daily conversations between students and local business leaders, many of whom are Hastings College alumni and/or members of our board of trustees. Meeting for 3 hours each day for 3 consecutive weeks, students are able to discuss with these business professionals such issues as the importance of community service, philanthropy, and social entrepreneurship. Student evaluations of these experiences are exceedingly positive, and the course has become very popular in a matter of just a few years. Doerr's (personal correspondence, January 26, 2005) own reflection on this class gives some insight into how valuable the experience has been for all involved:

> One student commented that he/she ... "was waiting for a class like this." I found that interesting. Are we doing enough throughout the curriculum of the college

to show students the relevance of the courses they are engaged in as it pertains to their ability to deal with [future] life issues...? My own vocation was an accident, perhaps with some divine intervention involved. It probably would have come out even better if there had been more guidance and counseling about my on value system and how different vocational choices would be impacted by those values.

The success of the Business as Calling course led us eventually to ask how this apparently effective model might be expanded to encourage men's involvement in service learning and vocational reflection across the curriculum. We also wondered what it was about the nature of the course material that was more attractive to men than to women. Might this outlier in our Vocation and Values Program curriculum provide an insight into how men and women think differently about vocational reflection and the notion of community service? We decided to engage this and other questions with a select group of male campus leaders in a special course entitled Men's Leadership Through College.

MEN'S LEADERSHIP THROUGH COLLEGE

The STS340: Men's Leadership Through College course was comprised of 12 sophomore, junior, and senior men, with majors ranging from chemistry, business, religion, history, music, and education. The class met for the entire fall 2008 semester, twice each week for 1- to 2-hour sessions. Our objective was twofold. First, Dr. Deffenbaugh introduced the men to a style of vocational reflection that seemed more consistent with the task-oriented, analytical mind-set demonstrated among the business students in Doerr's classes. The students were aided in this endeavor through their reading of Friedman's (2008) text, *Total Leadership*, which is designed to encourage business professionals to revise their understanding of success to include a balanced commitment to self, family, job, and community. The men in this course were asked to work, both individually and as a group, through Friedman's chapters and to reflect in weekly journal entries on what they learned about themselves and their values. Students were also required to agree on and commit to a shared community service project.

A second objective of this course was to provide a context for a series of group and individual interviews to be conducted by Dr. Ron Chesbrough on men's and women's attitudes toward, and motivations for, community service. The results of this research are summarized below. The full set of research data is compiled in *College Students and Service: A Mixed Methods Exploration of Motivations, Choices, and Learning Outcomes* (Chesbrough, 2009a).

RESEARCH

The overall design of Chesbrough's research took an exploratory mixed methods approach and initially focused solely on gender dynamics in how students in the sample described their motivations toward service and toward their learning from service. This focus expanded as the research unfolded.

Initial investigations centered around focus group interviews, with the men in the class exploring their reasons for involvement in service during college, their choices of specific service involvement, and their self-described learning from service. These focus groups occurred over an 8-week period roughly every other week. Co-instructors of the class also observed a group exercise wherein the class was asked to select a particular service involvement from among several options and to give reasons for how and why they arrived at a specific project.

Following the conclusion of male focus-group interviews, similar consultations were conducted with female students, with the same questions being asked about motivations, choices, and learning outcomes of service. These were followed by a mixed-gender focus group interview comprised of roughly half of the members of each previous group. Finally, individual interviews with four men and four women from the original focus groups rounded out the qualitative data-gathering phase.

In a subsequent quantitative phase of the research, emergent themes from interviews were used to create a survey for measuring student responses to similar questions about motivations, choices, and learning outcomes from service. The survey was administered online to 1,004 full-time undergraduates at Hastings College and received a response rate of 470 students, roughly equal parts male and female. Data from completed surveys and earlier interviews were compiled and analyzed, revealing a number of compelling findings.

Findings

Data were analyzed in four basic categories: motivation to serve, choosing service, description of service, and learning from service. Findings are reported here across these categories, specifically in relation to gender differences and similarities in response patterns.

In the category "motivation to serve," men were more likely than women to indicate external factors as an inducement for becoming involved in service. The literature on gender difference in college would support this finding of discrepancy between men and women. Sax (2008) reported substantial differences between men and women at entry to college regarding their likelihood to engage in service without some form of external motivation, such as a course or team requirement. Using survey data from over 270,000 students at over 393 campuses, Sax found that 73.1% of women held a commitment to helping others to be very important or essential, compared to 58.9% of men. When predicting future volunteer work, a similar gender gap emerged, with 34.6% of women predicting involvement in volunteer or community service work compared to only 17% of men (Sax, p. 43).

One logical conclusion from a comparison of these data to the findings of this study was that women are predisposed to become involved in service during their college years for intrinsic reasons and without external motivation. In contrast, men are more likely to become involved, at least initially, if prompted by some external incentive, such as a course requirement, or by being part of a team or an organization.

In the category "choosing service," men reported that the amount of time they had for service involvement was limited and that this factor led to the selection of projects more often than not when service was selected. In the survey, those men reporting that they had not engaged in service in the past year cited not enough time as their chief reason. Similarly, when asked why men are less frequently involved than women in service during college, respondents of both genders cited not enough time as among the top three reasons for male noninvolvement. Also in response to these two questions, respondents of both genders indicated that men were generally not aware of service opportunities and that no one asks for their participation as reasons for male noninvolvement. The group of top four answers to this question was rounded out by the response "just not interested," again a high-frequency response for both genders when they were asked about male noninvolvement.

Returning to the work of Sax (2008) regarding gender difference in college, she noted the following uses of leisure time among men and women responding to a national survey of over 270,000 students (Table 1).

In this large sample of college men, males reported spending considerably more of their leisure time exercising, watching TV, playing video/computer games, and drinking beer. Men in focus groups in the Hastings College research

Table 1
Gender Differences in Leisure Time Among First-Year Students, Fall 2006

	Women (%)	Men (%)	Difference (W-M)
Activities (6 hours per week)			
Exercising or sports	44.0	58.9	−14.9
Watching TV	22.6	30.8	−8.02
Reading for pleasure	12.2	8.5	−3.7
Partying	18.9	25.6	−6.7
Playing video/computer games	3.8	22.0	−18.2
Activities (frequently or occasionally)			
Drinking beer	37.3	48.5	−11.2
Drinking wine/liquor	47.8	49.6	−1.8
Smoking cigarettes	4.9	5.7	−0.8

Note: Weighted national norms abstracted from Pryor et al. (2006).
Source: Sax (2008, p. 31).

project reported essentially the same phenomenon when asked why their peers were less likely to become involved in service. As one student commented about his male peers, "sometimes I worry that those students spending their time playing video games and living on Facebook are completely out of touch with the real world—why is no one inviting them, challenging them, requiring them to get involved?"

Based on the evidence, it would seem that men have as much time as their female peers to engage in service during college but choose often to use their free time differently. Thus, their reported time constraints are not as real as they are apparently perceived. The fact that men claimed to be unaware of service opportunities or had not been invited to participate might be evidence of either a supported or accepted social norm of male noninvolvement in service. It appears also to indicate a need to reach out more effectively to men in the promotion and marketing of service opportunities.

The category "description of service" sought to explore how men and women describe their service experiences. Again, substantial differences were found based on gender. Women were more likely to view service as an activity based in emotional and subjective reality and to see service as an inherently personal commitment based primarily in relationships. Men were more likely to view service as a rational/analytical activity and one based in objective realities. The majority of males described service as impersonal, a manifestation of global/societal duty, and an individual, as opposed to a relational, activity.

The earlier work of feminist theorists, such as Chodorow (1978), Gilligan (1982), and Noddings (1984), would have predicted these outcomes of difference based on gender. These authors made the case that female development does not necessarily follow the same path as that of men and argued that many of the student development theories of the late 20th century did not adequately account for gender difference in development (Pascarella & Terenzini, 2005, pp. 43–44). Noddings particularly proposed an alternate framework for ethical analysis with her concept of caring as a construct within which women think, reason, and act in matters related to social responsibility and ethical response to need. She suggested that women tend to think about and respond to the perceived needs of the other in a personal and purposefully subjective manner. It is a matter of personal commitment as one enters into a caring relationship with the other.

Similarly, Gilligan's (1982) model of women's moral development proposed an alternate conception of the developmental processes for women to that of the "one size fits all" models of her predecessors. Gilligan observed consistent discrepancies between the traditional theories of moral development proposed by Piaget, Erikson, and Kohlberg, on the one hand, and women's concepts of self and morality, on the other. She suggested that the problem lay in the inherently gender-biased nature of the traditional theories, all of which had relied almost exclusively on studies of male subjects and which purported to explain a universal development process for both men and women (Gilligan, 1977, 1982). Gilligan argued that these traditional theories did not adequately or accurately describe women's experiences or bases for moral reasoning. Kohlberg's theory, for instance, focused on the "subordination of the interpersonal to the societal definition of the good" (Gilligan, 1977, p. 489), when, in fact, women's perceptions of self were "tenaciously embedded in relationships with others" (1977, p. 482). Women's moral judgments, she concluded, were "insistently contextual" (Gilligan, 1977, p. 482).

In the Hastings College study, these distinctions were clearly played out for men and women in response to the question regarding perception or description of service and arguably in previous questions regarding motivations to service, choice of service, and learning from service. Women tended to focus in their responses on relationships, personal connections, and subjective thought processes, whether in reference to motivation to serve, definition of service, or learning from service. Men tended to focus on objective decision making, societal good, and ethical obligation. These distinctions were conspicuous in focus-group discussion and individual interviews.

"The guys feel like it's their duty to correct things and achieve justice," one woman remarked. "Women are more apt to choose their involvement based on an emotional reaction, not a sense of power imbalance or a need to 'correct' something." Another young woman framed it this way: "Women approach things more emotionally while men approach things more logically and rationally, and I don't know if it's wrong when you say that, but I think that." These distinctions were also evident and measurably significant in survey responses. Distinctions continued to be evident in measurements of learning from service. In this category women were more likely to report learning in the areas of social issues, community, caring, and love. Men were more likely to report learning in the areas of social justice, organizations, and duty.

Implications

So what do these findings mean and what are the implications for educators and practitioners in higher education? We feel that we are able to draw the following conclusions. Some extend beyond gender issues to larger considerations for involving students in service. Several of these implications were previously discussed by Chesbrough (2009b).

Encouragement. Educators should recognize that gender does play a role in how students think about, choose, and describe their learning from service involvements during college. In seeking to involve more male students in service, educators should be careful to avoid affirmation of a stereotype based in fact—that men are less likely to serve than women—and should seek to reach out and market service opportunities to male students. Men reported in this study that they did not feel invited to serve or were unaware of service opportunities. These are perceived obstacles to service involvement that are easily removed.

INTEGRATION. The Hastings College study demonstrates that men, students earlier in their college career, and those who had not served substantially prior to matriculation were more likely to become involved in service because of a requirement. However, once involved, they were likely to continue and even expand their involvement. Educators should strive to introduce service opportunities to students early and often and to find ways to integrate service into orientation programs, first-year seminars, and residential programs.

LANGUAGE. In recruitment to service, language is important, particularly where gender is concerned. One service learning director recently reported removing the word *service* from a course description and replacing it with *work*. Coincidentally or not, the course enrolled more men than was typically the case. Men and women in focus-group discussions pointed out on numerous occasions that they gravitated toward certain conceptions of service more than others and that differences did tend to exist between men and women in what drew them to service involvement. Educators should craft language to describe service opportunities in ways that appeal to established motivating factors from this and other similar studies. This might mean crafting language related to career exploration and advancement, social obligation, or personal fulfillment.

TYPES OF SERVICE. According to results of this study, educators must be aware of the types of service projects being offered, particularly in the recruitment of men, students early in their careers, and those who have not served previously. Short-term projects are more likely to attract involvement from these groups. Special service days, college-wide or residential unit tasks, and one-time projects delivered in the venues described above may be the key to early involvement and the cultivation of a service ethic among students less likely to serve. Purists in the service world might argue that this is a "dumbed down" version of service, with little potential for reflection, learning, or impact. The aim, however, is to promote awareness among students who might not have otherwise expressed an interest and to make it clear that all are invited to service. It is important to establish that service is not simply the purview of that core of students on campus devoted to social justice causes and community involvement.

REFLECTION. In terms of learning from service, most research into the impact of service on student learning has found that learning is maximized by adding a reflection component to the service experience (Astin & Sax, 1998; Pascarella & Terenzini, 2005). This is a long-established fact in the service learning world, but it is often neglected in practice, particularly for the kinds of early, one-time projects described above. Even for these experiences, a brief conversation during or following the service activity can serve to plant a seed, raise a question, or excite further interest among participants. Providing this opportunity assures that it will be more likely that participants will enjoy maximum advantage from the experience.

FUTURE STRATEGIES

Given the above conclusions, it is apparent that men and women are attracted to service opportunities for quite different reasons. Whereas women are generally seeking to develop relationships and understanding, men are more likely to be interested in solving very clear problems. In hindsight, we can see that many of the learning opportunities that were available to students through the Hastings College Vocation and Values Program were designed, albeit unwittingly, to appeal to the kind of experience and reflection that is more attractive to women than to men. Long-term projects in which students are working closely with members of the local or global community are, on the whole, founded more on an ethic of care than an ethic of duty. By contrast, courses like Doerr's Business as Calling offer male students an opportunity to reflect on civic engagement and personal responsibility in a manner that is more attractive to them. It is little wonder that up to 90% of the problem solvers who have enrolled in this class over the last 5 years have been men.

As Hastings College looks toward continued success with its Vocation and Values Program, we will need to keep in mind that educational opportunities for service and vocational reflection will have to be more diverse than they have been in the past. As suggested above, new marketing strategies will need to be employed as we seek to engage more of our college men in service and vocational reflection. Although student groups have addressed a number of social problems through the creation of outreach organizations like Food 4 Thought, it is evident that there is a need for more task-oriented projects that appeal to college men. For example, male students might be encouraged to become more involved in our local chapter of Habitat for Humanity or in the Hastings Literacy Project. There has also been discussion among some faculty about entering into a partnership with the Red Cross to create a student disaster relief assistance organization. It is an unfortunate reality of living on the Great Plains that such service opportunities will eventually present themselves.

At the curricular level, discussions have begun among faculty about ways that we might engage more of our business and science students in vocational reflection by providing opportunities related to career exploration or advancement. For example, our premed students might be encouraged to take advantage of service projects recently established at the University of the West Indies in which they can spend 3 weeks working with orphaned children afflicted with HIV. Business majors might be instructed in various social entrepreneurial projects. A minor field of study, coordinated through our Vocation and Values Program, might also be implemented to provide business and science students with core courses in service learning, leadership, and ethics. These could be supplemented by other offerings relevant to each academic discipline. As in Doerr's Business as Calling class, these might include the limited assistance of dedicated alumni—doctors, lawyers, business professionals—who are willing to serve as mentors in special internships designed to incorporate vocational reflection.

The Hastings College Vocation and Values Program has in the last 7 years transformed the academic landscape of the campus, and we are gratified by the many successes that we have enjoyed. However, as the research above has demonstrated, there is still some fine-tuning that needs to be done. Though some might object that gender studies like these only serve to perpetuate well-established stereotypes, the conclusions that we can derive from this research are nevertheless clear: men and women interpret and value their experiences of the world in quite different ways. It is our responsibility as educators to be aware of these discrepancies and to address them creatively for the benefit of our students.

References

Astin, A.W., & Sax, L. (1998). How undergraduates are affected by service participation. *Journal of College Student Development, 39*(3), 251–263.

Chesbrough, R. (2009a). *College students and service: A mixed methods exploration of motivations, choices, and learning outcomes.* Unpublished doctoral dissertation, University of Nebraska-Lincoln.

Chesbrough, R. (2009b). Students and service: Who participates and why. *Student Affairs Leader, 37*(21), 1–4.

Chodorow, N. (1978). *The reproduction of mothering.* Berkeley,CA: University of California Press.

Friedman, S. (2008). *Total leadership: Be a better leader, have a richer life.* Boston: Harvard Business Press.

Gilligan, C. (1977). In a different voice: Women's conceptions of self and of morality. *Harvard Educational Review, 47,* 481–517.

Gilligan, C. (1982). *In a different voice: Psychological theory and women's development.* Cambridge, MA: Harvard University Press.

Noddings, N. (1984). *Caring: A feminine approach to ethics and moral education.* Berkeley, CA: University of California Press.

Pascarella, E.T., & Terenzini, P.T. (2005). *How college affects students: A third decade of research.* San Francisco: Jossey-Bass.

Pryor, J.H., Hurtado, S., Saenz, V.B., Korn, J.S., Santos, J.L., & Korn, W.S. (2006). *The American freshman: National norms for fall 2006.* Los Angeles: Higher Education Research Institute, University of California, Los Angeles.

Sax, L. (2008). *The gender gap in college: Maximizing the development potentialof men and women.* San Francisco: Jossey-Bass.

Section B.
Involving Men in Athletics and Fraternities

6

Mentoring Luther College Male Athletes for Reflection and Discernment

Stu Johnston, Peter Wehr, and Jordan Grimm

Introduction (Stu Johnston)

Our project at Luther College focused on providing reading, reflection, listening, mentoring, and service opportunities that have not been previously available to men on campus. Additionally, we aspired to make these opportunities more attractive to young men.

The desire for men to participate in vocational undertakings is contingent on several features: first, a safe space for men to feel comfortable in sharing their thoughts, beliefs, and values and to be respected by their peers is of utmost necessity; second, men need to feel they have common ground with the other participants, which is augmented by the presence of mentors and role models whom they feel comfortable with and have common interest with; and, last, young men respond best by actively participating in the project.

Our project had the following goals:

- to read, before tackling vocational discernment, Marx's (2003) *The Season of Life* and hear the experience of a man who has listened, heard his calling, and offered a new definition of masculinity, which is the foundation of vocational discernment in college men;
- to provide a safe space for men to think about vocation and to begin to think about their true selves and how to serve the common good;
- to experience testimony from other men who have been in their shoes, who have progressed in their own vocational discernment, and who are willing to share their journey (hopefully this would provide an adequate foundation to begin imaginative listening);
- to offer a structured volunteer/service-learning program to athletes that would likely attract more men; and
- to provide reflection, either in written or experiential form, after activities, to plant the seeds for discerning vocation.

Luther College

Luther College is a private, liberal arts college located in Decorah, Iowa. Luther College is affiliated with the Evangelical Lutheran Church of America. Most of our students come from the Midwest, and many of our students are involved in co-curricular activities, including music ensembles and athletics. Decorah is a town of 8,200 residents, and Luther College is one of the largest employers in Decorah.

Men and Vocation

As we think about young men and vocation, we believe that there need to be discussions about masculinity prior to examining discernment. It is in our belief that many young men come to college with a narrow, arguably unhealthy, and ultimately destructive sense of masculinity. We believe that it is necessary to name and challenge this view of masculinity and offer a healthier conception of masculinity. After addressing misconceptions of masculinity, our discussions delve into topics that involve vocational discernment.

Our project allowed participants the safe space to pay attention to their vocationally discerning "gut feeling." In this safe space, participants connected with older role models and potential mentors. Through a directed reading, monthly student athlete meetings, and increased opportunities of service, there was an increase in imaginative listening to, exploration of, and exposure to how these men could serve the common good.

Why Male Student Athletes?

Our project focused on male student athletes. During discussions with the coaching staff, it was clear there was not a strong focus on vocational discernment on campus for student athletes. After meeting with the football coaching staff, there was an especially strong interest in our pilot project and in it being implemented into their existing program. Luther's new head football coach, Mike Durnin, started in January 2008. During an initial meeting, it was very apparent that Durnin endorsed our efforts. Additionally, vocational discernment connects well with his philosophy of developing the complete student athlete.

Before vocational discernment can begin, male student athletes need to understand false masculinities in order to comprehend the definition of true masculinity. Men are influenced by multiple forces that can pull them in the wrong direction at times. As a result, they can lose the ability to listen for their callings. Offering a new definition of masculinity helped the men participating in the grant to understand these outside forces, thereby enabling them to do some imaginative listening, free of false masculinities.

Our pilot project consisted of four efforts. It included a summer directed reading, a service project component for all student athletes, vocational discernment through film activities, and a vocation dinner series.

Pilot Project: Directed Reading

Our directed reading, *Season of Life* (Marx, 2003), provided content for the structured discussions, reflections, and service opportunities. *Season of Life* describes an unconventional way of coaching and offers an alternative view of the definition of masculinity. Joe Ehrmann, the influential coach of the Gilman Greyhounds, who are highlighted in the story, discusses his position that many men are socialized to accept and to live out "false masculinities" (Marx, p. 36). Ehrmann's three components of false masculinity include: "athletic ability, sexual conquest, and economic success" (Marx, p. 36).

Ehrmann offered an alternative he calls "[s]trategic [m]asculinity" (Marx, 2003, p. 124). He stated that this strategy consists of two components: relationships and discerning a cause higher than oneself. He talked about developing enduring relationships that are grounded in love and meaning. Athletic ability, power, prestige, and wealth mean nothing if people cannot build successful relationships with others. Ehrmann explained that people need to think of others first and must have a purpose beyond themselves.

During the academic year, in monthly discussions, members of the football team began to explore issues of masculinity and serving others. Members of the football team were divided up into smaller groups by academic standing and each group met with one of the coaching staff. During these monthly meetings the coaching staff led discussions revolving around themes of masculinity and serving others. The coaching staff were provided a list of questions or open-ended statements, gathered from the book, to start the discussions for that particular evening.

Feedback from the student athletes was positive. Peter Wehr, a student leader during the project, writes:

> While at first players were unsure of the unconventional meetings, some learned to appreciate the outlets for discussion. As a member of the football team who was well aware of what was going on behind the scenes, I had the same mentality that I did at the conference. I was along for the spiritual journey and was eager to see where it would take me. Along the way, I heard such comments as "Those sessions were actually kind of cool" and "There's a real importance to relationships and keeping teammates close."

It is clear from the feedback that the student athletes responded positively to the discussion regarding false masculinity but also to the environment. Many student athletes said they felt comfortable talking about the issue in that setting, because they knew the other people well, felt they could trust them, and experienced the process as a team. The student athletes also responded positively to having a coach lead the discussions. This was an environment they were comfortable with—an older male leading a meeting with younger men. Student athletes mentioned that it was helpful to hear what someone older has experienced. Student athletes see coaching staff as role models.

Another unplanned result of the power of the message in the selected reading and discussions was the sharing of this information by the participants. Many of the student athletes passed the selected reading on to others, including their parents, grandparents, siblings and high school coaches. The student athletes and the coaching staff requested that we continue with a summer reading for the following year.

Pilot Project: Luther Athletes Serving Others (Peter Wehr)

On Friday, February 15, 2008, Stu Johnston and I embarked on a journey to Saint John's University to attend the 5th Annual Conference on the College Male. At the time, it seemed to me that I was just along for the ride. As a sophomore at Luther College, I was unaware that such a conference even existed. However, I was familiar with the conference co-host, the Lilly Endowment Inc. Lilly grant flyers littered the Luther College residence halls and pillars of the Student Union, all of them boasting words that my friends and I had come to dread: "A Sense of Vocation."

My head football coach at the time had given Johnston, a counselor on campus and the recipient of the grant, my name as a student athlete that he felt embodied the characteristics that Johnston was looking for to serve as his student intern. I was a member of the football team, which is highly visible in the Luther College community, and I was also involved in both Student Athlete Advisory Committee (SAAC) and ecumenical organizations on campus, making me a public candidate for the job. Johnston explained to me that male participation in vocational programs across the country was at an all-time low. I was part of the minority. A handful of organizations had gone about the difficult task of doing research on the matter, some of which would later be presented at the conference. Their findings generally supported the suspicion that college-aged males were reluctant to become involved in vocational programs.

Saint John's University was not the only institution that was concerned with this trend. Thinking back, I too had noticed that few of my male friends attended church or chose to participate in the programs, which were noticeably dominated by women. Certainly, the observations could not be simply attributed to the fact that more women attend Luther than men, could they? Johnston explained that the essential purpose of the grant was to increase male participation in volunteering and other vocational activities. After meeting with him on several occasions, it became apparent to me that we had an opportunity to make a real difference on the Luther College campus.

At the conference I came to realize that the declining participation of males in vocational programs was in large part due to a greater social problem. The culture among young men in the United States was somehow discouraging their participation in these programs. Due to reasons unbeknownst to those who were observing the waning trend, a culture of underachievement had developed among young men in the United States. Some male students even bragged about the lack of studying they did. Vocational programs were not "cool." People have to ask themselves, "Why?"

The sociological explanation for the behavior of the college male is gray and cannot be cleanly identified. A multiplicity of factors must be considered. Young men and women are socialized by several influences, including their friends, family, and the media. Norms, mores, attitudes, values, and social roles all determine how people live within society. Yet, how are men socialized differently than women in regard to the desire to develop themselves holistically? The answer is too broad to simply identify.

Johnston and I were inspired by the work of Augustana College at the Annual Conference on the College Male to construct a program that would combine athletics and service opportunities. By focusing on sports teams, we were provided with a controlled sample of Luther College's student population. In addition, male athletes were of particular interest because several studies emphasized this population in their research, such as the aforementioned study conducted by Joe Ehrman relating false masculinity and athletic success. Choosing Luther athletes also allowed us to provide a way to recognize the community service that student athletes were already doing. Each individual's invitation would be based on his affiliation with his or her team. Athletes would be motivated by their peers and coaches to do service while simultaneously becoming more well-rounded individuals by furthering their own spiritual development through service.

THE LUTHER ATHLETES SERVING OTHERS TIMELINE

Luther Athletes Serving Others (LASO) was conceived on a napkin at Marty's, a café on Luther's campus named after Martin Luther. Little did Stu Johnston and I know that a simple acronym on a paper napkin would soon become as prevalent throughout campus as the Lilly grant flyers.

The LASO service learning program began on October 12, 2008 with the LASO Fall Kickoff. Children from around the community were invited to play games with the college athletes. Johnston and I ordered 100 cookies in preparation for a huge turnout. Over 60 athletes showed up on the Preus Library lawn, anticipating the fun and games, and, although we had a low turnout of children, the impact was immense. I learned an important lesson that day: Success cannot be measured in numbers (or leftover cookies). Any participation on part of the student athletes is a valuable contribution to the program.

THE PROGRAM

Athletes at Luther College are locked in a constant "give-take" relationship with the community. The community attends events, provides meals, and finds a sense of identity in sports teams. The team receives gratification and motivation by striving to perform well on the court and on the field, thereby lending to the community a sense of pride and purpose. There is a spiritual message that underlies wins and losses that can only be satisfied by giving back to the community that raises an athlete. Community service benefits men and women in all aspects of their lives. As a young man, I am a brother, a son, a future father, and an active figure in our community. Given that action develops character, LASO's mission is to focus on these acts of service and teach young athletes how to nurture an array of relationships by presenting to them more opportunities to serve.

Coaches at Luther College encourage their athletes' involvement in community service. As a result, some student athletes were already involved in service projects in some way or another. Yet, for many others who wanted to get involved there were few outlets available to learn about service opportunities. Furthermore, those student athletes that were previously involved in service were seldom recognized for their sacrifices. The program provides a means to give student athletes more opportunities to serve as well as the recognition they deserve.

A distinct mentality motivates LASO. Rather than asking athletes to come to LASO, the organization uses its skills and enthusiasm to go to them. Service is referred to as "service opportunities" because each student is given the chance to do service according to his or her own internal motivation and desire. Within each team there will inevitably be a certain degree of peer pressure to participate in a service opportunity. However, students are not forced to participate; rather, they are positively coaxed by their teammates. We believe that subtle efforts to bring service to students are the most effective. By providing the means and atmosphere to do service, LASO supplies the student athlete with the right conditions to develop as a member of the community and to benefit as an individual.

The LASO program itself builds on the spirit of competition that resides within each athlete. Like a game, the rules are logical and straightforward. Every service hour completed by an individual student athlete awards their team one point. Then, in order to give thought to the impact of the volunteer work he or she has completed, the student athlete has the opportunity to fill out a brief reflection sheet for an additional hour, or one point, to be tallied to his or her team total. Reflection sheets encourage students to think about the skills, talents, and enthusiasm they bring to the service opportunity. Students are asked to identify the skills they brought to the project, to rate their feeling of satisfaction, and to think about what they gained from the experience. Without some form of reflection, students would not fully contemplate the impact of their actions on both themselves and others.

Individual and team totals are recorded, and rewards are given to the top performers for a job well done. The top three individuals with the most service hours are recognized at the end of each semester, and the team with the most points at the end of the year also receives recognition. Because larger teams would have obvious advantages over smaller teams, rewards are based on team averages. Team hours are compared by taking the sum of the service points divided by the number of individuals who are signed up on the team. Thus, the team total is the average number of hours per member. Whichever team has the highest team average at the end of both semesters wins the game.

A "point-person" is designated as the LASO spokesperson for each team. He or she is asked to provide program updates to his or her teammates each week by highlighting upcoming service opportunities and team point totals. Perhaps the point-person's most important responsibility is spreading enthusiasm about the program's events. As team leaders, the point-people's promotion of the program was key for all teams' success and involvement. In fact, after the initial round of LASO competition the team with the point-person who had the most enthusiasm and took the most initiative for LASO ended up with the highest point average at the end of the first semester. The top three individuals with the most service hours were also members of that person's team. This example illustrates the power teammates have to influence each other to give back to the community.

All students who signed up for LASO were given a T-shirt imprinted with the LASO logo and with the words from a poem by Edwin Markham, which were selected from the book *Season of Life* (Marx, 2003): "All that we send into the lives of others comes back into our own" (p. 21). The T-shirts not only served as an incentive to sign up but also advertised the program throughout the campus and athletic complex. The LASO emblem began to pop up around Luther as the project gained momentum. Posters made by the Luther College Photo Shop with an image of LASO athletes doing service were juxtaposed next to an image of the same athletes on the field or court. Above the images and next to the LASO emblem were the words, "Making an impact in the game and the community." Posters were then placed strategically around campus. Families of the students exhibited in the posters were sent letters of appreciation and praise for their son or daughter's commitment to working on the field and off the field in the community.

THE PEOPLE BEHIND THE PROGRAM

LASO is a unique program in that it functions through the collaboration of three separate, autonomous departments on campus. The program merged the talents and leadership of Student Life, the Career Center, and the Athletic Department. All departments provided invaluable perspectives on how the program ought to function in terms of best practice.

Johnston and I represented Student Life—he as the overall supervisor and I as the student liaison. Johnston played a pivotal role in the program. His experience as a staff member at Luther College for nearly 23 years gave the program the wisdom to function well within the existing academic and athletic setting on campus. Obviously, without his prior involvement in the American Men's Studies Association and close relationship with Gar Kellom, director of the Men's Center for Leadership and Service at Saint John's University, the funding and proposal for the program would not have existed. Furthermore, his passion for men's studies and expertise provided the energy that put the program in motion.

As Johnston's intern, I served as the "face" of the program. LASO's availability to student athletes and promotion in student life were among my chief concerns. I made efforts to promote LASO throughout the Luther campus and the Decorah community. When anyone on campus or in town inquired about the program, including the student newspaper *Chips*, it was my responsibility to provide them with information about LASO. To ensure that each student athlete experience would be enhanced by the program and its initiatives, answering questions about the program and promoting it within the football team and student athlete community were some of my principal duties.

Lisa Vander Molen, a student worker in the Career Center, worked as a liaison for LASO contacting various organizations and people in the community of Decorah. As the intermediary between LASO and the community, she ultimately planted the seed in the minds of Decorah residents that a new service organization was on campus. In addition, she tracked student involvement, individual and team points, and names of LASO members. Her care and diligence were critical to the function of the program.

Jennifer Myhre, special assistant to the athletic director, worked as the link between LASO and the Athletic Department. Among other contributions, she posted information in the athletic complex, researched National Collegiate Athletic Association rules and programs, helped coordinate activities, and communicated with coaches and athletes. Myhre's contributions were imperative in order to affectively relay information between LASO and the Athletic Department.

The Program by the Numbers

By November 2008, 228 student athletes had signed up for LASO. By the end of the 2008–2009 academic year, a total of 990 service hours were compiled, not including the extra hours awarded for filling out reflection sheets.

Review

The best quality of community service is that both parties benefit. It is hard to say who benefited more, the Decorah community or the college students. Nonetheless, one important notion is clear: nearly one thousand hours of community service were completed that otherwise never would have been accomplished if it were not for the efforts of the student athletes.

In order to increase participation in events, we found that service opportunities must have the following characteristics:

- Service opportunities must require only a low-level of commitment. Student athletes are stretched thin between classes and training. Long-term or weekly commitments were not particularly attractive to LASO members. Additionally, service locations ought to be close to campus and be no more than a five minute drive away.
- Community service should be fun. Student athletes are active people and games or other means of competition are great incentives. In order for students to sacrifice their valuable time they must benefit in a direct way.
- Service must be easily accessible to student athletes. The mode of signing up for and getting to events must be simple and fast. LASO brings the means of participating to athletes rather than asking athletes to seek out such means.

As an organization that was created primarily to increase male participation in vocational programs, LASO must make new efforts to appeal more directly to the male athlete population on campus. Currently, female student athletes are more involved than men—the same phenomenon that the grant is making efforts to explain. The key is to identify service work that men feel comfortable doing and to continue to encourage participation.

My Contribution as Student Leader

Initiating a new organization was more difficult than I had expected. LASO was possible only due to the devotion, hard work, and collaboration of the program team. The program's challenges tested my faith in myself and at times in other people. LASO provided me with insight into my own behavior as a male, and voiced the sociological stimuli that motivate some of my thoughts and actions. My friends and I came to dread the Lilly grant's vocational themes because at times it felt the program was only adding more weight to our academic and athletic demands. The pressure of being the man that society defines as masculine is, at times, overwhelming.

Men must learn to maintain the balance between work and play. It is my opinion that men are so pressured to become involved—to fit the mold that society devises for them—that some choose to underachieve and subconsciously rebel. Instead, men need to live a life of balance. Men's senses and lives are more overwhelmed today than ever before. Modern society is full of excess, including commercials, the Internet, cell phones, computers, cars, iPods, capitalism, politics, fast food, extracurricular activities, nightlife, fashion, and consumption. In addition, people are bombarded with messages that attempt to define masculinity and femininity within a society.

To get men more involved, "lighter" service-learning opportunities must be promoted. There is a great deal of faith in focusing only on the present rather than rushing to look toward the future. Matthew 6:34 (New King James Version) reveals, "Therefore do not worry about tomorrow, for tomorrow will worry about its own things." LASO asks students to focus on today through service that will offer benefits later in life. Ecumenical vocation activities can seem overwhelming in comparison.

While no solid evidence can be found for the decline in male participation in college, the remedy is clear. It is not the young men who have faltered. The college cannot wait for young men to come to them. It must strive to bring vocational programs to them in whatever style best meets their needs.

Pilot Project: Vocational Discernment Through Film (Stu Johnston)

During the month of January, Luther College has a 3-week long January Term. This is a time when students take one course, and the typical academic workload is somewhat less time-consuming. During the month of January, 2009, a pizza dinner was offered with a feature film and an informal discussion. The student leader for the project invited the football team to the evening activities, the discussion was led by the grant coordinator, and we had 25 members of the football team in attendance each week.

One of the movies, *Fight Club*, was selected from films listed on the Programs for the Theological Exploration of Vocation (PTEV) Web site (http://www.PTEV.org). The other film selected, *Good Will Hunting*, was a suggestion from one of our student leaders. Questions were proposed prior to the start of the movie. Afterwards, the grant coordinator led a discussion about the film. In *Fight Club*, issues related to "Can one only find oneself when one is willing to lose everything?" as well as "Can one who has not hit bottom discover her or his true way in life?" The discussion also moved into the issue of where men can gather safely. In the film, part of the attraction of *Fight Club* is the men in the film feeling connected as a group. One of the participants asked, "Where can men gather?" We discussed what might feel like safe places for young men, including belonging to an athletic team or even gathering as a common group to watch a movie.

In *Good Will Hunting*, the discussion was begun by just processing the film after the grant coordinator discovered most of the men had not seen the film prior to the evening activity. The issue of independence and interdependence in human life was also discussed in addition to loyalty and wanting the best for one's friends. The men in the group could identify with the idea of feeling called to something and knowing that others were hopeful they would pursue that calling, even though it could take them in different directions than those of their friends.

Feedback from the student athletes was quite positive. Participants felt it was a safe space to talk about the movies and to explore the deeper meanings of the movies and how they relate to their own lives and the process of vocational discernment. Participants talked about the comfort factor in relation to knowing the other people in the room, which allowed a greater ease of communication. The participants strongly encouraged the grant coordinator to offer this program again the next year.

Pilot Project: Vocation Leadership Dinners (Jordan Grimm)

The vocation leadership dinners began when the head football coach chose ten players he considered to be leaders on the team. There were two freshmen, two sophomores, and six juniors. Five players were on the offense, and five players were on the defense. The coach was present along with Stu Johnston, a guest of honor. There were three dinners, and they were all on campus. The guest of honor for the first and last dinners was Todd Ondell. Ondell has his EdD, teaching in the business department at Viterbo College in LaCrosse, Wisconsin.

Imagine the first dinner: ten large college football players sitting around a fancy dinner table where the only conversation is occasional pleasantries. There were distinctly questioning looks on all of the players' faces. Finally, Ondell started off the dinner by saying, "Yesterday was the most perfect day of my life, and today is going even better because I chose to make it that way." He continued as follows:

> I make the decision every morning to make today better than yesterday. It's my choice; I realize to have a perfect day I will give something to someone and expect nothing in return—a smile, opening of a door, or even the benefit of the doubt.

After these first few words, everyone in the room was transfixed on Ondell's words. He continued to talk about leadership and what it means to be a good husband, father, and friend. Throughout the dinner he would ask each individual a question that tied into what he was talking about. Each player was fully engaged, and the feeling in the room was very comfortable. He ended the dinner by writing out the word "leadership" on a large sheet of paper. Then Ondell flipped the page and wrote a large "L." He asked the players to shout out all of the words that they could think of that had to do with leadership, starting with the letter "L." Ondell continued to do this for the rest of the letters in the word "leadership." Then he said that the following day each player should pick a word from the list we had comprised and try to focus on that word for the rest of the day. The next day each player was supposed to pick a word from the next letter, and so on, until he came back 2 months later.

The guest of honor for the second dinner was Mark Lovelace. Lovelace is a former Division One basketball coach and is now the co-owner of an insurance agency in Decorah, Iowa. He is also a Luther graduate of '92.

Lovelace had a much different approach than Ondell. He started with an introduction of himself, explaining how he used to work as a Division One basketball coach, lived in downtown Chicago, and was always very busy. He rarely saw his wife and newborn son, but he was doing what he loved, basketball. Lovelace explained that he saw he did not have "balance" with that lifestyle and had to reevaluate himself and his career choice. Lovelace had been a basketball coach and a part of the game for so long that he nearly felt lost without it. After a detailed introduction, he opened up the discussion by offering us the opportunity to ask questions, which really changed the atmosphere into a casual conversation over dinner.

Throughout the conversation, Lovelace's main focus was on balance. He was able to connect his life story to what all the players were going through at that time. Because he was a graduate of Luther and very involved in sports while he was enrolled, Lovelace was able to connect with the players. As the time passed, the conversations became more personal as we all began to dig a little deeper. Players were sharing their own battles with achieving balance and understanding their identities. The conversation continued until the allotted time had passed, and the coach explained that, if anyone needed to, he was welcome to leave to do homework or for any other commitments. All of the players looked around the room at each other, and not a single person got up to leave. Almost simultaneously one of the players asked a thoughtful question that led right back into the discussion. The players ended up staying well past half an hour later. All were disappointed when the conversation ended.

Todd Ondell returned as the guest of honor again for the third and final dinner. The focus of the last dinner was goals. We started off the dinner by separating into two distinct groups—one with the offensive players and the other with defensive players. Each group thought of specific goals for the next football season. Then Ondell brought both groups together and had all the players think of team goals. He explained that good goals are ones that benefit the team. Each individual goal should be what is best for the team not what is best for each individual player.

After we shared our goals as a collective group, Ondell tied the discussion to the relationship between a husband and a wife. He expressed how important it is to have goals that are congruent with one's spouse. Ondell also showed how relevant goals are when working for a company and how that relates back to being a part of a football team. The wide range of vocational subjects prompted conversation about all sorts of things, such as marriage, vocation, and masculinity. As the conversation progressed, Ondell began to talk less and less. After a while, the only people talking were the players. The conversation lasted for almost three hours, and no one wanted it to end until it became too late and the group reluctantly dismembered.

I believe that the benefits of these dinners are vast, fostering healthy male relationships and personal reflection. The dinners provided men with a safe and comfortable place to open up to healthy male interaction. Furthermore, it provided an excellent example of masculinity for the players by introducing them to both a mentor and role model. While it is common to assume that college age men should be the ones doing the mentoring, college is actually a vital time in a man's life where the guidance of a mentor is crucial. In closing, it was the relationships that players built with each other and with the mentors that made these dinners so valuable.

WHAT WE HAVE LEARNED (STU JOHNSTON)

First, there need to be discussions regarding masculinity before there can be conversation about vocation. Many of our young men are basing their ideas of vocation or of a calling on a false sense of masculinity. When this is addressed—when young men are given a language to name false masculinity and a process for understanding a healthier vision of masculinity—then true, honest vocational development can begin. Second, there needs to be a safe space for men to gather to discuss issues of masculinity, relationships, and vocation. Much of the positive feedback that we received from the participants was how comfortable they felt talking about these issues with others they trusted. Third, as people interested in the development of young men, we need to go to spaces that may feel less safe to us. We need to leave our offices and meet with men where they gather, including residence hall lounges, athletic facilities, and group meetings, that may seem somewhat out of the ordinary for us but are spaces where young men feel at home.

And, finally, collaboration across campus is vital. Our pilot project involved the Counseling Service, Career Center, and Athletic Department, which typically are not common collaborators. These offices do have a common interest in the development of all students, so, although they may not always speak the same language, there may be surprising alliances in development of college men.

Reference

Marx, J. (2003). *Season of life: A football star, a boy, a journey to manhood*. Washington, DC: Simon and Schuster.

7

Bringing Fraternity Brothers and Alumni Together at Augustana College

Rebecca A. Poock

The Center for Vocational Reflection (CVR) at Augustana College, Rock Island, Illinois, was established on campus in 2003 as a place where students could recognize who they are called to be. Students at the CVR engage in a process of self-discovery and community awareness based on five main questions for reflection: (a) What are my skills, gifts, and talents? (b) What are my passions and values? (c) What are the needs of the community? (d) Who am I called to be? and (e) What's my story?

The most significant effort of the CVR has been to embed vocational reflection within the curriculum of most academic programs. Through Senior Inquiry, students are expected to be reflective as an integral part of the capstone program. The majority of all Augustana students will engage in reflective activities before graduating. In addition, the CVR recognized the significant impact that cocurricular student groups had on students' identity formation. Greek life is one of the largest groups on campus that the CVR had not reached with regular programming. Twenty-five percent of Augustana male students participate in the fraternity system. Many men mark their participation in fraternities as among the most significant activities in their campus life. However, data from the Called to Serve assessment project indicated that 24% of fraternity members felt that they did not have a vocation. Again, 29% of men active in fraternities disagreed with understanding vocation as what they are meant to do with their lives. Fourteen percent of the fraternity members disagreed with the statement that coming to an understanding of their gifts and abilities is essential to their vocational understanding. And finally, 14% of males on campus feel overwhelmed by the idea of vocation. Identifying this need in our Augustana community prompted the following proposal.

The Proposal

The CVR recognized that inquiry into who one is called to be is most fruitful when done within the context of relationships. The depth to which students reflect can be best attributed to a welcoming environment, consistent contact, and asking the questions that lead to vocational reflection. With disparity in our male students about vocation, the CVR targeted the fraternities as a necessary group. Thus, the Fraternity Alumni Network (FAN) was created and implemented. Augustana piloted FAN to strengthen vocational reflection among male students through intergenerational mentoring relationships with Augustana alumni. The

FAN focused on intentional one-on-one time as well as periodic networking with all participants in the program. Taking steps to ensure the success of the mentoring program, the CVR approached FAN through seven key points: evaluate, identify, recruit, equip, engage, celebrate, and assess.

Program Review

Evaluate. There were two key groups of people the program would be serving—fraternity students and fraternity alumni. Initial work was done to ensure that, indeed, a need was apparent for vocational reflection with male students. Also, the CVR needed to ensure that the fraternity alumni would find the experience engaging and helpful. The idea was presented to a Greek Council meeting and received an overwhelming positive response. Students believed this program would help them personally as well as help the perceptions of Greek Life on campus. Senior fraternity members who would graduate before implementation of the program expressed regret that there was not something like FAN sooner. Fraternity men were quick to say that networking with alumni is one of the most significant benefits received from involvement in Greek Life. This network benefits both their professional life as they seek employment and their social connections as they move to new communities. Unfortunately, these benefits primarily are received after students graduate from Augustana. The students recognized the benefits of FAN reaching students before graduation and accompanying them through vocational reflection.

With students interested, the CVR connected with a fraternity alum. He was already mentoring a student and approached the CVR for resources to help him. Through his conversations with alumni fraternity brothers, the feedback echoed the students' sentiments. There were more alumni like him who were interested in mentoring relationships and were eager to find ways to give back to Augustana. With the audiences of both fraternity students and alumni on board, the CVR pursued the next steps in creating FAN.

Identify. Leadership of the program was crucial in keeping the CVR, fraternity students, and fraternity alumni connected. Initially, the director and program associate of the CVR envisioned FAN; however, with a new staff member added to the CVR team, the community engagement coordinator became responsible for coordinating the program. Fraternities would be represented by a student project leader, who would coordinate leaders from each of the six fraternities. Seven students would be public leaders for FAN. The alumni connection provided an opportunity with someone who had mentoring experience and a passion for this new program.

The student project leader's role helped keep the student perspective in mind as the program was implemented. Answering the question, "What's in it for me?" assisted the designing of FAN as the student shared students' viewpoints. He also would create marketing materials for the fraternities and be the major recruiter for participants. From the inception of the proposal, the student leader was a part of thinking creatively about how students and alumni connect. He would manage details of the program, plan the end-of-year celebration, and assess the success of the program.

The alumni leader would need to be active in the Augustana alumni organizations and help recruit alumni participants. He offered much enthusiasm and experience to a mentoring program with Augustana students. (Unfortunately, he was unable to continue this position, and an alumni leader to replace him has not been found.)

The staff coordinator would be responsible for supervising the student leader and managing the administrative pieces of the program. Communication with alumni was the staff's responsibility as well as leading the vocational reflection with alumni and students at large gatherings.

RECRUIT. FAN was to launch in fall 2008, with some initial work done by the student leader. In the spring prior, the student leader recruited six fraternity students to represent their individual fraternities. Marketing and communication strategy was to be organized in the summer by the student leader. Unfortunately, as the new staff member was hired, there were 3 weeks before students were to return to campus, and the student leader had not done any work over the summer. The goal was to recruit 24–30 students with the FAN chairs leading recruitment in their own fraternities. In the fall, the student leader met with every fraternity and presented information on the mentoring program. Between poor communication and lack of organization, the FAN chairs never materialized, and recruitment was solely the student leader's responsibility.

Meanwhile, the CVR requested a list of alumni near campus or within driving distance who would be appropriate for the program. Alumni Relations created a list that included 150 prospective alumni for FAN, some as near as Rock Island and others in downtown Chicago. A letter and application were mailed to alumni, with a response requested by the end of September. After phone call and e-mail communication, by mid-October, 20 alumni applications were received.

Although the program was targeted at junior and senior students, the student leader was not having success recruiting many upperclassmen. The decision was made to open applications to sophomores as well, and the student roster swelled with applicants. Because of the delay in alumni response, 17 students were notified of their acceptance into the program in mid-October.

Once participants were recruited, the staff coordinator set the criteria to match alumni and students. First, being in the same fraternity was a clear factor in matching students and alumni. If the fraternity matched, then the next step was determining the match in interests (i.e., major, job experience, hobbies, sports, music). Although not a significant factor, locations of the student's hometown and alum's home were considered. With many of the alumni coming from the

Chicago area, students would not be able to meet face-to-face with them often. However, if the student's hometown was a suburb of Chicago, then the likelihood of face-to-face meetings over breaks increased. As the process unfolded, there were not equal matches of fraternity alumni participants and fraternity student participants. And there were fraternity brothers who did not match in interests. Both students and alumni were contacted to discuss the options of matching with an alum/student that was not from his respective fraternity.

This prompted alumni and students to opt out of the program. They were interested in connecting with fellow fraternity members, so the number of participants decreased. By the end of the matching process, FAN had 17 matches, totaling 34 participants.

EQUIP. E-mail correspondence seemed the best way to communicate with alumni and students, so letters went out electronically to both parties identifying their matches. FAN planned to have an introductory meeting at Augustana's Homecoming in October, but, with the delayed response and matching communications, many alumni were not available to meet their students over that weekend.

Preparations were made for the staff coordinator to travel to Chicago to meet alumni mentors twice over the late fall. Quad Cities mentors would connect with each other once in the local community. The purpose of these mentor gatherings was to have the men reflect on their mentoring experiences and their expectations for the relationship they were beginning with an Augustana student as well as equip the mentors with the tools they would need to succeed. The majority of the mentors were in their 40s and brought a diverse array of experiences with their mentoring. Many reflected on the impact of their fathers or other male relatives, and some shared the impact that a professional during an internship had on their development. Discussion moved to peer mentors when fraternity stories bubbled up in conversation. Some alumni were still in contact with their fraternity big brothers, who connected with them during initiation and membership activities. Others mentioned that they regretted not having a distinct mentor in their lives during their college years, but they hoped they could be one for a student now.

Utilizing Zachary's (2000) *The Mentor's Guide*, the staff coordinator established expectations of the mentoring relationships and expectations of FAN. The groups reviewed the old paradigm of mentoring, an authoritative, mentor-driven relationship, and compared it to a newer model of a joint effort of mentor and mentee contributing and benefitting from a mentoring relationship. The alumni were also asked to reflect on vocation and the sense of recognizing who they are called to be. Again, alumni responded with honesty and integrity, and they reflected on how helpful the conversation would have been when they were in college. This was a key point in encouraging them to be that person that asks the questions that lead students to reflect on their callings. The guidelines of communication were set. At least two contacts a month, whether it was by e-mail, phone, or face-to-face meeting, were expected. It was clear that the relationship would not develop if intentional communication and time set aside were not priorities. Also, with the lack of a formal meeting face-to-face, at least once before the mid-year gathering, mentor and mentee would meet face-to-face. Unfortunately, only one-third of the mentors were able to attend one of the sessions, but materials were sent out to equip them with follow-up e-mails.

The student project leader coordinated the on-campus orientation meeting with the fraternity students. The luncheon was arranged for times that students would be available during the week. These two sessions primarily connected the students with the expectations of the program. There were some miscommunications about what FAN was and what was required. Many were looking forward to connecting with someone from their fraternities, and others were encouraged by connecting with someone in their intended professional fields. The student leader presented information at the two meetings, with most of the focus on networking with alumni. The staff coordinator shared the goals of the CVR to help students recognize who they were called to be. Only half of the students attended either meeting. The student leader committed to following up with the other half face-to-face to convey the expectations of the program.

ENGAGE. Before the mid-year gathering in January, students and alumni were to have been in contact at least four times. With 12 out of 17 alumni residing out of the Quad Cities area, most of the pairs introduced themselves over the phone or online. Those who were paired with alumni from the Quad Cities found it a great benefit to be in close proximity. A couple of the matches were with alumni from south-central Illinois, which further deterred a face-to-face meeting. The staff coordinator and student leader communicated with the participants to assess connections and participation. By December, five of the alumni and student matches had made no connection at all.

The mid-year gathering proved to be a unifying event for the program. With much of the network functioning in pieces, the gathering provided an opportunity to meet people connected with FAN and solidify the purposes for the program. Nine alumni and 12 students were present. Many of the pairs had not met each other face-to-face until then, so the physical presence of the person they had been connecting to was rewarding.

Jon, the student, and Nick, the alum, were matched from different fraternities, but their connection sparked at the mid-year gathering. Jon had been abroad fall term, so the communication was all through e-mail for the first part of the program. Ironically, Nick was leaving on business to the same part of the world. Their face-to-face meeting brought the similarities of their personalities to the forefront; they also discovered more of the same interests as they spoke in person. The fraternity difference made no difference to them. It was the school connection and personal connections they made that impacted their relationship.

Ben, the student, and Kent, the alum, were matched from the same fraternity. Kent admitted to disconnecting from the fraternity for awhile, but his relationship with Ben triggered a renewed sense of belonging at Augustana and his fraternity. This pair found much success in communicating online and quickly moved to frequent phone conversations. With Kent's child being a first-year student at Augustana, he found many opportunities to see Ben as part of the family visits to campus. Ben shared his appreciation for Kent's "real" perspective and renewed loyalty to his fraternity.

Unfortunately, there were alumni and students who attended who did not have their respective mentee/mentor present. They shared their frustrations about communication difficulties and time management issues. Some of the alumni found that students did not respond to e-mails or phone calls. They speculated on the students' commitment to the program. Some students also commented on their alumni and asked of their commitment to the program. Messages not returned signaled to students that the busy life of the alumni was more important than the relationship they hoped to build.

Conversation was guided by the staff coordinator as participants reflected on their personality traits and values. These two exercises offered examples of the reflection the CVR frequently does with students one-on-one. The mentors and mentees then shared with each other their reflections. Another part of the conversation circulated around the Parks (2000) book, *Big Questions, Worthy Dreams*, which the alumni received in the mail to read for the gathering. This text identifies the shift in young adults' reflection on the future and the impact that mentors can make on a young adult's development. Many of the alumni did not read the entire book and found it inaccessible to a person removed from studying and textbooks. Overall, the response from those who did read some or all of it found it to be helpful to discern the differences of young adults today and young adults when they were in college. The CVR intended to have participants reflect on that same issue to emphasize the diversity of students' experiences and backgrounds but, also, to examine the similarities men have in reflecting on their vocations no matter in what time of life they find themselves.

CELEBRATE. FAN ended the year with a review of the program and thoughts for the future of the program. An end-of-the-year celebration was scheduled for the beginning of May, with new fraternity members welcomed into fraternities and finals not quite upon students. With four alumni and three students, it was a disappointing attendance to close the year. One alum came from outside the Quad Cities, and the rest were from the area. Another disappointment was that the student leader did not attend the final gathering. The staff coordinator reflected with those who came and shared about the CVR's response to the year with FAN.

ASSESS. Assessing FAN includes the strengths and weaknesses of the program. From a mid-year evaluation and personal feedback from the participants, the CVR was able to assess the success of the program.

FAN was able to motivate alumni to reconnect with campus and particularly with fellow Augustana fraternity brothers. Many shared at the final celebration that they were on their upcoming homecoming reunion committees or on the alumni board. Alumni's connections with fraternities strengthened the memories of when they were in college and encouraged them to reflect on what it was like to be in their early 20s again. This proved to be helpful because students found it encouraging to look at fraternity brothers who lived in similar shoes and who were men who found the students important. The spirit of service and community was reflected in the mid-year evaluations. Participants also found the CVR's focus on calling to be helpful as matches talked about the present and future situations. Many of the alumni reflected on the diversity of jobs they had throughout their careers, with some relating to their Augustana majors. Others compared their time spent weekly and how that did or did not reflect their values. Students shared their thoughts on activities they participated in at Augustana and how those affected their future plans; decisions were based not solely on majors and classes but on how their whole experience impacted who they are.

Some weaknesses of the program were primarily with communication. Although the staff coordinator contacted alumni through e-mail and phone calls, there were three alumni who never responded or communicated with their students. Some alumni never came to campus to meet their students. There were four students who stopped communication with their mentors without explanation. The student leader of the program lacked organization and innovation. He did not have the connections with students to keep the morale of the program going, and his other school activities became a bigger priority to him as the school year went on. Another challenge for the program was the number of mentors far from campus. Most of the students who had mentors far from campus agreed that it would be better to have someone in the area to talk with and make a better connection. Because the network was based primarily on the commitment of individuals, it was difficult to account for mentor/mentee communication frequency and continued commitment.

Overall, did FAN accomplish what it set out to do? Yes. Men were engaged in reflection both formally and informally throughout their participation. The CVR was able to connect with students in fraternities that they otherwise were not connecting with. Alumni were reflecting on vocation in ways they had not before, and they encouraged the students to do the same. The year ended with energy for the coming year and hope for change with some of the challenges the program presented throughout the year.

FAN Now

FAN did continue into the following year. Six alumni returned to the program to either be matched with new students or continue mentoring students from the previous year. A returning FAN student became the new student leader and worked with the staff coordinator throughout the summer. He contacted fraternity councils over the summer and prepared the applications before students returned. Alumni were contacted again by using the database through Alumni Relations; however, Quad Cities alumni were primarily targeted. Those beyond the Quad Cities who were invited included those from the previous year. This new target resulted in a much older crowd of alumni with some in their late 70s and early 80s. Fifteen alumni responded, but the student response was low. The student leader had to identify specific individuals who would be willing to participate to match every alum with a student. Recruitment ended with 15 matches.

The group did meet at Homecoming, with most of the alumni and students in attendance. The program reviewed vocation, calling, and mentoring. The midyear and final celebrations are scheduled for the coming year. No time commitment was stressed with pairs, but a commitment to the relationship was stressed. The student leader and his mentor discussed the effort that both have to make for the relationship to succeed. The future of the program depends on the commitment of alumni and students and the leadership of the student leader. The influence that FAN has had on 64 men in their personal lives will hopefully impact their larger communities.

References

Parks, S.D. (2000). *Big questions, worthy dreams: Mentoring young adults in their search for meaning, purpose, and faith.* San Francisco: Jossey-Bass.

Zachary, L.J. (2000). *The mentor's guide: Facilitating effective learning relationships.* San Francisco: Jossey-Bass.

Section C.
Building New Programs

8

Engaging St. John's University Men Through International Service and Research

Gar Kellom, Corbin J. Cleary, Alvin Thomas, Jessica Nelson, Ashleigh Leitch, Michael Wallace, and John Van Rooy

Introduction (Gar Kellom)

As the host institution for the Lilly Endowment grant and the site of the men's center that was sponsoring this grant proposal, St. John's University had a unique opportunity to create a pilot project that would add to the thinking about how to involve college men in vocational discernment activity. Work in this field had been ongoing as a part of the Center for Men's Leadership and Service, which was established to create a space that college men would call their own to design their own projects for service, research, and leadership. One early study of those interested in volunteer activity was undertaken by Kevin May, the president of the student senate, and Mark Osborne, the vice president. As part of a men's research class, they decided to canvas all first- and second-year SJU students in the residence halls door-to-door, asking them if they had volunteered and if so why and, if not, why not.

The results of their survey were surprising because it revealed that the college men they talked with had two distinct preferences for volunteering. First, working on projects that required some physical activity seemed to be a top priority. Not surprisingly, they identified working on school construction in Belize (a long-term spring-break project in Campus Ministry) and Habitat for Humanity. Somewhat unexpected was the second preference—of working with children. It was not surprising, therefore—when the men's center piloted a Saturday school for college students to work with grade school students in Ames School in Saint Paul—that there was a good response. Today, it is the longest-running service project in the men's center, annually involving over a dozen students who commit to spending Saturdays tutoring children and working with parents.

Several projects were attempted as part of the grant, all of which yielded valuable insights into ways to increase men's involvement: coed service trips to Trinidad and Tobago in January 2009 and 2010, an all-male service/research trip to India and Nepal in summer 2008, a coeducational service/research trip to India and Nepal in summers of 2009 and 2010.

This chapter captures some of this work and the collaboration of students in the research. Corbin Cleary has summarized some of the insights from the service trips to Trinidad and Tobago in both years. These trips were designed with the help of Kevin May and Mark Osborne to take students to work in orphanages in the Caribbean, where there have never been male volunteers.

Alvin Thomas, a Morehouse College student who was the first Morehouse participant in the men's center exchange between the two schools, coauthored the work on Tibetan monks (Thomas & Kellom, 2009). His serious and detailed analysis of vocational discernment by Tibetan monks is a powerful example of how deeply and seriously each student devoted himself to this project. They completed and published the research project but also were impacted profoundly themselves in their own theological reflections. Jess Nelson and Ashleigh Leitch coauthored some reflections of Nepalese monks and Tibetan sisters from the 2009 trip to add to the study.

Finally, with over 80 students involved in these international service and study trips during the grant period, there were many reflections written and a great deal learned from student accounts of how these experiences have impacted their vocational discernment. A fuller account of the themes of these reflections can be found in the final report of the grant to be submitted to the Lilly Endowment later this year. Two reflections are included as samples. First Michael Wallace, who was a freshman during his participation in the India and Nepal trip, wrote of his experiences for the Asian Studies Program newsletter. Lastly, John Van Rooy, one of the participants in the first India and Nepal group, has written an account this year that looks back on his yearlong experience as he prepares to do further graduate study in South Asian studies. The writings of these two men serve as bookend student experiences and begin to give a flavor of the richness and depth these experiences have had for college men.

As this is being written, thanks in part to the testimonials and writings of those above, another full group for the 2011 Trinidad and Tobago trip is forming, and 130 students have expressed interest in the 2010 India and Nepal Program. Over a dozen of these have written a research grant to the Freeman Foundation to fully support summer research in Nepal on topics such as continued interviews with Tibetan Buddhist nuns. The grant has been successfully funded, and these researchers will be joined by more male volunteers to help keep the summer program going, even after the Lilly grant has ended.

THE 2009 AND 2010 CARIBBEAN SERVICE TRIPS TO TRINIDAD AND TOBAGO
(CORBIN CLEARY)

By most accounts, young men who are enrolled in universities across the country volunteer at rates that are usually much lower than those seen among woman enrolled in the same universities. There are, of course, exceptions to these generalities, and these exceptions demand intensive analysis to determine why college-aged men become involved with volunteer opportunities.

At St. John's University, a service trip entailing volunteer work in Trinidad and Tobago is sponsored each year by the Men's Center. Because St. John's University is paired with a sister college—the College of St. Benedict—the trip was not exclusively designed for men but was designed so that half the members of the service group are men. When compared with other service trips offered, this ratio of men to women is quite high.

Every year, over winter break, the Men's Center sponsors a group of students to attend a 13-day cultural immersion and service trip to Trinidad and Tobago. The service element of the trip is focused on working with two orphanages near Port-of-Spain: Cyril Ross Nursery, a nursery run for HIV-positive children, and Amica House, an all-girls orphanage managed by a group of Catholic nuns.

The men on this trip studied nearly every topic; majors included accounting, political science, philosophy, mathematics, and biology, and, in addition to these, two members were also completing the preparatory curriculum for medical school. The male members of the group also possessed a variety of differences in religious beliefs, but most members described the importance of these beliefs in encouraging their volunteerism. Alec Torigian, one of the participants who volunteered at Amica House, described his desire to volunteer, "My faith and upbringing [created my interest in volunteering]. My parents and my youth group taught me the importance of spreading Christ's love through service."

Perhaps even more important than the men's own reasoning were the ideas they expressed regarding the means in which to encourage more men to volunteer. Jack Ries, a junior mathematics and Hispanic studies major, expressed his belief regarding men's volunteering, claiming, "Men should know how valuable and important their skills are to the world and all of those in need." To encourage more men to become involved with volunteering, it seems that just that should be done. They should be informed as to how important their service truly is, and, on this trip, the service of men was seen as especially important at Cyril Ross Nursery. At the nursery, the presence of older men (older than the oldest male child; age fifteen) is virtually nonexistent. The sudden arrival of three excited college men, ready to play, run, and in some cases roughhouse, provided the young boys of the nursery with a chance to experience male relationships.

In addition to presenting to men the importance of their volunteering—in order to increase their recruitment in service programs and volunteer opportunities—perhaps the most success is seen by individual recruitment from man-to-man. College-aged men have a natural tendency to do something if their fellow male peers are doing it, and this is seen especially at men's institutions such as St. John's University. To recruit more men, then, perhaps the easiest and most effective method is to have some men personally recruit and involve other men within the program. That connection of man-to-man allows for a bond to be formed that is then only strengthened through the actual works of service done during the volunteering expedition.

The poor volunteering numbers for men, though worrying, are not something that has to continue. Instead of accepting the lack of service work done by the college-aged male, strong pushes should be made toward recruitment focusing primarily in three areas: emphasis on personal beliefs, as is seen in those statements of men who say their faith inspired their service; importance of what men have to offer in their service work; and, finally, encouragement of college men by other college men to volunteer. Through these three methods, this trend can, in some sense, be reversed, and more men will begin to experience the rewards of service work and volunteerism.

THE 2008 INDIA AND NEPAL MEN'S RESEARCH AND SERVICE PROJECT
(ALVIN THOMAS)

Saint John's University (SJU) was founded by Benedictine monastics who have developed close connections with Tibetan Buddhist monks about the common experience of monastic life for men (de Dreuille, 1999). Brother Aaron Raverty, an anthropologist from Saint John's who has traveled to Tibet, Dharamsala, India and Nepal is one example of the ongoing exchange between men of different faith traditions who share a common monastic life style. He collaborated on some of the planning to establish connections for this project.

The idea for our project was developed on a sabbatical granted by the St. John's University Board of Regents to Dr. Gar Kellom to explore the cross-cultural nature of vocational discernment with monastics of different cultures and faiths. Broadly conceived, the project was to involve students in research and service by having them interview Buddhist and Benedictine monks and sisters and discover any patterns that might exist for how they decided to become monastics. To my knowledge, there is little research on the vocational discernment of Tibetan Buddhist monks and none that is cross-cultural in comparison.

Plan for a Study

This study was undertaken at the intersection of two fields. First, Tibetan Buddhism and Tibetan culture, as carefully studied by religious studies scholars (Tucci, 1988), is now undergoing a dramatic change since the relocation of the Central Tibetan Administration of the Dalai Lama to Dharamsala, India, in 1959. Throughout its history as one of the world's great religious traditions, Buddhism has adapted as it moved out of India, where Siddhartha Gautama first envisioned the *middle way* to Tibet, China, Japan, Korea, Southeast Asia, and the West. Currently under way is one of those periods of great transition, with the movement of a large refugee population, the destruction and reconstruction of monasteries (Department of Religion and Culture, 2000), and a significant new impact of Tibetan Buddhism heretofore hidden away in the high Himalayas. Few are now unfamiliar with this tradition, because it has often been at the center of international media attention.

Second, there is a convergence of Eastern religious traditions, such as Tibetan Buddhism in America (Eck, 2001; Queen, 2000), with the establishment of colleges such as Naropa University in Bolder, Colorado, centers for the study of Tibetan Buddhism in most major metropolitan areas, and several large refugee communities. The second largest of those is in Minneapolis/Saint Paul, Minnesota and has resulted in rituals such as the creation of the sand mandala and performances of traditional dance and music at colleges like St. John's, where they have been easily accessible to large numbers of college students (Gandhi, 1974).

It was arranged for 15 students (14 from St. John's and 1 from Notre Dame) to interview 35 Tibetan monks as part of the monthlong service/research trip to India and Nepal. The monks ranged from age 21 to 40 years, and most had family origins in various parts of Nepal and India, with Amdo (one of the three traditional provinces of Tibet and the birthplace of the 14th Dalai Lama, Tenzin Gyatso) being a very commonly reported birthplace. All the monks are presently in Dharamsala, India—some sent there by their head monasteries located in other parts of India or Tibet. The monks for this study were chosen by a Tibetan from Dharamsala, India, who is a volunteer coordinator from Volunteer Tibet, an organization aimed at sourcing and organizing aid and assistance to Tibetans living in refugee status in India. He recruited those monks who wanted to learn English and had the time to do so within the brief window during which the small team would be visiting.

A bit of creativity was chosen for this project that would allow the students to meet both goals—that of data collection and that of teaching English to monks. Each student worked with two monks separately each day to produce an individual writing sample from each of the monks. The general guide to the writing sample was divided into three parts: (a) Tell me about yourself, (b) How did you become part of the monastery? and (c) How did becoming a monk affect your life? This kind of partitioning allowed for manageable examination of the issues during the discussions as well as providing ample time for immediate feedback to the monks, bearing in mind the language barriers.

The interview questions were drawn from a pool of questions developed during a brainstorming session with the student interviewers and the researchers. In multiple separate sessions, student interviewers were briefed on the process of data collection via ethnographic interviews. These sessions served as a training program that helped infuse some standardization into the data collection process. Students worked with their monks to help them improve English competency, and they eventually emerged with a writing sample. The students also kept journals of their experiences. These journals were the window into the relationship that developed between each monk and student, and they also served as a kind of touchstone to the final writing sample that each monk provided. Each student journaled his own thoughts about what the monk was saying or was attempting to communicate during their meetings, especially regarding nonverbal cues. Thus, the logical progression of data collection had the teaching and conversation becoming the interview, the writing sample serving as the transcribed interview, and the students' journals serving as the data collector's reflections.

This research project was guided by thoughts and themes nestled in the overall topic of vocational discernment. The project aimed at examining the factors, patterns, and commonalities that emerged from ethnographic interviews. We hypothesized that particular themes, such as family, educational, and political issues, would be of interest to the research; however, the analysis of the data for revealing the most common concepts would be the final determinant of what themes would be examined in this presentation.

From this data, we obtained some very interesting demographic information and formulated six themes. We based these themes solely on the frequency with which they appeared in the writing samples and the stories of the monks as reflected in the students' journals. After an analysis of the demographic data on the sample, we analyzed these themes in the following order: (1) study of Buddhism, (2) religious altruism/realization, (3) monastery life, (4) good education, (5) family issues, and (6) political issues.

In this sample of 35 monks, ages ranged from 5 to 21 years for the chronological age at which they joined their monasteries. The data on present age and age when they joined the monastery were recorded for 25 participants. Of these 25 monks, 15 joined in their pre-teenage years (12 years or earlier) and 22 joined before their 18th birthday. Of the 25 monks, nine joined monasteries in their teen years, with 6 of that number in their middle to late teens.

These numbers are revealing. The volunteer coordinator explained, "The basic starting point of becoming a monk is giving up everything or renouncing." He accepts that not even he was ready yet for that kind of sacrifice and commitment. For many boys who are placed in monasteries at young ages at the will of their parents or that of the family, it is an imposed sacrifice. The coordinator pointed to disparities in a few points of interest between the boys who were sent to monasteries and those who joined of their own volition. He estimated that, in Tibet, of the boys aged between 7 and 9 years of age who were put into monasteries by their parents, 90% remain true to their vocation and stay for life. He points out that, in India, however, in the same category of boys, 90% disrobe or go back home. Speaking on the topic of teens who join monasteries of their own volition, he estimates that in Tibet approximately 90% remain as lifetime monks and of teens in India, 80 to 90% stay. He states emphatically, therefore, that it is far better to have boys join monasteries later rather than earlier if they live in India. It is also evident that, if the boys are in Tibet, there may not be too much difference in rate of disrobing.

On the other hand, the estimates seem to suggest that there is some underlying issue that may help explain these disparities besides the ability to make one's own choices and the maturity and capability to reason abstractly, which favors teens in the decision-making process. Both the young boys and the teenage boys from Tibet who join or are made to join monasteries have very low rates of disrobing, while their cohorts born or raised in India show dramatic differences. The coordinator sums up the truth of his estimates in this way: "When it is our choice, we are more likely to stay." One could venture further, though, that young Tibetan boys are influenced by the stark reality and immediacy of their social, national, and political situations and thus are readier to make the sacrifice or the renouncing that the coordinator spoke of. The boys in India are more removed from the naked reality of the national and cultural crises and may not identify as readily with this level of sacrifice or even the culture or the attempts at preserving what is left of it. Thus, it may begin to become apparent that the national and cultural identities of these young Tibetans are being slowly diffused. Along with that, the coordinator pointed to a dramatic decrease in the rate of boys joining monasteries in regions with which he is familiar. He estimated that, in 2008, there may have been only one monk from any one family or none at all, a departure from the norm of the 1960s and 1970s when there were many monks, because each family had one or two monks. In the 1980s and 1990s, boys had stopped becoming monks, and there were fewer every year as boys opted to seek higher education.

Of the 25 monks whose ages were reported, 9 joined in their teen years but before their 18th birthdays. Most of these ranged from 13 to 15 years old. Only two joined at 17 years and one at 18. The data support the idea that it is in the teen inductees into monasteries rather than child inductees that vocational discernment occurs more credibly. As a result, we will, for the duration of this presentation, focus primarily on the teen category of monks and launch our examination of the data from that point of view. This breaks out into our six themes.

The Study of Buddhism

In conversation with the general secretary of the Tibetan Government in Exile, one researcher sought clarification of the first theme of the study of Buddhism as a reason why young men join the monastery. He was told, "Monks should join with the purpose of benefiting other human beings and making them happy. That is the point—to live to benefit the world—other sentient beings." Many of the monks who were interviewed cited the opportunity to study Buddhism as their primary motive for choosing monastic life. This avenue was viewed as far nobler and more beneficial, both to the individual and to all sentient beings, than merely being a lay Buddhist. One monk suggested, "If you want real happiness, you have to become a monk." He went further to espouse a profoundly simple thought, "Nobody wants suffering—not even killers and robbers." In the West, a criminal is often labeled and devalued to the point where his or her being human is almost negated. To these monks, however, every sentient being deserves happiness. Moreover, to be of any assistance to these and other beings, the individual who would embrace this philosophy has to be willing to renounce everything, because, as a monk, "You can't have a wife and children because you can become jealous and kids can give you problems." A monk has to be willing to live above all these influences because his vocation is no part-time affair that can be picked up and laid down according to the currents and flights of fancy that often govern daily secular living.

The discipline and the stoicism that is monastic life, coupled with the philosophies of peace, contentment, and coexistence characteristic of the Buddhist way of life, provide one avenue to young Tibetan men who are seeking answers to the existential questions, Who am I? and Why am I here? The general secretary's words assume a ring of Socratic wisdom when he says,

> ... you only have 100 years. If you spend your life making others miserable and causing pain, what is that? Your life is no use. But if you spend your life making things better for others, that's a life well spent. We are here such a short time.

In light of this statement, one would think that a torrent of young men wanting to be monks would be a welcome occurrence, but the general secretary was quick to post a caveat to his position. He cites the Dalai Lama when he says that they are interested in the quality of the monks they get rather than the mere quantity. He adds, "A lama must be realized. It should be that, when he speaks, his words bring happiness to others."

The attempt by monks to inform others of their culture and philosophy becomes apparent in their dedication to the goal of benefiting all sentient beings, demonstrated by their voracious appetite to gain knowledge and the languages, especially English. The intention of the students to learn the language is to become sufficiently proficient to be capable of sharing the Buddhist teachings and the intricacies of the accompanying philosophy with Westerners. To appreciate how free these monks are to undertake this task, one is reminded of their right to renounce and the austere sacrifice that they take willingly unto themselves.

Religious Altruism and Realization

Monks acknowledge, "The Buddhist monk's duty is to help another person, kindness, affection, love, good ideas, [and] good leadership." This religious altruism, often along with some form of religious realization or change, was another key factor in the decision-making process that resulted in monastic life for these monks. Those who cited the study of Buddhism as key to their decision to take monastic vows relished the study of Buddhist philosophy and the ritual-related sutras and scripts, while those who cited religiously altruistic factors seemed more honed in on the service aspect of the philosophy and the practical and immediate benefits to all sentient beings. It should be understood, though, that neither one of these paths is philosophically or religiously superior to the other. In fact, both these characteristics of the Buddhist monk's life are so carefully intertwined that it may often seem that there is no concrete difference. The two are symbiotic, though for the sake of this presentation we have examined them separately but only as it pertains to their function as factors that influence the decision for monastic commitment.

Some monks spoke of a call to join the monastery, while others told of having a burning passion for others and for sentient beings, but both seemed to have found their answer in Buddhism. "I had many questions and no answers," one monk simply put it. While another, still in keeping with an almost existential theme, declared, "I became a monk in this life to get good knowledge this time and to help other people and animals in this life. I can benefit all people and animals in this life." Referencing his belief in rebirth and thus his past life or lives, the monk seemed on a mission to prepare himself to be of service not just in this life but in his successive lives as well. The aim here is not at learning sutras or scripts for the sake of learning or for spiritual self-efficacy but rather for mastering those rules and thus being reborn in a position that would be of ultimate benefit to all beings in their quest for happiness.

The monks believe that life as a monk will help them be reborn as a human being in the next life, because monks follow the rules of Buddhism more strictly than do laypeople. Hence, if one is gravely concerned with the afterlife or afterlives, then it would not be a far cry from logic to expect that many would seek this monastic lifestyle, even with all its stoicism. Referencing the estimates of the coordinator of Volunteer Tibet, however, one could conclude that many young Tibetan boys and men are not as particularly concerned with afterlives as much as they are with the numbers of those seeking monastic life continuing to dwindle. It simply is not possible for a layperson to be able to devote the requisite time and energy that the monk is able to do on a daily basis. The demands of secular life make an already difficult task impossible. Thus, it becomes the vocation of the monk to gird up those in the rest of society and the world at large who in their quest for happiness have chosen more secular means, which paradoxically leads to even more unhappiness and suffering, according to the monks' explanation of their philosophy. To be a monk is to be happy, and, to be happy, one has to be a monk, these devotees seem to say.

In the search for happiness, one can get so engulfed with what is perceived as differences that one ends up using his life to cause misery and pain to others, and, to quote the words of the general secretary, "What is that? Your life is of no use." One monk explained that the red robes they wear as monks are only a small difference from other people saying, "Skin does not matter, inside all humans are the same." Many people never come to this realization and go blindly on their chosen paths to perceived happiness, often leaving in their wake a field of wasted lives, wrecked spirits and dreams, and crippled souls. Some monks, it seems, have an innate passion for people and other sentient beings even before they are fully immersed in Buddhist philosophy. Many of the monks confessed that they "became ... monk[s] because [they] have compassion for people. [They] wanted to make people happy." They believe that their chosen vocation was the best way to make people happy, the best way to reduce suffering, and the best way to get closer to Buddha.

Did these men feel the compassion they report before they joined the monasteries? Is it a result of their embracing of the teachings and philosophy of Buddhism? Or, even more, is their behavior an environment-seeking one?

Environment-seeking behavior means that these men have actively or passively sought out an environment that was most conducive to their aptitudes and passions. Either of these could be true, but because most of the monks' indication that their compassion toward all beings was a driving force behind their decision to become monks, I conclude that theirs is environment-seeking behavior in many cases. These young men are a more compassionate, more emotive, gentler, peace-loving, and nurturing kind, who, understanding the paradoxical state of human beings and the interrelated fates of all sentient beings according to karma and rebirth, seek a path that allows them to intervene, as it were, on behalf of paradoxically entwined people. Their compassion either drives them to Buddhism or maybe, inversely, Buddhism draws them in with the opportunity to express their compassion for all beings in a structured and socially acceptable way. Most monks can usually point to no other way of helping people and animals in this life or the next than through being a Buddhist monk.

Monastic Life

Monastic life is one way to give much of oneself without the hope of hoarding anything material in return: up for breakfast at 6:00 a.m.; 6:00 a.m. to 8:00 a.m., temple; 8:00 a.m. to 10:00 a.m., meditation, Dharma, teaching; 10:00 a.m., debating about Buddhist compassion; 10:00 a.m. to 11:00 a.m., reading books; 11:00 a.m., lunch; 2:00 p.m. to 4:00 p.m., teaching Buddhism and grammar; 4:00 p.m. to 5:00 p.m., relax, bathe, and take a walk; 6:30 p.m., debate group. This is the daily routine for one monk in a monastery. Though not every monastery has exactly the same routine, it would not differ drastically. Those monks who were not affiliates of any particular monastery in the area had more relaxed schedules and more free time, which they often spent by taking English classes or learning to use the computer. What was explained previously regarding the virtual impossibility of living the true Buddhist monk's life becomes immediately clear when one examines the very circumspect schedule that governs the life of the monk in the monastery.

Monastic life is characterized by discipline and control. Asked why he decided to stay in the monastery after many years of life there, a monk gave an answer that was similar to what most of the others proffered. He said that he had an initial attraction to Buddhist philosophy and that had guided his decision to join. He would later explain that the discipline and self-control inculcated through the philosophy he learns allow him to resist distractions and temptations to leave. This stoic life of self-control and discipline moves very quickly for young monks, from being taught Buddhist philosophy to what one monk describes as an "art of living." Monks cite the development of control over one's mind as a welcome benefit from this vocational choice, and thus they argue that their lives become more meaningful. Modern lay Buddhists cannot make such a strong definitive claim because they, according to these monks, "pray for good business, but monks do not pray for worldly things but take refuge in the wisdom of god."

The differentiation between modern and old lay Buddhists is made because, according to one monk, today, to be a serious practitioner of Buddhism, a person must leave home and must have many years of free time. Monks, therefore, are free to focus all their energy on their vocation, while lay Buddhists have no choice but to divide their energies and attention. In old times there were many yogis and hermits, but today there are fewer. To say that sacrifice and renouncing are integral parts of the Buddhist monk's lifestyle and therefore play a very important role in this vocational decision is an understatement that was examined repeatedly. Unavoidably, though, this issue will be reiterated because it is a critical and interrelated portion of the lifestyle and the vocational decision-making process. Like the lotus flower, out of the muck and struggle that many of these young men often have to tramp through, many emerge as beacons of stoicism, perseverance, and peace, thus gaining them the respect and admiration of their communities and their countrymen.

Life in the monastery is a plethora of statues, teachings, temples, texts, community, chants, ceremonies, sutras, scripts, schedules, rules, and more. One monastery had 3,000 monks, an abbot, a chant master, pilgrimages, novices, the Three Jewels (Dharma, Buddha, Sangha), meditation, prayer in the halls, and mandalas. But what really keeps monks from disrobing once they have settled into the task of shouldering this hefty vocation? The data reveal that possibly the most influential factor is the skill level of the monks in relation to the skill-set demands that exist in the secular world. The skills that monastery life and Buddhist philosophy embrace are usually diametrically opposed to those that would be critical to successful navigation of life outside the monastery. A monk describes monastery life thus, "Monastery discipline is good and clean. I will never forget my monastery's kindness in this life." The seemingly idealistic world that is the Buddhist monastery is a far cry from what one obtains in the rough, sometimes heartless world outside the monastery. Many of the monks confess that they have "no qualifications to work outside the monastery because [they] join[ed] so young." They argue that, though they love the monastery and the life that comes with it, they really "know no other life besides being a monk ... didn't know anything about business or anything outside monastic life."

It appears, therefore, that most monks either lack the motivation to want to disrobe or maybe are too deficient in skills to dare venture into the outside world. Additionally, one could proffer the argument that, after having grown accustomed to the structure and relative comfort of the world of the monastery, it would take an act of great upheaval or one that challenged very convincingly the life and philosophies that these young men have embraced to cause disrobing. Such a change could be most expected from a monk who had monastery life imposed upon him or one who never got to the point where he began to identify in a personal way with the teachings and philosophies he was taught. Once these factors had been positively accounted for, it would become fairly difficult, if not impossible, to tell whether the love that monks expressed and felt for their monastery and their chosen lifestyle was a function of cognitive dissonance or a love that grew out of regular circumstances.

Good Education

It cannot be denied that monasteries provide some form of education. One could suggest from the stories and comments of the monks that the level and content of the education provided may be a bit circumscribed within a very religious and Buddhist foundation. In spite of this fact, while many of the skills and much of the knowledge may be apprised as devalued capital in the outside world, for many of these monks this may have been one of their few opportunities for an education. This "good education," or at least the opportunity to earn one, was yet another of the decisive factors in the vocational discernment process for many of the monks. One of the data collectors commented this way on the enthusiasm of the monks assigned to him, "It was awesome to see the two monks when they got something or understood it. Their faces would light up and they would kick their feet. Their thirst for knowledge is almost enviable." This exhilaration with and for learning was one that would be played out many times over because other data collectors returned with similar stories of monks for whom the learning process seemed almost a palpable and honest experience—one that the teacher could visibly observe with little difficulty. If one were then to compare these reactions to the stories of wholesale woe and disappointment often reported by Western teachers, the situation would seem to suggest a devaluation of the educational experience in the West at the expense of the results, which is often wanted all too instantly. One could venture to conclude that the West values the destination more than the odyssey, while these monks, at least from my limited vantage point, savor the educational journey far more than the West does. Of course, I could be charged with overly romanticizing the monks and being overly critical of my own culture, not to mention being guilty of just plain generalizations.

Generalizations and all culturally romantic notions considered, there is a deep love for knowledge and learning among the monks and among the families from which they came. At age 13 one young man was urged very strongly by his mother to join the monastery. For him, monastic life "[was] the only way to get an education." Another was sent to the monastery at age eight by his parents for the primary purpose of getting an education. These kinds of scenarios played themselves out in quite a few of the stories that were recorded, and in most of the cases the children were offspring from poorer nomadic villages that supposedly offered very rudimentary education. If one had aspirations beyond the herding and nomadic lifestyle, then an education beyond that level was necessary. More often than not the best alternative for that kind of education would be the monastery.

Describing an environment of extreme poverty in his nomadic East Tibetan province of Amdo, a monk relived his desperation to get out—to escape the poverty and seeming desolation. He remembered always reading children's books as he tended to the animals on the farm, a testament to his love for learning. Becoming a monk was always a thought, and it always seemed in his estimation like something that would be a beneficial undertaking. To find a more altruistic slant to such a story or to at least be able to find what Western minds such as mine would term a Buddhist motive, one would have to do a bit of interpretation. There were some stories, though, that would need far less interpretation to reach the same ends.

He narrates that "one day [he] was reading a story about Tibetan kings, and [his] aunt scolded [him] for not doing [his] work." This love for learning would continue to be tested because he would later spend 3 years at a small monastery close to his nomadic village. There were no teachers there, so he left for Lhasa with the intention of becoming educated and being able to return to help another group. He had taught many young Tibetan monks the Tibetan language before, but he thought he could be of far greater use if he had a firm grasp of Buddhist philosophy, so he sought to continue his education in that direction. In his case, the desire for self-improvement assumed a symbiotic relationship with the desire to return and be of service to others; hence, the hybrid of the two desires was an altruistic act and one that, from my vantage point, was rooted in Buddhist teaching as explained by the monks I met. Education thus is not merely for its own sake but rather is done with a higher charge of service in mind.

Family Issues

Do struggle and suffering of any kind serve to strengthen the resolve of the monk regarding his vocational choice? Does this suffering serve merely as hardship and just a hurdle to be overcome, or does it perform character-building actions? Does the resolve that is supposedly built by suffering weaken over time? Many of these questions were answered in varying degrees as I examined the data before me. The impact of family issues on the decision of the monks was a critical category of inquiry. In some cases family issues of various kinds drove young boys into monasteries, while in other cases the strong emotions that come with familial ties threatened to undermine the vocational choice.

With one older sister and two younger brothers, aged 15 and 8 years, one young man, 21 years old, decided to take up monastic life because he felt a calling to that vocation. We met him shortly after he had made his decision and was newly arrived at his monastery. As noble as the intention was, it conflicted with long-held tradition that the eldest son inherited the responsibility of caring for the family and continuing the lineage. There was immediate conflict with the family patriarch, who was described as a quiet man who worked in the army. While the father eventually quietly acquiesced to his son's decision and supported him, the situation raises the question: What happens when traditional duty and one's calling seem to butt heads? Judging from the resolution of the impasse, it seems, at least in this case, that the calling won out if the devotee was intent on embarking on the noble undertaking. It may be possible that, although tradition had to bend to personal religious passion in this case, the presence of two other sons, though younger, may have softened the blow caused by this assault on tradition. The young monk talked about being continually wracked with guilt because his family had to support him financially through his decision. He made it clear that, in his culture, it is important to honor one's parents and care for them, but he had no idea how he was going to repay them.

There is considerable external social pressure that intends to keep young boys true to their vocation whether or not they made the choice freely. The pressure of knowingly bringing dishonor to one's parents and family, as opposed to the honor that they hoped for, has to be a considerable weight to bear and should function as a very powerful deterrent to those who would consider disrobing. However, to reference the astounding estimates that the coordinator of Volunteer Tibet had provided, how does one reckon these two disparate occurrences? The story of the eldest son who, against tradition, took up monastery life may provide an interesting explanation. In both cases there seems to be a weakening of the power of social sanctions. Could it be that the younger generation of Tibetans does not feel as guided or bound by tradition and customs as do the older generations? An explanation along these lines would, if only parsimoniously, begin to account for the stark differences in the estimates given for the number of young Tibetan boys who, put into monasteries from 7 to 9 years old, disrobe, as opposed to their cohort who grew up in India. There may yet be life in this explanation because quite a few monks in this data set provide support for the idea that there is an eroding of tradition and with it the waning of the power of social sanction, norms, and mores that the old guard lived by.

One older monk leveled a few indictments against the younger generation of Tibetans, saying "Some young people think that we lost our country because we have been too passive," a response to the indictment that some of the young—more than likely the lay Buddhists—had leveled against the old guard. This denunciation flies in the face of tradition and the essence of Buddhist philosophy and thus serves as a telling sign of the erosion of the power of social sanctions and traditions that are discussed here. An older monk added that "in old times a man who could spread peace and compassion was considered masculine. Now focus has shifted toward money and materialism." No matter what the outside culture believed, the monk thought, it was always best to work toward peace and compassion. In that light, then, the structure and discipline of the monastery become even more important if it is to be the last bastion of Buddhist and Tibetan culture and tradition. If one does aim at protectionist policies regarding culture, then a minimization of interaction, or at the very least a controlled interaction with other cultures, is advisable.

The family still remains the ideal place for conveying culture and tradition, but, when families do not function normally, the monastery seems to fill in the position as surrogate. In the instance of domestic violence, the family structure is compromised and dysfunction ensues. One monk, whose story of domestic violence I have examined under a separate theme, undergoes a kind of Cinderella story. After the death of his father, who was "not a good man" and the subsequent passing of his mother, providence would have it that he would eventually end up at a monastery. There he would experience the love, acceptance, compassion, and nurturing that he had been longing for. The family atmosphere of the monastery would serve as a haven from cruel fate for yet another monk. At 12 years old he was still reeling from the death of his father when two of his seven siblings, aged 2 and 3, also passed. He recounted, "When I saw such a very sad situation, I decided my own self to become a monk, my mother was very happy." With the family being assaulted by tragedy, the monastery became a refuge for both the young monk and the honor and hope of his mother. In these situations the family structure and the congenial, nurturing atmosphere of the monastery become a welcome and very capable surrogate for the young boy who is leaving the besieged family.

It appears that most monks, regardless of the circumstances under which they joined the monastery, eventually grow to love and appreciate it. "Pressure from [my] parents" was the reason for my joining the monastery, a monk wrote, but he would allude to his love for the Buddha and his respect for the Dalai Lama and his teachings and Tibetan Buddhism as the key reasons for his decision to stay. He was 13 years old when he joined, but he has "obviously grown to love his life as a monk even though he did not choose it," a data collector observed. The teachers and uncle of one monk agreed that he should be a monk, and soon he was in a monastery. His present view of the decision is that "it is OK. Yes it is. Not wrong. I like being a monk and doing a monk's job." A possible drawback to putting boys into monasteries at a very young age is that they have no frame of reference when they do become old enough to question the decision that was made on their behalf. One monk has no memory of life before the monastery, because his grandmother decided to enroll him in a monastery while he was still in kindergarten. He has grown into the decision, though, and enjoys or maybe has learned to enjoy his present life.

POLITICAL ISSUES

To attempt to examine the concept of vocational discernment regarding Buddhist monks without including the political situation and its effects on that process would be irresponsible. The monks describe the political situation in Tibet as one in which it is difficult to freely practice one's religion. This lack of religious freedom is underscored by the physical destruction of the temples or in other cases the detaining of the abbots and other leaders, the terrorizing of the monasteries through repeated ransacking and raids, the usurping of the rule of the monastery by the Chinese government, or a combination of these and other tactics. Relating his experience with the political situation, one monk communicated, "I could not join my local monastery because it was destroyed by the Chinese invasion. Only two monks remain because of Chinese occupation." Another monk added that "from the late 1990s the Chinese policy toward the Tibetans and Dalai Lama became intolerable." The monks served to echo what I had heard so many times on my trip from many different sources that were supportive of the Tibetan plight. A young monk proposed that "this makes it impossible to live an ideal monk's life ... under such unjust laws and orders, no sensible being, especially a religious person, can survive without ignoring the world around [him] and [his] destiny as well as [his] comfort." Anyone still living in Tibet or Lhasa who seriously desires to take up monastic commitments has to be willing to face what many of the monks described as almost insurmountable odds, often to the extent of being prepared to bleed and possibly die for that choice.

Even those monks who have, through craft or providence or both, managed to get out of Lhasa and into India to join monasteries say that they have to worry about the families they left behind because these families often suffer physically the brunt of the young man's decision. One monk was very near tears as he told us of his aged parents whom he had to forsake. He told of not being able to communicate with them because all communication channels were monitored by the Chinese government and the family could face serious penalties for that action. Not just communication but movement, too, was especially restricted. A young monk told of how he skirted the restrictions in order to take up his monastic life and explained, "I could not go to Lhasa without permission of the Chinese government. My uncle was a very clever and smart man and bribed the official in the area with cheese, butter, and fruit."

A monk told his story of coming to India to be a monk. It turned out to be such a powerful tale of suffering, determination, and fortune that it seemed to parallel only the plot of a very well-written movie. The indomitable spirit of the narrator shone through most brilliantly as he retold his trials, before commenting that his journey really was not all that terrible considering the fact that he was lucky to have come through alive while many other Tibetans did not. Speaking through a translator, he told of the severe poverty that his older brother who had escaped his village. His brother excelled in Chinese at school and was thus able to secure a job from the Chinese government in a law office. While his older brother worked in the secular world, this young man sought a vocation as a Buddhist monk.

It would take four arduous attempts before he successfully made it to India. His first attempt was made with a group of 15 people. After a long trek through the Himalayas, they got to Nepal, where there was a bridge guarded by a Chinese camp. Just across that river lay his desires for religious freedom. No sooner had they begun to cross the bridge than they were seized. The rest of the night would be a nightmare they would all have to relive for the rest of their lives. They were held for the entire night and tortured throughout their detainment. He told of being forced to hold his arms outstretched in front of his body while supporting the weight of heavy, flat, metal objects. To ensure that the torture had its intended effect, cigarette lighters were positioned directly under his outstretched arms, so that when his arms inevitably grew too fatigued to support the heavy weights, they would be burned.

Early the following morning they were loaded into jeeps and conveyed to another prison camp. They were issued a stiff warning, because it was their first offense, but they received some leniency and were released. They were sent back to Lhasa. After about 4 or 5 months, he was at it again, and, with another group, he made his second attempt. A jeep took the group to the base of the mountain from which they hiked for 13 days through the Himalayas until they made it to Kathmandu. They were identified by police in the area and taken to a detention center. Through a translator they explained to their captors that they were only trying to see the Dalai Lama. The police discussed the situation among themselves and then told the group that they would be put on a bus that would take them to see the Dalai Lama. So strong was their conviction and desire to escape and take up monastic life and start a new life in a Tibetan community that they naively believed the story without question. Along the way to the supposed destination, two detainees who were familiar with the route realized that they were heading in the wrong direction. They were headed for Tibet.

They were handed over to the Chinese police and spent 2 days at a prison camp before being returned to Tibet. Utterly disillusioned, the young man joined a monastery in Lhasa and abandoned his hopes of ever being free to practice his religion. It was a full year before he tried again. His time at the monastery did not hold the best of memories. There was very little food, the educational opportunities were very poor, and the building suffered frequent forays from the Chinese police. With a group of 47 Tibetans, he began his third escape attempt, and this one, like the others, was set for failure. Packed in a truck, they drove to the mountains before beginning a 20-day march through the Himalayas. This attempt was made during the winter, and they had to deal with the season's harsh conditions. They slept during the day to avoid the worst of the winter conditions and walked all through the night. One of the nuns who was with them fell ill, and a monk broke his leg. Both seemed like harbingers of the eventual failure of this trip. The group had to take turns carrying the injured until they happened upon a small village where they left the sick with a bit of money to cover their care.

After another lengthy hike, there was one mountain peak left to cross, and the group could see their promised land. They spied what they thought was a small village of nomads in the distance and made their way toward them, hoping for some desperately needed rest and recuperation. The encampment turned out to be Chinese police who had been tipped off by the injured members of the group when the Chinese had raided the small village. The young monk-to-be was taken into custody and again returned unceremoniously to Tibet—a third failed attempt. Why he would not have simply called it quits and settled for what he had obtained as far as a vocation in Lhasa is a testament to pure, unadulterated passion for his beliefs and a kind of dogged determination that is husband to bravery.

His lengthening criminal record made it difficult for him to return to his old local monastery, so he lived with a family in Lhasa for 1 year. During that year he was informed by some Tibetans that there was an alternative route with a chance of success far greater than those routes he had been taking before, but it would be longer. He made up his mind to try a fourth time to get to India and left with three other monks. Again, they set off by jeep for the mountains, and, after 7 days of driving, they hiked for 30 days through the mountains. Falling on hard times, they traded with some nomads, giving some of their warm clothing for food because, after only 1 week, their supply had run out. They reached Nepal safely, and again their attempt at escape seemed like it would be foiled when they were discovered by police. One of them managed to elude capture, but the others were taken to a detention center and interrogated.

The escaped monk did not forsake his brothers as may have been thought but rather alerted the Tibetan agency of the capture and imprisonment of his three fellows. This action may have tipped the scales of providence in their favor, because the agency promptly dispatched a representative to ascertain the circumstances under which they had been detained. Jaded by prior negative experiences, they believed their aide to be an undercover policeman and thus refused to converse with him. A second representative was sent, and this time the group, strained and stressed by the situation and the history that gave it birth, broke down, explaining among their tears the difficulties of their journey to Nepal. A bribe from the representative to the guards ensured safe passage to India for all the travelers and at last a miracle seemed to have occurred. Finally, after three fruitless attempts, the young monk would get his wish to worship and learn in a Buddhist monastery that was not censored by the Chinese government. He "looked so peaceful sitting in front of me. Speaking with him helps me keep perspective, and will for a long time," said the student researcher as he looked almost in awe at the narrator of an autobiography almost too incredibly genuine, human, and touching to believe.

Vocational Discernment Among Tibetan Buddhist Nuns in Dharamsala, India: A Companion Piece to The 2008 India and Nepal Men's Research and Service Project (Jessica Nelson and Ashleigh Leitch)

We interviewed eight Tibetan Buddhist nuns during a weeklong stay in Dharamsala, India. The nuns ranged in age from 25 to 42 years old, and most had family origins in various parts of Tibet and India. All the nuns are presently in Dharamsala; some were sent there by their head monastery located elsewhere in India while others left Tibet to pursue greater religious and cultural freedom. The nuns for this study were chosen by a Tibetan Buddhist monk, Tsultrim Gyato, who coordinated our stay in Dharamsala. He recruited nuns who desired to improve and practice their conversational English.

INTERVIEWS

We were partnered with a nun with whom we spent extensive time over the course of the week (about 10 hours over July 26–31, 2009) in conversation and conducting informal interviews. The six other nuns in the study were interviewed more briefly in shorter, less extensive interview sessions.

The general interviews included name, age, birthplace, information about their family, age they joined the monastery, why they joined (did they make the decision or did their parents?), what their parents thought about their decision if they chose, why they thought women should become nuns, and what they liked about being a nun.

As we became more aware about Tibetan/Buddhist culture, we asked the interviewed nuns more questions in regard to whether they went to school before becoming a nun, were their siblings (especially sisters) educated, what ages their siblings married, had they ever wished they had gotten married, were any of their siblings nuns or monks (and, if so, and they had joined before she took her vows, did that influence her decision to be a nun), and were they active politically (if so, had they been arrested or involved in demonstrations in India/Tibet).

DATA COLLECTION

The data collection techniques used for this research included conversations and personal interviews conducted by us. During these interviews, we took notes and quoted the nuns' responses; we also made interpretations based on nonverbal clues and our previous knowledge of the subject being discussed when the language barrier created confusion. We recorded these conversations, interpretations, and our own personal reflections in journals and in transcribing summaries of the interviews.

RESULTS

This research was guided by the idea of vocational discernment and aimed at discovering the factors that encouraged the sample of interviewed women to devote their lives to the monastery. Another aspect of the research was to investigate the effect of the interviews on us.

The hypothesis was that the factors that encouraged the women to become nuns would be similar to the themes described in Thomas and Kellom's (2009) study. These themes were the study of Buddhism, religious altruism/realization, monastery life, good education, family issues, and political issues.

From the data, it was found that, although the themes were similar, Tibetan women have different cultural expectations than Tibetan men, and thus there are some succinct differences. The main themes we found were the study of Buddhism, education, and the desire to help others/religious altruism.

This research contained a sample of eight nuns between the ages of 25 and 42. Of these, three took their vows in their preteen years (12 years old or younger), four joined in their teen years (13 to 19), and one joined in her 20s. Six joined monasteries before their 18th birthdays. The range of ages that they became nuns spanned from 6 to 24 years old.

The main themes as to why Tibetan Buddhist nuns join the monastery are as follows: for an education, to study Buddhism, to help others, and to have a more meaningful life. Also influential in their decisions were the difficult life of Tibetan lay people, political issues, no desire to get married, and the desire to improve their own lives and have more time for themselves. All of these issues are deeply interwoven into the fabric of Tibetan culture and society, and thus, culturally, a woman often has the ability to dictate her own life only after she has taken her vows to become a nun.

Study of Buddhism

One of the nuns explained that she enjoyed being a nun because it allowed her to study Buddhism and to pray. If she had stayed in Tibet with her family, she would have had to stop her studies to work on the family farm. She also mentioned that, by being a nun, she avoided the "craziness" of family life, such as marriage and children.

Four other nuns expressed similar religious reasons as to why they decided to become nuns. One said that "women should be nuns because it's a good opportunity to study and practice Buddhism and to study women's status in society." She also explained that she likes to teach other people Buddhism. The other three alluded to the difficulties of Tibetan lay women. One stated that, "If we become laymen we can't practice [Buddhist philosophy]." Another said that she became a nun "because it's good for humanity and also to practice Buddhism and philosophy ... if we become lay people we can't practice." Similarly, another said, "[I am a nun] because I like this way. I want to make my life meaningful. Also, I want to practice the Dharma." She also mentioned that lay people do not have enough time to study Buddhism and that the ability to receive an education is one reason women should become nuns.

Education

Only two of the women interviewed had attended school prior to becoming nuns, and one of those nuns received a Chinese education. A stark reality for Tibetan women is that becoming a monastic is often their only opportunity to be educated. Not only that, but as the Chinese continue to oppress the Tibetan people and culture, an authentic Tibetan and even Buddhist education can often only be achieved outside the borders of Tibet. Therefore, Tibetan women must not only join a monastery but must also escape Tibet in order to receive an adequate education in both their culture and religion. These are some of the reasons why more and more Tibetan Buddhist nuns are appearing in Dharamsala, India; the location of the Tibetan Government in Exile.

For many of these nuns, a monastic life is often their only opportunity to be educated. Because of this reality, when women choose to be educated, they often are also choosing a monastic life. One nun put it simply, "I am a nun to learn." Another nun said, "The opportunity to be educated is one reason women become nuns."

Another nun, faced a similar situation. Although her family origins were in India, she explained that "in home, no chance to study, need to work on farm. Very hard life." Therefore, the desire to be educated encourages many Tibetan women to adopt the monastic way of life.

RELIGIOUS ALTRUISM AND THE DESIRE TO HELP OTHERS

Tibetan women who are not in the monastery typically have a difficult and strenuous life of farming, cooking, raising a family, and so on. Because of this, they cannot devote much time to religious altruism and helping others. Therefore, another main reason for women to become monastics is to have the time to help others or religious altruism. The interviewed nuns mentioned having time for various types of religious altruism—such as educating people in Buddhism, practicing Dharma, and helping the poor and sick—as a key reason why they joined the monastery.

One said, "Nuns [are] very happy because everyday prayer, help other people, kind to other people, meditation.... If people sick, help them wash clothes, make food, give food." She also went on to explain that she was not upset about giving up the opportunity to have a family, "Marry no. Maybe marry but everyday don't help other people, no time ... baby, husband ... no time to help other people."

A main portion of religious altruism is to alleviate the suffering of others as well as one's own suffering. A nun explained how being a monastic could alleviate suffering, "I think nuns happy and enjoy. No worry. Myself. Maybe I marry and I have baby, then I worried and suffering. I alone, then I help. I get enough time to help other people, poor people. I get free time. If I married, then I carry baby and look for house and do food—very, very suffering. I'm free. Then I'm very happy."

DISCUSSION

THE SITUATION FOR TIBETANS

The current situation in Tibet—the difficult lives of Tibetans, the political climate, and decreased religious and educational freedoms—is an important context as to why Tibetan women choose the life of Buddhist monastics. Life for the majority of lay Tibetans is very difficult because the majority of the population is agro-based and thus makes a relatively small amount of money for a highly labor- and-time intensive endeavor. Lay people in Tibet are often so consumed by doing things just to survive that they often do not have the leisure of having time that they can devote to education, practicing Buddhism, or helping others. Not only that, but life for lay Tibetans is also difficult because the Chinese government imposes strict measures of oppression against the Tibetan people, such as limiting freedom of expression, censoring Tibetan communication, destroying religious temples and books, and forcing Tibetan children to attend Chinese schools.

Due to the harsh reality for many Tibetans—especially in regard to the political situation—several of the nuns we interviewed were active participants in protests and demonstrations for a free Tibet and for an end to Chinese occupation and oppression. One of the nuns interviewed was arrested in front of the Chinese Embassy in Delhi, India, for protesting against the Chinese occupation of Tibet when a Chinese official visited India. Another was involved in a demonstration in Lhasa, Tibet, in which around 1,000 people circumambulated a large monastery with signs that read "Free Tibet!" "We Want Freedom!" and "Chinese Go Out!" The Chinese broke up the protest with guns, knives, and tear gas, killing and injuring many people who were armed with only stones and sticks—things they picked up from the ground. This nun—and several others from her nunnery—managed to escape; however, because the Chinese had warrants out for their arrest, they could not return to their monastery. Of these nuns, two were arrested and imprisoned for their involvement in the protest, while three managed to escape to Dharamsala, India.

Despite arrests and narrowly avoided imprisonment, both women continue to protest several times a month. They say they do this to help their people and their country and to raise awareness about the injustice that is occurring in Tibet.

Impact on Researchers

After spending a week doing interviews and learning more about the nuns and the situation in Tibet, we discovered that we took more away from the week than some incredible stories, new friends, and a passion for Tibet. We found that we were deeply impacted by the strength, devotion, commitment, and conscientiousness emulated by the nuns we interviewed.

Through these conversations and newly formed friendships, we found that we were inspired to search for and pursue what makes our lives meaningful. This was shown on a large scale through a story of a nun that risked all she had ever known for what she believed in, revealing the need to live and work for something bigger than herself and to find a vocation that "makes life meaningful." On a small scale, an instance of a nun carefully carrying ants outside rather than smashing them, reminded us to live conscientiously and to respect and live symbiotically with nature. Other lessons that we were taught were to keep perspective, especially in regard to the sacrifices one often has to make in pursuit of one's goals. For example, a large sacrifice in Western culture is often nothing compared to the sacrifices many of these nuns had to make, including arduous and dangerous journeys through the Himalayas in which they had to leave their loved ones and country to be free to practice their religion and culture.

We learned to make the most out of the opportunities we have been given: education, the vast number of vocations available to us, and so on. We also learned that, despite all of these opportunities, we must remember to live simply, live with respect, work for what drives us, and, at the very least, do small things to alleviate the suffering of those around us.

FUTURE RESEARCH

The present study, although enlightening in its findings and implications, is really only a small preview of other research that can be conducted on this topic. Limitations in the present study include the limited number of nuns interviewed, the brief amount of time spent with some of those interviewed, and the language limitations of the researchers.

Future research in this area could encompass an investigation into the link between the age vows are taken and the age women are expected to marry, the availability of education or study for girls in the lay population, and a comparison between why Tibetans become Buddhist nuns and why Westerners become nuns (Buddhist or otherwise). Other future research on this topic could include a comparison between why men versus women join the monastery and research into whether increased opportunities for women—education, vocation, decision not to marry, and so on—decreases the number of women who join the monastery.

REFLECTIONS ON VOCATIONAL DISCERNMENT: INTERVIEWING BENEDICTINES AND OTHER BUDDHISTS (MICHAEL WALLACE)

Stepping out of the New Delhi airport, I was immediately bathed in heat and the noise of busy streets, both of which still permeated the nighttime city. It was refreshing to be outside, even in the heat, and away from the inquisitive officials in the airport. This was the start of my monthlong experience of India and Nepal last summer. The trip was led by Gar Kellom, the director of the Men's Center at St. John's, and included six other people from the College of St. Benedict and St. John's University.

The first week of the trip was spent touring three major cities in India—Delhi, Agra, and Jaipur—known as the Golden Triangle. The first city I toured was Delhi, a sprawling city that holds the capital of India, New Delhi. I immediately met India's chaotic streets and ceaseless noise caused by an overabundance of people. There seemed to be no traffic laws, or, if there were, no one followed them. Evidently, the lines of the street determining lanes were solely for decoration, and the rare traffic light was spotted only a handful of times. The tour guides led my bus through the myriad of streets to a number of different places of cultural and national importance, all the while giving me incredibly detailed explanations of the history around me. The first place I visited was a memorial to the most important modern historical figure of India, Mahatma Gandhi. There, I followed Gandhi's last footprints to the place he was assassinated. While in Delhi, my group also visited an elaborate Sikh temple, where I learned about Sikh traditions and met some of the most hospitable people during the tour of India.

Leaving Delhi, my group rode the tour bus through the hot, flat desert to Agra, where the Taj Mahal was built. The Taj Mahal is a mausoleum built by a Mughal emperor for his wife. It is by far the most elegant building I have ever seen. It stands alongside several mosques in perfect symmetry. The beauty of the Taj Mahal can't be completely captured by pictures or art, one must see it personally. While I was touring the Taj Mahal, the astonishingly well-informed tour guide told me the rich story of who the mausoleum was built for, which added to the already amazing experience.

The last place in India I visited was Jaipur, also known as the Pink City because of the pinkish color of many buildings. Here I had the opportunity to ride elephants, learn about Hinduism while visiting a Hindu temple, and visit the Neerja Modi school, one of the leading schools in India. The Neerja Modi school and the Men's Center cooperate to give college students internships in teaching. This is only one option for interning through this trip; other options include working for the Kathmandu Guest House in Nepal or teaching at a school in Southern India. All students on my trip had an internship or a research project in India or Nepal. Three students who recently graduated bought one-way tickets and stayed at the Neerja Modi school, two have returned since, and one will come back in December. After touring the school and dropping off a member of our group (two others returned to the school for their internships), I headed for Nepal.

Nepal borders both India and China and lies among the foothills of the Himalayans and the Tibetan Plateau. The first city I visited was Kathmandu, the capital of Nepal. Dozens of restaurants lay within a 10-minute walk from my hotel, the Kathmandu Guest House, and shops of Nepali clothes, teas, and other goods are abundant. The Guest House is also a great place to meet people from all over the world who are also traveling around Asia. The majority of the group had internships organized by the Guest House itself, ranging from helping a local Nepali museum display its art to creating a scarf business within the Guest House itself. When I wasn't exploring Kathmandu, I was meeting new people at the Guest House.

My favorite part of this trip was its flexibility. Gar Kellom created a general outline of the trip, allowing the group to fill in the details. After spending a few days exploring the temples and life of Kathmandu, the group decided to travel to a city in the mountains called Pokhara and to whitewater raft on the way. The whitewater rafting was an exhilarating experience, and the lush green hills of

Nepal were the perfect background for the ride. I stayed one night in Pokhara, a gorgeous city nestled between the Himalayan mountains that also lies along a lake. The next day, the group and I went on a 1-day trek into the mountains, through vibrant jungle hillsides and quaint rice farms, until I reached a village and stayed the night. I returned down a different path and back into Pokhara the next day, where I stayed for another night.

After returning to Kathmandu, half my group went to Dharamsala, India, to see the Tibetan Government in Exile, and half started internships in Kathmandu. I stayed in Kathmandu and had the unique opportunity to visit a Tibetan Buddhist monastery for 4 days. At the monastery, I taught English, learned about Tibetan Buddhism and the Tibetan culture, and continued an ongoing research project interviewing Tibetan Buddhist monks. My visit to the monastery was a deeply spiritual and enlightening experience. I left the monastery with a broader view of monastic culture. Before I knew it, I was in the Kathmandu airport, heading back to the states.

The Men's Center's summer India and Nepal trip was an incredible experience. I learned a lot about the cultures and religions of India, Nepal, and Tibet. Kellom organized the trip so that there was room to choose what the group wanted to do. Instead of taking a 1-day trek, the group could have taken a 3- or 4-day trek. The many internship options also added to the experience. I only wish I could have stayed longer!

REFLECTING ON A YEAR IN INDIA, 1 YEAR LATER (JOHN VAN ROOY)

"In the twenty-first century our global society will flourish or perish according to our ability to find common ground across the world on a set of shared objectives and on the practical means to achieve them" (Sachs, 2008). These words, written by renowned economist and global thinker, Jeffrey Sachs, capture my motivation for applying to the MA program in Languages and Cultures of Asia (LCA). With the imminent onset of the Asian Century, a regional expertise in Asia will be of utmost importance in helping the global society to flourish. I believe the ability to find common ground and achieve shared objectives on a global scale is largely dependent on a broad understanding of languages and cultures.

The nine months I spent in India after completing my undergraduate degree allowed me to experience the importance of linguistic and cultural knowledge in building global relationships. First as a research assistant interviewing Tibetan monks and later as a volunteer teacher at a high school, I had the opportunity to form inspiring relationships that encouraged me to learn more about the history, languages, and cultures of India.

Upon returning to the United States and reflecting further on my experience in India, I decided to shift my academic focus from Latin America to South Asia. My passion for the Spanish language has inspired a passion to learn Hindi and Urdu. As an undergraduate, I had the opportunity to live in Chile and Colombia.

This living experience taught me that language is the door through which one understands culture. The strong emphasis on language acquisition is a significant motivating factor for my desire to apply to the LCA program.

In addition to achieving fluency in more languages, I am interested in deepening my knowledge of conflict studies and peace education. Particularly, I would like to focus on the relationship between India and Pakistan. A project I have in mind is to do research on Kashmir and investigate how the conflict there might be mediated through interreligious dialogues and the implementation of peace education in high schools. I feel that the areas of expertise represented by the LCA faculty and the opportunity for interdisciplinary collaboration provide a ripe environment to engage this research interest.

My long-term vision for pursuing an MA in the LCA program includes several potential career paths. One route is to work at the governmental level as a diplomat or policy maker. A second career interest is to pursue a PhD in LCA or some other Asian-related field and teach at the university level. A third option is to work in the nongovernmental sector, focusing on international development and education. Should I attend this graduate program, I believe I would be well prepared with a strong foundation to successfully pursue any or all of these career paths.

When reflecting on how to best use my time and talent, I return once again to the writing of Sachs. He has provided me with the inspiration to lay the groundwork necessary for the flourishing of global society in the 21st century. Sachs writes about the importance for a new approach to global problem solving that is based on cooperation among nations and the ability to be dynamic and creative. In whatever career I end up pursuing, I hope to take on this challenge and be the change I wish to see in the world.

References

Brooks, C. (2008). *A study of gender imbalance in PTEV (programs for theological exploration of vocation) programs.* Paper delivered at the 2008 Conference on the College Male at Saint John's University.

Coffey, A., & Atkinson, P. (1996). *Making sense of qualitative data: Complementary research strategies.* Thousand Oaks, CA: Sage.

Crotty, M. (1998). *The foundations of social research: Meaning and perspective in the research process.* Thousand Oaks, CA: Sage.

Clydesdale, T. (2007). *The first year out: Understanding American teens after high school.* Chicago, IL: University of Chicago Press. An assessment of all 88 Lilly programs is also underway by the same *author*.

de Dreuille, M. (1999). *From East to West: A history of monasticism.* New York: Crossroads.

Department of Religion and Culture, Central Tibetan Administration. (2000). *Destruction and reconstruction: The story of the rebuilding of monasteries of India, Nepal and Bhutan.* Dharamsala, H.P. India: Indraprasta Press.

Eck, D.L. (2001). *A new religious America: How a "Christian country" has become the world's most religiously diverse nation.* New York: Harper Collins.

Ghandi, R.S. (1974). *Locals and cosmopolitans of little India: A sociological study of the Indian community of Minnesota.* Bombay, India: Popular Prakashan.

Hammersley, M., & Atkinson, P. (1995). *Ethnography: Principles in practice* (2nd ed.). London: Routledge.

Johnson, A.G. (2000). *The Blackwell dictionary of sociology* (2nd ed.). Oxford, UK: Blackwell.

Kellom, G. (2004). *Developing effective programs and services for college men.* San Francisco, CA: Jossey-Bass.

Lincoln, Y., & Guba, E. (1985). *Naturalistic inquiry.* Thousand Oaks, CA: Sage.

Manning, K. (1992). The ethnographic interview. In F.K. State & Associates (Eds.), *Diverse methods for research and assessment of college students* (pp. 91–103). Lanham, MD: University Press of America.

Merriam, S.B. (2001). *Qualitative research and case study applications in education.* San Francisco: Jossey-Bass.

Queen, C.S. (Ed.). (2000). *Engaging Buddhism in the West.* Boston, MA: Wisdom Publications.

Sachs, J. (2008). *Common wealth: Economics for a crowded planet.* New York: Penguin Press.

Thomas, A., & Kellom, G. (2009). Vocational discernment among Tibetan Buddhist monks in Dharamsala, India. *Journal of Ethnographic and Qualitative Research, 3,* 251–268.

Tucci, G. (1988). *The religions of Tibet.* Berkeley: University of California Press.

9

Deep M-Pact:
Mentoring Gustavus Men for Masculinities of Meaning and Making a Difference

Christopher Johnson and Benjamin Hilding

As at many colleges and universities that have been part of the Lilly Endowment's Programs for the Theological Exploration of Vocation (PTEV)—and, it seems, in the broader culture—male students at Gustavus Adolphus College are less likely than their female counterparts to be engaged in activities and practices that foster exploration, reflection, and discernment of vocation. They are also less involved in religious life, community service, leadership formation, and other vocation-related aspects of the Gustavus experience. In response, Gustavus has begun an extended, multifaceted project called Deep M-Pact: Mentoring Gustavus Men for Masculinities of Meaning and Making a Difference. This project—including the annual Deep M-Pact Men's Retreat, which will be the focus of this chapter—grows out of the idea and practices of Gustavus as a mentoring community.

Context: Vocational Reflection in a Mentoring Community

As a residential, church-related (Evangelical Lutheran Church in America), liberal arts college of about 2,500 students, Gustavus' mission to educate young people for fulfilling lives of leadership and service in society is rooted in the conviction that every person is called to responsible ethical action and leadership in community life. Our Deep M-Pact project builds on the work of the Center for Vocational Reflection (CVR), which was launched in 2001 to implement our PTEV initiative. The CVR's animating vision is to influence the ethos of the college such that the invitation to reflect on life as a vocation becomes inescapable for everyone in the Gustavus community.

One of the ways that vocation has been spoken of at Gustavus is as a calling to live out one's distinctive gifts, passions, and senses of faith and meaning in ways that benefit the community and help to address the world's needs. It is the shape that one's daily life takes in answer to the big questions of identity, purpose, and meaning—questions, such as Who am I, and why am I here? What's my place in the world, and how can my life make a difference? What do I really care about, and what does my life really stand for? To think of one's life in terms of vocation is also to tell—to live out—a certain kind of story of that life and of the way things are and ought to be. Since it has to do with one's identity and place in the world, it ultimately grows out of and expresses key senses of the self and of what it is to be a human being. Thus, vocation[9] is also spoken of as an overarching self-understanding that sees the self as

- *gifted*—both in terms of discerning and nourishing one's gifts, talents, skills, competencies, strengths, interests, and passions and in terms of knowing that one's very life is a gift to be cherished and shared with others. It grows out of and expresses a capacity to live one's life with a posture of awe and gratitude (theologically, a posture of grateful response to grace), rather than one of entitlement or fear or cynicism.
- *free*—that is, free *from,* for example, the pressure to conform to social norms and practices that are damaging to one's spirit or destructive of community, or from the need to earn God's favor through good works, or from prejudice and narrow-mindedness—and free *for* a life of meaning, passion, and purpose in service to the neighbor and for a hope-filled life of courageous willingness to take risks for others and to stand up for justice.
- *nested* within realities and relationships that are greater than oneself: community, for example, or a cause that evokes care and action, God, or a hopeful future. Vocation expresses a sense of the self, not primarily as an isolated, independent, individualistic unit but rather as fundamentally relational, interdependent, and interconnected with one another and with Creation.
- *having agency and efficacy*—that is, as someone whose decisions and actions are meaningfully his or her own (e.g., at least partly within his/her control and subject to rational deliberation) and do in fact matter in the lives of others. Vocation expresses a belief that one has a role in the working out of the meaning of things, a conviction that one's life really does make a difference to those around him/her and to the world.

To have a sense of vocation is to see the self through the lenses of a certain kind of story of what it means to be human, a certain kind of story about the way things are and ought to be. Grounded on this foundational conception of vocation—as having to do with ways of understanding the self-in-community—Deep M-Pact invites consideration of new ways of imagining what it is to live the human story, particularly as males. It invites the entire campus community, moreover, to explore "the profound and dramatic transformation in what it means to be male or female in the 'new global commons' in which we now find ourselves. In this sense, we are called to think of Gustavus as a mentoring community in which we welcome and celebrate our shared growth toward full 'humankindness.'"[10]

---

[9] This formulation of a distinctively (but not exclusively) Lutheran understanding of vocation is thanks to our Gustavus colleague, Dr. Darrell Jodock, the Drell and Adeline Bernhardson Distinguished Professor of Lutheran Studies.

[10] From a correspondence with scholar, author, and educator Laurent A. Parks Daloz following one of his visits to campus in connection with the Deep M-Pact project. Larry's con-

An important aspect of the CVR's work to infuse vocational reflection throughout the Gustavus experience is known as Gustavus as a Mentoring Community—a conceptual "big tent" based on the work of Parks (2000) and Daloz, Keen, Keen, and Parks (1997). The emphasis on mentoring in the Deep M-Pact project, as we will describe below, is tied to our ongoing exploration of what it means for the college to be not just a community of individual mentors but a mentoring community, one whose shared values, narratives, and practices collectively orient its members toward lives of contribution to the greater good.

College students are ripe for exploring questions of identity, meaning, and purpose in their lives and are often eager for their teachers and advisers to help them to wrestle with these questions. But, Parks (2000) argues, "many young adults, even those who are regarded as privileged, are often being cheated in a primary way. *They are not being asked big-enough questions.* They are not being invited to entertain the greatest questions of their own lives or their times" (p. 138). Deep M-Pact is designed, in part, to help us as a mentoring community to be more intentional and effective in asking big-enough questions of our male students and to equip them to ask those questions of themselves throughout their lives. At the heart of Deep M-Pact is the conviction that many men at Gustavus (and in society) need and want to be mentored toward understandings of masculinity, manhood, and humanity—ways of being and knowing themselves as men and as human beings—that are markedly different from the versions they more typically imbibe in the media and the popular culture.

THE DEEP M-PACT PROJECT

Within these vocational and institutional contexts, then, the CVR helped to create the Deep M-Pact project, the centerpiece of which has been an annual Deep M-Pact Men's Retreat. As of this writing, there have now been two of these off-campus, overnight retreats. The primary focus has been on intergenerational mentoring of sophomore men, who often are at a crucial time of transition intellectually, spiritually, socially, emotionally, and behaviorally. The aim is to contribute to the sophomore experience as a time of initiation (into, e.g., life-giving narratives and models of masculinity, capacities for reflection and meaning-making, and a sense of agency) and of inoculation (against, e.g., postures of indifference and apathy, destructive patterns of behavior, and distorted or shallow understandings of masculinity).

---

sultative collaboration with us across the first year of the project included two scholar-in-residence visits to campus. He was a special guest facilitator for the first Deep M-Pact retreat, where he "workshopped" ideas in his forthcoming book on men's development and models of masculinity. His residencies also included several class visits, a major public presentation, a chapel homily, meal conversations, and workshops and consultations with coaches and captains in men's athletics, student leaders, and Student Affairs staff.

Retreat Design and Implementation

Several core values and considerations have helped to shape the planning, design, and implementation of these Deep M-Pact retreats:

Intentionality

Planners convey to participants that the retreat isn't just one more thing clamoring for their attention and time and that they have been intentionally sought out to take part. Participants are invited by the college president in a letter informing them that they had been nominated by a faculty member "who recognize[d] in you important qualities of leadership, reflection, and service, which will make for significant contributions to the retreat, to the College, and to an endeavor involving college men across the nation." Since one of the hallmarks of a mentoring community is that its members truly see one another both for who they are and for who they can become (Parks, 2000, pp. 128–129), these invitations help them to know that they have been seen. Participants are told from the beginning, "You matter, and it matters that you are part of this," emphasizing two key aspects of the notion of vocation at Gustavus: that of having a sense of agency and efficacy and that of fundamental human interconnection and "nestedness" in realities beyond oneself.

Intergenerational Mentoring and the Power of Story

A core feature of the Deep M-Pact retreats is intergenerational mentoring—tied to the campus-wide work as a mentoring community. At the retreats, the core group of sophomores is accompanied by smaller cohorts of prominent and well-regarded junior and senior peer mentors and faculty/staff (older-adult) mentors. There have also been invited guest speakers at each retreat.[11] In each case, the focus was on the exchange of ideas and questions, insights and challenges prompted by their presence among us, rather than on their status as expert or special guest.

---

[11] The first year, Larry Parks Daloz facilitated a discussion of major ideas from a forthcoming book of his on models of masculinity and male identity development. The working title for his book, his retreat presentation, and ultimately a major public presentation on campus was *From Armored Boy to Wise Old Man: How Men Grow Up ... or Don't—Men for the 21st Century.* His engagement with us around this project drew from anthropology, mythology, developmental psychology, philosophy, experience, and popular culture to explore and critique two common constructs of masculinity: the *armored boy* and the *puer aeternus*, or the eternal boy. He also offered a vision for ways of being male that are more capable of engaging the full humanity of men and women in responding to the unprecedented perils and promises of these

The power of story is the fuel for much of the intergenerational mentoring that takes place on the retreats and a key factor in the absence of hierarchy or "elderarchy" in the relational dynamics of the retreats. Regardless of age, people *are* the stories of their lives. So the opportunity to share and reflect on one another's stories is a key part of the intergenerational encounters that characterize the Deep M-Pact retreats. One student participant commented

> A very important part of the retreat was the bonding between the students and the professors. I found our conversations about male identity to be very helpful. I was not only given an opportunity to explore the meaning of being a male but I also got to explore my own identity throughout the whole process. Hands down, the conversations were the most meaningful aspect of the retreat.

STATIONS

The retreat itself is built on a framework of structured activities, presentations, discussion, reflection—individually and in groups, including long, lingering conversation over meals and around the campfire (for discussions of a mentoring community's "practices of the table and of the hearth," see Parks, 2000, pp. 154–156)—and good doses of unstructured downtime. Within that framework, a core element (which plays on the basic observation that "guys like to do stuff together" and may communicate better when shoulder-to-shoulder rather than eye-to-eye) is a series of four experiential-learning stations or break-out sessions through which the men rotate in small groups throughout the retreat. These sessions are more than simply an opportunity for male bonding around shared experiences, however (which can happen just fine when men play video games together, thank you very much). The reflective component associated with each (and infused into the retreat as a whole) seeks to demonstrate that the quality of men's relationships can be even deeper when based on a sense of shared values, purposes, and questions. The mix of activities in these stations has included the following:

- Service-Learning. Through the Hands of Woodcrafting. In this session, one of our faculty/staff mentors, a professor of music and wind-orchestra conductor who also designs and builds artisan furniture, reflects on the creative (and for him, spiritual) process of working with wood. He showcases furniture pieces he has created to show how his avocation complements the art he creates through music and then guides participants as they work in pairs to construct simple

---

complex times in the global commons. While his ideas and the book have continued to evolve since his visits to Gustavus, his many rich contributions and provocative springboards for the thinking, conversation, and action in this emerging project have been invaluable.

wood birdhouses that are later donated to local nature centers. The juxtaposition of crafting fine art and wielding hammers invites reflection on, for example, the intersection of one's passions with being of service to others, the importance of honoring the "muse" or sources of inspiration, and the role of creativity and imagination in leadership (Parks, 2005).
- Men in the Kitchen. Led by a student chef and working in small groups in shifts that correspond to each of the mealtimes throughout the weekend, the men exercise their creative, collaborative, and culinary capacities in order to prepare, serve, and clean up after each meal. In addition to developing some basic domestic skills, the men use the occasion to reflect on, for example, gender stereotypes, the nature of work, confidence and courage with which to counter inward inhibitions and external resistance, and sources of nourishment for self and service.
- Team-Building and Effective Leadership. Through a series of team-building exercises led by a Gustavus staff member, this session seeks to build relationships and strengthen capacities for trust, confidence, creative problem solving, and cooperation as the men learn to rely on each other for effective teamwork. Issues for reflection include independence and interdependence, "followership," shared wisdom and collective folly, conflict resolution, fear and trust, and alternative conceptions of leadership.
- Loafing in the Beauty of Nature. This session, led by a guest naturalist, invites quiet attention to place. It cultivates awareness of beauty and of the "sacred ordinary" that surrounds us in the quiet spaciousness of the southern Minnesota prairie and in the contours of everyday life. It prompts reflection on the inner and outer landscapes of our lives and underlines the importance of mindful presence for integrated, healthful lives that are fully awake to caring for the common good.

Interwoven between the breakout stations are large- and small-group discussions, each of which is fueled by a set of prompts tied to a topic area. Both students and teachers facilitate these discussions, reinforcing the intentional reciprocity of the community of learners.

The first breakout station invites the men to flex their ability to think aloud together by focusing, relatively safely, on their lived experience in their everyday contexts. Titled simply Men at Gustavus, this session invites consideration of such questions as, What is the stereotypical male at Gustavus? What pressures do you feel as a male at Gustavus? How do you react? Do you have any interests or passions that you believe might cause you to be ridiculed if you were to express them publicly? Do you do them anyway? What grounds or supports your choice to do so? How do men create community?

The second of these discussion sessions, Influences, begins in small groups, where the men brainstorm with each other about what they see as negative and positive influences that men can have on other men, on women, and in society. They are then invited to journal individually and share in a paired deep-listening conversation about key influences in their own lives, in response to the following prompts: Think about someone who mentored you or in some way was a role model for you as you grew into your understanding of what it is to be a man. What are among the special qualities of your mentor/role model? How has this person influenced your sense of your masculinity or your understanding of what it is to be a man? Finally, in the large group, discussion revolves around such questions as Why is it important for men to have role models/mentors? How might we contribute to "Gustavus as a mentoring community for masculinities of meaning and making a difference"? To conclude this session, the men are invited to write a letter to a role model or mentor (preferably the one they wrote about in their journals) with a word about how this person has been an important influence for them, a memory of some key experience they shared, and gratitude for the role this person has played in their lives.

The third major discussion session, Involvement and Goals, picks up where the previous session left off and orients the energy and momentum of the retreat toward the Now What? Facilitators of this session ask, Where are the men? Why aren't more men involved? How can we bring what we've learned and experienced here back to the Gustavus community? To help the conversation and energy to become more solidly grounded, the men reflect in their journals and then in a paired deep-listening conversation on the following questions: What is one of your biggest, boldest, most life-giving dreams? What is one of your important goals in life? What inspires, nourishes, and drives you toward those dreams and goals? What, if anything, might be holding you back, and how might you respond in ways that could help you to move forward? From whom might you find help and support? How are your own dreams and goals related to your involvement at Gustavus?

Finally, returning to large-group discussion, the men brainstorm specific ways to link their insights about men's involvement with their individual and collective goals: How can we apply the questions, insights, challenges, and discoveries of the retreat to getting more guys more involved at Gustavus? What do we do now, and where do we go from here? What support do we need, and how can we get it or build it? In what direction should the Deep M-Pact men's initiative go?

Outcomes

One of the retreat participants' first major answers to this question of the future direction of the initiative was to launch a new campus organization, the Men's Leadership Team (MLT). Much of the MLT's work so far has been focused on consciousness raising and education for the campus about constructs of gender; understandings of privilege, complicity, and oppression; and calling men and women alike to greater action, service, activism, and reflection. They have fostered collaborative action and education around issues of sexual assault and violence against women, developed several service projects on campus and in the surrounding communities, and hosted guest speakers and community-forum series.[12]

A more recent and still-emerging answer to the Now what? question has taken the shape of Peer Action-Learning Circles.[13] The circles, each consisting of three to four sophomores and co-facilitated by a student and faculty/staff mentor, were launched at the second annual Deep M-Pact retreat as a way to provide ongoing structure and mutual support. Each circle, which will meet at least once a month through the rest of the school year, extends the retreat's safe, courageous space for reflection, learning, challenge, and support around issues and goals of the members' choosing.

Program evaluations and anecdotal observations have shown the following outcomes among the men who participated in these retreats (student comments are in parentheses):

- Increased familiarity with the idea and language of vocation, and increased capacity to think about one's life in terms of vocation ("The retreat really got me thinking about the bigger, deeper questions, and about how I want to define my life and how I want to be a better person.");
- Increased sense of agency, including a clearer understanding of one's own gifts, talents, interests, passions, and capacities for making a difference for others ("The retreat reinforced my calling to help others live meaningful lives through my talents." "The retreat helped me to open my eyes about my own passions, and the learning circles have helped me to make the decision to follow my calling to teach.");

---

[12] One of the challenges this group has been working through with great care, openness, and maturity is the reaction from some quarters to their name (Men's Leadership Team), which has been perceived by some as suggesting that their purpose is to secure the structures and benefits of patriarchy by working to keep men on top and out front. In order to make clear their resolute commitment to being egalitarian, inclusive, and mutually empowering in their purposes, work, and relationships, they have organized several community forums, listening and discussion sessions, collaborative projects, and consultations with faculty and guest experts to learn as much as possible about the issues that are at stake and to discern the best way forward. A key outcome is their recent decision to change their name to M-Pact, drawing on the wellspring of the project that gave them birth. It should also be noted that, alongside this challenge—and partly because of the way that they addressed it—another response to the MLT was its being selected for the annual campus-wide Magnusson Service and Leadership Award in the spring of their first year in existence.

[13] Building on the initial success of our Lilly Endowment-funded work on the Deep M-Pact project, an additional grant from the C. Charles Jackson Foundation allowed us to train student and faculty/staff mentors on the theory and implementation of peer action-learning circles. For more information, see Marquardt et al. (2009).

- Deeper, more nuanced and positive understandings of masculinity and manhood ("This retreat was awesome! This weekend was the largest group of men I have ever felt so completely at home with. I grew up with two sisters, so ladies were always around. Some of my best and most "real" friends have been girls, and I expected to look around and see girls at this retreat because of the gentle and down-to-earth emotion that we had going on—as men! This was a wonderful experience. And I've never seen so many men being so gentle with cats!" [There are several resident cats and other farm animals at the rural retreat center where the event was held.]);
- Increased interest in ways of living that will benefit others and contribute to the common good ("I was extremely empowered during the retreat to start actually getting involved on campus and to target the problem at its source. I found new ways to think of problems, new ideas for MLT, and a bunch of new friends that share a lot of the same passions that I have.");
- Greater familiarity with and appreciation for practices of reflection, retreat, deep listening, and discernment; and
- Strengthened understanding of the importance of mentors and mentoring ("This was extremely helpful. Hearing the facilitator share his own problem and solution was deep stuff, inspirational to know that everyone deals with issues and that no one is perfect." "It was very helpful, because they have been through many life experiences. They provided us with thought-provoking questions that helped us to think about our own lives.").

Key Learnings

While it is, of course, still very early in the life of the Deep M-Pact initiative, the following important learnings seem to be emerging.

Make it personal, and make it matter. Personal invitation, word-of-mouth encouragement, and the like are important ways of overcoming what seems to be an otherwise deep-seated reluctance of men to go outside their normal spheres of activity and interaction. Conveying to each of them the message that "you matter in this" is crucial—as is the signal that they will benefit in ways that are important to them and to their larger networks of belonging. The men on the retreat repeatedly expressed their gratitude for the chance to engage with other men around substantive issues and to contribute to efforts that will benefit others. To put it bluntly, it's a chance to show one another that being a college guy is about more than drinking, video games, and sexual conquest. In spite of all the ways that they have been conditioned by the wider culture to accept narrow conceptions of masculinity and to pursue thin versions of what is commonly thought to constitute "success," their thirst for what Parks (2000) calls big-enough questions is real, as is their desire to make a difference in the lives of their local and global commons.

CULTIVATE SAFE, COURAGEOUS SPACE IN COMMUNITY. As important as each individual is to the effort, college men also still seem to seek a sense of belonging, security, and validation from a group. The Deep M-Pact retreat acknowledges this group instinct but demonstrates that being part of a group of men can be about so much more than they might typically think. Rather than being presented with a pack mentality that reinforces negative attitudes and destructive behaviors, they experience ways of being together with other men that allow them to lower their guards and be authentic with one another. The time, space, and permission afforded by the retreat setting for these men to be present with one another in meaningful conversation about stuff that matters are among the most powerful aspects of the experience.

In this regard, careful listening is a crucial hallmark of the retreats and of Gustavus as a mentoring community. O'Reilley (1998) wrote of the power of close listening:

> One can, I think, *listen someone into existence*, encourage a stronger self to emerge or a new talent to flourish. [And in learning to listen well, one can also learn to be *listened to*], "to be able to stand being heard. It's frightening because true attention ... invites us to change.... Attention: deep listening. People are dying in spirit for lack of it. In academic [some would say stereotypically male] culture most listening is critical listening. We tend to pay attention only long enough to develop a counterargument; we critique the student's or the colleague's ideas; we mentally grade and pigeonhole each other. In society at large, people often listen with an agenda, to sell or petition or seduce. Seldom is there a deep, openhearted, unjudging reception of the other.... By contrast, if someone truly listens to me, my spirit begins to expand. (pp. 17–21)

These retreats create a safe, courageous space for men to uncover important aspects of their truest selves and to bring to light the better angels of their natures. Older students and faculty/staff mentors make important contributions by modeling open, honest exchange, willingness to "go there" in talking about sometimes difficult issues, depth and thoughtfulness in exploring important questions, and commitment to engaging with others from postures of trust and trustworthiness. By supporting and challenging one another to create a shared space of attuned hospitality to the depth dimensions of the self and the other, these men discover the strength that comes in vulnerability, the vitality that comes with authenticity, and the groundedness that comes with a more expansive imagination of the self. According to one student participant:

> There was something about the setting that allowed an authentic, lively energy to come out that I have never encountered elsewhere. I was very blessed by the deeply personal things shared with us by our respected professors. I was blown away by the openness, sincerity, and power of the mentoring that took place.

There were so many incredibly wise faculty [members] eager and excited to open up their hearts and share their hard-earned wisdom with the younger generation of men. In the discussions we shared, I found new definitions of masculinity being wrought, rich definitions [of masculinity] that claim [for males] special versions of both tenderness and strength and that have since revolutionized my way of living.

GROW AN ETHOS OF SHARED INTERGENERATIONAL COMMITMENT. The combination of student and older-adult voices in exploring together the big questions has been a key factor in our success. Bringing students and faculty together has the potential to cause participants to slip into assumed roles and expectations, so the project's success over time will depend on the genuine commitment to the values, aims, and purposes of the project from both the students and the adult mentors. "The retreat 'taught' all of us something," Benjamin Hilding recalls:

> It served as an opportunity for older students to mentor younger students and for older faculty to mentor younger faculty, as you might expect—but also for the students to teach something to the faculty and staff (like when [a student participant] was in the kitchen showing Professor Douglas how to cut carrots). We were all teachers, and we were all students. The age and occupational divisions were blurred at the retreat, and that was pretty special. Uniting students and teachers in a common cause outside of the classroom bettered the overall Gustavus experience for both students and teachers. For me, after being a student leader in this initiative, I was inspired to develop a new and improved personal approach to the classroom, to my Gustavus contributions and involvement, and to the greater community. This side-by-side, rather than top-down, method of learning inspired me to become a better student, a better leader, and a better man.

CONCLUSION

The public television comedy series *Red Green* does a masterful job of poking fun at stereotyped images of what it is to be a man, especially in the rugged north woods: Talk of fishing, trucks, and duct tape—the "handyman's secret weapon"— abounds on this show. Each episode ends with the all-male cast gathering for the opening of the regular meeting of the Possum Lodge by bowing their heads for the Man's Prayer:

> I'm a man.
> But I can change.
> If I have to.
> I guess.

For the guys at Gustavus, and on these retreats, it's not a matter of changing who they are as men but of becoming more fully and truly who they are as human beings. As Daloz (personal communication, November 4, 2008) put it:

> This work is transformative work. The challenge before us is to move away from the traditional conditioning we all share in which men were presumed to be the "generic" human and privileged with power over women, to a new kind of partnership as full equals with women.... We men need to own our inner work of becoming complete as humans in male form. It's not about shedding our maleness, our "armor," if you will; it's about transforming it into an inner, grounded, mature strength with which we can celebrate our shared growth toward our full humanness.

Reflection on the big questions within a mentoring community opens up the space to do this transformative work, to consider more humane and truthful ways of being in the world. Our hope is that over time, Deep M-Pact will help to extend the work of our vocation initiative and of the college as a mentoring community by more intentionally engaging men in this transformative work.

So far, the men of Deep M-Pact are stepping up to the challenge.

References

Daloz, L.A.P., Keen, C.H., Keen, J.P., & Parks, S.D. (1997). *Common fire: Leading lives of commitment in a complex world.* Boston: Beacon.

Daloz, L.A.P. (2008, October 27) "From armored boy to wise old man: How men grow up ... or don't—Men for the 21st century." Public lecture at Gustavus Adolphus College.

Marquardt, M.J. (2009). *Action learning for developing leaders and organizations: Principles, strategies, and cases.* Washington, DC: American Psychological Association.

O'Reilley, M.R. (1998). *Radical presence: Teaching as contemplative practice.* Portsmouth, NH: Boynton/Cook.

Parks, S.D. (2000). *Big questions, worthy dreams: Mentoring young adults in their search for meaning, purpose, and faith.* San Francisco: Jossey-Bass.

Parks, S.D. (2005). *Leadership can be taught: A bold approach for a complex world.* Boston: Harvard Business School Press.

10

College Men and the Heroic Imagination: Reflections on the Gustavus Adolphus Deep M-Pact Project

L. A. Parks Daloz

It's Orientation Day for the first-year students. On the men's floor, the guys gather in a ragged circle for introductions. "Just take a few moments to share who you are," says the dorm advisor. Feet shuffle, eyes sweep across the floor, deathly silence. Finally, "Well, I'll go. I'm Bob. I live in Benson. I play soccer." Relieved nods around the room. A moment later, "My name's Sam. I'm from Grand Falls. I like to play Ultimate." His eyes scan the circle looking for a receiver. Then, "Ben here. I come from Mankato. Pre-med." Eyes back to the floor. And so on. It's all over in 15 minutes.

Meanwhile, down on the women's floor, the advisor corrals her charges and gives the same instruction. "Hi! I'm Allison, from Minneapolis. I love music. My mom and dad took me to see Phantom last summer...." "Oh my God!" a girl across the circle breaks in. "Didn't you just love it? I saw it too! It was awesome." Smiles around the room. "Yeah. I was like.... Oh. My. God," and she rolls her eyes. Then, "I play soccer too." "You do? So do I!" another girl breaks in. And they are off to a bubbling conversation. Toward the end, nearly an hour later, a shy young woman leans forward slightly. "I'm from Boston," she says. "It's a long way, and I'm kind of nervous." Almost immediately another woman says, "Oh, I'm from San Francisco. I feel, well, anxious, I guess. But I guess we'll get used to it." And three others break in to reassure them. "We're here for you," they say. "We're here for you."

Like most of the studies in this volume, the Gustavus Adolphus College project grew out of a concern that significantly more women than men seemed drawn to positions of leadership, especially in areas of community service, vocational discernment, and spiritual reflection. This trend has been widely observed at other colleges as well. In the Wabash study, for instance, male students reported being primarily interested in being entrepreneurs, making money, and working in a prestigious occupation, while showing less interest than women in learning about other cultures, preserving the environment, and helping others (see chapter entitled "Vocation and the PETV Initiative at Wabash College," page 158). Nationally, women are significantly more likely to value such activities as helping others, taking social action, and promoting racial understanding (Sax, 2008).

This is of particular concern at Gustavus because of the college's strong institutional commitment to the formation of graduates with a deep allegiance to the common good and the well-being of all Creation. It has been estimated that as many as 80% of those in non-sport student activities are women. It has not always been so. Not surprisingly, then, the college is asking, Where are the men?

There have been a lot of tentative answers tossed out: Service work just isn't a guy thing; entering boys are less mature than the girls; young men still feel pressure to be primary providers and soft jobs don't pay the bills; feminism has tipped the scales to favor women; postmodernism has dissolved the authority structures that favored men; and more discursive teaching methods disadvantage men. But similar trends are well under way in elementary and secondary schools, where girls now outstrip boys in almost every category. Is this due to video games or overmedication of obstreperous boys or the effects of endocrine disruptors on testosterone or the general devaluation of traditional values in the culture? Clearly the explanations are multiple and complex. And clearly the issue is rooted in a far wider context than the Gustavus campus or even of college campuses across the country. The whole world is shifting under men's feet.

The Three Pillars of Manhood

Traditionally, down through history and across virtually every culture, to be considered successful, men must do three things well: procreate, provide, and protect. In fact, anthropologists tell us that these three pillars of manhood have upheld virtually every society on the planet for millennia: We men are expected to procreate offspring, the more fruitfully the better; provide for our families and tribes, the more lavishly the better; and protect them, the more fiercely the better (see Gilmore, 1996).

But the world has changed and the rules are not so clear any more. A global economy has shattered our industrial base, high technology has devalued manual labor, the rich-poor gap has become a chasm, birth control and expanded education for women have spawned a feminist revolution, environmental consciousness has cast doubt on unrestrained providing, and the looming climate meltdown has torn the future from men's grip. In an overpopulated and increasingly urban world, it no longer makes sense for a man to sire as many children as he can, especially because women have a greater voice in that decision; in a society where a single income has lost its potency and women share the workplace, fewer men can be the sole provider; and in a shrinking and more complex world, protection is rarely about just being tougher. The three pillars of manhood that for eons have sustained men's sense of worth are crumbling.

At the same time, Venus has been rising in the east. For years we have rightly been concerned with ensuring that women have full respect in the home and an equal chance in the workplace. Legislators have passed laws to equalize opportunity, educators have redirected curricula and resources to eliminate gender bias, and employers have changed hiring policies to crack the glass ceiling. And it has worked remarkably well. By the turn of this century, girls were surpassing boys at school in every academic area except math. More than a quarter of practicing lawyers and doctors, almost half of all medical and law school students, and over 55% of all professionals now are women. Colleges report that, within 5 years, barely one-third of entering students will be male. Already some schools are quietly lowering the admissions bar for men. Meanwhile, in the recent recession (dubbed the "mancession" by the press), 80% of the unemployed were male, and some, predicting "the death of macho in the workplace," have suggested that what drove the whole economic mess was an overdose of testosterone (Salon, 2009). Although women still earn less than men and public power remains disproportionately in male hands, a recent *Time* poll measured dozens of dimensions on which women have drawn alongside or trumped men (Gibbs, 2009). From a historical perspective, the changes have happened at whiplash speed.

But we have failed to notice what is happening with men during this time. With few realistic and enticing images of manhood, boys are increasingly drawn to the fantasy triumphs of video games, opting out of school leadership and dropping out of college altogether at an accelerating rate (Kimmel, 2008). Men are drinking, taking drugs, and committing suicide in growing numbers. Meanwhile, the U.S. male prison population—at 15 times the female figure and the largest in the world—is rapidly bankrupting state after state.

For better or worse, most men have drawn self-worth from what we can do, from what we can earn, and from our personal physiques and public power. Despite the dramatic changes, most societies still expect their men to uphold those three pillars. After all, marriage is for procreation, isn't it? It may be all right for women to bring home dessert from time to time—but the bacon? And while we may tolerate a few female generals, in the trenches it's men only. So when these traditional expectations shift—as is increasingly the case—we should not be surprised that men feel confused, depressed, and profoundly threatened.

Whether Islamic fundamentalists or Tea Party members, men faced with crumbling identities and fearing the loss of power feel betrayed, and some are striking back. This is not good for either sex, but clearly there is no going back. Nor can we simply shrug and hand the power to women. The world will be no better off with women in charge than it was with men. As tempting as it might be for us to step back and say, "Be my guest" (and as seductive for women to accept), that's no solution.

The solutions lie in recognizing that we live in axial times: The old ways of being male are no longer adaptive for the drastically altered world we live in, yet we have not yet forged a new, more adequate manhood for the 21st century—one that affirms women as full and equal partners, the purpose of work as the enhancement of the common good, and brute force as the last option for resolving conflict. In the end, the task is neither to restore the three pillars nor to demolish them. Rather it is to transform them, to give them new meaning. Consider the following scene.

> Then, sometime during the first semester, you visit the first-year dorm. On the women's floor, most of doors are open, girls flit from room to room in groups. There is a steady burble of sound, mostly talking, whooping, laughing. For the

girls, it is the conversation itself that seems to matter. Topics vary, but mostly they are about people, relationships, who is seeing whom, what's going on about campus.

On the men's floor, half the doors are closed. Occasional explosions of male laughter break the silence, and muffled electronic beeps and squawks seep through the doors. You walk down the corridor and glance into the open rooms. In one, a boy sits alone on his bed playing a guitar. In another, two guys are playing cards; in another a group is hunched intensely over a video game; in another three guys sprawl shoulder to shoulder on a couch, talking together at the wall. Mostly they are talking about what they are actually doing, or telling stories, or occasionally just horsing around good naturedly.[14]

The Deep M-Pact Project

It is against this backdrop that the men of Gustavus have created the Deep M-Pact project to inoculate and initiate young men into a new, more adequate form of manhood—a lab, one might say, for growing men for the 21st century.

Most societies recognize some version of the notion that men are made, not born. That is, masculinity does not just occur naturally. As anthropologist Gilmore (1996) says, it is not "purely psychogenic in origin but is also a culturally imposed ideal to which men must conform" (p. 4). Manhood is not automatically conferred; it must be won. For this reason, most societies have instituted some form of initiation, some set of tasks to transform boys into men, and tests to mark that passage. For the most part, however, our culture has done this badly, relegating that function at best to a letter in sports, a high school diploma, or a driver's license and at worst to a first sexual conquest, getting dead drunk, or a prison sentence. None of these says much to a young man about what it means to be a good, adult male.

So it seems appropriate that the Gustavus project recognize itself as a form of conscious initiation into manhood for boys who mostly haven't given the whole thing much thought before. And that's where the wisdom of the term *inoculate* comes in.

Male initiation took on a kind of glowing significance during the men's movement that flourished from the mid-80s to mid-90s. Too often regarded as a panacea in a radically individualistic culture, it was often badly over-romanticized. The fact is, the purpose of initiation in most cultures is to perpetuate the wisdom of the tribe and to pass on the secrets and stance of men from generation to generation. Moreover, this is frequently done in a way that most contemporary Westerners find appalling in its brutality, incipient misogyny, and exploita-

---

[14] For this and the preceding vignette, my thanks go to Barbara Larson-Taylor, Assistant to the President for Special Projects at Gustavus Adolphus College.

tion. In a time of dramatic change, it is essential to recognize that discernment rather than mere transmission must lie at the heart of male initiation. Some things about being male are worthy to be passed on, but some are toxic and require inoculation.

For this reason, the project's care in designing a mentoring environment for men takes on particular significance. If discernment is to be practiced, it had best be practiced in community. Although mentors have been around for eons, the idea of creating a conscious mentoring environment is still fairly new. It builds on the recognition that mentorship is an ancient and powerful way to cultivate human development, particularly during the transition from youth to adulthood. But it recognizes that, in Parks' (2000) words, "if a young adult is going to be initiated into a profession, organization, or corporation as it is presently practiced and defined, a mentor who guides the way is enough. But if they are going to be initiated [into these] ... *as they could become,* then only a mentoring community will do" (p. 134). An environment like this is not merely made up of a single significant elder as in the traditional mentoring relationship but recognizes the transformative power of the community when it is aligned and committed to a particular goal or set of values. Thus, it is likely to consist of a number of wise elders who hold the long-term values of the group, of more experienced people who share these values, and of peers who are fellow learners. Moreover, there is often shared work that manifests the values of the community, and there must be safe space in which reflective conversation can take place, so that all members can deepen their respective understandings of the work that unites them.

The work of the Deep M-Pact project as a mentoring community, then, is the formation, transformation, and empowerment of the men on the Gustavus campus, with the goal of increasing their participation and leadership in such areas as community service, vocational discernment, and spiritual deepening. To understand this work, let's step back a bit and look at one particularly salient aspect of male formation.

THE HEROIC IMAGINATION

I recently spoke with a young man shortly before he left for basic training with the Army. I'll call him Art. Art plans to apply for the Special Forces so that he can work with village people in places like Afghanistan to clear safe havens for the establishment of democratic institutions. This is a noble and courageous impulse. In the liberal and highly educated community that reared him, it is a road less travelled, and surely that's part of what motivates him. But it is also a road that calls at some point to almost every young male from an early age. I asked him if he had ever read about knights as a boy.

"Oh yes," he replied. "When I was very young my mother wouldn't allow us to play with guns, but my friends and I used to dress up as knights, and we would set up castles and bash each other with sticks. And then my dad would come out dressed as an ogre and beat us into submission," he added with a grin. "So yeah, there is a little boy in me who always wanted to be a soldier." The desire to be a hero, "to fight for the right" in a noble and honorable way, to answer the call of duty, and to have power in the world is deeply imbedded in the male soul.

The image of the knight holds this desire for many boys and is transformed for adult males into lives as doctors, entrepreneurs, teachers, politicians, statesmen, and, of course, soldiers. Note (and weep) that the season's best selling video game is called "The Call of Duty: Modern Warfare" and is widely played on campuses. For many young adult men who have not yet chosen a career, it has an almost archetypal power.

As a matter of fact, it is likely that the real knights of old actually were twentysomethings. That's the time when men have the best bodies for fighting and when they have to establish their position among their fellows. With a lot of footnotes to back me up, I have become convinced that a prime element in the formation of the young adult male imagination is combat. For the most part, of course, men do it in sports these days, but it's still all about the pecking order in the vaunted male hierarchies—the football captain still gets the dames. And if there is any doubt about the endurance of this image, I refer the reader to the ads during the next Superbowl.

But note that in the 20s is also the time when the call to a noble and even self-sacrificial adulthood is surging. A proper knight engages in noble quests and battles evil on behalf of fair maidens. That is, he dons his armor in order to do good, to protect the innocent and the vulnerable—both out in the world and inside himself. Tender on the inside and crunchy on the outside, he lives on the edge and takes crazy chances to test his armor. Recall that little boy inside Art, who has always wanted to be a soldier.

Jungians have dubbed this boy the *puer aeternus*. We know him as Peter Pan. He intends never to grow up, flits from one grand adventure to the next and loves to fly. Yet properly stewarded, that grandiosity of his can make him a visionary. This is the wonderful idealism that springs from adolescent souls and drives them to join the Peace Corps to save the world. It's also the same force that, improperly stewarded, drives Don Quixote tragically mad. But for many young males, adventure, risk, and high ideals (*Semper fi!*) are big.

At the same time, still possessed of his armor, he needs to keep reassuring himself that it is in good working order. The best way to do that is to engage in tough challenges. In particular, if he can suffer terrible pain without buckling, he can reassure himself that he is, indeed, a big boy, as he was told he'd be if he didn't cry. This is tricky because, in some cases, overcoming adversity only hardens the armor; in others, it builds character.[15]

---

[15] Speaking of tough challenges, in a previous Men's Conference, Kyle Long of the Wabash project did a wonderful riff on the students, comparing them to Achilles and making the point that young men love to see their lives as a process of overcoming challenges. Indeed, if one sees

But here's what I believe is the single most important thing to know about men: All of their mothers are women; they have achieved their identities as males by pushing away from their mothers and reaching out to their fathers. For a thousand reasons, this creates a particular challenge for men—especially when there is not a strong, connected male presence to catch them. Thus alone or only partially caught, they compensate by forming armor (fight) or by refusing to grow up at all (flight). Most of them do a bit of both. They become, at some level, armored boys. What both defenses have in common is that they value separateness over connection and distance over intimacy. In the great developmental dance of interdependence, men learn early on to be more comfortable doing stuff shoulder to shoulder than talking about it eye to eye (see Baker-Miller, 1976; Chodorow, 1978; Dinnerstein, 1976; Gilligan, 1982).

At the same time, men retain a deep need to connect. Says family therapist Real (1997), "My work with men and their families has convinced me that boys are fundamentally just as relational as girls and women" (p. 184). The bottom line is that boys and men are still human beings and, as such, long to connect. It's just that, as Real says, men have been "stuffed with the privilege of insensitivity" (p. 184). And they use that privilege to retain what they like to think of as their independence at what too often becomes an unbearable cost to themselves and an indefensible cost to the rest of the world.

> When my son was five years old, he went through a period of punching me and pulling my hair. One morning as his energy began to rise, he started in. At first I tried to ignore it, thinking it best not to reinforce it. That failing, I pushed him back and said, "Hey, that hurts!" He stopped for a few moments, and then began again. But in that interim I had a chance to realize that what he really wanted was to connect. So I turned and hugged him. Instantly he hugged back. "You know what?" I said to him. "Next time you feel like punching me, why don't you just hug me instead?" "OK, Dad," he chirped. The punching never happened again, but there has been a good deal of hugging ever since.

So with all this in mind, what is the power and promise of the Deep M-Pact program for the formation of a new expression of manhood? How might this perspective on male development help men to sharpen and deepen their understanding of the effectiveness of these programs for men, and more, to better understand some elements of how men grow into mature manhood?

---

the *Iliad* and the *Odyssey* as a single story of male development, it is significant that the young Achilles is all about armor, while the wily Odysseus sheds his armor as he returns home to reunion with the feminine.

Transforming the Three Pillars

As I suggested at the outset, the assumptions of infinite resources, endless growth, rigid sex roles, and unconstrained violence no longer hold in the changing world. But they are among the assumptions that have formed men's notions about manhood for at least the past 20,000 years and are too much a part of them simply to delete. The task, in this axial time, is not to eliminate but to transform them, to give them new meaning.

How, then, might the procreative drive to sire offspring be transformed into a constructive impulse to care for the larger world? How might men understand themselves as a part of the ongoing creation of life in a larger sense? Men have always been creative, from the first axe flaked from flint to the Apple tablet. They have invented democracy, conceived economic cooperatives, composed soaring arias, and concocted a dazzling array of ways to imagine God. How then might they turn their courage to creating a flourishing life for the coming generations—slowing climate change, devising more adequate economic structures, or forging new ways to understand themselves more richly as a species among species?

Similarly, rather than providing simply for themselves or immediate families, how might they imagine themselves as a part of a larger commons, a safe space in which they will thrive, not in spite of others but because of them? In fact, the economic radical individualism that has shredded our social fabric is relatively new. Historically, men have hunted together, shared fishing rights, created shared enterprises, and provided liberally for the common good. They know how to do that. What is called for now is to extend that knowledge to a world of diminished resources and limited space. It means cultivating a new economic imagination, a more complex orchestration of resources and products. Moreover, how do they do this in an interdependent world, in full equality with and inclusion of women, in regulated exchange with other nations, in awareness of the imperative of a sustainable prosperity?

And finally, I have asserted that much of male consciousness has been formed by combat, by the knowledge that, when it comes to conflict, young men are the ones who will be asked to sacrifice their lives first. Indeed, world around, when young males have nothing better to do—and sometimes when they do—they will fight. And society will thank them for it. Think of Art again and his Green Beret. But the costs are obvious. A recent news program carried a report that more American veterans have died by their own hands since the current wars began than have died on the battlefield.

This is not to say that the world isn't dangerous or that they died in vain. But war is increasingly a technical response to an adaptive challenge (see Heifetz, Grashow, & Linsky, 2009). How might the imperative to protect one's immediate family or tribe be transformed to a recognition that, until all are safe, none will be secure? There is no dearth of oppressed people, children, women, or the planet itself. But men need a larger understanding of what it means to be safe—and from whom or what? What's the threat—poverty? terrorists? corporations? evildoers?

men? or violence itself? The work before men is to transform their longing to be heroes from a knee-jerk lunge to battle into a restrained discernment between enemies and criminals, acting with nonviolent means when possible and appropriate force when necessary.

What Has the M-Pact Project Done Right?

The project has done a lot. Simply the act of bringing young adult men together in a conscious way for the purpose of learning from one another, reflecting on what works and what does not work about being a male at this time in history, and pooling their strengths to make a difference is transformative work. Here are some final reflections on particularly noteworthy elements of the project.

Cross-Generational Mentoring

In addition to the power of a mentoring community mentioned earlier, bringing men of different generations together rewards all ages. In many settings, age can be a barrier to close communication, but when the larger frame is something that all hold in common, age recedes in importance and the conversation can focus on what they share—their manhood, in this case. Moreover, held in that larger frame, the differences emerge as edges against which new learning can happen.

And while the benefits of mentoring are often hailed for the younger partners, in fact, whether a sixth-grader is mentoring a third-grader or an éminence grise is mentoring a mid-lifer, almost universally the older ones will say the experience was rich in learning for themselves as well. Thus, when they are candid about their failures and doubts so the younger men can experience their groundedness and humility, the elders may find new meaning in passing their hard-earned wisdom on to the next generation. In this way, each is able to move toward a more connected realization of their shared humanity.

The truth is that men actually are capable of tenderness if the circumstances are right. The sadness is that too often the only time they can do that is with women—particularly women who evoke the tenderness they may have known with their mothers. So, an important part of the work is for young men to let down their guards and risk compassion with other males.

Participating in Shared Work

Men famously work together shoulder to shoulder more readily than eye to eye. They are more comfortable doing stuff while they are talking. This wisdom shows up especially clearly in the artful design of the station activities in the men's retreat. All four topics perched at the edge of conventional macho activity: cooking, creative art, cooperative leadership, and contemplative presence in nature. As such, they invited the cultivation of a layer of sensitivity and feeling just beneath the outer armor and summoned a deeper humanity—both toward the self and toward others—that was new, at least for some of the young men. At the same time, all the activities were led by experienced and competent men, legitimizing them as fully male. To remind young men of the long history and extraordinary achievements of male creativity (requiring a very real measure of courage) is to nudge the future toward a more spacious understanding of the traditional injunction to procreate and to broaden the options of how to provide.

CRITICAL REFLECTION

The follow-up series of reflective conversations about being male—the inoculation—brings important balance into the larger work of initiation by encouraging a deeper level of both what is positive and what is toxic about conventional masculinity. When carried out in a safe space, particularly when led by more experienced males who have done some of the work of consciousness deepening, this is an essential complement to the experience itself—getting language around it. But the context in which this is done is enormously important. Coming out of the retreat with a healthy recognition of the value and power of men at their best, thoughtful yet critical conversations will have far more leverage than misguided attempts in a sterile classroom to shame men into realizing how oppressive they have been, particularly if it is done in the presence of wounded and angry women.

At the same time, it is known from the *Common Fire* study (Daloz, Keen, Keen, & Parks, 1997) that positive engagement with otherness can be a powerful stimulus to the development of a larger sense of "we." Many of the activities in the M-Pact project involved opportunities for people to meet and get to know people markedly different from themselves. Although women were rightly excluded from the men's retreat and subsequent reflection, enormous value can be gleaned from a well-designed engagement in conversation with women as "other." I heard a number of people (many of them women) wondering aloud whether the prevailing female-centered bias of so many of the service activities on campuses might not cause men to dampen their fires in a well-intended but perhaps misguided desire not to burn their female colleagues. Such a discussion might be a good first step in more profound conversations in which each gender strives to get beneath its own armor and seeks a shared understanding of its common humanity.

THE HEROIC JOURNEY AND THE YOUNG ADULT DREAM

The project's emphasis on storytelling by young and old alike is based on the powerful insight that men reinvent themselves as they revisit their stories throughout their lives. Whether they rename their experience at 45 in a more profound and positive way than they did at 22 depends in part on whether they have had the opportunity to retell their stories in settings that welcome the deeper questions. Conceptual tools, such as Levinson et al.'s (1979) "young adult dream," Campbell's (1968) "monomyth," Parks' (2000) "worthy dream," or metaphors, such as armor and the eternal boy, can serve as a kind of ongoing initiation to help men frame and mark their growth.

GATHERING AROUND THE FIRE: DEVELOPING PURPOSE AND AGENCY

One of the most memorable moments of the men's retreat was the campfire. The men stood around that fire late into the night ducking the smoke and telling their stories, reinventing themselves, getting down, shedding armor, risking vulnerability, reaching to connect with other guys, and discovering their knowledge about what matters in life. It is no accident that this happened best around a campfire. Fire has been a part of human evolution since well before it enabled our species to spread across the globe. Life is most creative at the boundaries—the edge places where systems meet. Sitting by a fire, men position themselves in that liminal space between light and darkness, fire and ice, and safety and danger, where life can thrive. Fire restores men's deep memory of what finally matters.

So it is appropriate that the men of Gustavus have chosen for their symbol a logo representing a man holding a candle placed somewhere between his belly and his heart (see Figure 1).

Figure 1. Logo for Gustavus men's initiative.

At the summary gathering of the 2009 Men's Conference at St. John's, a young Gustavus man spoke eloquently to the orienting question: Where are the men? "It's as though our fire has gone out," he said. "We just hang out and go with the flow. Well, fire doesn't do that. We need to, you know…" and he reached up with his hand as if struggling to wrench the words from the air, *"we've got to find ways to light that fire again."*

REFERENCES

Baker-Miller, J. (1976). *Toward a new psychology of women*. Boston: Beacon Press.
Campbell, J. (1968). *The hero with a thousand faces*. Princeton: Princeton University Press.
Chodorow, N. (1978). *The reproduction of mothering*. Berkeley: University of California Press.
Daloz, L., Keen, C., Keen, J., & Parks, S. (1997). *Common fire: Leading lives of commitment in a complex world*. Boston: Beacon Press.
Dinnerstein, D. (1976). *The mermaid and the minotaur*. New York: Harper & Row.
Gibbs, N. (2009, October 26). What women want now. *Time*, pp. 25-27.
Gilligan, C. (1982). *In a different voice*. Cambridge: Harvard University Press.
Gilmore, D. (1996). *Manhood in the making*. New Haven: Yale University Press.
Heifetz, R., Grashow, A., & Linsky, M. (2009). *The practice of adaptive leadership: Tools and tactics for changing your organization and the world*. Boston: Harvard Business Press.
Kimmel, M. (2008). *Guyland*. New York: HarperCollins.
Levinson, D., Darrow, C., Klein, E., Levinson, M., & McKee, B. (1979). *The seasons of a man's life*. New York: Alfred A. Knopf.
Parks, S. (2000). *Big questions, worthy dreams*. San Francisco: Jossey-Bass.
Real, T. (1997). *I don't want to talk about it*. New York: Scribner.
Salam, R. (2009, June 18). The death of macho. *Foreign Policy*, 27-34.
Sax, L. (2008). *The gender gap in college*. San Francisco: Jossey-Bass.

11

Vocation and the PTEV Initiative at Wabash College

Anne Bost and Sonia Ninon[16]

Founded in 1832 in the heart of Indiana, Wabash is a small liberal arts college for men, dedicated to educating "men to think critically, act responsibly, lead effectively, and live humanely" (part of the college's mission statement). The 900 students are governed by a single rule—The Gentlemen's Rule—which states, "A Wabash man will live both on and off campus as a gentleman and a responsible citizen." The emphasis on obtaining gainful employment after graduation is strong, as evidenced in T-shirt slogans such as the one worn by Career Services student workers: Career Services. Because one day you'll graduate.

In some ways, Wabash men are a peculiar group. Our students matriculate to a small college that offers no woman peers. Instead of female companionship, our students are promised to become part of a brotherhood of Gentlemen. The promise is palpable in admissions brochures: "As a freshman you immediately become immersed in a feeling of brotherhood, an all-for-one, one-for-all mentality. An extraordinarily deep bond forms between the men of Wabash" (Pope, 2006). The brotherhood is nurtured by requiring all men to live in college housing through the end of their sophomore years (with the exception of men who commute from home), with about 60% in fraternity houses.

In an environment laden with tradition and emphasizing close student/faculty interactions, Wabash students come to see themselves as special—no longer boys but confident Wabash men. Our men pride themselves in demonstrating what they consider to be their superior intellectual abilities, and they believe that Wabash makes these abilities even more robust. They are, in general, stereotypically masculine, with almost 80% involved in intramural and club sports and about 40% playing at the varsity level ("Future Students-Athletics," 2010). Yet, there is a sensitive side as well. The beginning embers of brotherly love are evident in weekly all-campus meetings, as the men rise to sing in unison: "Dear Old Wabash, thy loyal sons shall ever love thee, and o'er thy classic halls, the scarlet flag shall proudly flash. Long in our hearts we'll bear the sweetest mem'ries of thee. Long shall we sing thy praises, Old Wabash!"

Why Pursue a Program for the Theological Exploration of Vocation Grant Project?

One of the aspects on which Wabash prides itself—and markets to its students—is its graduates' ability to land jobs or professional school slots. Recruit-

---

[16] We offer special thanks to Matthew Grennes and Jacob Surface for their research contributions to this project as well as their helpful comments in the writing of this chapter.

ing materials talk about "the thousands of doctors, lawyers, teachers, and corporate executives who used Wabash as a launching pad for successful careers" ("Future Students-After Wabash," 2010). Admissions brochures also feature the extension of the Wabash brotherhood into the professional world: "No matter what your career interest, there's sure to be a Wabash alumnus to help you get started" ("Future Students-After Wabash," 2010). Survey data confirm that Wabash's career focus infiltrates faculty/student interactions. In 2008, 82% of Wabash seniors reported talking often or very often about career plans with a faculty member or advisor. Thus, discussions about careers often are ongoing at Wabash. Yet, the extent to which such discussions encourage our men to think about deeper vocational issues is less clear.

Why? Our suspicion at the start of this project was that the desire to be strong—and, perhaps equally important in the mind of an 18-year-old man, to be perceived as strong—may limit deep vocational conversations among our men. At Wabash, freshmen quickly learn the college motto, "Wabash always fights." In parallel, they embrace upperclassmen's views on the process of becoming a man at Wabash. Through pledge fathers (upperclassmen in the fraternities) and other peer relationships, young students grasp the idea that one becomes a Wabash man by never giving up, by being loyal, and by building strength of body and mind. This strength is symbolized by the college's mascot, a giant with bulging biceps. Although Wabash men generally talk freely about conventionally strong or masculine aspirations, we were unsure of the extent to which they discuss weaker topics, such as discerning one's calling.

In his book *Beleaguered Rulers: The Public Obligation of the Professional*, May (2001) describes the "deeper questions of professional identity.... Who am I? Whom shall I be? ... What am I? A mix of technician plus entrepreneur? A careerist making my way in the headwinds and crosswinds of the corporation? Or something more?" As a campus community, Wabash helps young men in many ways to connect with potential employers (including loaning out interview suits), but questions remained: Are Wabash men afforded opportunities to think about the "something more" as they choose their career paths? How do they make vocational decisions? These questions led us to an investigation of the state of vocational reflection on our campus, under the umbrella of St. John's University's larger Programs for the Theological Exploration of Vocation (PTEV) initiative.

How Did We Design the Vocation Project and Why?

A few years ago, a coworker piloted a Summer Business Immersion Program at Wabash. Although the program succeeded in granting business experience, it was largely unsuccessful in getting Wabash men to talk about their passions and values with respect to their professional aspirations. From this and other examples, we realized that if we wanted to initiate fruitful vocational conversations among Wabash men we were going to need a new approach beyond the standard course method or Career Services activities.

In short, we needed a back door entry—a way to get college men talking about vocation in a nonthreatening environment. Wabash's culture celebrates student research, and students are accustomed to being asked for their opinions on student-investigated research topics. We therefore decided to couch the vocational investigation in the context of a student research project. The idea was to use the qualitative research process as an avenue for initiating peer conversations that might otherwise have been awkward to pursue. We designed the following structure to have concentric circles of impact: (a) We would select five Wabash men (a senior, a junior, and three sophomores) to mentor intensely, hiring them as researchers tasked with the job of learning about the state of vocational discussions at the college. They would use their networking skills on campus to infiltrate a variety of campus groups, establishing formal interviews to learn about their peers' vocational thoughts. As part of the research preparation, we would nurture our researchers' own vocational reflections. Through reading and writing assignments and discussing their peers' answers to a scripted set of questions about vocation, our researchers would spend a year thinking about how one makes vocational decisions. (b) The research interviews would serve as a nonthreatening way of cultivating vocational conversations with a wider group of Wabash men. In effect, we would find out about how Wabash men were thinking about vocation while simultaneously initiating the very kinds of vocational conversations we think would be advantageous. (c) The research team would use their increasing awareness of vocational issues to help local high school freshmen begin to think about their own vocational journeys. The high school students—all young men—would be selected by their guidance counselors as ones who have college aptitude but were not yet sure of whether they would attend college. As at the college level, the interactions with the high school men would be in the form of interviews designed to encourage vocational reflection. The high school component of the research project would give our students a mentoring opportunity (hopefully further developing their own vocational reflections) while also encouraging the high school students to begin to reflect on their life goals. (d) Findings from the interviews would be shared with staff/administrators to inform program development.

What Were Our Goals and How Did We Pursue Them?

We developed the PTEV project with the following goals in mind.

Goals for our Wabash research students

- Investigate May's (2001) "deeper questions of professional identity" (p. 7) through research, readings, and hands-on mentoring of local high school students.
- Deepen the men's vocational discernment by providing structured opportunities to talk with peers and mentees about the relationships between passions/callings and careers.

Goals for other students

- Facilitate vocational reflections among Wabash College men by initiating small group discussions.
- Facilitate vocational reflections among local high school young men by providing college mentors to engage in conversations about passions and careers.

Institutional goals

- Inform programming by investigating the paths by which Wabash students make vocational decisions.

WHO WAS INVOLVED IN THE PROJECT AND WHAT DID WE DISCUSS WITH THEM?

At Wabash, our researchers interviewed 29 undergraduate men. Because of Wabash's living unit niches, we included members of four different fraternities as well as independent men. The interviewees represented first-, second-, third-, and fourth-year men from different racial and geographic backgrounds. All interviews were conducted on campus in 30-minute focus groups, ranging from 2 to 10 people per group. In the interviews, we asked about passions instead of vocations or callings, because the latter terms are not understood by all of our students in the same way. Participants were asked to respond to the following questions: (a) What are your passions? Why? (b) Why did you decide to go to college? (c) Do your passions influence your career considerations? (d) What factors are important in your career considerations? (e) Do you believe that your career considerations should benefit the common good? (f) Are you taking steps to accomplish these career goals? If not, what steps should you take?

The interview questions for the high school freshmen were similar to those for the college men. However, to facilitate the mentoring process, we spread the high school interviews out over the course of 4 months.[17] As preparation, the researchers each wrote their own responses to the interview questions. The monthly 30-minute interviews covered the following. Session 1: What are some things you are passionate about? If you could do anything, what would you do? Why? Session 2: Last time we talked about your passions and your ideal activities. Do your passions influence your career considerations? Do you think college would help you in this path, or not? Session 3: Do you believe that your career should benefit others? How could you impact the world around you now? Session 4: How do you follow your passions into a career that serves the common good? Are you taking steps to accomplish your career goals? If not, what steps should/could you take? What things can you start now to prepare?

---

[17] We obtained written parental and student consent to participate in the interview program. The principal also gave written consent for us to run the program on the school property.

We met weekly with our researchers to debrief about what they were hearing in the college and high school interviews. We also assigned the research students both individual and group work. The latter typically occurred late in the evenings and provided a rich time for the men to brainstorm together before meeting with us. In addition, for team building, we hosted the researchers for several meals.

What Did We Learn?

Through this project we learned a great deal about what current Wabash men value, how they make their vocational decisions, and how they experience Wabash as a place in which to refine those decisions. Much of this information is more relevant to our own Career Services, first-year program coordinators, and administration than to a general audience. However, a few themes may be of broader interest.

First, we rediscovered the importance of mining the data sources we already had. Most institutions have reams of survey information about their students that rarely if ever see the light of day. Our college is no exception. A number of commonly used surveys, such as the College Senior Survey[18] and its companion freshman survey, have questions about students' career expectations and values. To better tailor the vocation project to our campus, we began by looking at Wabash men's answers to these questions. In some cases, the surveys confirmed what we thought we knew about our student body. For example, compared with peers at other institutions, Wabash freshmen placed more importance on having administrative responsibilities or succeeding in a business of their own and less importance on volunteering in the community. These data fit our sense of the professionalism/service disconnect among our students. We also were not surprised to find that Wabash men strongly valued raising a family. There were some new, intriguing findings, however. A larger percentage of our men placed importance on developing a meaningful philosophy of life as seniors than they did as freshmen. In addition, over the course of their 4 years here, about 15% of our men decreased the extent to which they valued becoming wealthy. Together, these data suggested that Wabash was altering at least some of the students' incoming vocational values. This information provided a contextual scaffold on which to hang our subsequent findings from the vocation focus group interviews.

Second, we learned about the multiple influences that interact to shape Wabash men's vocational choices. Six major influences were prominent (see Figure 1).

Notably, the three influences in the lower half of the hexagon share a common denominator: Family. In some cases students' vocational paths were an outgrowth of relatives' interests: "He developed these passions because it was a way for him

---

[18] The College Senior Survey is offered by the Higher Education Research Institute. See http://www.heri.ucla.edu/cssoverview.php

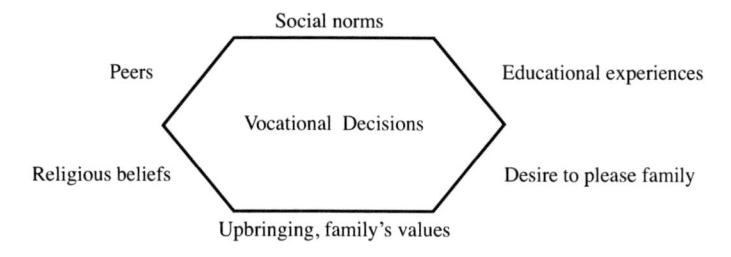

```
                    Social norms
         Peers    ╱─────────────╲   Educational experiences
                 ╱                ╲
                 ╲ Vocational Decisions ╱
                  ╲                ╱
   Religious beliefs ╲────────────╱  Desire to please family
                    Upbringing, family's values
```

Figure 1. What influences Wabash men's vocational decisions?

to connect with his father. He said that through doing these things he grew closer to him." In other cases decisions were based on preparing to have one's own family some day: "It feels like I am building toward something by going to school and that is to have a large family." Especially for the Christian men, the idea of becoming fathers was central in their thoughts about not only what job they would pursue but what type of man they would become. One Catholic student summarized, "For me, I want to be a good person, and I associate that with fatherhood." In addition to family influence, participants talked about how their peers, religion, and the expectations of the community at large (social norms) impacted their vocational decisions. As one Wabash man said, "The relationships you have, the time you are at in your life and other outside factors all have an effect." The interviews revealed to us the complexities that our men face as they try to find their vocational paths. The college is but one voice among many vying for students' attention as they think about careers. Understanding the interrelationships among the voices is important as we think about how to further heighten and deepen our young men's vocational discernment.

Third, we learned that even if college men talk with their peers about their passions and life goals, they may have trouble connecting those conversations with career decisions. One of our researchers summarized this way: "These discussions are happening at Wabash, but they are happening in hidden ways. I believe from the interviews and personal experience that students are having [vocational] conversations among peers, professors, and faculty; however, they are occurring when the student is not consciously evaluating his vocation." Another echoed his assessment: "I would immediately support the notion that these conversations are occurring here; however, students are unaware of their importance and they do not know what to do with them." Our task as educators, then, may be not only to provide safe opportunities for men to reflect on vocational issues but also to guide them in connecting the dots between those reflections and their career choices.

How Did This Project Have an Impact on College Men?

How Did Our Project Benefit the Student Researchers?

As we had hoped, during the course of the PTEV project, our research students began to have a fuller understanding of a number of professional roles. Yet, the biggest benefit we saw for the team was in their increasingly deepening vocational reflection. The men began to think more broadly about vocational exploration, piecing together May's (2001) career elements of "Who am I? Whom shall I be?" (p. 7) with their own passions, values, and paths. These young men also seemed to become more comfortable talking about these issues with peers. Given the peer influence on vocational decisions at Wabash, the ability to talk about personal vocational ideas—and not just about manly career aspirations—may be as important as the initial step of thinking about such ideas.

Throughout the vocation project, we encouraged our research students to reflect not only on their own vocational paths but also on how they were experiencing the research program. We generally did not give specific writing assignments for their reflective journals. Rather, we invited them to write about any topic they desired, as long as they wrote at least weekly. Their journals provided a structured time for them to reflect and gave us insight into aspects of the program that we hoped were influencing them but in which we did not have a direct hand. The late night student-only research team sessions were a good example. These sessions, led by the team's student manager, proved to be effective not only for getting the research work done but also for bonding the men. As one sophomore wrote, "I usually have a good time working with the other research guys. We joke around a lot and still get a lot of work done, which is pretty good considering my near-workaholic standards on that sort of thing. It seems like the conversations we end up having about Wabash and vocation are the most valuable, however. I get to bother a senior about what has made him want to go into Teach for America and probe a couple of Economics majors on the true value of money in life. While I am slow to admit it, it does seem as though these conversations have given me a different lens through which to consider not only vocation but life as a whole. "

Other excerpts from the journals provide additional glimpses of how the men's thoughts developed as the program went on. Their writings exhibit both the enthusiasm and the uncertainty that come with wrestling vocational decisions. Following, we include excerpts from two of the researchers' journals, allowing them to reveal their journeys themselves.

Wabash Man 1

Entry 1
Now that I know the codes [identifying themes from the vocation interviews] for my own considerations, it has become easier to sort out exactly what I want out of my

life and future vocation and why. For this reason, it makes it a little easier to accept an unpaid internship in the ridiculously expensive New York City because life isn't all about making money; it is about following your passions. Of course, you still need to make some money, but I am working on that end.

Entry 2
As I reflect on what matters to me, I keep returning to a core set of values. This weekend allowed me an opportunity to meet facilitators and officers of our national fraternity, grown men with jobs and families who volunteered their time to help us try to return to the more important aspects of our fraternal lives. Seeing the passion that these men had for the values impressed upon them by their experiences in [fraternity name] was reenergizing. I no longer feel as though I am alone in desiring a more rational, responsible approach to life among my fellow college males. The facilitators challenged us to be the change that we want to see. I feel reassured that I am on the right path in that suggestion.

Entry 3
One of the latest things that I have learned, or rather changed, about myself is my need to connect with people as friends. I have found a very tight-knit, respectful group to associate with at Wabash and they have aided me greatly in improving my personal, social, and academic being.... Whatever my vocation is in the future, I know that my ability to connect with coworkers and colleagues on a personal level and share similar values, especially regarding work ethic, will be key to my professional success.

Entry 4
I [now] define vocation as the set of all values that influence future lifestyle choices. Since engaging in this project, vocation has expanded from a pigeonholed definition of religious service or future career choice for me to a decision-making process that reflects what [I] want out of life. For me, such prioritization has become more important as family and personal time have become a more integral, valued part of my lifestyle.

Wabash Man 2

Entry 1
So far this vocation investigation has been insightful not only from a researcher's perspective but also from a personal perspective. We have been probing students to understand and envelop the idea that a vocation is not limited to religious activities but can include all the other aspects of their personal lives. I am currently attempting to develop more of a viewpoint on how we can help others open up their perspectives on vocation.

Entry 2
I have begun really breaking down possible career paths after college. I know this sounds weird that I can go preach to a freshman in high school to start thinking about it, and then as a junior in college finally sit down and tell myself that I need to think about it. However, I think I am settling on a very fulfilling path.... Through these interviews and reports, I have tried to break down other people's ideas and situations and determine why they like that passion or career. When doing this with mine, I found something interesting. I think the most important part of my calling is the common good theme. I seem to be infatuated with the idea that I can go out into the world and keep the bad things from happening.... I don't know if this feeling had recently been brought out due to the projects I have completed at the Center,[19] but I know that they definitely didn't hurt.

Entry 3
I now define vocation as "life." Originally, I categorized the term under the heading of religion, and I believed it to only include spiritual life. However, now after researching it and breaking down the term, I understand that it incorporates much more than that. Vocation is your job, your family, your volunteer work, your hobbies, and once again your religion. To sum it all up again, vocation is your LIFE.

How Did the Interviewees Benefit?

We do not yet know the full impact of the vocational conversations, but early anecdotes suggest that the interviews sparked new thoughts for at least some participants. Over the course of the four interviews, the high school men in our program began to think more concretely about how their interests and values might fit into a future career. For example, in one of the early sessions, a high school student mentioned that he liked building things in his backyard but had no ideas of what career he might pursue. After talking with his college mentor (our researcher), he realized that his passion for building could be fulfilled as a construction worker. He subsequently sought and completed a job-shadowing program in the construction field. Another young man from a farming family began to consider education as a path to improving his family's agricultural tradition—a new idea for him, because he had expected to go straight to farming after high school. One of our researchers described his final interactions with him this way: "In the interview, I managed to have the student lay out some real long-term goals that he had. I also walked him through the thought process that links everyday choices to achieving short-term goals, which in turn leads to achieving long-term goals. I stressed to him that this thought process does not happen naturally, so it is important to keep those goals in sight while making day-to-day de-

---

[19] Center of Inquiry in the Liberal Arts, at Wabash College. For more information, please see our website at http://www.liberalarts.wabash.edu

cisions. I also stressed that I was not necessarily advocating one path or another, but that it was up to the student to decide what was most important to him in the long term and plan his decisions from there."

Tangible evidence of how the interviews impacted the Wabash interviewees is more difficult to obtain. One exchange, however, feeds our optimism that the vocation questions kindled new thoughts at Wabash as they did at the high school. One of our researchers talked about asking a follow-up question highlighting a passion/career divide of which the interviewee had previously been unaware: "I asked, 'Your passion is in art. Why do you want to be a doctor?' This question seemed to stump him. He almost seemed to realize that his passions didn't really coincide with his career choice." While we can't be sure that exchanges like this one reverberate in the thoughts of the participants, we hope they do.

WHAT WERE THE CHALLENGES?

As with almost any college, one of the most limited commodities at Wabash is time. Recruiting interview participants took much more fervor and time than expected. The most efficient means, which we underutilized, was contacting presidents of student organizations and asking them to do the recruiting for us. For anyone interested in a similar program at other institutions, we recommend tapping into existing student hierarchical structures to increase focus-group participation. Time constraints also presented another challenge: In this pilot program we limited each college focus group to one session rather than to a more sustained series of vocational conversations. In our opinion, the model we used with the high school men and our small group of researchers was more effective. For those young men, vocational reflection became a required priority; it didn't fall prey to busy schedules, left to be considered in the spring of the senior year. Rather, consistent time slots were devoted strategically to connecting passions and current pursuits with long-term goals. The interviews with Wabash men worked well for initiating the conversations about vocation but probably would have been even more effective as a springboard for a series of similar conversations. In variations of this approach, focus groups could be built into existing all-college courses or Career Services programs, creating intimate small groups purposed with talking about vocational paths over the course of the 4 college years.

It perhaps also is worth noting that we are two women, overseeing a men's vocation program. We wondered if the gender difference impacted our young men's vocational thoughts or comfort in speaking, so we asked them. One of our men responded as follows: "Looking back on our training, I do not think that having women mentors changed my perception of vocation or my journal entries. I have had two women faculty in class, one of whom I have had for three classes, and have developed relationships with other female faculty and staff members on campus. These have all played into my self-perception and vocational considerations as my relationships with males have. I do wonder if a discussion with female peers would have changed my considerations. I expect, however, that I would have been slower to reveal my more inner thoughts in such a scenario." His answer fits with our perceptions of the gender impact. The presence of women—especially college-aged women peers—may make some college men reluctant to share private vocational reflections. Although we were able successfully to mentor our five young men, we believe part of the success was the dual method of requiring vocational conversations with us but also weekly men-only small group discussions without us. In this way we prompted the men to discuss specific vocational elements but did not intrude on their peer-only discussions. A similar dual approach might be useful at coeducational colleges. That is, pairing mixed gender conversations with separate men's-only conversations could prove a nice balance of differential perspective and comfort, especially if each men's-only group retained the same small number of men each time it met.

Conclusions and Take-Home Points

Our experiences suggest that collaborative research may be an effective means of initiating vocational conversations with college men. First, at the campus level, the research process can open doors to conversations that otherwise might be awkward or impossible. In the medical profession, young doctors quickly learn the value of wearing a white coat. The coat is a symbol to the patient that very personal conversations will be safe with this individual. In much the same way, a college man who dons the metaphorical coat of an academic researcher is afforded a similar benefit; the research provides a socially appropriate entryway into talking about sensitive topics with his peers. At the campus level, then, the research serves two functions: It catalyzes vocational reflection among the men who participate while at the same time gathering student-level data for the administration to use in programming decisions.

Second, for the men who conduct the interviews, the research provides consistent opportunities to think hard about their peers' comments about vocation. This in turn informs the researchers' thoughts about their own vocational paths. Research team meetings become an opportunity to think about vocational options from a distanced perspective—that of the unbiased researcher—and then to apply those thoughts to their own more personal reflections. Because of the trust bestowed by interviewees, proper training of the student interviewers is imperative. Just as a medical student cannot interact with patients without significant training, college men must be thoroughly versed in the ethical and professional constraints of qualitative research before beginning interviews. From a vocational mentoring standpoint, this required training is ideal. It not only supplies a reason for the young men and mentors to meet regularly but also leads freely to discussions about what it means to be a professional (in any profession) and to identify and use one's talents well. In short, conversations about becoming good researchers marry well with May's (2001) ponderings: "Who am I? Whom shall I be?" (p. 7)

Why Did Our Approach Work at Wabash, and Would It Work at Other Colleges?

As educational consultants at the Center of Inquiry in the Liberal Arts, we work with lots of colleges and universities. If there is one thing we have learned from our work beyond the PTEV project, it is this: Campus culture matters. Each campus has its own history, its own traditions, and its own way of viewing education. This means that any attempts to improve college men's education—including their vocational education—must work within the constraints of the campus culture or have a very good reason for departing from it.

Wabash's culture values independent thought and creative exploration of ideas, leading to an abiding commitment to student/faculty collaborative research. Each year the college hosts a campus-wide event called the Celebration of Student Research and Creativity at which Wabash men present independent work ranging from song writing to microbiological lab research. Wabash also is a place where students have an active voice in campus decisions. Leadership resonates with our men, and they are accustomed to having their opinions sought. In fact, they expect that their opinions should be sought. For this reason, Wabash's campus climate lends itself very well to focus-group interview research. For a campus like ours, the focus-group interviews about men's vocational paths provided a helpful avenue for initiating deeper vocational reflection across the college. In essence, formally researching college men's vocational journeys gave us the chance to initiate the types of conversations we felt our men needed to have but likely were not having. The approach we used may be particularly beneficial for other small colleges that (a) are committed to student research in various academic fields, including the social sciences; (b) value student/faculty mentoring collaborations; and/or (c) have a similar culture of involving students in administrative decisions.

References

Future Students-After Wabash. (2010). Retrieved January 19, 2010, from http://www.wabash.edu/admissions/after

Future Students-Athletics. (2010). Retrieved January 19, 2010, from http://www.wabash.edu/admissions/life/athletics

May, W. (2001). *Beleaguered rulers: The public obligation of the professional.* Louisville, KY: Westminster John Knox Press.

Pope, L. (2006). *Colleges that change lives: 40 schools that will change the way you think about colleges.* London, UK: Penguin Books, Ltd.

12

Micro-Grants and Adventure Travel:
Engaging College Men in Vocational Discernment at Georgetown College

Bryan Langlands and Coran Stewart

Enveloped by the gentle hills and horse farms of the bluegrass region of central Kentucky, Georgetown College is a small, Christian, residential, coeducational liberal arts institution. Our undergraduate population is 1,335 and ninety percent of those students live on campus. Of those 1,335 students, 44% are male. In 2006 and 2007, Georgetown participated in conversations that developed into the Lilly program called Involving More Men in Vocational Discernment Activities: Identifying and Implementing Best Practices. We were excited to have been chosen to participate in this pilot project because of our interest in increasing male participation in our campus programming.

Over its two-year duration, our Involving College Males project has consisted of two distinct programs. The first program is a micro-grant initiative that has provided micro-grants to male students who applied for one either to help fund their work with a currently existing service/ministry project or to start something new. The second is an adventure travel program in which we have used funds from this grant to help subsidize: annual mountaineering and white-water-rafting expeditions, an alternative spring break trip to Camp No More Deaths (providing emergency humanitarian assistance to migrants in the Sonoran desert near the Arizona/Mexico border), and a homeless simulation weekend experience in downtown Lexington, Kentucky called the Plunge to Poverty. An important part of each of these trips was the intentional group debriefing and/or written reflection we had involving deep questions about what is most important in life and life goals, talents and passions, and/or vocation.

Getting male students involved in the adventure travel program was not terribly difficult. Our initial thought was that by advertising our adventure travel opportunities through e-mail, on-campus calendars, and especially by personal invitations through word of mouth we would successfully recruit males for our trips. This initial thought turned out to be largely correct. We ended up having solid numbers for each of the adventure travel trips that we took. For the mountaineering trip that we took in September 2008 (to Grandfather Mountain, North Carolina), we took nine male students and one male staff person. For the mountaineering and white-water rafting trip that we took in October 2009 (to Grandfather Mountain and to the Chattooga River on the South Carolina/Georgia border), we brought sixteen students (thirteen of whom were male) and two male staff persons. For the alternative spring break trip to Camp No More Deaths (Camp NMD) in March 2009, we brought six students (three males) and two male staff persons. For our Plunge to Poverty immersion, we brought fourteen students (six males) and three staff persons (two males).

Engaging male students in the micro-grant program, we initially thought, would be a little more difficult. Since signing up for a micro-grant program does not have nearly the curb appeal that a mountaineering and white-water-rafting trip has, we sensed that we would have to be more intentional about recruiting male students to fill out a micro-grant application. Although there ended up being some truth in that initial assumption, our male students responded as well as we could have hoped to our micro-grant program recruitment efforts. Basically, we advertised to male students by telling them "Free money!" Naturally, that possibility caught their attention. We spread the word about the micro-grant opportunity through campus e-mails, word of mouth, and announcements at our weekly student-led worship gathering. Once a male student expressed an interest we e-mailed him a micro-grant program application to fill out (this application is included at the end of this chapter, see pages 181-182).

We received nine applications during our recruiting phase for the micro-grant program. Each of the nine applicants was informed that his project had been approved and that he had been awarded $500 in seed money from which we would reimburse him for expenses incurred during his work. Of the nine grants that were awarded, seven students ended up using at least some portion of their allotted funds. One of the two students who did not use any of their micro-grant funds transferred to another college a month after his grant was awarded. The other student was never able to get his idea of collecting used baseball gloves and sending them to a mission partner in the Dominican Republic off the ground.

Of the male students who did utilize their micro-grants, what follows is a list of the kind of ministries/projects they led: taking pizzas and drinks to a downtown park in Lexington, Kentucky, and fellowshipping with homeless folks there; painting the inside of the AMEN House (our local food pantry and clothing closet); funding travel to Bolivia and orphanage construction there; funding a dinner for students who traveled with a fellow student who preached at a conference in Louisville; purchasing Bibles that a student gave away; funding the youth ministry programming for a local, rural youth ministry (a church for which the student served as the youth pastor); and underwriting a local benefit concert (the proceeds of which helped to fund a service trip to Brazil).

Although the adventure travel and the micro-grant programs were distinct, we discovered that there ended up being some crossover participation between the two programs. Of the nine male students who filled out an application for a micro-grant, five of them also participated in one of our adventure travel trips.

REFLECTIONS FROM STUDENTS WHO TOOK PART IN THE MICRO-GRANT PROGRAM

What follows are reflections written by students who participated in at least one of our two programs. For a couple of students, we have provided their answers to the questions on their micro-grant applications, their reflections immediately following their micro-grant work (their post-experience reflections), and their final reflections on the entire program. In all cases that are listed below, the answers to application questions were written in spring 2008. The different post-experience reflections were written at various times during 2008–2009. All of the final reflections were written in November or December 2009. Our hope in providing all of these reflections for a few students is to give the reader some sense of the growth our students experienced through these programs.

Answers to the Application Questions from Student #1

A ministry that I am planning on being a part of is Andrea's Home of Hope and Joy, which is an orphanage in Guayamerin, Bolivia. I am not starting this project but rather being one of many who give of their time and money in order to see it through. Construction has already begun on the orphanage, and the grand opening will be on June 14, 2008. This is a very exciting time in the life of the founders, Gary and Jerri Zimmerman. They are building the orphanage in remembrance of their daughter Andrea, who lost her battle with cancer at age 29, leaving behind a husband and two children. When complete the orphanage will house 150 Bolivian children. The goals of the orphanage are:

1. Establish and maintain (through child sponsorships and other donations) an orphanage/Christian school for 150 children.
2. The children who will be cared for and raised in the orphanage will learn English, master the computer and learn a technical and/or trade skill.
3. Upon their departure from Andrea's Home of Hope and Joy at the age of eighteen, the children will have learned a trade or skill to ready them for the adult world. If the child chooses, he or she will be encouraged to pursue university training upon graduation from high school.
4. Once the orphanage is established, it is the goal of Love In Action International Ministries [LIAIM] to raise the standard of living throughout the community of 45,000. We will accomplish this through various community outreach programs directed through the orphanage and by working with the local evangelical churches.

I have been on two previous trips with the Zimmermans in which I helped with the construction of a church in Santa Cruz, Bolivia.... My trip will be from July 25–August 6, 2008, and will cost $2,100. I will be working this summer to earn this money and doing fundraising with the hope that grants like this will help defray the cost of the trip.... Vocation to me is a calling from God of what someone should do with [his/her] life. I believe that God has a plan for all of our lives. I believe he has called me to Bolivia as a full-time missionary. This trip is just another step in my preparation for life in Bolivia. When will I get there? How will it come about? I have no idea, but I am willing to trust him. I give him my life to do with it whatever he wants. I have promised him that where he calls, I will follow.

POST-TRIP REFLECTION FROM STUDENT #1

I have used all of my grant money.... I went to Bolivia this summer with Love in Action International Missions. I had been to Bolivia three times previously, but this trip was unique in that I went to a new area of the country and worked at an orphanage. The orphanage was still under construction, so there were no children there, but we were able to meet three different families whose children might go to live at the orphanage. Since [my] trip, the orphanage has started accepting kids, and several kids have already moved in. This was an amazing trip in the sense that I will be able to (and will) go back years from now and meet the kids who I helped build a home for. I feel called to full-time missions work in Bolivia. This trip helped me give to the Bolivian people before I have the ability to permanently move there. This trip helped solidify my calling to Bolivia. I would like to thank all the people who helped make this trip financially possible for me. I could not have done it without you.

FINAL REFLECTION FROM STUDENT #1

The trips we have taken over the past few years will be ones I will remember for many more to come. They were exciting trips where new relationships were formed and I was stretched, physically, spiritually, and relationally. Physically, the trips to Grandfather Mountain pushed the envelope of what I have done before. Spiritually, the time we have taken each trip to talk about life and God have helped me to grow. Relationally, I have been taught patience and love for others.

With regards to my vocational calling, I feel like the most beneficial trip has been my trip to Bolivia, which one of the [m]icro-[g]rants greatly helped in making possible. I have felt called to missions work in Bolivia for some time now, but this trip was the first time that I was able to go and work at an orphanage. The organization I am hoping to work with focuses on building orphanages in South and Central America.

It was great to go down and see exactly what they are doing. I am still confident in my calling to live in Bolivia. I would be most excited to coordinate with short-term mission teams from the United States, being their point man on the ground in Bolivia, and making sure all the logistics of the trip once on South American soil were taken care of. I am grateful for the support which the [Lilly] [g]rant has offered me in the further exploration of what it is exactly that God wants me to do with my life.

Final Reflection from Student #2

This money has helped me be able to provide opportunities for the youth I serve at our small rural church here in Scott County. Whenever an idea for something that required monetary funding was planned, this fund was available to help provide a means to support the idea. Being able to do these activities with the youth has helped me understand that I want my vocation to be fellowship oriented.

I like spending time with people, learning to love them well and provid[ing] support where it is needed. With the youth, I am able to relate to their stories, answer questions and concerns, ask them questions about their life in return, and teach them about how one can understand them to be a Christian in their community.... This has made me interested in pastoral opportunities [such as] chaplaincy, campus ministry, and Christian education.

Final Reflection from Student #3

This grant has allowed me to have opportunities I did not know would ever be available to me. It has allowed me to go on a mission trip to be in the trenches of modern day border wars. In this way I have seen up close and personal the suffering of people as they attempt to find a better life for them and their families. This grant has also allowed me to start a ministry to feed the homeless people who congregate in Phoenix Park in Lexington. Without this grant I would have had a much more difficult time attempting to get food to the park.

Both of these ministries have been very effective, and I have learned a great deal from both of them. They are both good ministries that allow students to positively affect the lives of others. They are the trenches of the war against evil and oppression. Christ was willing to be in these trenches and so should we.

Reflections from Students Who Took Part in the Adventure Travel Program

Arizona

Our decision to participate with Camp NMD stemmed from some positive feedback we had heard from a friend who had volunteered there a few years ago. Camp NMD partners with other humanitarian relief groups to provide emergency water, food, and first aid to migrants in remote regions of the rugged Sonoran desert. We participated with Camp NMD during our week of spring break in March 2009. Our camp was a small tent village located on private land near the small town of Arivaca, Arizona. The campsite was approximately 30 miles in from the U.S./Mexico border. After a day of training at the historic Southside Presbyterian Church in south Tucson, our primary activity for the week involved transporting gallon jugs of water to remote sites along well-traveled migrant trails.

POST-TRIP REFLECTION FROM STUDENT #4

> Though I am well-traveled for someone of my age and have spent a great deal of time doing service work, no journey has ever radically altered my perspective as our work with No More Deaths [Camp NMD]. Not only was I physically exhausted after days of hiking in the 90-degree desert, I was mentally and emotionally exhausted. We encountered almost a dozen people in a time of their greatest desperation, hoping for a chance to feed their families. Such desperation and strength of will was something I had never seen before, and from that I knew that as a follower of Christ it is my duty to bring His love to this situation.
>
> Our camping arrangements were not exactly luxurious. We slept in a tent [that] was unbearably hot in the daytime and unbearably cold in the nighttime. We ate little meat and had no electricity. As I sat in discomfort, I felt that I could be in no better situation to do this work. Though we slept in the cold, the migrants likely were sleeping in arrangements much worse than ours. Thanks to this I was always painfully aware of my brothers and sisters traveling across inhospitable lands for days, and I was filled with compassion and determination to help.
>
> What stuck out most prominently in my mind as I left the camp on Friday was the connection I felt with the migrants. I always thought of immigrants as these faceless, anonymous people whose lives were completely different than mine. While they are considerably different, all I could remember were the similarities. Most of them were other Christians, with spouses, children, and grandchildren. They loved their families as I love mine and sought the means to provide for them. They also believed in the love of God and believed that by his power he would provide for them. At that time I felt more love and kinship with those distant brothers and sisters than most of my country. Such a love can only bring me to continue to fight for them and for their right to live a fair life.

FINAL REFLECTION FROM STUDENT #4

> The work that I have been involved in through the Lilly Foundation has been a clarifying and almost overwhelming experience. I have spoken to men and women who have nothing and are so grateful for anything that might be given to them. I have walked in the hot sun for miles to bring aid to people that I will never meet. I understand better who I am, but more importantly, I understand who those people are that I am trying to serve in my Christian vocation.

The meaning of the term Christian vocation has also shifted for me. I realize that my vocational calling does not exist in the confines of my own mind or for my own ambition. Rather, vocation is what calls me to places I cannot fully imagine or understand until I have been there. My future may be uncertain, but I am ready for whatever it may bring. Camp [NMD] and Feeding Friends in Phoenix Park [Georgetown College student-initiated homeless ministry in Lexington, Kentucky] have reshaped the limits on what I will do in pursuit of God's kingdom.

Post-Trip Reflection from Student #5

My experience in the desert gave me the opportunity to minister to the "least of these my brothers" that Christ speaks of in Matthew 25 by being in a position to give food and water to those who hunger and thirst. I was given the ability to be inviting to the stranger. I was reminded of the flight of the young Christ's family to Egypt in order to escape persecution, and I was led to wonder who might have given them aid as they crossed the desert. Knowing that some people crossing the desert bear the names of Maria and Jesus made the parallel all the more powerful.... The walls being built on the border force migrants into the desert which, while beautiful, is also inhospitable. It is also unfortunate that many conservative Christians have aligned themselves with those who are intent on keeping migrants from trying to find a better life. It seems we have forgotten the special place of the poor and the alien in the laws of God. In Leviticus, God demands, "The alien living with you must be treated as one of your native-born. Love him as yourself, for you were aliens in Egypt. I am the LORD your God." My experience with [Camp] NMD was one of practicing love for the alien in this land.

The power of community was incredibly evident at [Camp] NMD. Just as the founders of the Sanctuary movement needed a large community during the 1980s, they continue to rely on a diverse group to carry out the mission of aiding migrants in need. We worked with Protestants of all stripes, Catholics, Quakers, and many unsure about religion. In a time when the Christian faith is divided by many who would rather hold on to certain doctrines than practice self-sacrificing love, it is refreshing to see such a diverse and eclectic group united in an effort to aid others. This environment provided a great place for important conversations around the fire and on our hikes. For the nonbelievers among the group, I think it was important for them to see Christians committed to actions rather than merely words.

My experience with [Camp] NMD opened my eyes to an issue I knew very little about before our trip. I feel like many of us in Georgetown are isolated from issues concerning the border[,] being as geographically removed from the border as we are. However, migrants are to be found in all communities, and a human rights issue as serious as this needs to be considered by all. It is my hope that what I learned from the members of [Camp] NMD and my firsthand experiences in the desert will allow me to be an advocate and a voice for these migrants in my own context. Oftentimes it seems that there is little that I can do as a college student; however, students are often a very socially active group. I plan to use my voice to wake students at Georgetown up from their complacency.... More and more Christians must become peacemakers and be the voice for those whose voices have been silenced and whose faces have been hidden by an unforgiving wall.

GRANDFATHER MOUNTAIN, NORTH CAROLINA

Grandfather Mountain stands 5,946 feet above North Carolina and offers stunning views in all directions of the Blue Ridge mountain range. As a part of the United Nation's international network of Biosphere Reserves, the mountain is home to 16 distinct ecosystems and is home to dozens of endangered species. Trails range from easy to strenuous, and, in many places, ladders and steel cables are necessary to safely traverse steep cliff faces. The overlooks and clear spaces along the trail system provide ideally suited spots for rest and conversation. After spending all day on the mountain, we returned to the cabin tired and sore.

At the cabin, as everyone sat on comfortable couches rubbing their sore legs, we reflected on our experiences during the hike. The conversation then shifted to deeper matters as we began a guided conversation on life passion and vocation. Away from the hustle and bustle of school and in the company of their peers, students were more comfortable sharing their thoughts and feelings. The next day was another strenuous one, spent (in 2008) white-water rafting and inflatable kayaking on the Nolichucky River in East Tennessee. In 2009, we rafted on the Chattooga River along the Georgia/South Carolina state border. Though these days ended with sore arms to match the previous day's sore legs, the adrenaline rush that came from navigating the rapids propelled us through our nightly conversations. The mountain we chose to hike and the rivers we chose to raft were selected because of our campus minister's familiarity with them.

POST-TRIP REFLECTION FROM STUDENT #6

I believe the conversations we held each night on vocation were very beneficial. Discussing questions about what is important to us, what we see our life mission to be, and what is holding us back, encouraged me to really think about the direction in which my life is headed. I started to think a lot about the motivations behind my goals. Even more important than the group conversations, though, I think were the private conversations that sprang up from the discussions. Talking with Billy [our guest conversation facilitator] made me ask a lot of hard questions about what I want to do in life. Because I really care about bringing the good news to the poor and being a champion for the least of these, and I also want to be a pastor[;] I think I was encouraged by Billy to see where these choices intersect. Billy encouraged me to look at the mission of the church today and how my life can fit into that and how I can be a leader in this mission. I am encouraged to see where the Kingdom is advancing and to be a part of it.

Post-Trip Reflection from Student #7

This trip was great! I loved the whole thing, even though it left me feeling extremely sore. I particularly liked the discussions that we had in the evenings, both the planned ones and the spontaneous ones that would pop up between the guys in the cabin. It was great being able to build relationships with a few guys that I may not have gotten to know as well otherwise. I feel like this really helped me to connect with them in ways that go deeper than just a casual conversation. Although many of the discussions didn't end with any real conclusions (they were about topics where practical conclusions probably aren't possible), it was great being able to see other perspectives and to really learn more about what others are thinking. After this trip, I will take back with me the need for building meaningful relationships with all types of other people and the knowledge of what a deep conversation can do in the process of building those relationships.

Plunge to Poverty Homeless Simulation, Downtown Lexington, Kentucky

The Plunge to Poverty idea was suggested to us by our applied anthropology professor at Georgetown College. He had participated in one previously and had a great experience. The Plunge took place over a weekend in November 2009. It involved deliberate attempts to divest ourselves of privilege and to walk a mile in the shoes of homeless folks in Lexington (population approximately 290,000). The first night we handed over our cell phones and wallets. We then purchased the clothes we would wear for the weekend from a thrift store. Later that night we slept on the floor of an unheated warehouse. The next day we were given $1 to spend for the day. We were told we could either fast, eat at soup kitchens, and/or collect and redeem aluminum cans as we walked the inner-city streets. That night, we came together and had a World Food Banquet (where 15% of our simulation participants received a steak dinner, 35% got beans and soup, and the other 50% ate only a handful of rice for dinner—these percentages reflect the realities of global hunger). We also spent time processing what we saw and experienced on the streets that day.

Post-Experience Reflection from Student #8

This weekend was truly life-changing. I use[d] to think I had a firm grasp on how blessed I am and didn't think twice about the poor when I saw them in passing. I was shocked to see how different it felt from the other side when talking about charity. I once was a huge proponent for this type of aid, but I failed to see its biggest flaw, the lack of relationships.... I have been guilty of this in the past. It means much more to these people if you take the time to get to know them instead of coming in on the holidays, posing for a photo op, and feeling good about yourself for the rest of the year. I never understood the disdain for those providing charity until I was on the other side of the fence this weekend. As I went from free meal to free meal, those who were serving never attempted to start a conversation with me, deciding instead to stand on the wall and stare at us as if we weren't human.

I'll never take my warm bed, good meal, and most of all the freedom and mobility to go where I choose for granted again. I'll also never pass a homeless person in Lexington, or anywhere else in the world, and pass judgment. Everyone has a story and everyone has something to contribute to society. I was also surprised at how accepting and warm the homeless community was to our group.... This truly was a life-changing experience. True change comes from creating relationships and sharing in the struggle. Being so close to Thanksgiving, I'll never take anything for granted that I previously did before this weekend.

Overall Project Assessment

It has been said that if you give a man a fish he will eat for a day, but if you teach a man to fish he will eat for a lifetime. This proverb reminds us that the greatest thing you can do for another person is not just to share your wealth and talents, but to help him discover his own. Our experiences taught us that this should be the philosophy underwriting any program wishing to encourage reflection on vocation with male students.

Our hope is that the micro-grant program has provided experiences that have helped to reveal to male students their own treasures of passion and talent. Our interpretation of the feedback given by students who participated in the micro-grant program is that part of what made it successful was the way in which it encouraged students to explore their own callings and dreams. We learned that a crucial part of our task involved figuring out how to coach and encourage male students to use the money to make their vision a reality. We also discovered through this micro-grant program that by giving ample opportunities for feedback we encouraged students to reflect on their experiences. Through this reflection, they have come to a better understanding of their vocations. It was exciting for us to read on each of these students' initial applications that they already had complex thoughts and ideas concerning vocation. Based on the feedback we received, overall, the experiences of our students who participated in this micro-grant program further engaged them in their vocational discernment.

While our program took a largely hands-off approach to the implementation of the students' projects, we have learned that there are cases where this may not have been a best practice. As we admitted before, a couple of our students' projects failed to take off. The particular project involving collecting baseball equipment had promise, but there proved to be many obstacles in the way of implementation. Students should confer with program leaders to discern the feasibility of their projects and to decide if any other forms of assistance will be necessary for their completion. If these extra steps are taken, we believe, a micro-grant program could be an even more effective practice.

The reflections related to our adventure travel program repeatedly point to the benefits of the guided discussions held and the conversations that grew out of those discussions. Conversations like these were possible because of the environment in which students found themselves. Taking time away from homework, the dorm room, and the comforts of the familiarities of campus life and journeying out into the wilderness engendered a kind of creative vulnerability in our students. Also, because our hiking and white-water-rafting activities were group oriented, a sense of community began to break down barriers that may have existed previously. That our debriefing facilitators were committed to listening as well as guiding provoked and nurtured excellent conversation. Ultimately, all of this served to create a safe space for male students to discuss vocation.

Our work with Camp NMD demonstrated that aligning adventure travel with a humanitarian aid program is also extremely beneficial. Students benefited from immersing themselves in the strangeness of a rugged desert environment, from the physical exertion involved in lugging one gallon water jugs out to migrant trail drop points, and from reflecting on our daily experiences each night around the campfire. Such immersion far away from home requires one to pay better attention and to trust others for help navigating new circumstances and unfamiliar space. In the desert, the eyes of students were opened to the hurting world around them. Here, students were again given an opportunity to discover their own riches by aiding others.

Based on our student reflections, the Plunge to Poverty immersion experience also proved to be a very beneficial weekend. During this Plunge, students were invited to become homeless for a weekend. We began by visiting a thrift store and buying the clothes there that we would wear for the weekend. Each night we slept on the floor in a cold warehouse and were only allowed to carry two personal items and $1 with us for the weekend (students were not permitted to carry cell phones). Students were broken up into small groups and sent out into the city on Saturday to complete a list of tasks assigned to them. These tasks included asking a stranger to borrow a quarter, rummaging through a garbage can or dumpster for something useful, collecting aluminum cans to redeem for cash, and so on.

If participants wanted to eat during the weekend, we had to go to a soup kitchen. The one meal provided on Saturday night was a World Food Banquet. This banquet culminated with a debriefing about our experiences on the streets during the day. Several of our students reported in their reflections that they will never look at a homeless person again the same way after walking for one day "in their shoes" (although part of our debriefing involved the ways in which we were not really in their shoes because we still enjoyed many privileges—being college students—even as we tried to divest ourselves of privileges that day). As in several of the other adventure travel reflections, a common feature of these Plunge reflections was the fatigue that students reported.

In conclusion, based on our experiences and the reflections of our students at Georgetown College, we judge the use of micro-grants as well as adventure travel to be effective practices for engaging male students in constructive life activities and vocational discernment. When students are given resources to implement a project of their design, they learn more about their personal strengths, weaknesses, passions, and resources. Providing micro-grants fosters the entrepreneurial spirit, encouraging those who have a vision to serve but lack the resources to make that vision a reality. Similarly, when students are given the chance to journey outside of their zones of comfort to an unfamiliar place (be it the borderlands, rugged mountaintops, or inner-city streets), the mundane aspects of daily college life fall away, and students are encouraged to learn, to act, to take risks, and to reflect deeply. Utilizing trustworthy leaders who could adeptly debrief and help students to unpack the experiences, emotions, and insights they were experiencing was a component that proved to be crucial for the success of these conversations.

GEORGETOWN COLLEGE MICRO-GRANT PROGRAM APPLICATION

Dear Male Ministry Students,

We are excited to inform you of a great new opportunity for you. Have you ever wanted to create and enact an [ongoing] ministry project but did not have the funds or the resources? Now, thanks to a generous grant from the Lilly Endowment to Georgetown College, you have the opportunity to apply for up to $500 to implement a project of your creation. The final amount awarded will depend on the number of applications received and accepted, but this is the anticipated amount. So, if you have an idea for a ministry project for our College community or for the neighborhoods surrounding the College or wherever, we encourage you to fill out this application and return it to Bryan Langlands. You can choose to host a series of events, raise awareness for an issue, start a ministry with needy folks in Lexington, or whatever. Be creative! Please just remember that this $500 will not be "pay," it will be used to reimburse you for money that you spend doing your ministry. The deadline to turn in applications will be Friday, April 25th, 2008, at [n]oon. If you receive a grant, you will be notified the following week. The grant money may be used anytime between May 1, 2008, and May 1, 2009.

_____ _____ _____
Name Year in School Major

_____ _____ _____
Telephone Number E-mail Mail Box #

On a separate sheet of paper please type your answers to these questions:

Please give a detailed description of the project you would like to create. How much money do you anticipate needing?
Is the project sustainable, could it potentially become a regular event even after the grant is expired?
Describe your walk with God at this time[.] What new things are you learning?
Give a definition of what "vocation" means to you[.]

13

Road-Tripping:
The Male Initiative Project at Davidson College

Karen Martin

Davidson College is a private, Presbyterian church-related liberal-arts institution for 1,800 students, located 20 miles north of Charlotte, North Carolina. With generous support from The Lilly Endowment, the college in 2001 unveiled its Office of Programs for the Theological Exploration of Vocation, known widely and fondly on campus as the Lilly Programs in honor of the Lilly Endowment. The office included two full-time staff—a director and an assistant director—as well as administrative staff. Programs included, among others, semiannual student retreats for conversations about faith and vocation, alumni summer retreats for similar discussion, mutual mentoring opportunities among students and faculty and staff members, fellowships for the exploration of congregational ministry and service, and numerous on-campus lectures and discussions.

Over time, new methods were needed to generate student participation, especially among male students, who seemed to be engaged in lesser numbers than women. The office of the Lilly Programs had developed a reputation among students as being centered primarily on introspective reflection, a characteristic that appealed to women but not to men, who seemed uncomfortable with, or intimidated by, such self-reflective conversations. The Lilly Programs office adopted several programmatic changes from year to year, with inconsistent success.

At the same time, the Davidson campus was changing, due largely to additional resources resulting from a large capital campaign: More programs were available to students, with more guest speakers and added discussions. Students began to report that they felt overprogrammed—put simply, they were overwhelmed by the richness of program offerings, and, while they said they wanted to participate, they felt anxious about balancing such participation with their rigorous academic schedules as well as with their social, athletic, and service pursuits. The college understands the complexity of this reality and is addressing it through the strategic plan adopted in October 2009 by the college trustees.

Project Background

When the staff of the Lilly Programs heard about grant funding available through the Male Initiative, they eagerly applied, proposing two related projects: a seminar series titled Faith, Reason and World Affairs and a special opportunity for male-only road trips.

The seminar series was constructed in a manner similar to previous series. Offering six seminars over the course of the 2008–2009 academic year, the series was designed to include topics that historically engaged male students at Davidson: global insecurity, global development, the environment, capitalism and entrepreneurship, the intersection of art and social conscience, and the intersection of writing and social conscience. The objective was to demonstrate how vocation can embody not only employment but also fellowship, civic engagement, faith, and community. Faculty members and community leaders were asked to lead the seminars, speaking briefly about their knowledge on the seminar topic and then opening the floor for questions and discussion. The seminars were scheduled to take place over meals in casual, comfortable settings on campus.

Attendance at the initial seminars was disappointing and seemed to reinforce previous patterns. Students, male and female, simply did not wish to add one more commitment to their schedules. Given this response, the seminar series was discontinued, and resources were redirected to support the Road Trip project.

Starting the Engines

The project was modeled after Road Trip Nation (www.roadtripnation.com), a global effort that began with four friends who had just graduated from college and were unsure about their future career paths. They piled into an old recreational vehicle and hit the road for three months to talk with inspiring people in order to find out how these people lived their lives, where they were on their life journeys, and how they got there. The friends filmed their interviews, their reactions, and their day-to-day observations. Because this fresh approach to life's big questions became so popular, Road Trip Nation took on a life of its own, evolving into a PBS television series, three books, a blog, an online community, and a traveling ensemble that visits college campuses.

Davidson had welcomed the Road Trip Nation crew to campus in the fall 2007 semester, energizing students, faculty, and staff, including Kristin Booher, who at the time was the Assistant Director of the Lilly Programs. "I thought, wouldn't it be cool for us to offer an opportunity for something like that?" she recalls.

The Lilly Programs launched two pilot road trips, at the request of two groups of women students who wanted to try their hand at navigating the open road. These trips were somewhat unstructured, allowing the young women to explore their collective curiosities about life beyond the familiarity of the Davidson campus. "We told them, tell us where you want to go, and what you want to learn—is there something in particular that you're struggling with?" Booher says.

One group videotaped its adventures; the other wrote a report. Based on these pilot experiences, the Lilly Programs office created a more structured Road Trip project—with a student coordinator, a competitive proposal and budgeting process, and specific post-trip reporting requirements—to be offered within the framework of the Male Initiative, starting the wheels turning for a distinctive group of male-only experiences.

Handing Over the Keys

Cameron Barr, a senior religion major, was appointed as the student coordinator. His responsibilities included marketing the program, compiling applications, tracking and distributing the funding, and ensuring that all of the participating groups reported their activities and results. Barr recalls thinking that the Road Trip project would be a unique way to generate excitement among male students. "The road trips encouraged them to tap into their entrepreneurial, creative spirit," he says, expressing the belief that previous student programs within the Programs for the Theological Exploration of Vocation did not consistently seek ways to allow students to explore their creativity. "Traditional programs on campus were not a big success, and we thought the Road Trip program was an exciting way to let students have more control over what they needed and hoped to learn."

To generate awareness for the road trips, Barr contracted Davidson's Office of College Communications to create four-color glossy posters that were placed at high-traffic areas on campus. He created a broadcast e-mail list of students and clubs that he thought might be interested in the project and added the names of every male student who had registered for previous Lilly Programs opportunities—retreats, fellowships, mentoring programs, and the like. He also relied on simple word-of-mouth advertisement, telling just about everyone he met about the Road Trip project.

Students, in groups of three or four, were required to submit two-page proposals, outlining who would take part, where they wanted to travel, what they wanted to learn, how that tied to their vocational goals, and who they planned to interview. They were required to submit a budget and later to submit a final report—an edited video on DVD—regarding their Road Trip experiences. The groups were directed to Davidson's offices of Alumni Relations and Career Services to determine the appropriate interview subjects with whom they could discuss their goals. They also were pointed to the Road Trip Nation Web site for resources for developing interview questions as well as tips for recording the interviews. Trips could be taken over winter or spring break. Expenses were to be paid by the students, and they would be reimbursed after they submitted receipts.

"Our group learned about it from the posters on campus," says Michael Mellody, who participated with three other students as a sophomore. "We were all good friends prior to the trip, and we would probably do something for spring break together as a group anyway—we thought, why not apply for the chance to see something new and learn something along the way?"

"It was one of the few programs only for guys," adds Christoph Pross, who was a junior when his group embarked on its road trip, "so there was quite a buzz about it in the Student Union."

Six groups of students, first-year students through seniors, submitted proposals for Road Trip participation. An advisory panel found that all six proposals were compelling and, because there was enough funding to support them, all were approved.

Getting Underway

The groups were given the latitude to decide the road trips' directions as well as the role that each student would play along the journey. One member of Pross's group, for instance, worked on campus as a videographer for the Office of Information Technology Services, so he naturally was tapped as the trip videographer.

"We played to our strengths," says Joseph Sills, who, due to his aptitudes for math and logistics, handled his group's budget and logistics. Most of the driving was in the hands of his friend Michael Majzoub, who owned the car they would take. The third group member doesn't like to drive, so he took responsibility for thinking through the interviews, ensuring that the group members were asking the most appropriate questions of their subjects in order to keep them focused on the group's theme.

Sills's group, a junior and two seniors who shared a common passion for community and nonprofit service, at first considered a journey including Washington and New York City because of the large nonprofit communities there. All three, however, previously had visited those cities. "We looked at this as a chance to see someplace new," Sills says. They repurposed a wall projector, typically used by one of the students to project video games onto his dormitory room wall, to get a literal big-picture view of the country. Using Google Maps, they searched for large concentrations of nonprofit organizations within the United States. They chose New Orleans as their primary destination, determined to learn how alumni working in nonprofits have been able to balance their work lives and their personal lives—especially as they continued to face the persistent, enormous tasks of rebuilding their city and assisting its residents in the wake of Hurricane Katrina. There, they met with an alumna who works for a nonprofit organization that evaluates daycare providers that have applied for subsidy grant funding. After they toured the devastation of the lower Ninth Ward, they traveled to Atlanta, where they met with an alumnus who works for a private foundation and another who worked for years with residents in low-income housing.

Sills remembers that the group had some difficulty finding alumni to interview in New Orleans; they learned that one alumnus who they hoped to interview had moved away from the city and another had changed jobs. "We did a lot of talking about what contacts we truly needed to make."

Mellody recalls that, of his all-sophomore group, he and one other were "most enthusiastic about the documentation," about recording the group's experiences; later they would split the editing duties. With a common interest in writing, the group proposed a road trip far ending enough from the Davidson campus to feel that they had gone away yet close enough that the gasoline costs would remain on budget. They chose Chicago as their final destination, at the end of a route that would take them through Nashville and Memphis, largely because those "seemed like cool cities" that they never had visited, Mellody says. The Office of Career Services provided them with names and contact information for a dozen Davidson alumni living in those cities who had pursued careers in writing and journalism. After several rounds of e-mails, the group made appointments with a history major who now works as a publisher near Nashville, an English major who works for a newspaper in Memphis, and an Internet-based content editor for a medical center in Chicago.

Barr's road-trip partners, all seniors with an interest in the ministry and religion, were neighbors on campus; two were members of the track team. "We started thinking about religion and vocation," he says, "and then when the economy took its downturn, we changed our focus—we wanted to see how, or if, people were reevaluating their lives in the wake of the recession." Also in their headlights was the upcoming Southern Conference men's basketball tournament in Chattanooga, at which Davidson—still glowing from an Elite Eight appearance in the NCAA Division I tournament during the prior season—was hoping to again make a strong showing. The group created a list of alumni, generated from the Office of Career Services networking database as well as from one of the seniors' nationwide fraternity contacts, who worked in industries particularly affected by the recession. They also sought to connect with psychologists and ministers. With Chattanooga as their final destination, they contacted alumni in cities located along the way and drew their route as their appointments were confirmed. "We knew we wanted to stick around the South, and the bigger the city, the more likely it was that we could connect with someone." They arranged to meet with a psychologist in Atlanta who was working as an organizational consultant and then added Birmingham once an alumnus in banking agreed to an interview. In Chattanooga they cheered for their Wildcats and met with an ordained minister who once was a real-estate developer and has served as chief executive officer for Habitat for Humanity International.

Pross, a student from Germany, partnered with three other foreign national students—from Ecuador, Greece, and Sri Lanka—to find out what career hurdles were, or were not, faced by some of Davidson's international alumni. They planned a trip north, through Washington DC, Boston, and New York, because none of the four had ever been to all three major U.S. cities. The group had to navigate its own set of hurdles pertaining to driving in the United States; because of the great distances to be covered and the students' varying familiarity with the rules of the American road, only two members of the group were comfortable navigating and driving. They also had to rent a car, because none of the students owned one. To balance the rental-car expense, they planned overnight stays with friends rather than securing roadside lodging.

They found some interview referrals through the Office of Career Services but had greater response contacting alumni referred by the International Student Advisor and through simple networking with Davidson friends who had graduated.

In Washington, DC, they connected with a recent graduate who had worked part-time at the Greek Embassy reviewing documents and now was interviewing for a role with a Congressional study group performing demographic/political research on Cyprus. In New York they met with alumni who were in graduate school at New York University Law School as well as the brother of a Davidson friend now working at a major international financial institution. Their Boston connection was a graduate student at Harvard.

A group of minority students—three African-American and one Asian—were interested in asking alumni about their life experiences as minorities who had attended a higher education institution that is becoming more diverse in its student and faculty populations but has not always been so. "We selected the (interview) subjects through the alumni database in the Alumni Office," recalls Mordecai Scott, a junior at the time. "We luckily [found] barely four, the required amount." One of the students hailed from Washington, DC, and another from New York City, so they chose to travel to those cities in order to stay with family and cut their road trip expenses. In Washington, DC, they met with an alumnus who is a section chief at the Federal Bureau of Investigation and another who worked for both Presidents Bush, most recently as a special assistant for economic policy. In New York City they met with a 2006 graduate—a member of the Wildcat basketball team—who now is a coordinator for the National Basketball Association's (NBA) International Basketball Operations, working with the NBA's player-development camps overseas and helping the NBA's international players transition to life in the United States.

The final group—three sophomores and a senior—focused on vocation and faith. They all were members of the Campus Outreach ministry, and the senior student already had committed to working for the Campus Outreach organization at another campus after graduation. Three of the group members had never visited the northeastern United States, so they decided to head to the New England area. They first connected with two alumni who work for Campus Outreach at the Virginia Polytechnic Institute and State University (Virginia Tech). From there they drove to Connecticut, where they met with an alumnus who founded a church in New Canaan and an alumna involved in Focus Ministries.

Mapping the Journey

"The opportunity to capture our road trip on video seemed more personal than having to write up something," Pross says. "That was appealing to us." His group's video includes footage of their approach to the 7,200-foot-long eight-lane Fort McHenry Tunnel under Baltimore's Inner Harbor and a comment from one of the group members off-camera: "This is an interesting cultural experience, being underwater. Back home, we cross rivers by boat—we don't go under them." Similarly, the group's DVD features an extra-long shot of the New York City skyline. "That was interesting, to watch how the environment transitioned from countryside to the city," Pross recalls. "A lot of times you fly into a city, and you never see that transition."

Inspiration from cultural landmarks proved a common theme among the groups. Joshua Arthur, a first-year student from Jackson, Mississippi, marvels on-screen about seeing the Statue of Liberty for the first time, at night: "As we're driving on away on the ferry, the water was rippling, the sky was dark, and the Statue of Liberty [came] up on the left.... It was like, *wow.*" He is almost breathless as he speaks to the camera, spreading his arms wide.

The group that toured New Orleans did not comment on camera about their impressions after seeing what remained of the Ninth Ward—and there was no need to do so. Rather, the DVD footage of their tour begins with a moment of silence and rolls, slowly, to the haunting strains of British singer-songwriter Imogene Heap's *Hide and Seek*. The electronic notes slide and linger as the camera pans empty lots revealing crumbled house foundations, caved-in structures, and driveways leading to nowhere.

Mellody and his friends documented their visits to some of the quintessential sights along the way, panning the exterior of Tootsie's Orchid Lounge and Layla's in Nashville and later King's Palace Café in Memphis. The group's DVD includes a sequence showing the friends staring out over the Mississippi River, one by one, leaning over the levee to touch the water, set to the Blink-182 tune *I Miss You* ("and in the night we'll wish this never ends/we'll wish this never ends"). As their car nears the city limits of Chicago, the viewer sees the sign for the Illinois state line approaching, then whizzing by, and gradually the edits reveal the Chicago skyline, the Chicago Art Institute, and UNO Pizzeria. The accompanying audio is Sufjan Stevens's lilting song *Chicago* ("I fell in love again/all things go, all things go/drove to Chicago"), which starts softly and builds to an upbeat multivoiced chorus, much like nightfall in the city itself.

Pross says his group's road-trip theme song was Jason Mraz's *I'm Yours*, the video of which, coincidentally, shows Mraz on a foreign cross-country road trip, traveling by airplane, automobile, truck, and boat to meet new friends around the world.

Clearly, the project's intention of providing students with a creative mode of expression, through the requirement to document their experiences with audio and video, worked. Most of the groups, in fact, submitted one-page written reports in addition to their edited DVDs, and the difference between the two reports is striking. When narrating their experiences on paper, the students tended to stick to facts: who took part, where they went, and who they met, with perhaps a sentence or two about what the group members learned, collectively, along the way. In contrast, the DVD reports allow the viewer to read between the lines, so to speak.

"The filming made the trip more fun, because it allowed us to capture something we knew we'd be able to look back on," says Mellody. "Sure, we filmed the big landmarks, but we also tried to capture the mundane things in the car or in the hotel."

The DVDs reveal a host of mundane situations: visiting the drive-through window at a fast-food restaurant, making Cheerios-and-jelly sandwiches at an interstate rest stop, eating ice cream, playing video games, sleeping in the car, celebrating a birthday, scrounging for change while approaching a toll booth, singing or lip-synching along with favorite music.

"We had hours of stuff that was useless," Mellody recalls, "just us hanging out, being four guys. It was tough to find the parts that would be interesting not just to us but to outsiders." He made certain, he says, to include touches of humor—specifically, spur-of-the-moment situations, "things you can't recreate."

The most difficult part of the documentation, say the DVD editors, was deciding what to keep and what to leave on the cutting-room floor. "We had to cut out the inappropriate things," Pross says with a grin. "There's a lot of that when you're four guys in a car." "We had to decide which scenes to keep and which ones to delete and how 'real' we wanted it to be," agrees Scott, who describes the editing process as even more enjoyable than the road trip.

The DVDs themselves differ in their styles. Some are titled (*Three Cities, Four Guys, One Car*) but most are not. Some are heavily edited, with special effects and music that matches each change of location, while others are simply edited in chronological order: establishing shot, interview, transitional shot, interview. Some include on-camera interviews with the group members themselves, reflecting at that moment about their experiences as they occurred. One group edited its video as a series of flashbacks. Every DVD, however, includes film footage of the road, with directional signs reflecting on the distance traveled and scenery rushing past to mark the passage of time.

The interview segments that made the final cut reflect what the students felt were the most poignant advice and lessons learned from the alumni:

- "What would I have done differently during college? I would have developed greater networks outside of the football team, met more people outside my comfort zone."
- "Enjoy Davidson while you're still there. It might be a little bit of a challenge (to be a minority student) but you come to make friends and understand that they like you and want to be with you for who you are. That's a great growth experience for when you get out in the real world."
- "Davidson's small town environment helps you ease into living life in a big American city. If forces you to focus on work and meet more interesting people in a concentrated environment."
- "Wipe everything off the table—what the world says you should do (as a career), what your parents say you should do, what Davidson says you should do—and ask the Lord, 'what should I do, Lord? Here am I.'"
- "Know that being a minority, because there are so few, you are in a privileged spot. You should take that as (an obligation) to do well, to excel. Use that as motivation. You have a great opportunity that many other kids would love to have. Don't take it lightly."

- "Learn how to learn. Learn how to study. Talk to your professors—don't think you know it all."
- "Develop the minds that God has given you. To be trained and taught how to think, how to grow in your ability to work through arguments, to follow lines of thought—take advantage of it. It's an incredible opportunity."

Switching Gears

Beyond the interviews and the physical process of recording and documenting the trip, the students say the Road Trip project allowed them to get to know one another—and themselves—a bit better, simply by placing them in unfamiliar environments.

"I never would have done something like this. I never would have thought about it," Mellody says six months later when asked to reflect on the project. "But it started me thinking about the future. I hadn't really thought about it that much." He adds that while the trip provided "no big revelations" about the group members themselves—they all lived in adjacent rooms on campus, so they largely were familiar with their respective idiosyncrasies—"it got us interacting in a different setting. In a dorm room, things can be the same, so we talk about the same things." He recalls eating dinner as a group at a seafood restaurant in Memphis. "We had a great moment, sharing things we'd never thought to share before: family issues, goals, aspirations.... It was an amazing experience."

"Being stuck in a car (with three other guys) is great because you're not going anywhere," adds Majzoub. "Things that seemed trivial before—now they're interesting. You can't walk away from the conversation; you have to stay present."

"Probably one-third of the trip was in the car," recalls Sills, "so that's where we had some of the best moments. Deep conversations, light conversations ... just a lot of fun."

The trips also proved to be real-life exercises in navigating group dynamics and responsibilities. Pross's group was composed of students from four entirely different cultural perspectives, who had to balance Pross's tendency for precision—thanks to his German upbringing, he acknowledges with a chuckle—with an Ecuadorian group member's preference to handle events as they unfolded. Staying on schedule became a very real issue, Pross says, remembering the unnerving feeling of trying to find a parking spot in Manhattan only minutes before the group was scheduled to conduct an interview.

Mellody's group once slept through the blare of their alarm clock, and there were times, he says, when they "definitely could have stayed in the hotel and slept all day." Because of their commitments, however—to their interview subjects, to themselves, and to Davidson—they were forced to refocus on timing and schedule.

"It was sort of risky, [eight] days together, going places we'd never been before," says Barr, who adds that the students in his group had been friendly but not close friends before their trip. "Now, they're two of my greatest friends."

Looking in the Rearview Mirror

In addition to forging fast friendships, the road trips provided food for thought and, often, hope for the future. The students learned, perhaps for the first time, what it means to be part of the Davidson family that is so often referenced on campus.

"For these people to invite us into their offices and have some remarkable conversations, that was really powerful," Barr says. "We were able to experience the density and camaraderie of the Davidson network, which gave us some confidence in the future.... If I were in Atlanta right now and looking for a job, [an interviewee] would be one of the first people I'd call."

"It was interesting to see how fortunate, or unfortunate, the [alumni interviewed] were, with regard to visa issues, family, and finances," recalls Pross. "What we learned was how important it is to keep going. Take a step at a time. Even if you have to turn over fifteen stones, you'll eventually find one that reveals a great opportunity."

After meeting with the alumnus who works at a grant-making foundation, senior James Garrett says that it was "encouraging to see that even if I don't want a job directly in the field—helping people, passing out soup, something really hands-on—even if I don't want one of those jobs, I can still work for a nonprofit and feel satisfied." He says he learned that "you've got to concentrate on what you can do best, because if you try to spread yourself too thin, you're not going to be helping anybody at the level you want to help them. You can pick and choose what fits best. You have to play to your strengths and do what you do, well."

Speaking to the camera on the DVD, Majzoub says what he took away from the project was knowledge that "while it's important to be doing something meaningful, and you can be fulfilled by your job, that can't be the only place you find meaning and fulfillment in your life. You need to construct your life in a way that you're coming into work already fulfilled.... It's really challenging; [you] have to ask in [your] private lives: where [am I] going to get that meaning and fulfillment?" In a discussion 6 months after graduation, he says that the road trip was the first time he realized that "pursuing [his] own interests is healthy." He admits he still struggles with balance—he talked about this via cell phone at 9:30 p.m. while photocopying work documents—"but now I'm very conscious of the need to develop some balance—I have fun sometimes."

Sills says that the trip provided perspective, a "switch in thinking" with regard to the nonprofit work that he does within the Davidson community, serving as a Spanish-language translator for clients at the local community service center. "I found a new joy in doing what I was doing," he says. "I can help people, and I can make the most of it."

"Our interviewees all discussed the benefit of making a bunch of different friends, talking to people that you've never talked to before," Arthur says to the camera, arranged on a tripod in order to capture the thoughts of all of his group members in one setting. "Personally, that's been something that's very difficult for me; to step outside of my comfort zone, my close circle of friends, because of the ignorance I've faced prior to coming to Davidson.... I'm going to be a more open person. I'm going to branch out. I think it's really going to affect my time at Davidson—and then my life after Davidson."

On the Road—Again?

The students involved in the Road Trip project unanimously sing its praises. Barr says he and his road trip cohorts have talked several times about recreating their journey at some point.

Mellody's group got together the following semester to watch its DVD and to reminisce. "We'd remembered the big things—the landmarks, the shows we saw," he says, "but we'd forgotten all the little things that were fun at the time but probably would have been gone (from memory) if we didn't capture them on tape." Their road trip, he adds, simply was a unique experience.

First-year student Damion Samuels calls the Road Trip project "groundbreaking work," adding, "I think a lot of other people would have wanted this opportunity."

Whether that opportunity will be available for other students is a question that remains. The Road Trip project ultimately may be a one-time experiment, the replication of which would be difficult for reasons largely pertaining to logistics, oversight, and funding.

There was some discussion about the substance of the project when it was introduced on campus; specifically, women students expressed resentment that the project was available only to men.

Additionally, the DVD reporting requirement of the project—while resulting in noteworthy, evocative products—likely was much to ask of students who already felt the time constraints of rigorous academic expectations. Beyond the hours of filming during the trips, one or more students from each group spent up to six hours in an editing suite compiling their DVD reports. One group, composed of seniors, simply did not have time to edit its report between the return from their spring break road trip and graduation.

In the future, the Office of Student Life may investigate future road trip opportunities; however, economic realities are such that additional programs outside of the current college budget are unlikely.

Davidson is grateful for the remarkable opportunity to offer the Road Trip project with support from the Center for Men's Leadership and Service at Saint John's University, as well as the Lilly Endowment. Its impact is evident in what Samuels said at its conclusion: "Going to the interviews made us look at our semesters in retrospect. Speaking to people got us looking at ourselves. All of that, together, helped us bond as a brotherhood—and that's pretty important." Truly, as Samuels reflected, the road trip "was a beautiful opportunity."

Section D.
Forming Men's Groups

14

THE LEAGUE OF EXTRAORDINARY GENTLEMEN AT THE UNIVERSITY OF PORTLAND

Josh Noem, Thomas Bruketta, and Jamie Grimm

The University of Portland (UP) in Oregon is a Catholic university in the tradition of the Congregation of Holy Cross, serving about 3,000 undergraduates. The League of Extraordinary Gentlemen (LXG) was founded by Campus Ministry at UP as a program to serve the spiritual needs of men on campus, and it invites men to grow in four key values: brotherhood, justice, truth and seeking authentic masculinity. The foundation of the program is small group meetings, once every few weeks, where 8–10 men gather with two adult mentors (faculty or staff) to essentially answer the questions: Who am I and what do I believe? The men are grouped according to class year, and the groups remain together for four years. In addition to these foundational regular meetings, which touch on the value of truth (sharing deepest-held beliefs), student leaders in the league plan an event each semester that touches on one of each of the other three values: brotherhood (social event), justice (service outing), and some kind of discussion about authentic masculinity.

HISTORY

In the early 2000s, the administration at UP recognized that campus demographics mirrored national trends when it came to male participation in higher education. Men were lagging behind women not only in enrollment but also in academic achievement and general engagement in extracurricular activities. In response, the university began to seek ways to meet the needs of male students at UP by prioritizing programming explicitly for men. This initiative was envisioned as a retention tool as well as a way to enrich the undergraduate experience for all students. Campus Ministry occupies a central role in student services at UP because of the university's distinctively Holy Cross tradition to educate both the mind and the heart. With a new hire in 2005, Campus Ministry took the opportunity to expand its presence on campus with a program to serve the spiritual needs of male students.

In fall 2005, Campus Ministry took the lead in gathering together a group of male students on campus to envision a program that would excite and engage men. In the first 2 years, a variety of approaches were taken, all led by staff in Campus Ministry: topical discussions at a local pub, service outings to help the homeless, rustic retreats in the mountains, Wiffle Ball socials, and an exercise group that offered a daily reflection and conversation.

Overall, however, none of these approaches really took off or seemed to engage men in an important way. There was a core group of 10 men who were consistently involved, and, within that group, there were between 4 and 6 men who seemed to always attend everything. It was clear that the approaches we were using simply were not generating interest. If the activities had been successfully engaging men, we would have seen that core group of men involving others, and leaders would have emerged to take the group in new directions.

Our evaluation of the Men's Spirituality Program over these first 2 years offered some important lessons. The 1st year included a small group of men who met every 2–3 weeks at a local pub for conversation. There was interest among this group for other activities, such as a day hike or afternoon of service. The group, however, was comprised of men who already had previously bonded among each other. While men expressed objective interest in service opportunities or getting away, when it came down to prioritizing it and planning on it, they had too much else going on. The pub meetings drew on—but did not establish—core relationships from which interest and investment in such a group would grow.

We focused the next year on an activity that would give the group a sense of purpose and cohesion, a common project. We also thought that regular meetings would help the group develop its own identity. That year, we gathered men to do a physical exercise regimen, coupled with a daily reflection and conversation. We met three times a week to do push-ups in order to be able to do 1,000 push-ups in 1 hour by the end of the semester These exercise routines also offered a brief daily reflection and prayer. Again, the group did not grow beyond a half dozen participants, and the engagement beyond the morning exercise routine—such as service projects and a rustic retreat—was minimal. Regular meetings and a common project alone were not enough to establish cohesion and a group identity.

We determined another significant factor in the lack of success in the Men's Spirituality Program over these 2 years. There are two all-male residence halls on campus, both of which are filled with spirit and energy. Men who were looking for alternative activities and ways to connect with guys doing "guy stuff" already had that need met with their peers in those halls. The activities and opportunities offered by those residence hall communities were better than those offered by Campus Ministry, because they were a natural outgrowth of the fellowship and core relationships established in the halls. The activities were conceived and implemented by male students or their resident assistants, and they drew on a web of relationships that permeated the hall. To these men, the Campus Ministry offerings were simply another peripheral activity, such as the ecology club. Therefore, we only drew participation from those men on campus who had a self-identified and explicit interest in male spirituality, and we all know that this is a small demographic among college men. We were failing to speak to the mainstream culture of men on campus, and we were not serving men on campus who could most benefit from engagement with Campus Ministry.

For the 2007–2008 year, the 3rd year of the Men's Spirituality Program, we decided to begin a group modeled after the Men's Discussion Groups offered at St. John's University. We studied a review of the St. John's groups (Longwood, Muesse, & Schipper, 2004) and invited a dozen freshmen males to consider the group.

These freshmen were recruited through personal invitation from residence hall staff, who were asked to identify men who might be interested in starting such a group. Two Campus Ministry staff members served as mentors.

We began meeting after fall break and on average met twice a month. The meetings were simple—the conversation unfolded in three stages. The leader shared his life story by answering the questions: Who am I and what do I believe? There was a time for clarifying questions and reactions to the story, then the conversation was opened up to whatever larger issues men connected with. The two staff mentors led the first two meetings, and students followed.

We called the group the LXG, and good energy and interest developed within the group, which was lacking in our previous Men's Spirituality Program offerings. The men bonded well, and there was good and easy conversation among participants at meetings even though these men did not necessarily relate to one another outside of this group. Leaders emerged, demonstrating an interest in putting time and energy into the group. There was an overall excitement about this group and where it was heading. The group was offering participants the chance to develop core relationships with peers, and these relationships seemed to be driving interest and personal investment.

After finding success with the pilot group in 2007–2008, we expanded LXG to the general campus male population in fall 2008. We gathered about 30 new members, spread throughout all class levels. We split these men up into four new additional groups, each paired with two adult mentors. These groups met on their own throughout the 2008–2009 academic year; evaluation of the success of this year is noted below.

In fall 2009, we again held an open recruiting night for the campus, and we recruited more than 30 new members, the vast majority of whom were freshmen. We split these new members into three new groups, each group with two new mentors. We now had a total of seven active groups for more than 60 men in LXG.

Word-of-mouth has been our best means of invitation. We ordered glossy business cards with our logo and recruiting night information and had members of LXG walk through the halls to invite freshmen. It is an intentionally soft sell that we use—a simple invitation to pizza and root beer and to hear men already in LXG talking about their experience.

The male spirituality program at UP, then, has grown considerably over the past 5 years as shown in Figure 1.

STRUCTURE

In spring 2008, we brought the freshmen from the first pilot group together and asked them to help us vision what the structure of LXG could look like. We had conversations about the core values of the group and what they would like the group to grow to be. The students really took ownership of LXG at that point and clearly felt that they were pioneers for a new movement on campus and breaking new ground. The structure, motto, and logo they designed were effective in cre-

LXG Membership, 2005-2010

Figure 1. LXG membership, 2005-2010.

ating a sense of group identity. The values they claimed for the group had roots in the university's mission and identity, so they were a good fit for our context. The following is a description of the structure that they developed for LXG.

LXG is grounded in four values that are reflected in this group's name: brotherhood, truth, justice, and authentic masculinity. The values are articulated in the form of an oath that the group receives and shares at the end of their first year:

> We are LEAGUE in that we are brothers, united to a common good and committed to fellowship through the strengthening of each man who stands amongst us. We will be transformed through our *brotherhood*.
>
> We are EXTRAORDINARY in that we champion justice and search for truth. Gentlemen of the League take responsibility for the good of others—we will serve others and the common good in our work for *justice*. We will also share *truth* with one another in the form of our deepest-held beliefs.
>
> We are GENTLEMEN in that we proclaim *authentic masculinity* and reclaim the hearts of men: we choose to act as men of integrity, peace and honor.
>
> Arching over all of these values is the value of ACTION—we are men who take action to cultivate fellowship, service and character.

These four core values of LXG (brotherhood, justice, truth, authentic masculinity) resonate well with the values of UP as a Holy Cross institution (community contextualizing teaching, faith, and service). While LXG draws on many disciplines (gender studies, service learning, etc.), it is a good fit for Campus Ministry for several reasons. Campus Ministry's mission states that it nurtures the faith development of the UP family and assists members of the campus community to "discover the deepest longing in their lives." Particularly with the example of the group mentors (one of whom will be a member of Holy Cross, ideally), the conversations about deepest truths that take place in these groups will include the Christian perspective.

Our logo bears the initials LXG, encircled by a laurel wreath of victory. This wreath is also found in the processional cross in the Chapel of Christ the Teacher, the main worship space on campus. Our motto is inscribed below—*virtus unitas valet*—which means virtue united prevails (see Fig. 2).

Figure 2. The LXG logo.

FORMAT

Regular meetings take place once every couple of weeks and follow a very simple format.

CHECK-INS

Everyone takes a moment to talk about how their past few weeks have gone and gives a high and a low for where they are right now.

LEADER'S STORY

Each week, one member shares his story by answering the questions: Who am I and what do I believe? The mentors will each lead the first two meetings, and, after that, everyone in the group will take a turn. Each leader will receive a guide with some questions to help him think through what he wants to say.

REACTIONS AND DISCUSSION

After the leader shares his story, anyone can follow up with questions or comments about what he said. These reactions then flow into a general conversation about a theme or topic or idea that is grounded in the leader's story but is discussed by everyone. The leader takes responsibility for identifying one or two of these main themes and introduces them for general conversation.

Extraordinary Action

The group may decide to close each meeting with each member choosing one extraordinary action he will take on in the weeks until the next meeting. Each person can state the extraordinary action he will do before the group meets next. It would be ideal if the action each person chooses reflects something of the theme or conclusion of that particular group meeting. The check-ins for the next meeting, then, can be an opportunity for everyone to say how they did in accomplishing their extraordinary actions.

During the 1st year, groups focus on the questions: Who am I and what do I believe? The 2nd year has a focus on relationships. After the first 2 years, groups can elect to meet without a mentor. By that time, they are well-established as a group and know the flow of the meetings and can handle conversation on their own if they want to. The 3rd year is about resiliency—what challenges, suffering, and setbacks the men have encountered and how they have persevered. During the last year, seniors are invited to help mentor a freshman group. For their senior group, they will talk about what they have learned from their participation in LXG and what they are being called to do in the world upon graduation.

The conversation in this group is bound by three rules: (a) *Confidentiality* is essential to building trust so that everyone knows that this group is a safe place where they can talk about personal experiences. A violation of confidentiality would be about the only thing that would prompt someone being asked to leave LXG. (If someone is in danger of harm, a mentor may be required to break confidentiality and will ask for permission to do so.) (b) *Commitment* is required from men in this group for the rest of their time at the university. LXG is unique in that it offers men the chance to sustain a level of brotherhood over multiple years—this long view offers the group the opportunity to depend on one another and hold one another accountable. (c) *Communication* is requested from the men to be as honest and open as they comfortably can. We also ask them to share in the group by using *I* statements in order to own their beliefs and feelings and experiences. These meetings are not a time to teach or preach, so we don't use language such as "we all should do this or that" or "it is our duty to act in this way." Instead, we simply own our experiences and beliefs by using language such as "when I was growing up, this happened to me that was important" or "I believe that we are created by God." Legitimate and sometimes heated disagreements may emerge, which is fine as long as the discussion unfolds in a respectful manner.

Events

We hold events throughout the course of the year that offer opportunities for gentlemen in LXG to get together to practice a core value.

The regular meetings are the primary place where men will practice the value of searching for truth and brotherhood. Two events offer men a chance to examine themselves as authentic men, one in the fall and one in the spring. In November, LXG gathers for Mansgiving—a common meal together where we hear a prominent male on campus speak about his experience. In the spring comes the Manquisition, a mock trial where cultural stereotypes are parodied along the lines of Monty Python's Spanish Inquisition skit (which no one expects). Opportunities for LXG-wide fellowship and service occur throughout the year, and the 1st year ends with an LXG tradition, the Toasts and Oaths Meal, where 1st-year members honor the group's experience with toasts and receive and recite the LXG oath for the first time.

Student Perspective

LXG has been an important place for students to share stories. Talking about personal experiences has helped male students find meaning and appropriate values for their lives. Following is an articulation of a student's experience in LXG, written by Jamie Grimm, class of 2011:

> At the beginning of my sophomore year the League of Extraordinary Gentlemen was merely the title of a movie starring Sean Connery. LXG was no more known to me than the personal agenda of Donald Trump. A friend introduced me to LXG and I joined blindly, not knowing the activities or agenda. To me at that time LXG was only about social interaction. It was not until my sophomore year was over that I learned what LXG represented.
>
> My group developed exceedingly well around the core values. At first we began sharing, being open and truthful with one another about our thoughts. Then, with the openness created, trust grew, which in turn developed into brotherhood that led to a greater amount of openness. The cycle continued, bringing us closer with each meeting. With every meeting came a new person's story, and with each story more experiences were shared and more lessons were learned. When leaving each meeting I felt a greater understanding for the person that shared the story. I also felt a greater general understanding of how my actions are seen by other people. With each meeting it became clearer to me what kind of person I would want to become.
>
> Through its core values, LXG provides a setting for men to grow. This growth as a person is the most important part of life. In fact, to me, to grow defines living. To continually strive to better oneself in every aspect of life is an admirable trait that I have always revered and constantly try to incorporate in my life. Through LXG I was able to experience the lessons learned by my fellow members and to incorporate those lessons and apply them to my life. The lessons learned in our

group meetings cannot be lectured or taught by professors, they can only be experienced.

The men that were selected at random and placed in my group, I now consider to be some of my closest friends on campus. Although we are all from different backgrounds and have different views on many aspects of life, we find common ground in our desire to grow and learn from each other's experiences. In LXG, we grow individually, we grow as brothers, and we grow as men.

Evaluation

We evaluated LXG in several ways. We had members participate in a research study led by the Brooks Research Group of the 14 pilot schools participating in the Lilly study. We also conducted our own pre- and post-experience survey to men in LXG. Finally, we had extensive conversations with the mentors of the groups.

Mentor Reports

An important way in which we evaluated the program was with extensive exit interviews with mentors after the conclusion of their year with groups. Having a mature, adult perspective on the group's experience was insightful.

Mentors report that LXG is succeeding in offering undergraduate men on campus an experience of depth and interiority that they normally would not encounter. One student said, "I have other close friends on campus, but I have said things in LXG that I've not shared with anyone else at UP." This experience of depth, according to mentors, encourages personal growth among members—mentors have seen students grow in empathy and their ability to engage in sensitive, personal conversation. One mentor said that he is seeing the men in his group grow in being comfortable with self-disclosure and being in personal, close relationships with other men. They are gaining the skill to be able to ask personal questions in a way that honors and respects the vulnerable nature of self-disclosure.

LXG also brings a diversity of men together for personal sharing, and this diversity also encourages growth. The general experience in the residence halls is that people sort into groups that have something in common. The LXG groups throw together men from a variety of different backgrounds. The mentors report that this diversity benefits men—they get the chance to get to know men that they would not normally engage deeply. This diversity offers a variety of perspectives that enhance and deepen discussions. Mentors report that men came into their 1st-year groups thinking that they knew each other and quickly realized that they did not. They quickly grew in their appreciation for a common depth or interiority that they all shared—this led to a sense of solidarity and fellowship. The fellowship, in turn, helped to create an even safer place for vulnerability and affirmation. "The takeaway was that these men became a band of brothers," said one mentor.

One result of LXG group meetings is a clarification of values that happens with the storytelling. The mentors report that they are modeling the clarifying questions part of the meeting at first, but then members start to follow up with questions of their own over time. Essentially, what is happening here is that members are being taught how to read into their experience—to examine their stories to see what contributes to meaning and depth. Seeing mentors read into their stories helps them start to read into each others' stories. And, more importantly, they start reading into their own stories—they start connecting dots and seeing how they have become the person they are now and how they'd like to become the person they want to be.

Mentors report that values are an important part of the conversations they have—values emerge as an explicit topic, and the development and focusing of values happen as a result of the storytelling at these meetings. One mentor said, "I appreciated the opportunity to walk with these men as they explored what defines them as human beings and as males. It is an honor to walk with them as they come to understand what it means to be a man in the world today."

It is also important that this value building happens in the context of community, because members are able to express commonality and solidarity with one another. They see that they are not the only ones that have certain experiences or thoughts, and they are able to affirm one another and find support.

Though LXG is not explicitly spiritual in its structure or language, it is giving men a chance to experience conversation and community on the deeper, personal, interior level that is within the realm of spirituality. Our experience is that most college men are not interested in gathering to talk about spirituality. In this sense, LXG is a foot in the door—it creates the space where men can talk about what is most important to them. For some, what is most important to them is spirituality or religion. For others it is not, but the group opens the door to the possibility of spiritual engagement for men who would not otherwise seek it out. One mentor said that, while the group's primary experience was personal sharing, not explicit conversation about spiritual questions, "the depth of sharing and the commitment and community these men had *felt* spiritual." Another mentor reported that he saw "something inherently spiritual in their search for meaning—in their search for important experiences."

On the question of whether or not LXG actually helps men mature and engage in campus life or if LXG attracts men who are already mature and engaged, mentors report that they think it is a little of both. Some men clearly would have had conversations of depth and meaning on their own, but other men would not have found this without LXG. Mentors conclude, however, that LXG accelerates this maturation and engagement for men. Freshmen and sophomores are having discussions and asking questions that mentors would expect men to have as upperclassmen.

The dynamic that happens between the mentors and the group is essential to the success of the group. Mentors model good group sharing and set the tone for the group. But, beyond that, mentors also provide a level of validation for these young men—just knowing adult males and being known by them is an important experience for these men. The modeling that mentors offer, especially in the first two meetings in the 1st year, really sets a tone and example for members to follow when it is their turn to lead.

Pairing of mentors is an important factor in group success. The groups that thrived had a mentor pair that really clicked. The pair worked together as peers and had a good balance between the two of them as introverts and extroverts. This made it a rewarding experience for the mentors—both to be part of the group and to work together with another staff member. The groups that did not thrive had a number of factors play into their experience, but one could have been poor mentor pairing. In both groups, the mentors were not the same age/experience level, so they did not connect as readily as they could have. Also, this mismatch led to the dynamic where one mentor was mentoring both the group and the other mentor. In addition to balance in age/experience, it seems to be a good idea to have variety in backgrounds from mentors—for example, pairing a celibate with a married person is fruitful because they have very different perspectives.

Pre- and Posttesting

We evaluated LXG by using an 11-item survey that included both open-ended and multiple choice items. The survey was distributed to all LXG mentors to administer to their small groups at the group's first meeting in October and at the group's last meeting in April. In the pretest, 19 students participated; 14 completed the posttest.

In our evaluation, the following variables were assessed: sense of community, ability to identify and disclose personal beliefs and feelings, acceptance of other's beliefs, and value of spiritual growth. It was predicted that a sense of community, the ability to identify and disclose beliefs, the acceptance of other's beliefs, and the value of spiritual growth would all increase as a result of participation in LXG.

There was a significant increase in men reporting that they felt a "strong sense of community" (58% pretest, 79% posttest). While there is some correlation between the students' participation in LXG and an increased sense of community, there are a number of other variables that could contribute to this as well: the natural socialization of students as they progress through college, participation in other groups, or simple maturation as the participants grow in adult social skills.

It may not be too far off the mark to attribute this increased sense of community to LXG, however. We asked men who reported a strong sense of community on campus to list the factors that led to that awareness. In the pretest, the top three factors were residential community activities in the halls, athletic events or activities, and clubs or student government. In the posttest, the top three factors were residence life, LXG, and clubs or student government. This increase is particularly notable because the question assessing this outcome was open-ended, not multiple choice.

It was not surprising to find that, in the pretest, residential communities and sports ranked high in developing a sense of community for participants. It was interesting to observe that in the posttest, sports fell off the top three list of factors contributing to a sense of community. This may suggest that, while sports are initially an important factor in building community among college males, it may take a back seat to other forms of community later on.

There were moderate increases (between 0 and 10% increases on a self-reported scale) in men reporting an ability to know who they are, identify their own beliefs, share their beliefs with others, and be open to the beliefs of others. There seemed to be no significant difference in the ability of the men to share their beliefs with their peers or with other men, though the general trend was an increase in their comfort in sharing beliefs with peers and a decrease in comfort in sharing beliefs with adults and authority figures such as mentors and teachers. Again, there might be a number of reasons for this growth because men are developing in many ways during these years. LXG doesn't seem to have hampered that development and probably contributed to it.

One significant finding of our study is that men in LXG reported small but consistent decreases in spiritual growth (a desire to grow spiritually, identify their sense of community with spiritual organizations, and disclose with spiritual mentors). This unexpected decrease may be due to the lack of explicitly spiritual language in LXG. We ask men to talk about their relationship to God, and they are welcome to state that they do not relate to God, but, aside from personal disclosure, there is no spiritual or religious agenda to the discussions. Many students and most of the mentors include religion or spirituality in their comments, but it is not mandatory.

The men in LXG participated in a study conducted by the Catherine Brooks Research Group that surveyed the men's approach to vocational discernment. Of the 27 students surveyed at UP, 15 (56%) answered the first survey and 11 (41%) answered the second. Eight students answered both surveys (30%). All responses to these questions showed a decrease in interest and experience with spiritual or vocational exploration activities. There was a decrease in the percentage of LXG men who consider themselves to be persons of faith or someone who thinks about how faith can shape his life, especially around vocation discernment. LXG men from UP reported decreases in all of the vocational and faith-life measures surveyed by Brooks.

One possibility for the decrease in spirituality is that, early in college, students often distance themselves from religion as a part of their task of establishing their identities as independent from their parents' traditions and familiar institutions. Future studies might reveal whether this trend persists for LXG participants—it may be that the kind of spiritual growth that LXG encourages is well-integrated into experiences of community and self-disclosure and may not emerge as specifically spiritual growth until later years. We will administer the same posttest to groups as they exit the program as seniors, and results from that survey will reveal the full impact of 4 years of formation in LXG.

Another explanation for the decrease in interest in spirituality is that because LXG is not explicitly spiritual, members may not associate their experiences with spiritual language. It seems as though if we asked men in LXG to describe a spiritual experience, they might think about some kind of experience of transcendence or prayer. It may not occur to them to describe as spiritual the process of coming to a greater awareness of self, of one's life story and its meaning, and of community. Future studies might do well to exclude religious as well as spiritual language in favor of language that identifies interiority, self-reflection, community, identity, and finding meaning in one's experiences.

We evaluated this decrease in interest in spirituality against the results of the spiritual social norms survey conducted by the Men's Center at St. John's University. The social norms survey did not track changes in spirituality through the year—it was simply a snapshot of the male perception of spirituality on campus midway through the 2008–2009 academic year. This snapshot reveals something distinctive about UP and its context in the Pacific Northwest.

In all but one spirituality measure in the social norms survey, UP men reported lower mean scores for themselves and their peers than the average of the seven participating schools. Men at UP scored themselves and their peers lower, except for the area in which they were asked about fulfilling their spiritual needs through attending religious services. In this area, they scored themselves and their peers higher than the average from all participating schools.

These results indicate that, more than at other universities across the nation, UP men see religion as the most important way in which any person might fulfill their spiritual needs. Indeed, among the four measures of how they fulfill their spiritual needs, UP men indicated that, for themselves and their peers, religious services were more important than nature, literature, or athletic events.

It is our conclusion that men at UP tend to see spirituality as more closely aligned with religion. Therefore, when asked if LXG fosters spiritual growth, members would be more likely to say that it does not, because there is no explicitly religious element to the program aside from what members disclose about themselves. It is our conviction, however, that the four values that LXG fosters—brotherhood, justice, truth, and authentic masculinity—are inherently spiritual. It is our hope that this conviction is vindicated when members are surveyed as seniors about the formation they went through in LXG.

Conclusions

Factors that contributed to the success of LXG at UP are as follows:

- *WE BASED THE GROUP ON RELATIONSHIP NOT ACTIVITY.* The fundamental thing LXG offers men on campus is a safe space together for self-disclosure. The other activities all flow from this core. When we tried to reach men by programming male-centered activities, it failed because there was no core of relationship to draw from.
- *IT IS EASIEST TO ESTABLISH CORE RELATIONSHIPS WITH FRESHMEN.* Freshmen have not established significant relationships on campus yet, even within their halls, so they are free to commit and bond with a group. Freshmen in LXG had, within the first semester of arriving at UP, found a group of fellow men who they could count on as having an interest in their personal development for the rest of their undergraduate experience. Starting as freshmen gave the men the chance to establish a circle of support that would support them in the long-term, and the 4-year commitment provided security for the men to be authentic with each other.
- *STORYTELLING IS ESSENTIAL.* What is more, it is important to offer men on college campuses the space to safely share personal stories, where self-reflection and interiority are not out of the norm. The act of telling and listening to personal stories encourages value development—students start to read into their own and one another's stories to find that which provides depth and lasting meaning.
- *ADULT MALE VALIDATION IS IMPORTANT.* Healthy, well-integrated male mentors model interiority, self-reflection, respectful personal conversation, and listening for the group.
- *DEVELOPING STUDENTS AS LEADERS IS ESSENTIAL TO RECRUITING AND DEVELOPMENT.* At least half, if not more, of the men who joined LXG this year joined as a direct result of one student leader's invitation. Letting students take control of the group's identity and values was also fundamental to our success so far.
- *DIVERSITY ENCOURAGES PERSONAL GROWTH.* College students self-sort and surround themselves with friends who share similar perspectives. Encountering other perspectives in a safe context of personal conversation helps men grow.

REFERENCE

Longwood, W.M., Muesse, M.W., & Schipper, W. (2004, Fall). Men, spirituality, and the collegiate experience. *New Directions for Student Services: Developing Effective Programs and Services for College Men, 107,* 87-95.

15

THE SIENA COLLEGE MEN'S SPIRITUALITY GROUPS

W. MERLE LONGWOOD

In the fall semester of 2007, Fr. William Beaudin, OFM, college chaplain at Siena College, and I agreed to launch an experiment in which we would serve as conveners/facilitators of a men's spirituality group at the college, modeled after the men's spirituality groups developed at St. John's University in Collegeville, Minnesota. We had studied the report on the St. John's experience (Longwood, Muesse, Schipper, 2004) and had had extended conversations with Fr. William Schipper, who provided detailed information about the St. John's experience in which he had been involved from near its beginning, during a visit to Siena's campus. We decided we would begin our experiment by making two modifications to the St. John's model. First, the co-facilitators would be a friar and a lay faculty member, in contrast to the experience at St. John's where both facilitators were usually monks in the Benedictine Order, the community that founded their university. We anticipated that, if we continued this program, we would encourage this same arrangement for recruiting co-facilitators for subsequently developed men's spirituality groups at Siena. Second, the initial group at Siena College would be comprised of college men from different classes rather than just the class of 1st-year students, which had been the pattern established at St. John's University. There was not any particular rationale for having this first group include college men from a diversity of classes, except that the young men who responded to the invitations we had extended came from different classes and there were not enough students from any one class to form a viable group.

The groundwork, including the recruitment of students, was completed during the fall semester of 2007, and the group held its first meeting early in the spring semester of 2008. At the first meeting, we facilitators emphasized the importance of confidentiality, commitment, and communication, following the model that had been successfully promulgated at St. John's University (Longwood, Muesse, Schipper, 2004). Those who came to the initial meeting agreed to meet every other week for the remainder of the semester, although, as the semester progressed, we facilitators noted that there was a far greater amount of absenteeism than we had hoped would be the case, given that everyone who came to the first meeting had agreed to make commitment to participate in group meetings a priority.

SIENA COLLEGE'S PROPOSED PILOT PROJECT AND ITS IMPLEMENTATION

When we learned that Siena College would be invited to propose a pilot project to participate in the Lilly Endowment Grant on Increasing College Male Involvement in Vocational Discernment Activities, under the auspices of St. John's Center for Men's Leadership and Service at Collegeville, Minnesota, we decided to incorporate this experiment at Siena College into a proposed pilot project and to expand on this initial effort, which we articulated in terms of the following goals and a summary of how they were (or were not) implemented.

In the fall semester of 2008 and again in the fall semester of 2009, we propose to establish at least two men's spirituality groups: one (or more) for first year students and one (or more) for upperclassmen.

We established a men's spirituality group for first year students in the fall semester of 2008 and again in the fall semester of 2009. The men who agreed to become a part of these groups have done so with an understanding that they are making a commitment to continue to be a part of their group throughout their 4-year college careers. The group established in fall 2008 began with 12 students and has continued with 11 of its original participants. The group that began in fall 2009 has 12 students and may invite 1 additional student, a Palestinian Christian not yet on the campus when the group was formed, to join this group in spring semester 2010. We did not establish any new groups for upperclassmen, but we have continued to recruit upperclassmen to fill the vacancies created by graduating seniors in the group that we established spring semester 2008, so it has remained as a group of approximately eight students. This group's initial problem of excessive absenteeism has not continued in subsequent semesters.

We will seek to identify potential members during the 1st month of the 2008–2009 and the 1st month of the 2009–2010 academic years through a polling of faculty, academic advisors, and friars-in-residence.

We decided to do this in October rather than in September each fall semester so that those who would nominate students would know them well. We were especially impressed by the number and quality of students who were nominated by the faculty who teach the two-semester Foundations Sequence for 1st-year students. Because these classes have a small number of students and are designed to be intensively interactive, the faculty members get to know their students well.

In each of these fall semesters, we will invite the identified potential members to a festive meal where we will show-case the men's spirituality program, drawing upon past members of the pilot program to speak about their experience of the men's group.

We did this in each of these fall semesters, and it was a significant factor in the successful recruitment of young men into these groups, which will be confirmed in the sample comments from 1st-year students that follow these comments on fulfillment of goals.

We will seek to find conveners/facilitators from within the friar community and lay faculty in the college, with a goal of always having each group served by two adult mentors. As we put together these teams of conveners/facilitators, we will attempt to have at least one friar serving in each of the teams of mentors.

We were successful in recruiting such teams of conveners/facilitators for each of these new groups. In fall semester 2008 we recruited Fr. Daniel Dwyer, OFM, professor of history, and Dr. Dmitry Burshteyn, associate professor of psychology, to co-facilitate the new group for that semester. In fall semester 2009 we recruited Br. Walter Liss, OFM, visiting instructor in computer science, and Dr. Charles Seifert, professor of marketing and management, to co-facilitate the new group beginning that semester. We achieved our goal of having one friar and one lay faculty member in each team of co-facilitators.

We will encourage the groups to meet on a biweekly basis throughout the 2008–2009 and 2009–2010 academic years.

Once the groups were formed and held their first meeting, each agreed to meet biweekly throughout the academic year. Under the guidance of the co-facilitators, each group determined the time it would meet, usually for about 1 hour each meeting.

We will plan a weekend, off-campus retreat for group members for spring 2009.

We did not plan any off-campus retreats, but we did arrange an end-of-the-academic-year dinner in May 2009, especially honoring the graduating seniors, for the group that began in spring semester 2008, and we arranged an end-of-the-semester dinner in December 2009 for the group that began in fall semester 2008.

We will plan a service-oriented activity for group members for spring 2009.

We did not plan a service-oriented activity specifically for the group members, but we are aware that several members in the group that began in spring semester 2008 are significantly involved in service-oriented activities. One group member, for example, has taken a major leadership role in moving Siena College to become a Fair Trade Campus and has won Student Senate approval for this plan.

We will plan to have some members from each of the groups attend the 2009 Conference on Men at St. John's University in Collegeville, Minnesota, and while they are there we will involve them in a workshop that brings together men from St. John's University, Siena College, and Rhodes College as part of a research project that has been developed and will be published by Fr. William C. Shipper, OSB (St. John's University), myself (Dr. Merle Longwood, Siena College), and Dr. Mark Muesse (Rhodes College).

Beaudin, Samuel Ogden (a student in our group), and I attended the 2009 Conference on Men at St. John's University. Due to a variety of factors, including Muesse's withdrawing from participation in the research project, the design of the research project has been changed, and Schipper and I will be conducting interviews on selected campuses during spring semester 2010 rather than attempting to bring college men from several campuses together at a single workshop.

Sample of Responses of Students Invited to the First-Year Student Recruitment Dinner

One Foundations Sequence faculty member made available comments provided by three students who had been invited and attended the Student Recruitment Dinner held on November 4, 2009. These are excerpts of the responses they wrote as they chose to tie in their attendance at the dinner to a class assignment, giving a sense of how the students being recruited perceived the importance of the men's spirituality groups in the lives of those students who spoke about what it had meant for them. Some went further and indicated how it would impact, or already had impacted, their own lives.

Student A

Recently I was invited to a men's spirituality group meeting. I had no idea what this event was pertaining to at first[,] but when I came to Siena one of my goals was to regain [my] religious side. When I received the letter inviting me[,] I was immediately interested and very excited. So I went to the dinner and sat down. I sat with a professor of business who is helping start this new program. He immediately started asking questions and talking to us all, making us feel comfortable. We ate a nice, catered meal and continued to talk until the presentation began. A number of current students stood up and talked to us about the program.... [O]ne of the presenters talked about spirituality as a whole. He said that when he joined this group he was having a hard time with a lot of aspects of his life and had lost faith in God. He talked about the importance of spirituality and the impact it can have in [one's] life. Spirituality, he explained, isn't necessarily a belief in a Catholic God or a Protestant God or Yahweh, but it is the belief that there is something bigger than yourself out there to help you, something that can carry you when times are rough. He said that he was a very angry person because of [the] sad events that he had to deal with[;] however, after he joined this men's spirituality group, he found out that he had hope for humanity [and] love returned to his heart and he became more in touch with God again. He started to do nice things again and preached the importance of religion to all.

This story really touched my heart. When my grandmother died [when I was] in ninth grade I lost a lot of faith and lost touch with my religion. When I came to Siena, I hoped the Franciscan brotherhood here as well as the spirituality around campus could help me find religion again. Unfortunately, it didn't. When we had to read about Francis and the leper or Francis and the wolf, I wished I had the kind of faith Francis had[,] this overbearing love for God that led him to devote his life to living in God's image. When he took the leper and kissed him, it showed that all people are equal in God's eyes and deserve his love, even those who are down and out. It showed that faith in the Lord can lead one to love all, even if it means possible irreparable harm.

So why am I choosing this as my outside event[?] Well, you see, I was that leper. I was the person who was down and out[; the] person who felt the world had turned against [him] and who was starting to lose all faith in God. It seemed, at times, that maybe I was the undesirable, that a higher power had turned his back on me and decided that I deserved no happiness. Well[,] this group is my St. Francis. It sized me up, noticed that I wasn't helpless, that all I needed was someone, something to save me. This group is the kiss on the hand, rejuvenating me and letting me know I am still loved by some.

So I was the first to sign up officially for the group.... I asked the professor at my table if I could sign up right away. I know I need this group. This will change my [life] or[,] at least, help me out in a time of need right now. I know this will help bring me closer to God and to the good, loving side of me that I prefer to show, rather than the quiet, miserable side the world has seen recently. As Francis showed, a little compassion and empathy, such as to the wolf, can lead to a much more peaceful and happy place. I am more than ready to help this world became happier and more peaceful, hopefully in Francis's image.

Student B

After being invited by a Siena faculty member, I recently attended a dinner about a local group formed on campus. The goal was to discuss a newly created group called the [Men's Spirituality Group] and to persuade any freshman, who was invited, to join. Friars and current members made their presence known by greeting anyone who walked in.... Once everyone settled down, the meeting began. Everyone listened to current members discuss what the group was about and how it ha[d] influenced their lives. The commonality in every story was the emphasis on how strong of an influence the group ha[d] made on their life decisions and how it ha[d] made them [better persons.]

Following the [members'] discussion of the group, the friars who were in attendance spoke on behalf of the group.... They talked about how God plays such an important role in life and how the youth here at Siena... should continue moving forward with His message.... However, the group does not just focus on the Catholic religion[;] it welcomes, with open arms, people of all faiths to the group. It shows just how loving the Franciscan religion [is] and how the group has a bigger meaning than simply trying to develop their own religion and would like to see the good in everyone.

Continuing with the Franciscan religion, one can look at a story[,] written by the man himself, Francis of Assisi[,] [e]ntitled *Blessed Francis Leads a Wolf to Become Very Tame*[.] Francis tells a story about how his village was deeply afraid of a wolf that was terrorizing the people outside of the border. Francis, being a man who put all his trust in God, went out to the wolf and used him to resolve this issue by making a compromise. By the power of God, the wolf agreed and Francis fixed any scare the village might have. Amazed by his accomplishment, the village was grateful and believed in Francis. As the story goes, the wolf ended up dying[,] and the village that was once [scared] became saddened by his absence. But the story, which may or may not be true, demonstrates the general idea that God and his power is something many can believe in. Once his power was displayed through Francis, everyone believed in this idea.

After receiving the invitation, I was very skeptical on whether or not I should follow through and actually attend the meeting. I would have felt guilty if not at least giving the group a chance, and in the end it was a great decision. After hearing what current members had to say about God and spirituality here at Siena, it became both captivating and appealing to a lot of the members in the audience. Comparable to Francis of Assisi, the power of God was fully displayed by both the members and the friars.... Almost every person in the audience who was asked to attend ended up joining the group[,] and [that] shows just how strong the relationship is between our community and God. The village that Francis saved from the wolf is very similar to the audience. They believed in God after Francis displayed how much He could do, and the audience, including myself, believed in God after hearing the stories from current members and how much spirituality can benefit one's life.

STUDENT C

Earlier this semester, I was nominated to join the Men's Spirituality Group on campus. On first thought, I thought that it was not for me because I am not a spiritual person and I did not feel like talking about my feeling[s] every week. I am not the type of guy that any of my friends would picture to join a men's group on campus. I decided to go to the first meeting because of the various letters and [e-mails] that were sent telling me to go. The way they pulled me in was with the promise of good food. Sitting down at a table with about [10] strange guys was not as awkward as I thought. Being able to talk about anything without anyone judging me was different than most things I have ever been a part of. Each person in the group then has [his] own impact on the society as a whole. In the Men's Spirituality Group, members are encouraged to develop a sense of who they really are.

Joining the Men's Spirituality Group on campus has taken examination of myself to a new level. I would not say that I am more [religious] but rather just more open to new ideas and expressing my feelings about myself.

These three responses illustrate how these 1st-year students invited to consider participation in a group perceived that those already in a group had found the experience providing significant opportunities to explore their own spirituality in the presence of their peers. In fact, a number of the benefits perceived by these 1st-year students effectively relate to the values that are highlighted in several of the statements that articulate what Siena College's mission and purpose relative to hoped-for impact on students' lives.

MISSION AND PURPOSE OF THE COLLEGE AS THE CONTEXT FOR SIENA'S PILOT PROJECT

Siena College is a coeducational, liberal-arts college with an enrollment of 3,000 undergraduate students, and 76% of the students live on campus. Its 166-acre campus is located 2 miles north of Albany, New York, and less than 3 hours from New York City and Boston.

Siena's founding tradition is Catholic and Franciscan and

> this tradition remains alive at Siena where it engages students, faculty, staff, and administrators of diverse backgrounds. Siena is a pluralistic community where the population includes not only Catholics, but other Christians, Jews, Muslims, Hindus, and secular humanists, to give some examples. All are able to own and contribute to Siena's Franciscan identity while recognizing that not everyone appropriates the tradition in the same way. The importance of the friars as witnesses to the Franciscan charism and to the continued presence of the founding tradition is crucial to Siena's Franciscan identity. The involvement of so many different members of the College in the reality of our Franciscan identity may set us apart from colleges where religious identity is more narrowly defined. (Siena College's Catholic Franciscan Tradition Statement)

The faculty and administration as well as the staff and services seek to "cultivate an environment that integrates the values and teachings of St. Francis and St. Clare of Assisi to enhance and support student learning and development and to prepare graduates for lives of discernment, civic engagement and professional growth" (Siena College's Student Affairs Mission Statement). The College's Catholic and Franciscan values "serve as a lens through which to view the world, our way of being in relationship with each other and where the potential of each student is affirmed" (Siena College's Student Affairs Mission Statement).

As a learning community, Siena College "is committed to a student-centered education emphasizing dynamic faculty-student interaction" (Siena College's Mission Statement), and our pilot project builds on that commitment. As a Franciscan college, Siena is committed to fostering "faith in a personal and provident God" as well as "a community where members work together in friendship and respect" (Siena College's Mission Statement). In our pilot project we provide a forum in which young men can explore their inner lives, articulate what they believe, and support one another in their quest for meaning and purpose in their lives. Our major innovation in this pilot project has been the development of a men's spirituality group program, which we believe enables men to explore their own experiences of spirituality grounded in a mutually respectful community.

As a Catholic college, Siena is committed to advancing "not only the intellectual growth of its students, but their spiritual, religious and ethical formation as well" (Siena College's Mission Statement). Making these spirituality groups available to our male undergraduates has enabled these men to take ownership of their spiritual, religious, and ethical formation through mentoring and peer support.

When we applied to become one of the institutions that would receive a grant as part of the program initiated by St. John's Center for Men's Leadership and Service at Collegeville, Minnesota, we were aware that we were not like a number of the other institutions that would be involved in this program that have already been involved in a Programs for the Theological Exploration of Vocation program. Nevertheless, we were confident that vocational awareness would continue to be a concern for many of us at the college.

THEOLOGICAL EXPLORATION OF VOCATION AT SIENA COLLEGE

At Siena College, we construe vocational awareness in the broadest sense as well as in a narrower sense. That is, we seek to assist students in their search for a sense of vocation, mission, or purpose of life. Our preliminary discussions with students indicate that most of them view vocation as something more than a job or a career. As they develop life skills (listening without judgment, sharing openly with others, helping others), we believe it helps them focus their lives. In the narrower sense, we anticipated that a few among those involved in the pilot project might explore their vocations more specifically in relation to a calling to ministry, the priesthood, or another religious profession. In this latter sense of exploration of vocation, because the college relies on the presence of Franciscan friars on campus to assist lay faculty, administrators, students, and staff in articulating and embodying the Franciscan vision and values of the institution, the college does have an interest in promoting specifically Franciscan vocations. A men's spirituality group program, we believed, could provide male students who might be entertaining a call to religious life with a positive experience of a spiritually grounded fraternity and a sounding board in discerning a possible religious vocation. At the very least, such a group would provide a safe environment wherein male students could explore those deeper desires that so often point one in the direction of his life's work.

Preliminary Assessment of the Pilot Project

Beyond the students' comments excerpted above, we have not completed our qualitative assessment of our ongoing pilot project. We plan to use a set of 23 assessment questions that Schipper and I have developed to use in interviews that we will be conducting on the campuses of several institutions involved in this grant on Increasing College Male Involvement in Vocational Discernment Activities to determine the effectiveness of the programs at these institutions.

As they relate to Siena College, a coeducational institution with a Franciscan tradition, these questions will assist us in discerning what the significance of the values that are specific to the Franciscan tradition might be in the interpreted experience of the men involved in the pilot project at Siena College. The findings we obtained at St. John's University were primarily qualitative rather than quantitative, which seemed appropriate for St. John's University then as it does for Siena College now.

References

Longwood, W.M., Muesse, M.W., & Schipper, W. (2004). Men, spirituality, and the collegiate experience. In G.E. Kellom (Ed.), *New directions for student services:* Developing effective programs and services for college men (pp. 87-95). San Francisco: Jossey-Bass.
Siena College's Catholic Franciscan Tradition: http://www.siena.edu/pages/3479.asp
Siena College's Mission: http://www.siena.edu/pages/1180.asp
Siena College's Student Affairs Mission: http://www.siena.edu/pages/2718.asp

16

MEN TALKING: THE "CORE FOUR" AND MORE
THE WAGNER COLLEGE MEN'S PROJECT

MILES GROTH, WILLIAM JOCK, ANDREW HAGER, AND KYLE GLOVER

INTRODUCTION (MILES GROTH)

The Wagner College Men's Project is notable in that, from proposal to implementation, its essential leadership was in the hands of the students its findings are meant to serve as I learned about best practices for working with college men. My role as faculty mentor has been to respond to individual student interest in the project when I identified it and to do what was necessary to make it possible for a cohort of such students to meet, talk, and reflect on what it means to be a man and to articulate what each perceives his calling in life to be.

Early in the spring semester of 2007, mention of the Lilly Endowment program in a class on the psychology of men led a student to ask me what participation in such a project might mean to him and to other men on campus. From that point on, in every case, it was a student's commitment to me—and then, more important, to each other—that gave the project its life. That student, William Jock, writes about his experience below. The students who first participated in the project—its "core four"—developed unique friendships, and by word of mouth the group expanded and continues to grow even during "life after Lilly."

This report on the Wagner College Men's Project consists of sections by key figures at its inception and as the grant period drew to a close during fall semester 2009. At that time, one member of the core four, Andrew Hager, prepared an overview of the project as it had evolved. Hager's contribution is followed by an account of the preparation and acceptance of the project proposal by William Jock. Another member of the group, Kyle Glover, who also spoke at the 2009 spring meeting of participating colleges at St. John's University provides some reflections on his experience with the project. Finally, I offer some closing comments on the results of the project and the newly formed Men's Center at Wagner College.

THE WAGNER COLLEGE MEN'S PROJECT (ANDREW HAGER)

While at work in my small home town in Maine during the summer of 2008, I was contacted by my friend and professor, Dr. Miles Groth. He came to me with a proposal, asking if I were interested in heading up a men's group on our small New York City campus. I quickly said yes, excited about the challenge and opportunity but at the same time anxious about what would be expected of me and what I would be able to contribute. While I knew I would be able to offer my own life experience and leadership skills, it was evident that our group needed a clear-cut mission, something we could always refocus on and come back to as a point of reference. It was then that former Wagner student, Billy Jock, was able to give us a hand, because he had already written a mission statement for the accepted proposal for a project here at Wagner submitted by Dr. Groth. According to the mission statement, the project would

- encourage men to model spiritually and ethically grounded manhood;
- reach out to young men, one by one, as individuals, to evoke the deep, underlying concern for their inner lives as well as their public personas;
- provide an environment on campus in which young men could take the lead in locating appropriate places, occasions, and means to discuss what is basic to their lives as men; and
- put in place structured opportunities for Wagner men to grow by mentoring young boys.

This was something I could not only work with but could take to heart and truly believe in myself! It was now my task to find a few other good young men at Wagner College who also believed in this mission.

The Group

Located in the fifth borough of New York City, Staten Island, Wagner College is on Grymes Hill, overlooking the Lower Bay of New York and the Verrazano Bridge. Our small liberal arts school consists of just under 2,000 undergraduate students with a male-to-female ratio of roughly 35/65. The notable gender ratio was a key reason for the formation of the pilot project. We (the core four) wanted to understand why men were becoming so outnumbered on our campus. More important, the few of us involved soon realized that the men on campus did not know each other. Yes, most people fell into cliques (about which many on campus had their reservations), but some felt completely disconnected from the other men on campus. It was time for us to explore ourselves and each other while forming intimate relationships. While Wagner College had a number of groups for men (fraternities, athletic teams, and various clubs), for whatever reason there was still a constant feeling of division among males. There was no common ground, no place in physical or psychological space, where men of all backgrounds and interests could feel a bond that was beyond special interests and cliques. Here the core four felt we could make a difference. While each of us had his own special interests, there soon existed a common bond among us that brought about a kind of synergy.

The fall of 2008 marked the beginning of my junior year and the project. A recent departure from playing football left me plenty of time to focus on finding guys on campus to carry out the Wagner College Men's Project. With an introduction from Dr. Groth, I was able to recruit a unique fellow by the name of Kevin Burke, a senior returning from a 3-year hiatus of sorts. Next I was able to add another senior, Dave Hammill, a guy well-respected across campus for his work in our green community and his overall friendly demeanor. Finally, I wanted one last member, someone my age, and found him in a fellow philosophy major, Jonathan Badiali, an insightful thinker, who rounded out the core four. With that we were able to begin our journey together.

The core four soon began meeting often, usually once a week for a few hours. The day or the time was flexible so as to make room for everyone, but it seemed that usually every Tuesday we would meet in the lower-level seminar room of Parker Hall, an old stone building full of character from the outside. The four of us would arrive, one by one, around 7:30 p.m., eat some dinner together, and propose different questions for the night's discussion. Each member had ample opportunity to speak and be heard while the wheels of the others' minds could easily been seen turning. Here it is important to note that we were meeting on our own time, under our own guidelines, with our own motivations. There were no incentives here for guys giving up time—no class credit, no T-shirts—just the satisfaction of exploring our inner selves and getting to know other men on campus on a much more intimate level. We were four guys who simply believed this was important.

Our first meetings began simply. We each gave some background about ourselves, telling as much or as little as we wanted. Surprisingly (to me at least), most poured their guts out, in relief it seemed. We all finally had a place to share ourselves with other open-minded men.

At every meeting our main focus was building relationships among each other and with ourselves. Ultimately, we felt the best way to accomplish this was through the simple, yet dying, art of conversation. This, of course, is face-to-face, unlike most communications in today's modern world, which take place through some mechanical means, such as a phone or a computer. Sometimes a topic (or topics) was chosen for discussion, based on current local or national events affecting the landscape of manhood or even more general areas, such as art, religion, psychology, and philosophy. Members were asked to speak their minds as freely and openly as possible while standing up for what they believed in, arguing their points, taking responsibility for their views, and, most important, keeping an open mind for reevaluating their views. Each of us was challenged on a weekly basis to dig through his lifetime of experience, thought and feeling, and put into words his position on a given subject. Our own thoughts, words, and actions seemed to prove more relevant than any blog or speech could. We were learning about each other and ourselves in the most personal manner. We were learning how we ought to live our lives, learning what our true callings were from men our very own age. It was often an arduous task, but it fully benefited the development of each of us and created bonds among us.

Word of our group began to spread around campus, and other guys began to attend meetings. A few meetings had eight or nine guys in attendance. As a small group on a small campus, we fully understood that changing the landscape of manhood for the good in America (especially on college campuses) would be an uphill battle for which there is no one simple, easy solution. I do, however, truly believe that the small but significant step of creating tight, intimate bonds among a few males in small groups is the place to start to understand college men and determine what may aid in their revival as responsible and active participants in the college and larger community.

I believe what is in place based on the Wagner College Men's Project will continue to flourish and grow, breaking down walls that have divided us. A change in the look of positive manhood in America must begin with critical thought, constructive emotion, and productive action, but, before this can happen, vital changes must begin with small groups of men such as our core four or more, sitting around a table, learning about themselves and each other and about what strong relationships with other men can mean to them.

Mentoring

At the same time, we began piecing together a connection with a local community service group, United Activities Unlimited. We were put in touch with a junior high school social studies teacher who linked us with four 8th-grade boys who were identified as at risk for one reason or another and were making that challenging move in adolescence from being a boy to being a young man. They needed a strong male influence in their lives. We set up contacts with the boys, whom we thought we could help and who at the same time could help us each learn about himself hands-on and in a reflective way.

In order to set up a meeting with one of the boys provided by a middle school teacher, each of us took a name and a phone number, hoping to contact the boy directly and in a personal manner through his parents. We wanted the boys to know that we wanted them to join us and that we cared about them as individuals. It was important to us that each boy knew he was wanted in this venture and that we were willing to devote our time to him. A small get-together was planned for us to meet up as a group and enjoy a laid-back morning of food and fun, including attending a Wagner football game. But, much to our disappointment, only two of the four kids were able to attend. We did the best we could with what we had, especially enjoying the day with a young, vibrant, and impressionable 13-year-old "Tommy" and attempting to break into the rock-hard, stoic personality of 15-year-old "Chip."

As the semester progressed, we planned and held more meetings with the kids, but, the entire time, our only steady attendee was fun and bouncy Tommy. He spent time with us on and off campus, from our own dorm lounge areas to the American Museum of Natural History, enjoying each meal along the way! Tommy was eager and enthusiastic, willing to try and do new things. We even taught him how to play Frisbee! For the four of us, guys who came from suburban or rural areas, this simple toy was a staple of our childhood, but our afternoon playing Frisbee with Tommy reminded all of us that not every boy is afforded the same opportunities. And while we knew that most kids, including Tommy, could have found the inexpensive toy, it was not something valued in his culture at his age. The simple tossing back and forth of a plastic disc was not valued there, something that many of us were taken aback by.

While we truly believed that our first mentoring efforts were not a complete failure, it was crucial to gain an understanding of why we experienced such a tough time. First, there was quite literally a lack of communication between us and some of the boys. Many of these boys had little, if any, access to a phone. For most, their family's financial system just would not allow for it. Few had landline phones, and those with a cell phone could use it only on a limited basis.

Second, and what we identified as the biggest factor, was the lack of support at home to participate in the program. With Tommy we witnessed a mother, grandmother, brother, and extended family, who encouraged him to be part of the program. For others, these support systems were absent. We could notice from simply talking to the mothers on the phone (none of these boys seemed to have a male figure in the home) that this was not a priority for them at the moment. This in some ways piggybacked on our lack of communication with the boys, since the mothers were unclear about whether the program would cost money, who exactly was involved, and what their child would be doing, even though this had all been outlined in a program letter and a consent form they received at school in September. None of us knew what these mothers had actually absorbed and what they had just brushed off.

Last, we understood that the local culture of the school the boys had attended for a few years to this point was already deeply engrained in many of the boys, and it would be a tough task to break down barriers or ask kids to do something that would be seen as uncool to their peers. Because we knew that our 15-year-old Chip was friends with our other two original prospects, it is likely that he was able to sway them into not joining us by using the simple but all-powerful tactic of peer pressure. We now understood that the ages of 14–15 may be too late to start mentoring at-risk boys.

Further Developments

Toward the end of September, with a number of meetings of the core four under our belts, we decided to look for another guy to help add new dynamics to the group. We saw that e-mail invitations did not work. With a specific guy in mind, I understood that the best way to communicate with him was to meet face to face. I introduced myself and gave him a rundown of our project. I explained to him why I thought it would be good for him, good for us, and good for the campus as a whole for him to attend. This approach, which is a standard with our group now, seems to work wonders. Nothing exceeds the power of talking to a guy face to face, looking him in the eye, and establishing a real connection with him. So it was that sophomore Kyle Glover, our fifth guy, was added.

The first semester of the project continued with much success. Our group fluctuated in size from week to week, almost always including our now core five and usually adding a few newcomers. Conversations varied from Wagner-related issues to broader political, religious, psychological, and philosophical topics. Perhaps our most compelling conversation, and the one that is continually revisited by us, was about what it means to be a man in America today. We felt that the topic related to ideas of our overall attempt to understand ourselves and each other as men. Time and time again we tested ideas and thoughts, bringing up stereotypes assigned to men over the past 60 years or so, and attempted to examine them in terms of today's world. Ideas would arise, and ideas would fall. Often, we simply could not come to a consensus about what it means to truly be a man in the world today. One should keep in mind that this came from the minds of students who were athletes, musicians, philosophers, scientists, artists, and historians. It was a subject that none of us took lightly and that we all thought about to ourselves and out loud, at meetings and in the dining hall.

We finally understood that this idea of manhood was a "white whale" we had all failed to capture. And so we were able to put aside what others expected of us and began to figure out what we expected of ourselves. None of us fit any ideal to the fullest. None of us could ever fully be able to fill another's mold. Our meetings set us free to form closer bonds with each other and open our hearts and minds to thoughts we had never before imagined we would talk about with other guys. We were inching closer to understanding the yearnings each male has in life and what he needs to do in order to fulfill them.

At the Inception of the Project (William Jock)

I was motivated to help start the Wagner pilot project primarily because of my reaction to perceptions about men that I had heard among peers, in the media, and in academia. At times I had felt shame at being a man, agreeing with people's negative generalizations and making efforts to distance myself from so-called hegemonic masculinity. However, by the time I became interested in starting the pilot project, I had begun to acknowledge a lack of understanding of these negative perceptions. Not only did I find many of the perceptions to be exaggerated or unfounded, but I also decided that the behaviors that deserved criticism did not deserve the anger that accompanied it.

I wanted to share the new pride and responsibility I felt about being a man by addressing these generalizations, dispelling the myths, and giving due attention to the characteristics and behaviors that endangered men's personal lives as well as the lives of those around them. I purposely sought to start a group of students with whom I was minimally acquainted and who, besides being men, had little in common with each other. I was largely concerned with addressing the perception that men did not talk about their feelings. Since this was one generalization in which I saw some validity, it was rewarding to watch my peers warm up to each other through common sentiments and novel personal perspectives.

In my postgraduate years, the lives of men continue to fascinate and concern me. My experience with the pilot project inspired me to start a men's group for the homeless and mentally ill members of the psychosocial club and soup kitchen at which I work. While this is a completely different experience from speaking with college students, the thoughts and feelings about what it means to be a man are consistent. Two words that always come up are *strength* and *responsibility*. I usually challenge men on this, asking: "Aren't these traits necessary to all humans, whether man or woman?" Few disagree, which leads me to probe them as to whether men have *more* pressure to be responsible and strong. Few respond. However, their experiences with drug use, depression, homelessness, crime, and divorce reflect their reaction to this pressure, though many people, including these men themselves, would attribute their behavior to weakness or irresponsibility.

Through these discussions and my daily experiences as a man, I have concluded that strength and responsibility are traits necessary to being a man. They are also traits necessary to being a woman, though men and women have different strengths and responsibilities based on what nature and society give them. Strength and responsibility are necessary for basic survival, but the words also have a spiritual application. I try to be strong and responsible in every situation, so for me it is both a matter of survival and a matter of spiritual growth. For me, spiritual growth is not detached from the practical applications of strength and responsibility, because for me spiritual growth is a practical matter. If I grow spiritually I will inevitably be more likely to survive in every sense of the word. If I grow as a man, I grow as a human.

IMPRESSIONS OF THE WAGNER COLLEGE MEN'S PROJECT (KYLE GLOVER)

What is the potential for men's groups on college campuses? To answer this I recall an experience I had as a member of one of these groups. A small group of us went on a retreat (one of three during the time of the project) to upstate New York, a refreshing breath of scenic air from the constant humming of New York City. Nestled away in the woods of Tivoli, New York, we spent the weekend learning about one another, especially pertaining to what we felt was our source of spirituality in life. Answers ranged from interest in the mystical druids of Celtic lore, to the irreplaceable feeling of connecting with a musical artist at a concert, to the awesome power felt when surrounded by nature. We spoke of what symbolized this spirituality to us. For some it was a piece of jewelry and for others an unforgettable memory. We found that among us a sense of spirituality had not been engendered by a set creed but by virtue of human experience. These conversations on humanistic spirituality continued throughout our stay in Tivoli, with each man giving a talk in a comfortable setting, deep in the woods, around the campfire, or playing cards with the group.

In one heartfelt story, a member of our group told us of how an emotional experience involving his uncle and football shaped him as a man. In front of his uncle, his toughest critic, my friend played one of the hardest games of his life. In the end the other team won but not before he gave his all to try and win. After the game, he went in tears to see his uncle, a man he respected so greatly he could hardly look him in the face. When they finally ran into each other, his uncle embraced him heartily to show his affection and how proud he was of how his nephew played. The story was emotional and by the end of it my friend's face was etched with feeling. Looking around at the other members of the group, I could see that not one of us was untouched. One of us was in tears. We spent time explaining how that story made us feel, with the man in tears explaining that the emotionality of the story overwhelmed him.

This is what strikes me as perhaps the greatest potential of these men's groups: the personal connections that can be fostered by not being afraid to share one's life experiences. When moved by stories such as the one told by my friend, we as men can begin to tear down some of the artificial walls of manliness that have been erected to deal with a sometimes unforgiving world. We can step off the stage and stop acting the role of man and instead begin to connect with the others around us, empowering us to become our own strong individuals. We can break down these empty walls and see the connection between each of us, our shared humanity. Strengthened by this humanistic spirituality, we may strongly have an impact on the world.

STATUS OF THE PROJECT AND PROSPECTS: LIFE AFTER LILLY (MILES GROTH)

The Wagner College Men's Project flourished, thanks to the jump start it was given by Gar Kellom and the largesse of the Lilly Endowment. The project's mission, early history, and feel have been described above by three of its founding brothers. I want to say a bit about what my part has been, what I have learned from the young men who initially participated in the project, and what can be expected in the coming years at Wagner.

I have always seen my part chiefly as a mentor and facilitator. These wonderful guys have been the leaders, and the project was alive and well because of their commitment to each other and to the project. The proposal for the project, which was essentially that of a men's spirituality group with a mentoring component, was the last to be received by the project selection committee. Wagner is now the first college after St. John's to have a Men's Center.

The meaning of exploring vocation refers to what a college man comes to see as his calling in life—what Joseph Campbell called one's "bliss," which one cannot help following. But how is a young man to decide what to make of his life at a time when the gender playing field is changing in remarkable ways and the economy is fragile? The answer these young men are finding is that their spirituality is of fundamental importance in navigating these times. Everything else is related to this and depends on it. Whoever says that our young men are shallow, unthinking, and harsh has not met one of the core four and their brothers.

Here they are: They are marked by their strengths. One challenges himself by unraveling the ontology of Jean-Paul Sartre and then heads to the weight room. He talks about law school down the road. Another probes the labyrinthine mines of myth and archetype as he works his way into the ways of thought of Nietzsche and Jung. He wonders if he might have been a dancer. Still another does fierce battle with reason itself, exploring its limits. His passion for system and argument is stunning in its austerity, but his demands for consistency and coherence are bracing and reassuring when so much today slips and slides on postmodern uncertainties. He is undecided about what he will do, being more concerned about who he is. One returned to Wagner after a year and a half of travel, work, and reflection. He graduated with a degree in history. He writes short stories and likes to quote Walt Whitman, Henry David Thoreau, and Thomas Wolfe, continuing to ponder what his calling is. He prefers writing letters to sending text messages and e-mails. Another studies physics and has made his garden grow on campus. He pioneered the sustainability initiative at Wagner and is now teaching science to adolescents at the high school level. One is interested in basic research in biopsychology and is doing just that in his 1st year following graduation at a major research university. One could find no one more committed to the classic approach of the natural sciences. Yet another is trying to understand the experience of homeless men. He engages in hands-on work with chronically "failed" males at a walk-in center in New York City, where he has set up a men's group within its existing program. Still another is already sure he will teach philosophy, knowing full well the long route to a PhD in the discipline and how few positions there will be available to him when he reaches the end of this part of his life journey. But teach he must, and teach he will! He is surely following his bliss. One of his friends in the group smiles and fondly describes him as an old soul in a young man's body.

What these young men have in common is the authentic pursuit of a calling, and I think taking part in the Wagner College Men's Project has in part led to this being their priority. Determining just what their bliss is or refining its sense, however, has been only one of the two most decisive effects of being part of the project. The other has been the formation of deep friendships. All but having disappeared in the 20th-century climate of competition among males, the stories of their friendships with each other and how deeply meaningful they are have been privately told to me by nearly all of the guys. Given a space to meet and talk with other guys, without needing to wear the standard-issue persona of masculinity, has made this possible.

The word bliss is closely related to "bless" and "blessedness." Its association with the numinous has a long history, which is in keeping with thinking of the Wagner College Men's Project as ultimately a spirituality group in the broadest sense. To say that the guys in the project are finding ways to follow their bliss is reflected in qualities they possess that refer to those early senses of the word. The qualities show up, I have found, in all these young men in various ways—a blithe spirit, kindness of manner, delight, joy, enjoyment, and strengths of every sort. They are facing soberly and with a hard-won optimism the serious challenges that life in the 21st-century global culture presents males of their generation.

Self-presentation is still, alas, subject to the demands made on men, young and old, to put forward a certain image of manhood. So, one may miss one of the Wagner men from the project on campus—unless one stops to talk with him. Then the countenance shines through the façade that society still forces them to erect. There is no typical core guy. Some practice Zen and meditate. A few are activists. One was a linebacker, a few play the guitar, one writes poetry, another is a long-distance runner, and still another is an avid gardener. Some like heavy metal and have been in the scrum of a mosh pit. Others listen to quiet blues and folk rock and groups I do not know the names of. If you are on campus and think you have spotted one of the core Wagner men, stop him and ask for directions. You may be surprised what he tells you.

17

WHAT MEN WANT AT DUKE UNIVERSITY: AN ADVENTURE TO SHARE—AN ACCOMPLISHMENT TO ENJOY

KEITH DANIEL AND JESSE HUDDLESTON

INTRODUCTION (KEITH DANIEL)

When Gar Kellom first contacted me in the summer of 2007, we connected immediately over the desire to see more young men involved in the journey of discovering their calling as Christians. Having enjoyed and directed Programs for the Theological Exploration of Vocation for several years on our respective college campuses, we understood that a sense of unqualified success meant finding and attracting more men into our communities of faithful followers, leaders, and Christ-like servants.

I remember that phone conversation with Kellom like it was yesterday. It was a typical humid summer day in Durham, North Carolina. I was sitting in my car while my 9-year-old son and 7-year-old daughter were at track practice. I shared with Kellom snippets of my own journey of discovery with a small group of men that began assembling weekly around a kitchen table to pray, discuss, and reflect on the meaning and consequence of being a Christian man in the world today. That men's group started in the early 1990s.

Today, nearly 2 years since our phone conversation, I find myself once again sitting in my car, reflecting and pondering the vision and reality of seeing more men fully alive in the pursuit of their calling in Christ. This time it's a crisp and cold morning in March. I am in the mountains of Virginia. I made the 3½-hour drive from Durham to Goshen, Virginia with my long-time friend, Gary. We were attending an annual Christian men's conference[20] and retreat at the Rockbridge Young Life Camp. This is my third time attending this conference. I was a speaker at the previous two conferences. However, this time I am here to listen and journey alongside 250 men who have traveled from all along the east coast in small groups to seek God's face and listen for God's voice of direction for their lives.

From a kitchen-table discussion that began nearly 17 years ago to the theater hall of a Young Life camp in the mountains of Virginia to the annual father/son luncheon at St. John's University, Collegeville, Minnesota, I continue to enjoy and wonder about the glory and ongoing battle to unlock the hearts of men. The Top Gun retreat experience is a time for going deeper in the quest to know God, our-

---

[20] The annual conference is called Top Gun: Walking with God. Additional information about the conference, future events, and related regional men ministries, can be found at http://www.zoweh.com.

selves, and other men more intimately, compassionately, and courageously. The retreat involves substantial time for silence, solitude, recreation, prayer, journaling, and conversations among men longing to know God and to make God known.

At the 2008 Annual Conference on the College Male at St. John's, I shared some of my journey and self-discovery in intentional community in a speech entitled, Unlocking Men's Hearts: In Pursuit of Christ. I spoke of the conditions that often lead men to places of isolation and how intentional Christ-centered relationships with other men can draw one out and serve as a key to unlocking one's heart from fear and distrust that often leads to desolation. I tried not to offer answers as much as to share insight from my experiences as a young man through college who had not been consistently pursued or shepherded by faithful men who encouraged or nurtured me to live life from the heart on purpose. Women played the predominant role of nurturing my faith and character, my mother being the primary force. While there were a few influential male figures, including my father, male role models were not nearly as influential and present as women during my youth through college years.

Now, having experienced intentional Christian community with men during my postcollege years combined with the insight and experience gained through the College Men's Initiative, I offer two practical responses for the aim of drawing more young men out into the arenas of service, missions, communal prayer, and vocational exploration that lead to transformation and life giving experiences.

> The thief comes only to steal and kill and destroy;
> I came that they may have life, and have it more abundantly.
> I am the good shepherd.
> (John 10: 10–11a)

An important first step to engaging and increasing male involvement is to invite men into a shared adventure. Perhaps there is nothing more compelling to the male psyche than the challenge of an invitation from another respected and trusted man, peer, mentor, coach, or teammate to step up. This invitation may often be heard as more of a dare than a simple request to offer their strength, their presence, their experience, and their heart.

A healthy masculine journey to faith and service calls for a bonding forged through the sharing and the building of relationships with other godly men. This can be observed across cultures. The challenge is knowing how to engage in a shared experience that honors the dignity of humanity by bringing out the best a man has to offer the community.

This first step toward growth and a more open heart to share and serve may begin with a simple invitation for men to prepare and share a meal together. Most men want to eat most of the time. Although the preliminary sessions of our pilot project were catered, we donned aprons, prepared pancakes, baked, and served chili dinners for informal information sessions as well as intense discussions of the life of Dietrich Bonhoeffer or the work of Howard Thurman. Food is essential for life. However, we didn't live by food alone. It was the discussion and conversation and probing heart questions that engaged the hearts of men and drew them out into the fresh air of listening, expressing compassion, and serving others.

Our biblical tradition supports the joy of feasting. Food is the staple of life celebrations. It is the best thing we can share. Make food an adventure in gathering men for reflection and action. Talk about what it means to eat to live, and what it means to eat together across cultures and traditions. Better yet, cook together. Have men don aprons and mess up the kitchen. Our PathWays program pivots on the meals and gatherings at the PathWays home, located in a poorer Durham neighborhood less than a mile from the Duke campus. We invite neighbors. We cook. We clean. We support local/neighborhood growers, producers, and establishments. We enjoy variety and are constantly scouting for new recipes and new venues to gather, while being frugal and mindful of overconsumption. This is not women's work. This is a place where men can and should meet and encounter service in its most basic form. Men are invited to the physical and spiritual table of sustenance while being challenged to examine and explore their desires, shared humanity, and destinies.

Our pilot project at Duke began by forging the following questions: What do undergraduate men want? In what are men currently involved? Why? We gathered data from a variety of sources and were not surprised to find Duke men participating in a variety of extracurricular activities, including sports, individual tutoring and service projects, singing groups, and the arts. However, we discovered that men were not being invited to consider their participation and commitment to sustained, regular engagement (outside of sports and recreation) for a communal cause, purposeful objectives, or experiences on our campus. Sport teams have practice for competition. Fraternities may review their mission/charter. Yet we discovered essentially no space where men were invited to take time to reflect. The men we surveyed valued shared experiences and opportunities to swap stories about college, life, and relationships. I argue that men need recurring "seasons" and a purpose to engage in and prepare for in order to get and keep them involved.

A second vital step toward increasing male participation and sustained engagement in vocational discernment and exploration is to offer rewards and opportunities for celebrating the masculine journey. The journey should involve intentional time for reflecting, bonding, laughing, and weeping together. From watching and reflecting on classic films, such as *Chariots of Fire* or *Amazing Grace* or *Antwone Fisher*, going kayaking, scaling Mayan ruins, or serving together in local and international Habitat projects, young men will participate, especially when encouraged by their peers and mentors.

In recruiting young men to step up for service, one needs a mature young person who is not afraid of rejection and therefore doesn't take "no" to mean "never ask again." One also needs someone who has strong social capital and is willing to use that influence to call on his male peers and acquaintances of diverse backgrounds and interests.

We were fortunate early on to find such a young man entering his sophomore year at Duke. Before Jesse Huddleston agreed to lead our College Men's Initiative pilot project, he was already leading and serving actively on campus in a variety of settings, including the United in Praise Gospel Choir and the IMPACT Movement (a national campus ministry), as well as coleading our Sunday evening student worship service at Goodson Chapel. Huddleston was and is a resident advisor, and he served as one of our PathWays Summer Interns, where he worked with the college ministry pastor for a large local church. In 2008, he was a Resident Advisor for our Duke LEAD® (Leadership Education And Development) Summer Business Institute. Finally, as a sociology major, Huddleston's senior thesis is on college men's volunteering experiences and gender role conflict. His research has shown the connections between spirituality and volunteering because fewer men are involved in both of these arenas, given the stereotype that these are more appropriate for women. He is a prime example of how strong peer leadership combined with adult mentorship, passion, and genuine support is critical for successful projects and experiences in generating and sustaining male participation and engagement in spiritual formation and active participation. The content and thoughts to follow are his firsthand accounts, research efforts, and experience studying, serving, and leading his peers.

Reflections (Jesse Huddleston)

Rev. Keith Daniel first introduced me during my sophomore year to the observation that women were more involved than men and invited me to lead an initiative for college men. He charged me with the task of not just answering the question generally but also working specifically with men on our campus to get them more engaged in vocation and spirituality. As a result, I have been involved in the task of coordinating for students the pursuit to better understand what young men want during this 2-year initiative. Originally, my thought was that the answer would be connected to an individual man's calling or purpose and thusly connected to a combination of things, two of which stood out: the people that men nominate as most important and the manner in which men utilize their time.

With this hypothesis in mind and the assistance of the PathWays program, I planned what we called Man Meals, a time where men would gather together over food and discuss issues related to manhood and purpose. We had three sessions over the course of a semester with different undergraduate students and faculty, all of whom were male. We provided delicious food and a comfortable location for open conversation, ultimately centered on discovering what men want.

After three sessions, it was clear that all men want to be great men. This sounds obvious, because every young man agreed that this was a desire that they possessed. However, when questioned further, each man approached the task of reaching greatness differently. As I facilitated the discussion, this led me to ask the second question to the men present in the room: Were they actually pursuing what they claimed to desire? The easy answer was no; the more complicated answer was that their energies were not directed purposefully. In conjunction with my original theory, I challenged the men in each session to consider about whom they cared most and how they spent their time.

In this instance, I believe that some of the men began seeing how inactive they were in actually reaching the proposed goal of being great men. They spent their time doing a lot of different things; however, it remained to be seen if these different activities actually catered to their maturity, growth, and development as men. It remained to be determined if the people that they gave the most attention and care to actually helped them to be better men.

After these three sessions, I decided to shift our approach from generally theorizing about the topics in random small groups to specifically reflecting and discerning the topics and more with a set group of young men. I prayerfully considered men with whom I had established trust and good rapport, inviting them to our group as an opportunity to discover great manhood. Eight men responded and attended our sessions regularly. We continued providing food because it was a good incentive; everyone has to eat. And it fostered a comfortable environment for creating community.

Every Monday, we gathered on one accord, ate together, and talked to each other about a variety of topics centered on what it meant to realize what we want and how to live as great men. We spoke about the differences between what society generally perceives of as man and the reality of what it is to be a man. We discussed the importance of having vision, the meanings of strength and success, and the risks of pride. We talked over issues of sacrifice, confession, and integrity. We openly reflected on how we should carry ourselves in our relationships with friends and lovers. And as we intentionally occupied our time with these subjects, friendships grew. We learned about one another, our interests, our hopes, our concerns. We became a safe space for each other, a place where confidentiality, support, and respect were always upheld. We were challenged constructively and pushed to think of ourselves and our worlds differently. We all grew as men.

As I facilitated this interaction, I grew closer with Mark Storslee, someone who worked with me in the 1st year of the initiative both professionally and personally. Professionally, Storslee assisted me administratively in coordinating the logistics of our plans together, paying for the food, reserving venues, etc. Aside from the weekly experience with the men, Storslee and I bonded even more by way of the hours spent reflecting about these topics and determining how we would present them to our eight guys. We naturally developed a big brother-little brother dynamic in which we shared significant portions of our life experiences with one another. In many ways, he made my experience so much more constructive, substantial, and memorable.

Finally, our men's group concluded the semester with a 2-day capstone retreat on the coastal shore of Oak Island, North Carolina. We stayed in a small beach house near Myrtle Beach and continued to reflect on the topics of manhood and purpose. During that time, we considered our own life stories and meditated on any pivotal moments that strongly formed our masculinity. We viewed the movie *Antwone Fisher* and made our own judgments about how the film correctly or incorrectly depicted manhood as we had defined it over the semester. Even more, we just had fun! We were at the beach! We ate some awesome food from a local Thai restaurant and had all sorts of random jokes and laughs. We went parasailing and covered each other in sand. So many good times were had.

We concluded the retreat by committing to remain as connected as we could over the summer and planning to continue our small group experience in the fall. Though some of the men would not be present for a variety of circumstances, all agreed that the group should persist.

Since then, our group has continued into the 2nd year of the pilot project, and we have continued building trust and rapport among others. Though some graduated and moved onto other things, we invited other men, and we have remained a solid and secure space for pursing great manhood. Typically, I prepare a topic for discussion with questions and scripture. I facilitate the conversation, but many times the men themselves facilitate, posing their own questions and drawing conclusions for each other.

An interpretation of my experience during this pilot project confirms some of what I have read and seen in research. The theories of Longwood, Muesse, and Schipper (2004) on men's spirituality mirror my own. In their community, they intentionally invite all 1st-year men to small group experiences with other current male students. This small group continues throughout their entire undergraduate careers, and they reflect about who they are and who they are becoming. They claim that most men were just as invested in their masculinity and spirituality as women. However, men express their interest differently and must wrestle with how spirituality and other related pursuits (service/vocation) conflict with their masculinity. Good and Mintz (1990) agree that gender role conflict can cause significant psychological distress, and this level of anxiety could potentially inhibit men from coming to terms with their identity, spirituality, vocation, and the like. With this in mind, Longwood et al. emphasize the importance of framing and contextualizing the small group experience without making it emasculated or effeminate. It is a time for men. Offering an excess of reflections about nurturing others or emotional connectedness, subjects stereotypically reserved for women, can make the pursuit of vocational discernment unattractive or irrelevant. It can foster a disconnection between men and these matters of substance. With this in mind, we sought to make sure that our framework was intentionally and comfortably masculine for multiple kinds of men. Though we did discuss topics that challenged social concepts of masculinity and male ideology, any kind of gender role conflict was pertinent, shared, and facilitated in such a way that would encourage participation.

My qualitative research investigates a related topic: the relationship between men's volunteering experiences and their developmental transition into adulthood. More specifically, the consistent components of men's volunteering experiences were sought to better understand what ought to generally comprise the college male volunteer experience, particularly given their placement in the life course. Furthermore, this study paid great attention to the gender conflict that might exist for male volunteers. Though volunteering and vocation are not the same, there are clear connections between the two because the reality of low men's involvement is true in both settings.

With the concepts of gender role conflict in mind, the results of this study indicate that the men experienced little to no anxiety as male volunteers. The men were satisfied with their experience and acknowledged their families, either biological or fictive kin, as persons that encouraged them to volunteer as they currently do. Also, they all had a level of control and leadership as well as a deeper personal connection with at least one person in their volunteering experiences. Furthermore, the male volunteers were all religious, nominating Christianity as their religion, while three were primarily involved in campus ministry as volunteers.

With regard to religion, it seems that being active in one's religion or spirituality can increase the likelihood of development by way of volunteering. Oesterle, Johnson, and Mortimar (2004) concur that religion is significant in the conversation of volunteering, because it provides direct opportunities to serve and volunteer. However, religion can create adherence to more traditional forms of gender ideology and then conflict with the greater opportunities to volunteer. In her work on religion and volunteering, Ozorak (2003) posits that religious schemas and gender schemas influence an individual's attitudes toward service in ways that predispose volunteering or not as well as what students take away from the volunteer experience. This seems to suggest that more research would be needed on a man's gender ideology as well as his religiosity to better understand and anticipate what kind of intrinsic response he would have to a given volunteering experience. However, this does not take away from the truth that the participants who were intrinsically motivated to live out their religion benefited from volunteering in an environment that complemented their religion. For instance, one participant explained his feelings on his religious context:

> I think spiritual life is incredibly important to the life of a college student. I think it's the first time in most of our lives, I guess for me going to boarding school is a different story, but finally people are away from home and I think to be honest, the freedom that people have, it's not like it's a bad thing, but it's like wow I'm actually in charge of myself a lot more than I thought I was. And there [are] a lot of questions that people have about what am I doing, why should I do it, what's the point of doing it anyway, and I think there is often, if there hasn't been one before, a spiritual impetus to explore and understand whatever's around us, whatever we're interested in ourselves.

This kind of complementary volunteering encourages further demonstration of that same religious profession. Further research on the vocational and spiritual pursuits of different kinds of men is necessary in achieving greater perspective and understanding of this issue.

Ozorak (2003) also raises an interesting point with respect to men's pursuits to volunteer. She explains that both men and women claim to follow their preferences of career choices. However, any preferences for nurturing people over achieving power and success as traditionally defined are acceptable for women and still suspect for men. These kinds of social concepts, if unchallenged, make it difficult for men who often fit outside of the social concept of what it means to be a man. Reconciling these distinctions could be necessary for men who adhere rigidly to the traditional stereotype of being a man. Some of the men in my qualitative research were more flexible in their idea of manhood, and that helped in their enjoyment of their volunteering experience. Similarly, our discernment group intentionally challenged the stereotypes of what men do and who men are as well as purposefully put our newly formed concept of men in God's hands. In this way, our idea was righteous and pure as well as relevant and personal. It has helped as we engaged each other in discovering our vocation as men.

My own validations on men's gender identity and volunteering, both through empirical research and personal experience, include much on this topic of college student development. These validations inspire me to continue asking questions and researching about young men's experiences. It has also helped personally frame my own perspective and understanding on how men choose or reject navigating a social sphere that tends to combat who they aspire to be. It seems to me that men must be able to reconcile who they are with what they are doing.

In fact, this crucial reconciliation is a part of the direction I had taken for the 2nd year with the men. We determined to shift gears from conversations and reflections to tangible actions, where we could apply what we had discussed. Be it more social or spiritual in nature, I believe that it is important that the men have opportunities to put into action and enjoy what we have discussed and discerned collectively. This helps them to negotiate and connect what they do with whom they seek to be. Last year, our theme was called What Men Want: Discovering Great Manhood. This year, the theme is called What Men Pursue: Discovering Great Manhood (Part Two). I have encouraged and urged the men to actively pursue this discovery of who they are and what God has for them with wisdom. In my mind, wisdom implies a mature application of true understanding and knowledge with the proper perspective. With young men, this maturity will only come after a continual and progressive blend of thoughtful reflections and actual deeds. Fortunately, I have had the joy of coordinating much of this experience with the help of many other men. I have definitely made it my own and that has had an impact on my maturity. I continue to encourage the men to authenticate their time together as well so that it is personal and pertinent to whom they are and with what they care about. So far, they have done this, and it has been a privilege and an honor to participate actively in this substantive process of communal discernment and engagement.

REFERENCES

Good, G.E., & Mintz, L.B. (1990). Gender role conflict and depression in college men: Evidence for compounded risk. *Journal of Counseling and Development, 69,* 17–21.

Longwood, W.M., Muesse, M.W., & Schipper, W. (2004). Men, spirituality, and the collegiate experience. *New Directions for Student Services, 107,* 87–95.

Oesterle, S., Johnson, M.K., & Mortimar, J.T. (2004). Volunteerism during the transition to adulthood: A life course perspective. *Social Forces, 82*(3), 1123–1149.

Ozorak, E.W. (2003). Religion and volunteer service among college students. *Review of Religious Research, 44*(3), 285–299.

18

Male Commitment to Gender Equity and Antiviolence: A National College Study

Edward Heisler and Michael W. Firmin

Violence against women is a significant problem on college campuses across the United States. The Centers for Disease Control and Prevention (2007) reported that 20 to 25% of college women experienced attempted or completed rape during their college careers. According to the National Center for Victims of Crime (2007), young women ages 16 to 24 experienced the highest rates of relationship violence in 2000. Despite the predominant amount of male-perpetrated violence experienced by their female classmates, campus men have largely remained on the sidelines in terms of formal attempts to curb this problem.

Sexism and men's violence against women sabotage campus goals of supporting the fulfillment of each student's potential. Having recognized this and many other costs of gender inequality and violence against women, many campus leaders have increased efforts to create safe, equitable, and respectful campus communities, free from sexual and domestic violence. As a result, interest in men's gender equality and antiviolence groups is growing. Small groups of college men are allying with women to end the repressive campus environments created by ongoing threats of men's violence, harassment, intrusion, and sexism. This movement toward men's involvement represents an exciting shift in social norms, because more men are identifying gender equality and antiviolence work as vocations or part of their larger purpose in life.

Nonetheless, despite an apparent rise in campus support for ending gender inequality and men's violence against women, student activists for gender equity and antiviolence often feel unsupported in their campus community. This illustrates a struggle that feminist women have articulated for years: Working for gender equality is an uphill battle, and campuses have yet to achieve that goal. This circumstance poses a number of questions related to engaging men: What causes men to care about sexism and men's violence against women as a social issue? Why would men commit to gender equality work despite a lack of support from the greater community? What can campuses do to create a supportive environment for gender equality and antiviolence groups?

These are key questions that guided an exploratory project at the 1st National Conference for Campus-Based Men's Gender Equality & Antiviolence Groups at St. John's University in Collegeville, Minnesota. The conference was a groundbreaking gathering of representatives from campus-based men's groups across the country, providing an excellent opportunity to gather data. Fourteen male students were interviewed in an attempt to further understand how and why men are committing themselves to promoting gender equality and ending violence against women. Their responses have implications for the way campus leaders approach the engagement of men and the way campuses think about encouraging gender equality and antiviolence efforts. Their statements can also inform the way one supports men as they identify vocations related to gender equality and antiviolence work.

Method

Participants

The present research study used a purposeful sample (Arminio & Hulgren, 2002), consisting of 14 participants from 10 colleges and universities across the United States. Participants ranged from age 18 to 23, with an average age of 20.5 years. Each participant was involved in campus-related activities associated with gender equality and antiviolence work for at least one semester. Participants included majors from women's studies to mechanical engineering. Eight participants identified themselves as Caucasian/white, three participants identified themselves as Black/African-American, two participants identified themselves as Latino/Mexican, and one participant identified himself as biracial. Twelve participants indicated they were straight/heterosexual (two students identified their sexual orientation as male), one participant indicated he was gay, and one did not disclose. Project participants were recruited through a posting on the conference Web page. Potential participants completed a personal statement before the conference as well as a semi-structured, personal interview while at the national conference. Interview questions focused on understanding the nature of each participant's commitment, perspective, and experience related to gender equality and ending violence against women. Questions included: How did you first get involved in work connected to gender equality and violence against women? What are the greatest challenges and rewards related to your involvement? How has your involvement impacted your life?

Procedure

The study followed the protocol for a phenomenological, qualitative research investigation. This is a research protocol that explores and reports the perceptions of participants, from their own perspectives, giving voice to how the individuals view their worlds and personal constructs (Bailey, 2007). Interviews were digitally recorded for later analysis. The interviews were semi-structured (Seidman, 2006), allowing the participants to relate their own perspectives, stories, accounts, and sentiments—explaining their phenomenological perspectives freely and without coaching. Coding procedures for analyzing the data utilized an inductive methodology. That is, preestablished axial categories were not imposed on the data. This was due to the exploratory nature of the investigation. Consequently, open coding (Maxwell, 2005) strategies were more apt for studying the phenomenon of interest.

The interviews were assessed by repeated review and appraising the data for frequent words, phrases, constructs, and ideas. Concept mapping organizational review (Gay, Mills, & Airasian, 2009) helped to provide an organizational framework for the data analysis. At times, original codes were combined in order to keep the number manageable, and some codes were later discarded if they failed to reflect the sentiments of most participants. Constant comparison among the transcript data produced a set of codes that eventually led to the themes reported in the present research article (Bereska, 2003). Themes were only reported if they represented the consensus of most participants interviewed in the study. Initials used in the printed version of the article are fabricated in order to preserve the confidentiality of the research participants.

Internal validity for the study was enhanced primarily via two mechanisms. One was to generate a data trail (Daytner, 2006). This is a qualitative research technique of systematically supporting each reported theme in a study with citations and direct quotes from the respective participants. It helps to ensure that the themes reported in a study are adequately grounded in the collected research data. Additionally, the data trail was submitted to an expert qualitative researcher who was independent of the data collection and analysis. This qualitative research methodology helps to provide an objective appraisal of the process and reported findings, helping to ensure that the study possesses adequate rigor (Merriam, 2002). The independent expert supported the conclusions drawn, helped to sharpen the accuracy of the present research findings, and provided valuable assistance in assuring the overall quality of research design and execution.

Results

Of the 14 participants, all but 2 strongly asserted that they would remain involved in gender equality and antiviolence work for the rest of their lives. For most participants, striving for gender equality and a world free from men's violence against women had become part of their identity and life purpose. Most men described a connection and self-identification with gender equality work similar to the following participant's account:

> I respect and love women due to seeing my mother and grandmother. I acquired the knowledge of what women go through in the world today. With that said, I just want to help in every way possible. Women are fighting for equality everyday. So as long as they're fighting, I'm going to be right beside them, fighting with them.... I feel as though if I wasn't doing this kind of work I wouldn't be being me, you know? (JA)

Participants specifically explained that involvement in gender equality and antiviolence groups anchored their deep personal commitment to the mission of such programs. As such, these men expressed a perceived calling to which they felt more than a passing attachment. It was not said to be a fad or hobby. Rather, it was perceived to be a long-term commitment or moral obligation. For example, another participant explained:

> I feel like since I know so much now I can never go back. I'm always going to be progressive from now on. So no matter where I go, if I'm in college or I'm working, whenever I feel like this issue comes up I feel like I can address it because I know how to. I've learned values and I've learned different skills that can help me address this issue. (HM)

Overall, the path leading to each student's commitment, though filled with unique details, suggested at least four common themes: knowledge and empathy, social/peer support and exploration of masculinity, guidance and encouragement, and self-improvement and altruism.

KNOWLEDGE AND EMPATHY

It was common for participants to describe a presentation on sexism and violence against women that initially caught their attention, challenged their thinking, and called them to action. However, participants reported that learning in this area extended beyond conference-based or other intellectual learning. It is interesting to note that a small majority of participants had taken classes related to gender equality and violence against women, but academic study was not the central focus of participants' commitment. It was, however, common for participants to allude to a sharp and continuous learning curve, whether it began with a campus group, class, or volunteer experience. Participants seemed to be gaining knowledge, even though the medium for their learning was not strictly a classroom setting.

Additionally, participants shared that knowledge was only the beginning of the commitment they experienced. For most participants, empathy for the harm caused by male dominance and violence against women was at the heart of their commitment. Presentation activities intended to personalize men's violence against women for the audience frequently formed the foundation of their passion. Ongoing discussions in groups and classrooms, along with friends, family members, classmates, and campus faculty/staff, built on this foundation. One participant stated: "It has opened my eyes to some of the things unseen, such as hegemonic masculinity and the terror that women are put through, especially by their male counterparts" (RA). Engagement of the mind headed the path toward empathy in the heart.

For all but one of the men, empathy was amplified by detailed knowledge of a woman they knew who had suffered male-perpetrated violence and gender inequality. For example, some participants grew up in households with domestic violence, and this strongly impacted the empathy they experienced: "My mother keeps me motivated[;] thinking back to the violence she experienced will always be in my mind. I will always remain involved in the fight for this issue" (BE). Many participants also had close relationships with a female relative or friend who experienced male violence. Often, this exposure served as a catalyst in the lives of participants. That is, the issue became real and personal: "One of my best friends was raped my freshman year. So I think that's what really propelled me [to become involved]" (NP). The subject went from the theoretical to the tangible and practical for the research participants. As such, close experiences with violence against women seemed to force participants to struggle with what had happened and relate to the harm that resulted. One participant explained:

> I had a sister who, four years ago, her boyfriend at the time turned violent against her.... My sister felt like she, like she did something wrong. She felt, you know, "Why, why did I stay with this guy?"... And just thinking inside it's like, "You know this is none of your fault at all." (BT)

In multiple cases, participants indicated they were not aware of abuse that was impacting someone close to them until they were involved in gender equality or antiviolence groups for some time. They were not necessarily naïve, but insulated until they participated in prevention programs that illuminated the dynamics and effects of abuse. One participant aptly explained: "As a student in Sociology and Gender Studies, I knew it was around and carried passion for those who experience it.... However, it directly hit my heart when I found out my mom was being abused" (ST). He continued to elaborate on how his awareness had expanded:

> It's hard for me because I feel like I victimized my mom a lot. She's very outspoken. If she doesn't like it, she'll say it. And it got labeled as "she's crazy" from my dad, my brother, and I. That's the toughest part is that I can be a part of that structure. (LK)

Men's violence against women often carries with it significant shame and secrecy. Furthermore, children experience male dominance, and unhealthy beliefs develop, such as *women are irrational* and *women are objects*, which support inequality and violence against women. This phenomenon can make it very difficult for men entering college to have an intimate understanding of the amount and impact of women's experiences with inequality and violence. Participants in this project suggested that, as their awareness of the inequality and victimization that women experience increased, they were more likely to take responsibility for making things better.

Participants further suggested that personal connections with women highlight the difference between seeing sexism and men's violence against women as a subject versus an experience. In order to do well in a class or on a paper related to a presentation, students are required to study gender inequality and violence against women as a subject. They gain knowledge and understanding, which they apply to various life situations. Participants suggested that these learning experiences piqued their interest. Once the heart was engaged, however, participants perceived sexism and men's violence against women as an experience that impacted their lives as well as the lives of women around them. As a result, knowledge and understanding led to empathy and deeper evaluation of the world. Whether in a classroom, a presentation, or a men's group, higher levels of thinking and commitment seemed to occur when men stopped seeing sexism and men's violence against women as a subject and connected the issue with real women that existed in their lives.

Though most of the men in this project had a very intimate connection to men's violence against women, coming from an abusive background or having a close relationship with a woman who was sexually assaulted or battered was not required to connect the issue with the everyday reality of women. Participants often referenced victimization and perpetration statistics for men's violence against women. As one student wrote in his personal statement:

> My experience in [a campus men's group] has both opened my eyes to staggering and devastating statistics with regard to sexual assault and rape on college campuses—nearly one in four women is a victim of sexual assault at some point in her college career—and filled me with an enthusiasm and determination I had never felt before. (PC)

Empathy for victimized women was said to have been enhanced through the personal connections participants made once they became aware of the immense scope of the issue. In this way, exposure to the real-life situation of women made cogent impressions on the males in the sample.

Participants also highlighted the fact that violence against women is predominately committed by men: "We have to face the reality that men are perpetrating ninety-five percent of the time, and women are primarily survivors of this issue" (AR). Each participant was asked what he thought caused violence against women. Participants almost uniformly identified socially constructed masculinity: "It's definitely masculinity I think ... socialization ... we promote rape culture. We promote violence" (TL). The sense of connectedness to the root cause of violence against women seemed to be a powerful influence. A participant expressed a sense of responsibility, as a man, to address it:

> I found that, as a man, it was my responsibility to take a stand and say that misogynist, male-dominant attitudes are not healthy attitudes for men or women. Also, because I am a son, grandson, nephew, cousin, and friend to many women, these issues are around me and I cannot sit by while they continue. (CG)

It appears that a deep personal engagement for the issues, through both participants' minds and hearts, and a strong sense of responsibility as men, combined to create the beginnings of a commitment to gender equality and antiviolence work rooted deeply in participants' identity.

SOCIAL/PEER SUPPORT AND EXPLORATION OF MASCULINITY

The influence of a strong leader, friend, or close relative played a significant role in facilitating all but one participant's initial commitment to gender equality and antiviolence work. Influence came from a variety of sources. As one participant recalled, "A few [teammates] told me to get involved; it seemed like a good cause. My advisor at the time recommended me to the program as well" (OR). Participants' experiences suggested that one of the most effective methods for recruiting student involvement was for students, faculty, or staff to personally invite men into the group. One participant recalled:

> After watching Don McPherson speak for the second time[,] I talked to [two student leaders] to receive more information about [a campus men's group]. They were the ones who strongly encouraged me to keep the conversation going and to get more involved. Without them I wouldn't be filling out this form today. (IJ)

Some participants suggested that male students who appeared similar and had similar interests made the difference in becoming involved. When invited to participate by a male student with whom they were able to identify, participants reportedly felt much more comfortable about becoming involved.

The concept of a *man box*, often described as the restrictive hegemonic socialization of men based on domination and control, appeared frequently in interviews. Participants suggested social support from a group of men was valuable for thinking about their role as men and living outside the man box. As one participant wrote, "It's very rewarding. I have learned a lot of things about gender equality. More importantly, I am stepping outside the 'hegemonic male box,' and that alone is an amazing feeling" (MG). Participants clearly sought the social connections and support provided by a men's group, not only to step outside the man box but also to do something meaningful. One participant explained:

> It's seeing a problem, knowing that there's something wrong and you want to do something about it, and you finally have an outlet to do it. You finally see other people who have been feeling the same way you have been feeling. (TC)

Social and peer support was of critical importance to participants for reasons including personal growth and influencing the greater campus. Each participant reportedly found support in some way from the men and women in their lives.

GUIDANCE AND ENCOURAGEMENT

Individual mentoring from adult leaders was said to have had a major impact on participants' commitment to gender equality and antiviolence work. Participants were cogently influenced by their mentors. One participant suggested that his mentors were "... like moms [to him]. They showed great passion for me to get involved. They saw that I had the resources to help football players to think critically about gender" (HT). Many participants described an intense appreciation for the way faculty/staff mentors and student leaders encouraged them, created an environment for them to grow, provided enough structure to make groups purposeful, and actually guided them through the process of becoming leaders and identifying this issue with their purpose in life.

Outside of their group, participants did not have the same support. Because women face sexism and the threat of physical and sexual violence every day, it is important to note that the lack of support participants described for their commitment to gender equality centered on discomfort. None of the participants mentioned fearing for their personal safety or feeling completely isolated on a campus. Actually, some participants received a great deal of praise, largely from individual women in their lives. Regardless, participants experienced discomfort from frequent resistance to gender equality on campus. For example, one participant recalled: "I have been shut down by men and women about critically analyzing gender. One man told me not to bring this feminist bullshit to the locker room" (OR). Participants' experiences with negative responses to their commitment helped highlight the importance of guidance and encouragement through strong leadership. Participants described being ostracized and ridiculed as well as feeling like they were going against the tide—many men in their lives were saying and doing things that directly contradicted participants' beliefs. Participants particularly noted a threat of isolation.

> Sometimes I will invent a fake job when people ask me what I do. I don't want to tell them I'm a rape crisis counselor. At a party they'll just walk away from me because they think I'm the downer ... or they'll constantly be trying to throw these rape myths at me. Sometimes it's just easier to be a guy, "I work at a desk job, it's really boring." (LJ)

The threat of discomfort and lack of support made it more challenging for participants to live up to their own expectations of themselves. Participants talked about difficulties in turning beliefs into practice. It can be much easier not to fight the tide. As one participant explained:

> It's hard to speak out sometimes. Like within the group it's easy because you all agree with the general idea anyway. But when you're out there, you know, you might get criticized for speaking out and that can be kind of hard. (DF)

This statement highlights the challenging connection between male privilege and commitment to gender equality. Participants tended to identify with male privilege as a concept, namely unearned benefits men get for being men. They described male privilege through examples, such as being able to walk alone at night, getting more credibility as a public speaker, and receiving higher salaries than women. Most participants did not connect male privilege to the challenges and values surrounding their daily commitment to end sexism and men's violence against women. Men grow up learning to expect male privilege. Aside from having power over women, these privileges can include the expectation of comfort both inside and outside oneself. When facing resistance, then, many participants seemed to struggle with having to give something up, such as the comfortable relationship with some of the men in their lives, to challenge gender inequality as the status quo. Participants sometimes seemed frustrated that they could not live up to their own personal expectations without some discomfort. These findings suggest adult leaders and mentors should help men identify and work through their own discomfort, using the lens of male privilege, as individuals and in a group. The findings also support a call to create accountable connections with feminist women on campus. Formalizing a commitment to feminist organizations and their mission statements would keep male privilege more visible in men's gender equality groups and help men's groups remain centered on their goals of ending sexism and men's violence against women.

Participants recognized, to varying degrees, that the resistance they experienced from many men and some women might be related to socialized complacency for structural sexism. Academic institutions, like other major institutions, often reflect normalized gender inequality. This can create environments that implicitly support resistance to gender equality work—and participants in the study reported resistance was high on their respective campuses. Many men are threatened by men working to end sexism and men's violence against women, especially when gender equality groups are challenging perspectives and institutionalized male privilege. Men committed to gender equality shook the status quo on their respective campuses—and received resistance due to the resulting discomfort. Facing an uphill battle, participants rallied around the support they found from their group on campus and focused on strengthening their ability to live in a way that reflects gender equality. Group leaders' guidance and encouragement also were major sources of inspiration.

Self-improvement and Altruism

Participants spoke of focusing heavily on self-improvement—becoming better men. They highlighted how their involvement in gender equality and antiviolence groups helped shape them. For example: "I've grown as a person. What matters to me and what I care about, it's changed because of this group. I respect myself. I respect others so much more" (LG). Participants illustrated how their involvement had improved their present-day lives. They talked about improved relationships with their mothers and other family members, more fulfilling relationships with their romantic partners, better relationships with other men, a feeling of purpose in life, and more fulfilling experiences at their colleges or universities.

> And to really make it personal, it's a group that makes me stay at college, at the school I'm at right now.... And it's like, I feel motivated when I go to the meetings. I feel like, "Oh, I got to catch up on my studying because I've been slacking a bit. I've got to step my game up." (SL)

For many participants, campus gender equality and antiviolence groups helped create a more supportive, respectful, enjoyable campus environment, where they felt more equipped to achieve their fullest potential.

Participants expressed a strong sense that their exposure and commitment to gender equality and antiviolence work would positively shape and impact their lives in the future. This sentiment was seemingly deep-seated and proactive. For example, one participant articulated, "Our favorite statement is 'The man who views the world the same way at age 50 as he did at age 30 has wasted 20 years of his life' " (LH). Continued growth and development were commonly referenced throughout the interviews. Participants similarly discussed having a sense of purpose and better relationships: "I think being involved with this will help me in the future become a better husband, a better father, a better partner" (MB). They further explained a number of expectations and goals they had set for themselves. Statements, such as "I want to be present for, you know, everything that my kid does" (KA), were common. Ultimately, a clear sense of purpose and identity connected to gender equality seemed to be at the center of the numerous self-improvement benefits participants described. Gender equality and antiviolence groups helped participants form the internal beliefs and values that would shape the rest of their lives.

A sense of altruism was a universal component of each participant's commitment to gender equality and ending men's violence against women. Some participants described growing up with an understanding of the harm caused by male domination and men's violence against women. Others shared a more recent path to their understanding of the terrible impact of women's oppression. In all cases, participants shared a desire to make the world a better place. One participant illustrated this when sharing his personal creed, "If you make an observation, you have an obligation" (PO). He further explained, "In other words, I got tired of seeing males treat women like animals and abuse them" (PO). Another participant said, "That's always my goal is to help someone. I don't care if it's one person, I've helped someone" (EW). Many participants spoke about the duty they felt to make the world a better place for women. They wanted to be a catalyst to change the world, and the change was both internal and external for participants: "I'm making a difference and stepping outside the confined box of what it is to be a man and realizing that these are problems in our society that we need to tackle" (JG).

Discussion

Campus-based gender equality and antiviolence groups were found to help men identify a greater purpose in life and possibly a vocation related to gender equality, contributing toward the creation of a world free from men's violence against women. In this context, the present research study provided insight into the motivation and experiences of men committed to such work and illuminated some opportunities and challenges facing men as they form deep, lifelong commitments to gender equality. Findings imply the following recommendations to those wishing to engage men on campus. These recommendations require fighting a strong current of normalized male dominance.

- The heart is central to facilitating commitment. Engage the mind to raise awareness, and connect campus men's lives to the pain, frustration, and sadness felt by women due to male domination and violence. Empathy is the most salient reason men make commitment, despite an evident lack of support from the greater community.
- Student leaders and adult mentors should personally encourage men to attend men's groups and become involved.
- Create a welcoming, challenging, and open space for men to socialize with like-minded men as a way to learn more about themselves and issues related to sexism and men's violence against women.
- Leaders and mentors should build personal relationships with group participants and guide them as they form strong personal commitments to the issue. Committed men should be challenged to find ways to shape their daily environments so they reflect gender equality. They will need help identifying and working through their resulting personal discomfort by using the lens of male privilege.
- Support participants as they recognize and embraced the deep personal impact their involvement could have on their lives.
- Help group participants cultivate an altruistic sense of identity and purpose for the rest of their lives.

The findings from the present study suggest that college men committing to gender equality and antiviolence work feel a lack of support from their campus environment. Insight from this project can help inform a conversation on how campuses can meaningfully support gender equality and antiviolence efforts. In many contexts, this will involve redoubling efforts to create an environment that serves as a model. Some helpful questions to consider for such a campaign might include the following: (a) What would our campus look like if it reflected the philosophies of gender equality and antiviolence groups? (b) What would the dorms be like? (c) What would be different about the athletic department and student union? (d) What sort of education and organizational policy and practices could begin creating those environments? (e) How could we support women's and men's efforts to organize around gender equality and ending men's violence against women? Support could take many forms, including staff and administrative participation in the groups, highlighting active groups during tours for prospective students and at first-year orientation, featuring the groups in literature about the campus, using institutional language that highlights equality, attracting media attention to the efforts of the groups, and funding. Students need resources, mentors, and approval from the campus community in order for these groups to thrive.

Aside from organizing campuses around gender equality, this project raises questions about what committed men can do to help create an equal world free from men's violence against women. Despite declaring a strong, long-term commitment, many participants had not thought very deeply about what they could do after college in order to create such a world. Project participants seemed to hold to the few examples of concrete activities they knew they could do. Some men talked about going to graduate school in a field related to gender. Others hoped to educate in some way about gender inequality and men's violence against women. Still others spoke about mentoring younger men. Overall, participants focused on personal changes they could make and a larger outlook for the world that they would like to see actualized.

Each participant's sense of purpose and altruism creates a significant opportunity for potential widespread action, but the lack of a deeply deliberated post-college plan of action threatens to limit his impact to a personal sphere. To maximize the impact of campus men committed to gender equality and ending men's violence against women, campus leaders should help men realize their potential as leaders and allies to women. Adult leaders must create on-campus opportunities to work toward transforming the campus climate through organizational practices and policies that will prevent sexism and men's violence against women. These opportunities should meet a parallel goal of preparing men to work outside campus to end sexism and violence against women. As campus men approach graduation and begin identifying work to end sexism and violence against women as a vocation, they must think beyond the few concrete examples of how men can be involved after college. Campus men should work to identify how they might have the greatest impact and strive to create those opportunities for themselves in the culture. Feminist women did the very same thing as they created the sexual assault and battered women's movements. Committed men can contribute to these movements by creating opportunities for themselves that are in line with feminist women's organizations and their mission statements.

Two more recommendations address this gap between commitment and action: (a) Embark on an in-depth study of feminism as part of the group's weekly process and (b) create structured partnerships between committed men and feminist women's groups on campus. Have conversations and create written statements with feminist groups about accountability. Commitment to the goals and mission statements of feminist organizations is critical to men's ability to partner with women as safe and effective allies in ending sexism and men's violence against women.

Guiding men to partner as allies with women also will help them learn and identify more clearly how they can use their talents and skills for the broader movement. Too few examples existed of men's groups creating strong and sustained allied connections with women's groups among the participants in this study, and conversation about accountability to feminist groups or organizations and their mission was rare. Understanding of and identification with feminism was also varied with this group of participants. A stronger focus on feminism, the dynamics of men's involvement, and close, structured, and accountable connections between committed men and feminist women might better prepare men for an ongoing commitment as they end their academic careers.

Participants in this project represented a wealth of positive and exciting efforts on campuses across the nation. In the face of a reality where men are commonly resistant or unengaged, participants were committed to changing themselves and working toward gender equality and a world free from men's violence against women. These men represent a shifting of momentum, a changing social norm.

Campuses and the greater movement to end men's violence against women can guide and encourage this momentum. Imagine a campus where male and female students are working together with faculty, staff, and administration to ensure their campus is an environment supporting gender equality. Efforts to change social norms by engaging campus men as effective, accountable allies with women represent great potential to actualize this vision.

Future Research

The present research study was an exploratory study of a salient need in contemporary higher education. Namely, men's involvement in violence prevention programs across American university campuses is a growing movement but also one where further empirical data are needed in order to better understand and serve the needs of campus programming. Future research studies should include survey data from regional and national samples. Such research should draw substantially from the findings of the present study. Good survey questions should be based partly in previous research findings and sufficiently grounded from empirically based conclusions (De Rada, 2005). The present study significantly contributes to this end.

Additionally, while the sample size of the present study was adequate for its intended, exploratory purpose, future studies should expand sample sizes in order to help bolster the present study's external validity. Ultimately, external validity in qualitative projects is achieved through replication (Firmin, 2006). Repeating the present study, therefore, at a variety of regional and national conferences will help show the interconnections among various participants and manifest clear patterns among reported data points.

Most of the participants were Caucasian, because this reflected the predominant race of the conference participants from which the sample was drawn. Further studies should expand this subject pool to include additional participants from racial minority populations. A study that focuses specifically on minority men would be of particular interest, comparing the results with the present findings. If samples could be adequately drawn, then a series of studies drawn from independent minority groups (e.g., African-American, Asian-American, Hispanic) would be useful in order to compare how different minority individuals might view their respective participations with violence prevention for women.

REFERENCES

Arminio, J.L., & Hulgren, F.H. (2002). Breaking out from the shadow: The question of criteria in qualitative research. *Journal of College Student Development, 43*, 447–460.

Bailey, C.A. (2007). *A guide to qualitative field research* (2nd ed.). Thousand Oaks, CA: Sage.

Bereska, T.M. (2003). How will I know a code when I see it? *Qualitative Research Journal, 3*, 60–74.

Centers for Disease Control and Prevention & National Center for Injury Prevention and Control. (2007). *Understanding sexual violence.* Retrieved from http://www.cdc.gov/ncipc/pub-res/images/SV%20Factsheet.pdf

Daytner, K. (2006, June). *Validity in qualitative research: Application of safeguards.* Paper presented at the 18th Annual Ethnographic & Qualitative Research Conference, Cedarville, OH.

De Rada, V.D. (2005). The effect of follow-up mailings on the response rate and response quality in mail surveys. *Quality and Quantity, 39*, 1–18.

Firmin, M. (2006). External validity in qualitative research. In M. Firmin & P. Brewer (Eds.). *Ethnographic & qualitative research in education* (Vol. 2, pp. 17–29). New Castle, UK: Cambridge Scholars Press.

Gay, L.R., Mills, G.E., & Airasian, P. (2009). *Educational research* (9th ed.). Upper Saddle River, NJ: Pearson.

Maxwell, J.A. (2005). *Qualitative research design* (2nd ed.). Thousand Oaks, CA: Sage.

Merriam, S.B. (2002). Assessing and evaluating qualitative research. In S. Merriam (Ed.), *Qualitative research in practice* (pp. 18–33). San Francisco: Jossey-Bass.

National Center for Victims of Crime. (2007). *Teen dating violence fact sheet.* Retrieved from http://www.cdc.gov/ncipc/pub-res/images/SV%20Factsheet.pdf

Seidman, I. (2006). *Interviewing as qualitative research* (3rd ed.). New York: Teachers College Press.

PART III.
FINDING NEW DIRECTIONS

19

VOCATION, GENDER, AND YOUTH MINISTRY: THE YOUTH TRACK

JEFFREY KASTER

Why are there two girls for every boy at youth ministry events? How does vocational discernment happen in teens? What assumptions about teenage boys are shared among youth ministry program directors? Questions like these became the foundation for a youth ministry think tank on vocation and gender. Through a grant from the Lilly Endowment, seven colleagues associated with Lilly-funded youth programs gathered three times in 2008–2009 for conversation about the impact of gender on vocational discernment among high school youth.[20]

It should be noted that the Lilly Endowment has invested more than 60 million dollars in Theological Programs for High School Youth since 1998. This initiative seeks to stimulate and foster an excitement about theological learning and inquiry and identify and encourage talented Christian youth to consider vocations in the ministry. Five of the larger Lilly-funded youth ministry programs were represented at this think tank: Candler School of Theology's Youth Theological Initiative (YTI); Duke University's Youth Academy (DYA) for Christian Formation; Gordon-Conwell Theological Union's Compass Program; Catholic Theological Union's Peacebuilders Initiative; and St. John's University School of Theology and Seminary's Youth in Theology and Ministry program (YTM).

The goals of this think tank on vocation and gender in high school youth included (a) becoming knowledgeable about gender theory and its impact on vocation among males; (b) sharing assumptions and hunches about gender's impact on vocation, spirituality, and theological inquiry within high school youth; (c) analyzing and compiling program data related to gender; (d) developing common assumptions on the impact of gender on vocational discernment in high school youth; and (e) sponsoring a common training or experiment related to gender issues and publishing the results.

---

[20] Think-tank participants included Dr. Elizabeth Corrie, Candler School of Theology, YTI program director; Dr. Fred Edie, Duke University, program director, and Ms. Katherine Hande Smith, program coordinator, Duke Youth Academy for Christian Formation; Dr. David Horn, Gordon-Conwell Theological Union, Compass program director; Ms. Megan Kennedy-Farrell, Catholic Theological Union, director, Peacebuilders Initiative; and Dr. Jeffrey Kaster, director, Youth in Theology and Ministry, and Ms. Juliann Heller, theology faculty, St. John's University School of Theology and Seminary. Dr. Joyce Ann Mercer, who coauthored *Lives to Offer* (Baker & Mercer, 2007), was invited to our first meeting as a theological consultant. Think-tank participants also participated in the 2008 and 2009 Men's Conferences at St. John's University.

This chapter will report gender participation data from our youth programs, data from the 2008 Wabash National Study and College Men, shared assumptions about gender and vocation, and a common training on gender and vocation with our staffs. Finally, this chapter will provide excerpts from four essays, highlighting key insights gained from this conversation.

RECRUITMENT AND PARTICIPATION DATA

Gender data collected between 1999 and 2007 from Emory, Duke, Catholic Theological Union, Gordon-Conwell, and St. John's School of Theology and Seminary reveal a significant gender imbalance in application and participation rates at these Lilly-funded youth programs. As Table 1 indicates, applications of females significantly outnumber those of males, a divide that continues in who actually participates in youth programs.

This data raised concerns and questions. The data show that many more females apply than are accepted into our youth programs. The conversation revealed that the goal of gender equity resulted in many highly qualified female applicants being denied acceptance in favor of accepting marginally qualified males. In our discussion it was acknowledged that males are given preference in our youth ministry programs, that highly qualified females are being turned away in favor of less qualified males, that our good intentions toward gender parity might be endorsing male privilege, and finally that our commitment to parity might be an uneven good. Dr. David Horn, Compass program director, Gordon-Conwell Theological Union, summarized the discussion:

Table 1
Application and Attendance Data by Gender (%)

	Male	Female
Applications		
YTI Chandler School of Theology 1999–2007	28	72
DYA Duke University 2005–2007	36	64
Totals	30	70
Attendance		
YTI Chandler School of Theology 1999–2007	40	60
DYA Duke University 2005–2007	36	64
YTM Saint John's University 2000–2007	34	66
Compass Gordon-Conwell Seminary 2002–2007	52	48
Peacebuilders Catholic Theological Union 2003–2007	27	73
Totals	38	62

The elephant in the room clearly is that, in order to maintain parity in gender mix in our programs, all of us seem to be universally obligated to live with a two-tier set of gender-based criteria. Is this fair, particularly for female applicants? More fundamentally, should there be parity in numbers?

WABASH NATIONAL STUDY AND COLLEGE MEN

At the St. John's University Men's Conference in February 2008, Dr. Charles Blaich (2010), director of inquiries, Wabash College Center of Inquiry, presented data from the Wabash National Study of Liberal Arts Education about the college male. This is a longitudinal study of 7,500 students from 26 colleges and universities, begun in 2006. The data from the study reveal that college men express *greater* interest than women in being entrepreneurs; making money; working in a prestigious occupation; influencing the political structure; exercise; and drinking. College men express *less* interest than women in learning more about other cultures and countries; preserving and enriching the environment; helping others; becoming passionate about an occupation; political and social involvement; promoting racial understanding; influencing social values; spirituality; and volunteering. Based on the research to this point, Blaich (2010) presented two provocative conclusions: (a) Statistically, men work less, are less socially concerned, and more financially motivated than women. He said that, from a faculty perspective, men might look like "second-class women." (b) In interviews, many men frame college as an epic struggle in which they successfully overcome adversity, yet they are happy to take an easy path when one is available.

This research sparked a rousing discussion among think-tank participants. Ms. Megan Kennedy-Farrell, Director of Catholic Theological Union's Peacebuilders Initiative, raised the following question: "What about the fact that our programs are primarily based on the themes that men are less interested in?" Dr. Fred Edie, Director, Duke University Youth Academy for Christian Formation reflected: "If the data are to be trusted, adolescent males are less interested in service learning, encountering difference, contemplative spiritual practice, or self-conscious reflection than females. They are more interested in 'doing' than 'being.'" He raised the concern about minimizing such practices from our programs: "My own theological and formational convictions suggest that engagement in such practices is critical not only to female but to male Christian identity." Dr. Elizabeth Corrie, Candler School of Theology, YTI, Program Director, stated:

> I have a clear and slightly traumatic memory of the list of things young males are NOT interested in resulting from this initial research—spirituality, grassroots organizing, volunteering/service and social justice. Those are exact terms to describe most, if not all, of our youth programs.

Ms. Katherine Hande Smith, Program Coordinator, Duke Youth Academy (DYA) for Christian Formation, connected the Wabash research with the application and attendance data: "I would not have discovered the possibility that our own programs might be contributing to male power and privilege, even as—paradoxically—they implicitly deter young men from applying."

We concluded the conversation by discussing methods of making our youth ministry programming more male friendly, such as using the word *challenge* more prominently in our application materials and on our Web sites. We also recognized the need to remain faithful to programming that engaged both male and female youth in gospel practices, vocational discernment, and social justice.

Assumptions

At our first meeting we also discussed with theologian Dr. Joyce Ann Mercer those sections of Baker and Mercer's (2007) *Lives to Offer* book that deal with vocational issues for girls and boys. At the end of the first meeting, we surfaced the following assumptions about vocation and gender among high school youth:

- Youth ministry programs seem to cater more to girls than to boys.
- Youth ministry programs may need to do more to adapt to the culture to attract males.
- We presume that boys feel a welcomed place in the church that girls do not.
- Males have specific challenges associated with vocation that are unique to them.
- We must take into account male genetic/learned behaviors around status, power, and dominance.
- Adolescents, both male and female, are struggling to find a voice to name and enact their vocations.
- The multiple meanings of the word *vocation* often lead to miscommunication.
- Sexuality, spirituality, and vocation are closely aligned. There is a fear associated with this.
- In order to take up faithful Christian vocations, males must unlearn certain things and females must learn certain things.
- Our youth programs are influenced by and perhaps contribute to male power and privilege.

The two salient assumptions were about youth ministry catering more to girls than to boys and the possibility of contributing to male power and privilege. A poignant moment happened during the sharing of these assumptions about vocation and gender. The think-tank program directors (representing decades of youth ministry experience) realized that these vocation and gender issues were virtually unexplored territory within youth ministry. As each additional assumption was raised and discussed, we recognized how little time we had spent thinking about these issues or enacting program adjustments based on these assumptions. Mercer commented how delighted she was by the conversation, while noting how rarely such conversations took place.

It was clear that this think tank sparked new and important questions. It was also clear that we had much to learn and think about. Before we left this first meeting of the think tank, we explored the possibility of creating a common training with our summer program staffs on gender and vocation.

COMMON TRAINING ON VOCATION AND GENDER

We continued to discuss a common training on vocation and gender through conference calls and e-mail exchanges during the spring of 2008. Corrie developed a process for the common staff training on vocation and gender that four of the five youth programs agreed to utilize with our staffs (college theology majors or graduate theology students/seminarians) during our summer institutes in 2008. We asked our staffs to read *Lives to Offer* (Baker & Mercer, 2007) in preparation for this training session. The process incorporated a fishbowl technique of an inner and outer circle of chairs. The inner circle talked, and the outer circle listened. The female staff went first and discussed the following questions related to Mercer's chapter, "Like Job's Daughters":

- What kinds of messages did you receive from your parents or other significant adults about being a young woman?
- How do/did these messages relate to your process of vocational discernment?
- How did your parents or significant adults in your life affirm or discourage your vocational choices (whether by the examples they set for you or by how they responded to your choices)?
- Are there any stories from this chapter on girls that particularly spoke to you? Any examples from prior work with youth? Why did they speak to you?
The male staff then entered the inner circle and discussed Mercer's chapter, "Isaac's Long Walk," through the same set of questions oriented to males.

In September 2008 think-tank members gathered in Indianapolis to discuss what was learned from this common process. Key findings across the youth ministry programs about the male staff included the following:

- Male staff were reticent to share their vocation stories.
- Living up to scripted expectations was a strong theme, particularly the expectation for material success. Race and ethnicity impacted these expectations.
- The "boy code" identified in the Baker and Mercer (2007) text was prevalent across cultures but seemed stronger for those men from Africa and Latin America.
- Male vocation stories included subtle and explicit references to the interplay of vocation, questions of sexual orientation, and violence.
- Listening to the vocation stories of females was important and meaningful to the males.

The key findings across the youth ministry programs about the female staff were as follows:

- The females voiced a strong need to have it all together. To be successful was very important. Material success (money) was a high value for parents.
- Vocation could appear to be a weakness.
- Family influence was mixed. Many women described their families as strongly supporting them to be anything they wanted to be. However, some women said they received the message that choosing a religious vocation was below their potential.
- Women pursuing ministry felt the need to constantly prove themselves.
- Many of the women found listening to the stories of the men very eye-opening.

This discussion culminated in new questions. We felt it was important for us to revisit the definition that we use for vocation and how we help young people through the process of vocational discernment or discipleship formation. We wondered how our programs actually encouraged youth to consider formal ministry as a vocational choice. Underlying our concerns were questions about the role of youth programs like ours to be active in dismantling patriarchies that exclude some and give privilege to others. We also felt we needed to explore both how to construct programs that attract males as well as females and how conversations about gender might be integrated into our youth ministry programming.

Essays

As a result of our work together in Indianapolis, we agreed to write essays about what we learned from our discussion of gender and vocation with our program staffs. What follows are excerpts from those essays that touch on key insights. We presented these essays at a panel discussion at the 2009 Men's Conference at St. John's University.

Unresolved Tensions or How Answering a Simple Question Left Me in a Moral Quandary (Elizabeth Corrie)

The preliminary findings of the National Study of the Liberal Arts Education quite clearly explain why more women are attracted to our programs then men. Young men interviewed in this study indicated that they were less interested than women in spirituality, volunteering, understanding racial differences and exploring other cultures, preserving the environment, helping others, being involved in grassroots civic engagement, and being passionate about their vocational paths. Instead, males tended to prefer activities that gave them the sense of overcoming obstacles and challenges—in fact, using the specific word "challenge" and the competitiveness, exertion, rugged individualism, and honor this term implied, appears to make an activity more attractive to young males.

I direct YTI, a three-week summer program in ecumenical, justice-seeking theological education, focusing specifically on spirituality, volunteering, understanding racial differences and exploring other cultures, preserving the environment, helping others, being involved in grassroots civic engagement, and being passionate about vocational paths as we seek to discern what God is calling us to be in the world. *We are that which men seem not to want.* Hence, it should come as no surprise that, after sixteen summers and intentional, even desperate, efforts to recruit males, our applicant pool has consistently included two to three times as many female applicants as males. We had our answer—our programs are "girly." So, with the mystery solved, why did this feel so unsatisfying?

If males are less interested in our programs, should we change our image or our programs to make them more appealing to males?

In thinking over the data presented from the National Study of the Liberal Arts Education and in reflecting on my observations of the YTI program and its impact on both males and females, I began to wonder if the solution to our problem of low numbers of male applicants might simply be one of marketing. After all, YTI is in fact quite challenging—we may not ask our students to climb mountains or [beat] another group of people in a competition, but we do ask our students to examine their faith commitments critically, to reflect upon their own participation in systems of injustice, to learn to get along with people that they may disagree with strenuously, to read difficult theological texts, to take risks to try new things and test new ideas—activities that require overcoming huge obstacles of prejudice, fear, and complacency. Perhaps simple changes, such as replacing the word *discover* with the word *challenge* in the YTI brochures would make a difference—that is, instead of enticing potential applicants with the opportunity to "discover how to engage, analyze, and address public issues from a theological perspective," we instead invite them to "challenge yourself to engage, analyze and address" these same issues.

What role can or should we play in transforming the church?

A perhaps more salient question lies in what impact our programs can or should have on the church. All of our programs were initiated with grants from the Lilly Endowment, as part of a larger vision, perhaps even mandate, to identify and nurture leadership for the church. While some of our programs focus primarily or exclusively on a particular denomination and others strive to varying degrees to recruit across denominations, all of our programs seek to encourage young people to follow vocational paths that answer God's call on their lives. For the sake of the church, we hope and pray that at least some of these talented, faithful young people answer a call to ministry within ecclesial settings.

Yet, what do we do when the leadership positions with the church remain difficult or, in some cases, impossible to attain for the young women we attract to our programs?

In Their Own Voices: An Exploration of Issues of Gender and Vocation Among Peacebuilders Initiative Alumni (Megan Kennedy-Farrell)

Since its inception in 2003, Peacebuilders has served over 330 youth from Catholic high schools and parishes around Chicago. Of those 330 youth, approximately 27% have been male. We know there are some structural factors that contribute to this imbalance, namely the change in single-sex education with more all-male high schools becoming coed and all-female high schools remaining single sex. However, there is more to the story. Despite our efforts to prioritize recruitment and even acceptance of males, we have not been able to come close to a balanced community. We have wrestled with these issues for years, but have never asked the male participants to directly comment on this dynamic until now. In three interviews with five males, striking consensus emerged around two questions: Why aren't more young men involved in Peacebuilders? And what allowed these particular young men to overcome those obstacles and participate in Peacebuilders themselves?

While the five males I was interviewing were involved in three different interviews and did not have the benefit of one another's answers, their responses to this question were all immediate and very similar. They said:

- "Guys are usually less likely to try something new or branch out."
- "Guys don't want to be seen as feminine. They want to be cool so they don't want to show their faith on their sleeve."
- "Guys think it's not cool or manly to give of their time to help others and volunteer."
- "Guys aren't as into faith or as open about it as girls. They aren't cool if they do faith activities."
- "Guys think it isn't manly to talk about their feelings."

After exploring their responses a bit, I introduced them to Baker and Mercer's (2007) description of the "boy code," a cultural script that "encourages bravado among males at the expense of emotional attachment and a 'gender straightjacket' that limits boys' ability to express themselves freely" (pp. 136-137).

When I asked the five males if this was accurate and something they had experienced in their own lives, they responded:

- Chuckling, "or ... all of the above."
- "Yes, I feel like I have to live up to this. The media puts us up to this. Other kids are thinking this too, and we know that other kids will put us down if we don't live up to this. So, fear forces us."

- "I'm laughing because this is so true. I do see this *a lot*—in movies, billboards and especially in middle school where I felt like I had to be a tough guy to be accepted."
- "On the surface very much so. Most guys won't tell you much about themselves unless they are best friends. Even then it's a bit of a mystery. You would almost be ostracized if you did talk about your feelings. Underneath the surface, guys do have a soft spot, but the surface is about a mile thick and it is nearly impossible to get through."
- "You see this the most with spirituality. No one talks about it. People are reluctant to even say if they pray. Being spiritual seems feminine. This is true in our culture and I've always wondered why."

These five interviews merely scratched the surface of the exploration of gender and vocation within Peacebuilders. The five young men I interviewed are not a representative sample of the total alumni community. If anything, they are probably the cream of the crop and their continued involvement and leadership in their schools and churches is evidence of this. While definitive answers did not emerge from these interviews, the similarity in responses was striking and I am left with the next three major questions:

- Is there a role we can play in equipping parents and congregations to support and nurture the "inner kick" that young men do have for a life of faith and justice?
- How can we support the creation of more [introductory experiences] for young men to build their confidence and affirm their desire to break out of cultural modes? Are there ways we can adapt our program or the description of our program to better reach those who might be willing to take a first step?
- How would other young male alums, who are perhaps not the cream of the crop, respond to these questions? How would their reflections and insights further our understanding of issues of gender and vocation among Peacebuilders youth?

FATHERS AND SONS: A VOCATION STORY (JEFFREY KASTER)

At Saint John's School of Theology's common training session a male leader in the fishbowl briefly sketched a story about his father's expectations for him as a man and its impact on his vocational call. At the time William was a senior theology major in college and was discerning a call to seminary and ordained ministry. He shared that his father did not understand him and actually considered him "different" because he was not interested in the traditional male sports of baseball, football, and basketball. He also briefly described a potentially violent incident where his father expressed anger over his sexual identity. This essay is a result of a follow-up interview with this young man.

William began by sharing a story about his sensitive nature and his emotionality:

> I remember my mom telling me a story from when I was three years old. It was some sort of preschool screening to see how kids would react when their parents left them. After we were dropped off, my twin sister just went off and did her own thing, but I just sat there and cried and cried because my mom had left me. The director told my mom, "Tell him when he is older, that he is going to feel emotions very deeply."

I asked William what message he got from his dad about who he was. He said his dad thought he was "fruity"! His father said things like, "stop being so sensitive." William described his dad as being very traditional in his understanding of gender roles. His dad grew up playing baseball, basketball, and football. His grandfather and his father greatly enjoyed watching William's older brother succeed as a baseball pitcher. William said he received the message when he was six or seven that to be a real man he had to play his father's games. The problem was that William didn't like baseball, basketball, or football. He liked swimming, tennis, and soccer. His dad called these country club sports.

William then shared the story of a confrontation he had with his father when he was in seventh grade.

> I don't remember exactly what the fight was about, but I do remember that I was mouthing off. I was sitting on my desk chair in my bedroom. I don't remember exactly what I was doing, but he came in and he started talking to me and I just kept ignoring him. He got upset and kicked my chair out from under me. He then asked, "Are you going to stand up for yourself and take care of yourself?" Then he asked me, "Are you gay?"

William said he didn't think this was abusive because he never felt like his father was going to physically hurt him but was simply trying to shake him up a bit. William understood that his dad was trying to figure out what was going on with him. William did say that this incident caused him to wonder what was wrong with him. As a seventh grader William wondered about his sexual identity.

William said:

> I was just devastated when I thought about this. I remember I was in 8th grade and I didn't speak for a week. I was always a talkative kid, like I am now. My teachers even asked me what was wrong. One night that week I remember my mom was helping me study when I just finally broke down and said: "I think I am gay."

William's mom said "I don't believe that being gay is anything you can help and I am going to be here for you no matter what." William said his dad came into the situation and he tried his best to reassure William. A short while later William's dad apologized for the incident with the chair. William explained that understanding his parents' love took the pressure off. He said he slowly came to accept his sexual identity.

When I first heard William share his story about his Dad kicking a chair out from under him and questioning his sexual orientation, I assumed William's story was mainly about sexual identity, violence, and rejection. I assumed it would be a psychologically rich story about negative parental influences on psychosexual development and vocational discernment. I assumed that it would simply highlight the psychological and spiritual damage inflicted by fathers on sons. Upon listening more closely, I was surprised to discover that although William's vocation story does contain the themes listed above, it is primarily a story about reconciliation. It is a vocation story about a journey of a father and son who finally "get each other." It is a story about a father's journey as much as it is a story of a son. I wonder if William's story is a common story? I wonder about the contours of vocation for those young men who experience violence but never experience reconciliation with their fathers? It raises interesting questions about the extent to which parental views on gender roles and sexual orientation impact vocational discernment. It is clear that there is much for us to learn about the influence of parents on the vocational choices of young men.

BAPTISM, POWER, GENDER, VOCATION: TRANSFORMING SOCIAL RELATIONS IN THE NEW CREATION (FRED P. EDIE)

As director of the [DYA], I invited adult staff members to participate in the fishbowl exercise developed by my colleague, Elizabeth Corrie. Their comments on gender and vocation, while reflective, were mostly unsurprising to me. Some women named patriarchy as a force that shaped both the messages they received about vocation as well as a barrier to their present pursuits of ministry vocations. Other women described pressure to be accomplished as women in roles traditionally ascribed to females *and* as professionals in roles traditionally ascribed to males. They felt pressure to have it all—great job, marriage, and motherhood. Some men suggested that ministry is perceived as an insufficiently masculine vocation. Perceptions of low social and economic status for ministry were ingredients to the messages received by both male and female staff; men and women alike testified that parents and other influential persons worried or complained about low pay and/or the waste of intellectual talent.

More surprising to me, however, were later observations from several staff reflecting on the fishbowl exercise itself. They commented how "un-DYA-like" it was, not because it employed creative pedagogy and not because it encouraged all members of the community to speak and [listen] but because, according to them, it assumed but did not name any theological grounds for interpreting gender in relation to vocation. Without such explicit naming they thought we remained stuck with our painful gender stereotypes even if our hope through sharing was to shed light on them. They wondered why Christian baptism, which serves as DYA's primary point of theological reflection, including its reflection on vocation, was not part of our conversation.

Since then I have sought to fill in that perceived gap—at least for myself. What *does* it mean to speak in baptismal theological terms of Christian vocation? And, more to the point of this essay, what does it mean to speak of *gender* in relation to baptism and vocation? And how might answers to these questions trouble the waters of traditional gender identities for both men and women serving or seeking to serve in the church?

I no longer think the solution to gender imbalances is simply to practice a more muscular and presumably more male-friendly Christianity. This is not to say that I cannot learn anything from sociologists; it is instead to assert the need first to claim baptismally transformed understandings of gender and the correlative ways of exercising power that baptismal life enacts before rushing in to fix a program. To be more specific, to register the disinterest or disinclination on the part of young men for engaging difference is not simply an innocuous observation about learning preferences or styles, it is a marker of male privilege. Young men are not interested in difference because there is relatively less need for them to come to terms with it—difference must, instead, come to terms with them. But communities like DYA that seek to invite young men to live into the new creation will necessarily engage them with difference as a means to leave behind the old sinful self. Men require engagements with difference so they will not, as has historically been the case, be left to themselves to do violence to their own self-definitions or to the rest of the world. Similarly, the reported preferences of young men for acting upon processes rather than participating within processes is consistent with male formation into the practices of direct and relatively unfettered exercise of worldly power. It is a product of living by the boy code. To reiterate, however, the baptismal new man is sealed with a new practice of power oriented to solidarity with suffering, mutuality, gentleness, and peace. Paraphrasing Hauerwas (Christian theologian Stanley Hauerwas) the new man must find the courage to do nothing out of the recognition that so much of his prior acting has done violence to those he has acted upon while presuming that he and not God is in control. Thus, simply because young men are formed into the mythology of the television show *Charles in Charge* does not mean that DYA must immediately embark upon a campaign to further male activism. It owes them instead an honest appraisal of the Gospel's judgment of worldly male power and privilege *plus* practice in exercising Christ's power of peace and reconciliation.

In addition, redescribing gender through a theologizing of baptismal power relations can only affirm the growing numbers of young women who are populating our programs. Perhaps like the Hebrew babies they will become so numerous as to threaten Pharaoh. Despite what our own particular statistics report, the church universal has so far failed to fully embody the social relations that unity in Christ prescribes and, consequently, it has also failed to gender women consistent with the new creation. Women have not claimed all that God intends for them because the church has failed to be the church. Our programs, therefore, and the women who attend them should not be regarded as problems but as epiphanies of the Gospel's promise.

Conclusions

Three main conclusions resulted from this dialogue. The first and most obvious is that further discussion and research are needed about vocation and gender issues within high school youth. Think-tank participants were in complete agreement that we were simply scratching the surface of many complex realities that impact vocational discernment in high school youth. The second conclusion flows directly from Edie's essay. We need to be much more intentional about exploring the theology of baptism and vocation and its impact on our understanding of gender, gender roles, power, and privilege. We realized that this is very infrequently discussed within high school youth ministry curricula. Certainly, we must become more aware of the cultural issues that influence male participation in youth ministry, but more importantly we need to challenge cultural gender norms in light of the gospel. A final conclusion stems from the fact that nearly all that was written and shared in this chapter about high school youth, vocation, and gender came from adults. The think-tank members were all knowledgeable adults who have work extensively with youth, and the Wabash research was with young adult males in college. However, missing were the actual voices of high school youths. The final conclusion is the need to listen to the diversity of voices of the young church. We should listen to what they think, believe, and feel about vocation, youth ministry, and gender issues. Listening to the voices of high school youth will be essential to understanding these issues and essential in crafting a curricular response that is faithful to the gospel.

This think-tank dialogue has attempted to identify real issues facing youth ministry without coming too quickly to action responses. It was our consensus that we entered unexplored or, more accurately, under-explored territory in this dialogue on vocation, gender, and youth ministry. We ended the think tank with more questions than answers. Questions that deserve further exploration include the following: Is the research on college males in the Wabash study applicable to high school males? Do these findings on male interests accurately portray reasons for high school youth ministry attendance patterns? How do cultural factors such as the boy code impact vocational discernment among boys? How do parental views, sexual identity, and violence shape vocational choices? Do our youth ministry recruitment practices support male privilege? Will changing our marketing attract more males?

It is perhaps fitting to end this reflection with a quote from Freire (1997) about the hope of authentic dialogue as an act of creation infused with love. It represents our deep and abiding care for youth ministry and for young people themselves:

Dialogue cannot exist, however, in the absence of a profound love for the world and for people. The naming of the world, which is an act of creation and re-creation, is not possible if it is not infused with love. (p. 70)

References

Baker, D.G., & Mercer, J.A. (2007). *Lives to offer. Accompanying youth on their vocational quest.* Cleveland, OH: The Pilgrim Press.

Blaich, C. (2010). Wabash National Study. Retrieved January 3, 2010 from http://www.liberalarts.wabash.edu/study-overview

Freire, P. (1997). *Pedagogy of the oppressed* (New revised 20th anniversary ed.). New York: Continuum.

**PART IV.
BEST PRACTICES FOR WORKING
WITH COLLEGE MEN**

20

Some Final Thoughts

Gar Kellom

The synthesis of best practices for engaging college men began with the first meeting of our research and theory team, which met in Chicago in 2007 before the grant period actually began. The discussion that began continued at each of the three conferences at Saint John's University. This chapter attempts to capture the essence of those conversations as well as the lessons learned from the pilot projects. For one who does not have the time to read about all the exciting projects and activities conducted at the pilot schools, perhaps a synthesis of best practices in this chapter and what might be applicable on one's own campus or in one's organization may be helpful.

Respected Peer Leaders or Pied Pipers

As the grant application was being written and the research and theory team began to map out the activities of the schools, one best practice seemed to emerge that most schools could agree worked to engage more college men. We called it the Pied Piper Practice because many campuses found that having an influential peer leader involved in the process of engaging more men often resulted in increased numbers and more meaningful interactions. At St. John's we hired men in the Men's Center each year and made them responsible for the recruitment and facilitation of service trips and activities. This is not different from hiring the most qualified residence assistants for work in residence halls.

Some of the more experienced pied pipers spoke at the conferences. Grant Wollenhaupt and Brett Saladin, two of our best leaders, explained to attendees how they approached this work. While maintaining that it was easy to involve more men, Wollenhaupt explained a multistage process that he used to contact and sign up men to participate in the Trinidad and Tobago service trip. His approach was highly personal, often using e-mail and Facebook. It included multiple reminders and in the end often a personal escort to the meeting to get a student interested initially. Whether presenting to student organizations, such as the Pre-med Club, on the benefits of working with HIV-infected orphans in Trinidad or giving personal reminders that deposits were due or reflection papers needed, Wollenhaupt or Saladin were often the face of the Lilly grant or the Men's Center.

On many small liberal arts campuses, where relationships are key and students know each other well, getting a program started takes much more energy and effort than sustaining it once it is established and a positive reputation has been created. Thanks to the work of Wollenhaupt and Saladin in the early years, the work of Corbin Cleary was easier as he recruited for the 2010 Trinidad and Tobago trip. Students are fond of saying, "I heard it was a great experience!" When others hear that, they do not need as much convincing, and the selection of quality participants is possible with larger numbers of applicants.

We built into the grant from the beginning a student leader from each school not only to play the role of the pied piper but to come to the conferences and share with other student leaders and attendees what worked for them and why.

There were some other best practices that may be helpful to address the most frequently asked questions about what works and why. The most often asked questions and most discussed topics early in the process were those relating to advertising and communication strategies. We have captured some of the best of these in the following section. The strategies are not unfamiliar to admissions departments, fund-raising professionals, or people involved in target marketing of constituents. They reflect much of the wisdom contained in the project case studies presented earlier in this book.

SUCCESSFUL METHODS OF RECRUITING MORE MEN TO ACTIVITIES AND EVENTS

USE MULTIPLE E-MAILS OR TEXT MESSAGES REPEATED JUST BEFORE MEETINGS

While it is tempting to assume that one or two e-mails or posters will communicate enough about an event, one standard best practice is to repeat communication efforts from multiple sources, especially just before key meetings.

SEEK NOMINATIONS BY FACULTY AND STAFF AND INVITATIONS

Personal invitations have worked well in many cases. Having hall staff recommend those men who may be interested in an activity and then sending them a personalized invitation will often make the recruited men more inclined to attend.

SEND A PERSONAL LETTER FROM THE COLLEGE OR UNIVERSITY PRESIDENT

One school enlisted the office of the president to sign a personal letter of invitation to men. This made the recipients feel very special and led to increased participation rates.

MEET FACE-TO-FACE AS MUCH AS POSSIBLE

Another consistent approach was to use relationships and face-to-face communication as much as possible. It was often on the recommendation of a friend alone that a man attended an event.

INVOLVE STUDENT ORGANIZATIONS WITH SIMILAR INTERESTS

Reinforcing electronic messages and posters with personal explanations at student organization meetings with similar interests worked well. For the St. John's Trinidad service trip to work with HIV-infected orphans, the Pre-med Club became the key recruiting group, and leadership still routinely comes from that group.

Use Facebook, MySpace, LinkedIn, and Other Social Networks
Using electronic social networks is the emerging mode of communication and invitations for college men. Posting pictures of past events and connecting with ever-increasing circles of students is very effective.

Hand Out Small Business Cards Inviting Involvement
The University of Portland's League of Extraordinary Gentlemen found that handing out business cards for the LXG with a personal invitation was unique enough to get attention and increased recruiting.

Tie the Events to Working for Justice as Well as Social Ideals and Values
As we will highlight below, tapping into values and beliefs held strongly by students can be very effective. Working for social justice, Habitat for Humanity, and other activities provide opportunities for practicing those beliefs.

Use the Peace Corps Challenge—"Toughest Job You'll Love"—or the Military Challenge—"Be All You Can Be"
Drawing on traditionally masculine themes of toughness or risk taking used by the Peace Corps and the armed services can sometimes be effective with college men.

Use the Latest Successful Super Bowl or Other Advertising Techniques
For the most expensive (and often the most traditionally masculine) approaches, advertising approaches like those used by advertisers around the Super Bowl and other major athletic events is often the best way of getting the attention of the sought-after target market.

Designing the Activities for Men: Pilot Project Ideas

As our theory team and pilot project leaders met and talked about engagement strategies, a third category began to emerge about what was working that had to do with the design of activities or vocational discernment projects themselves. It may seem obvious to many, but involving more college men should include having college men themselves design the events or activities to which they are being recruited.

We observed a pattern on our campuses, which also appears in the Brooks data (see Chapter 2), that many schools have placed the responsibility for vocational discernment or volunteer activities in areas that were not frequented by men. Over the years, at St. John's and its closely affiliated women's College of Saint Benedict, alternative spring break trip planning and the planning and administration of other volunteer activities had gravitated to the women's campus. It was obvious that there was a skill and talent for this planning and administration there (and perhaps less responsibility being taken by the men) that had allowed the responsibility to shift to women's spaces. The consequence was a drop in male participation rates. It did not seem to be a conscious decision, but, over time, the change of where things were planned (i.e., away from more male spaces) had resulted in a reluctance of college men to see that those activities were for them.

One of the main reasons for establishing a Men's Center at St. John's in the student development area was that it created a space for college men to brainstorm and design activities they were interested to participate in. Such spaces now serve to add more gender balance to campuses with women's centers so that there are places where programs are planned for both men and women. Our motto is "Bring your best ideas, and we'll help you accomplish them in the Men's Center."

To help focus on the idea of empowering students' ideas, we used the metaphor of the center as a "green house," since we often saw it as a place where men's ideas were hatched and nurtured, with some growing and developing and some simply dying a natural death. It should be said at the outset that the activities did not need not to be exclusively for males, but, in order to enhance male participation, they typically started with some ideas that men are interested in and with some male leaders. This has led to larger numbers of males participating.

A perfect example is our service and study trip to Trinidad and Tobago. A St. John's student from Trinidad responded to an open invitation to suggest programs for the Men's Center. He stormed into the center one day, demanding to know why no one in the school had a study-abroad, volunteer, service learning, or any other kind of trip to Trinidad. He argued that over 30 students attended our schools from that country, yet no one on campus seemed to have any interest in and consequently any knowledge of that part of the Caribbean. I asked Cheval Morrison to design such a program, and the rest is history.

Morrison discovered that one of the best gender studies departments existed at the University of the West Indies and that there was great need for students to volunteer in orphanages there, in particular one for orphans with HIV-AIDS. Over the years his leadership and that of several other pied pipers have led to an annual service trip that is always 50/50 in its gender balance, because it has been seen from its inception as a men's program. There is rarely any difficulty getting enough female participants, but because the program begins in the Men's Center, has men recruiting for it, and has a long history of male participation, it also fills up with men.

Other examples from the pilot schools of designing activities for college men involving college men in the process have been described in the chapters above but are worth repeating in this summary for those looking for a short list of ideas to try to engage more college men. It should be noted how different the ideas are and how they are tied to the uniqueness or mission of the campus they come from.

- Road trips modeled after *Roadtrip Nation* and designated seminars (Davidson College)
- Faculty mentoring and fraternity alumni mentoring network (Augustana College)
- Engaging athletes through structured readings (Luther College)
- Designating a space for men in the College Men's Initiative and skydiving as an activity (Duke University)
- Retreats with team building, "take-the-hill" activities, and cooking together (Gustavus Adolphus College)
- All-male service trips with research, trekking, and rafting (St. John's University)
- Service trips working with high school youth and college men (Wagner College and Wabash College)
- Micro-grants soliciting student ideas and tapping into student initiatives (Georgetown College)
- Classes for men (Hastings College and Morehouse College) and training faculty to involve more men (Hope College)
- Spirituality groups (Siena College, University of Portland, and Wagner College)
- Working with high school males in a network of Lilly schools with high school programs (Youth Track)
- Men's groups working to end violence (Edward Heisler and the November 2009 college men's conference at St. John's)
- Including prayer, rites of passage, readings, or rituals in activities
- Building partnerships with women's groups
- Working through charismatic groups already alive with spirit (Magis, "Our God is an Awesome God")
- Working with returning veterans

Processes and Key Themes

As we compared projects and shared experiences, several more important key themes emerged that began to create a more complete picture of how to engage college men. Following are some of the most frequently occurring themes.

Creating Safe Male Spaces, Sacred Spaces, Sacred Time, or a "Cultural Island" on or away from Campus

The retreats, men's groups, male service trips, research projects, and other activities where men could be with men were consistent and common themes. In a research project run by students at St. John's, even before the Men's Center was established, a group of students was assigned to interview "Johnnies" about their most profound experience in the 4 years they were there. The responses had a remarkable similarity and were basically some version of this statement: "Late at night after the women go home and the studying is done, we get a chance to drop the mask, be with our male friends, and be ourselves." Men feeling fulfilled when they have the chance to share openly with other men in a safe and confidential space came up as a theme on campus after campus, whether in Greek groups, athletic teams, service projects, or residence hall floors.

It is more common for colleges and universities to make residence hall spaces and student organizations coeducational and seek equal opportunity for all students to participate, but there may be a loss in not having spaces where just men (or just women) can share with each other on a more personal level.

BUILDING CONFIDENTIALITY AND TRUST

More often than not, those working on the projects spoke of the necessity of developing trust and confidentiality with the men they worked with. Sometimes, through the establishment of ground rules or mission statements for projects, the fundamental respect and dignity of the participants became a key ingredient and one of the important aspects of the success of the project.

FACILITATING DISCLOSURE, DEEPER SHARING, AND REFLECTION AND ALLOWING MEN TO "GO DEEPER"

Kimmel (2009), author of *Guyland* and many other works on men and masculinity, was asked at one of the conferences what he saw to be the key to working with college men. He responded with one word—disclosure. With confidential, safe, all-male spaces created through the pilot projects described in this book, another key element is allowing for men telling their own personal stories.

As a way of testing this theme with schools not in the Lilly grant, the author was invited to organize a retreat with his own fraternity at his alma mater, Lawrence University. There was new leadership and a need to rebuild the chapter after having lost the fraternity house in a new housing plan implemented at the university. Terry Franke, also an alumnus and now chairman of the board of trustees of the university, asked alumni for ideas on how to rebuild the chapter. I responded with the idea of disclosure as part of the all-male, already existing fraternity group and, together with Franke, created a retreat for actives and alumni to get together and share their personal stories about why they joined the fraternity and what it had meant to each of them. It was called the brotherhood group. Following is Franke's response after that retreat (Delt Update: A Great Story):

> [Reenergized] and [repurposed] [are] perhaps the best way[s] to describe the new Delts. We had a meeting on Wednesday night with Delts and their new pledges. We started the meeting with discussion with the fraternity's [p]resident about the goals he had shared at the October meeting[,] and then we had five alums tell short stories about themselves.

> The retreat and telling personal stories were key[s] to the [repurposing] of the group. Delts are now about a group of guys who support each other, not a group of guys who happen to live under one roof who quite honestly didn't care that much about the group. Losing the house actually helped them. I could tell that the actives were different than when I last saw them at the Board meeting in October. We had the new pledges participate in the telling of their stories with actives and alumni as well. The new pledges are a great group of guys. One in particular, from Appleton, stood out as a leader. He is already organizing two new initiatives in the community.

What is so significant in this story is that initiation ceremonies may not be the only way of building Greek groups after all. It may be more about creating spaces for disclosure and deeper sharing. The Delts are exploring the possibility of this approach with other chapters and implementing this approach through the national organization.

Mentors and Mentoring, Intergenerational Communication, Acknowledgement, Affirmation, and Validation of Younger Men by Older Men

In the spirituality groups at St. John's, Siena, Wagner, or the University of Portland or in the classes or projects at the other schools, we have seen a hunger for college men to share in the wisdom of the previous generation, a need for intergenerational interaction. Perhaps Groth (2010) has put it best, as follows, having studied this aspect of men's involvement in depth (see also the report of the Wagner project):

> During more than [30] years of teaching, advising[,] and mentoring, first at an all-men's Benedictine college and for the last [16] years at Wagner College, a [coeducational] liberal arts college closely associated since its inception with the Evangelical Lutheran Church in America, I have identified [16] best practices for working with college men. All of them are means of forming a mentoring relation with my male students. They are *being perceived as open, available, responsive, patient, accepting, validating, [noninterventional], lighthearted, authentic, questioning, spiritual, intimate, confidential, proactive, tactile[,] and playful.* These practices were confirmed as effective during the period of the Wagner Project funded by the [Lilly] Endowment.

Becoming Part of Something Bigger than Oneself, Allowing Bonding to Occur as Men Share Activities of Deeper Authenticity

It is embarrassing to say what we overlooked as our own St. John's pilot project was undertaken to determine the reasons why Tibetan Buddhist young men became Tibetan Buddhist monks. Initially we suspected that there were six basic reasons for that involvement: education, the monastic lifestyle, politics, economics, and family problems. In a conversation with the head of the Dalai Lama's Government in Dharamsala, we heard that the answer to our question was quite simple: "There is only one reason why you become a Buddhist monk, all others are false: to help other people." Although we call it religious altruism in the chapter on the St. John's project, it may often be an aspect of engagement we easily overlook, namely, engaging college men in the most meaningful activities of our time.

A long-time leader of student development organizations in the United States, Phyllis Mable was often fond of saying that "young people simply yearn to be a part of something bigger than themselves" (personal communication at Longwood College, July 1984). There could be no better example than the last political campaign with throngs of college students working in grass roots organizations and in social networks to have an impact on the future of the nation and the world.

Conversations were most inspiring for participants in the grant overall and in the specific projects when we spoke of expanding men's roles to increase connectedness, to inspire hope, and to engage in activities of care. Around selfless activities and participation in the common good meaningful brotherhood and fellowship develop. We use words such as holy-ethical friendship, character friendship, and friendship with God and recall the relationships the disciples had with Jesus as models of meaningful male bonding that young men are seeking. Without taking the depth of our work into account in this fashion, it does not seem that we can do an adequate job of addressing how to engage college men.

Journey and Pilgrimage Out of the Comfort Zone

Larry Daloz in his engagement with the St. John's conferences and the Gustavus Adolphus project has done more than anyone to raise this aspect of engagement to include reflection on history and mythology. The endless movie remakes of Robin Hood, King Arthur, Alexander the Great, Genghis Khan, and others remind us that this is the time for an odyssey in young men's lives, and being engaged in the great journey is perhaps the key metaphor for engaging college men drawing on an unconscious motivation.

For Daloz, what is central is the fantasy of flight or escape, where vanishing is the incomplete story (for example, in *Born to Run*) and the completion of the journey is to return home again. Mentors play a key role in the journey. We recall that Mentor was the teacher who taught Telemachus, the son of Odysseus while Odysseus was on his journey. We may also think of the relationship between Yoda and Gandalf in the *Star Wars* and *Lord of the Rings* epics.

Through understanding our mythologies, both ancient and modern, we get a richer picture of the ingredients of best practices for engaging college men. That the epic journey of self-discovery is deeply moving to so many young men is evidenced by the popularity of movies such as the recent award-winning movie *Avatar* (2009) or its predecessors, *the Lord of the Rings* trilogy (2001–2003), the six-part *Star Wars* series (1977–2005), or even the Cohen brothers movie based loosely on the *Odyssey*, *O Brother Where Art Thou* (2000).

It seems clear that there is a journey to the forest or wilderness in most of the world's great traditions. The passages describing Jesus in the wilderness or the Hebrews' journey to the promised land are biblical sources reflected in modern journeys. Hesse's (2002) *Siddhartha*, based on the life of the Buddha, and the story in Indian mythology of Rama or the Pandava brothers (Narayan, 2006), who go to the forest to find themselves as men and literally wrestle with demons before returning to society, also remind us of the universality of this quest.

Why Do Best Practices Work?

While there are many ways to analyze the findings of the various approaches described in this book, a few stand out. The participants in the program approached it with a commitment to be interdisciplinary. While not exhaustive, some examples follow of how this was done.

A Data Analysis Perspective to Understanding Best Practices

Perhaps the best way to grasp what works and why is to look at the data from each campus. For example, at Wabash College, the Center for Teaching and Learning in Theology and Religion has consistently shown great success in the preparation of men for the ministry and also high numbers of men volunteering in service projects. Preliminary discussions with William Placher (Chair of the Religion Department at Wabash) indicated that the college environment may have established norms for its male students to participate in these activities.

Charles Blaich, Director of Inquiries at the Center of Inquiry at Wabash, is presently engaged in a National Study of Liberal Arts Education, a large-scale longitudinal study to investigate critical factors that affect the outcome of a liberal arts education. Data are being collected from over 4,500 students in 19 schools to learn what teaching practices, programs, and institutional structures support liberal arts education. Some of them are Programs for the Theological Exploration of Vocation (PTEV) schools, and Blaich has offered an analysis of data that would help identify what works with men and why. He offered the opinion at our first conference that the data collected on the learning environments on each campus showed that what worked on one campus may not necessarily work on other campuses and that the best way to determine successful practices on each campus is through research on the outcomes of projects tried there.

A very interesting laboratory to help us understand what is going on with college men and what works in vocational discernment can be learned from looking at the men's college perspective. Although only a handful of all-men's colleges remain in the country (a topic itself worth further elaboration at another time), all four of them are actively involved in articulating what the ideal educational environment is for college men. Wabash is one of them. Morehouse, Hampden-Sydney, and St. John's University are the other three.

Morehouse College is engaged in the process of assessing the uniqueness of their all-male college environment for its students. Having received a $1 million grant from the Mellon Foundation to address the issues of African-American men in higher education, Morehouse is eager to pursue a research direction to articulate what it means to be a Morehouse Man. They are identifying 20 indicators, such as leadership, service, spirituality, and character development, that they hope will clearly explain how men develop while on their campus. The new president of Morehouse, Robert Michael Franklin, is a minister who has said he wants to intentionally enhance the moral development and spiritual aspects of the Morehouse experience for men.[21]

We arranged a meeting of the men's college presidents for March 2010 so they could meet together at the American Men's Studies Association Conference to share their thoughts and discuss with conference attendees how men's colleges intentionally enhance men's moral and spiritual development. Student representatives from Morehouse, Hampden-Sydney, Wabash, and St. John's were also invited to share their thoughts on how an all-men's college environment makes a valuable contribution to engaging college men. A video of the presentations of the presidents of men's colleges is available from the American Men's Studies Association (www.mensstudies.org)

Men's colleges can be examined for the environment they have fostered that makes spiritual reflection, vocational discernment, and religious practice more normative. Preliminary studies at three of the campuses indicate that a different social norm has been established that encourages spiritual reflection and participation in religious activities and discernment opportunities. In an age when women's roles are changing so rapidly and women have more and more opportunities to undertake roles that have not been traditionally available to them, college men may need to redefine what it means for them to be men. This leads some gender scholars, such as Kilmartin (2000), to say that a redefinition of one traditional masculinity into multiple masculinities more attuned to the uniqueness of each young man is needed. His text is widely used in introductory courses for its clear explanation of the development of men's gender roles. The real goal may be to help each boy or college man to find his true self and to answer the questions: Who am I? What is my core purpose? What is my passion? What do I do about it? and What does the world need from me?

Perhaps the best example of the data analysis approach to increasing men's engagement is Sax (2008), who presented her data at the second conference for pilot

---

[21] Preliminary studies investigating men's spirituality from a social norms perspective have also been carried out at Morehouse as well as at the University of the West Indies and St. John's as part of the PTEV grant.

schools at St. John's. By analyzing Cooperative Institutional Research Program (CIRP) data (CIRP, 2010) on more than 8,000,000 college students, she has illustrated a much more complex picture of what works with college men and what works with college women. For example, when seeking to enhance the spiritual development of women and men, the data show that athletic participation often has a low correlation with spiritual development for women and a high correlation with college men. The scenes of college men praying before games or giving credit to a higher power after scoring points are easy to recall and may be part of the explanation for this correlation. College women, on the other hand, are more often seen as groundbreaking pioneers when participating in athletics and even challenging more traditional views of spirituality by their involvement. Similarly, taking gender studies classes for men is seen as enhancing men's spiritual awareness, while for women the opposite seems to be taking place. Sax's thesis is that it is necessary to get the data on what happens with men and women regarding their college engagement and use those data in designing strategies for increasing participation.

While Linda Sax does not provide explanations beyond reporting the data, a bigger picture seems clear: Some things work well to increase the engagement of men and women, while some things work better for men. It is wise to know the differences based on sound statistical data.

A Gender Studies Perspective and Socially Constructed Masculinity: Men Don't Want to Talk About It

The most obvious explanation for why some of the best practices mentioned above are working is related to a basic component of gender studies: the social construction of masculinity. Both Brannon and Pleck (1978) and O'Neill, Helms, Gable, David, and Wrightsman (1986) have similar descriptions of what constitutes traditional masculinity as it has been constructed in modern society. What it means to be a man and how it is consciously or unconsciously adopted by college men is heavily affected by the pervasive influences of the media, the culture, male and female peers, and family members.

Research over several decades concludes that, when men exhibit traditional masculinity, they are disconnected from their emotions and affections. For O'Neil et al. (1986), there are four measurable scales of traditional masculinity: restricted emotionality, restricted affectionate behavior between men, conflict between work and home, and a commitment to success and power. Brannon and Pleck (1978) put it clearly with their four pillars of masculinity: the "big wheel," the "sturdy oak," "no sissy stuff," and "give 'em hell." Jackson Katz portrays this reality well in his film *Tough Guise* (2000), which shows collages of television advertisements, music, and sports events, and in his recent film on professional wrestling, *Wrestling with Manhood* (2004).

Although decades of women's studies document an increasing flexibility in the roles that women can play in society and liberation from traditional expectations of behavior, there is much less evidence to show that men have gained a similar flexibility from the traditional roles they are expected to play, despite the rapid changes for women. As Obie Clayton of the Morehouse Research Institute articulated at the first conference on the college male: "Women's roles are changing, so men's roles need to change."

The consistent picture from a gender studies perspective is of men disconnected from their emotions and affections and enticed by an ethic of power and success, which leaves them also disconnected from their faith life. As a closer connection to one's true self, feelings, and inner life is a prerequisite for vocational discernment and faith development, this perspective can give a partial explanation for the disproportionate number of women involved in PTEV programs. Experiences in PTEV and campus ministry programs, service projects, and other activities that create safe places and time for reflection and tools for men to discover a deeper faith life and connection with their emotions and each other would therefore not only be liberating and deeply fulfilling but would become part of the solution to the real gender box that men find themselves in today.

A SOCIAL NORMS PERSPECTIVE: MISPERCEIVED MASCULINITY

Men do want to talk about masculinity and spirituality, but they often do not think their friends want to. Social norm theory provides a theory of human behavior that has important implications for men's health promotion and prevention. Used extensively to explain college students' drinking behavior, the theory is based on the premise that a person's choice of behavior is influenced by perceptions of how other members of a social group think and act. This results in behavior that is based on an individual's perception of social norms, which, in the case of masculinity, are based on core beliefs about the manner in which masculinity is enacted socially. Specifically, integrating Brannon and Pleck's (1978) four core beliefs about masculinity into gender role conflict theory, a social norm approach predicts that men will endorse a more traditional conception of masculinity for others than they will for themselves.

Gender role conflict theory has an extensive history of over 25 years of research. One of the oldest instruments used in the psychology of men and masculinity, the O'Neil scale (O'Neil et al., 1986), has been used in over 250 studies and has been correlated with a number of intra- and interpersonal contexts (all the information on other studies is available on O'Neil's website at the University of Connecticut and in Levant and Richmond's (2007) "A Review of Research on Masculinity Ideologies Using the Male Role Norms Inventory." In general, a stronger endorsement of masculinity on the scale has been correlated with depression, low self-esteem, anxiety, drive for muscularity, lower intimacy, positive attitudes toward sexual harassment, rape myth acceptance, and hostile attitudes toward women.

Several years of research on college men at St. John's supports the contention that men's perceptions of social norms about masculinity do restrict men's behavior. Steve Hoover of Saint Cloud State University and I have been collecting data on this phenomenon among college men that may help explain what is going on with them and what works and why in order to develop successful programming. We have been administering the O'Neil scale (O'Neil et al., 1986) to college men on our two campuses and to some of those participating in the grant projects. We are finding not only a significant endorsement of traditional masculinity but also a sense that college men do not necessarily endorse or perform traditional masculinity as much as they think their friends do. In this study, items from the O'Neil scale were administered to college men in two formats: how they themselves would respond to the items and how they believed the typical college male would respond. Social norm theory in the context of traditional notions of masculinity predicts that men will indicate a more traditional attitude toward gender role for others than they will for themselves. The implications are that most college men do not endorse many traditional aspects of masculinity, but, because of their perceptions that other men do, they modify their behavior to be consistent with the perceptions of socially enacted masculinity.

With all due respect to Real (1997), psychologist and author of *I Don't Want to Talk About It*, we think our research shows that men actually do want to tell their stories and share with each other (and probably those close to them) on a deeper personal level, but they often think that other men do not want to or that somehow it is not masculine to do that. Research, then, points to the likelihood that men's groups may work because they provide a safe place for men to get under the mask, take off the armor, discontinue the posturing, and be who they really are where they will be treated with respect and dignity.

A Spiritual Development Perspective to Understanding What Works

College students are deeply interested in spirituality. Building on the recent work of Astin and Astin (2003), which shows that there is great interest in spirituality among the majority of college students, recent work on spirituality and religiosity has been published by Chickering, Dalton, and Stamm (2006). Their work articulates many dimensions of college students' religious life and also takes a close look at understanding what is happening during James Fowler's stages of faith development. Fowler (1995) postulated 6 stages of faith development in his work *Stages of Faith*. Lisa Stamm (2006) suggests that greater focus is needed on the time between the stages of adolescence and young adulthood in Fowler's model. She suggests incorporating Parks' (2000) work on faith development for the college years. Parks proposes a young adult stage between Fowler's adolescent and adult stages entitled "young adult faith," which she says is typical of college students. In the adolescent stage young people may tend toward an uncritically embraced worldview and beliefs and values in the form of an ideology. In the young adulthood stage "the emerging faith associated with this stage involves the capacity for self-reflection, the relativity of one's inherited worldview and the rejection of literal interpretations of faith stories and myths" (see Chickering et al., pp. 56–58). She urges college faculty and staff members to be more sophisticated in their understanding of the diversity of the faith formation process and mindful of the importance of intellectual development as well as the quest for and practice of faith in the world of work. While the study says little about gender differences of college men and women (except for the fact that women are consistently more interested in faith formation than men), it does give a clearer picture of this developmental stage. Such an approach might lead to an improved understanding of the spiritual and religious development of young men.[22]

What does it mean to focus specifically on the spirituality and religious development of boys and college-age men? Some will say that a disproportionate amount has already been written by men and from a male perspective and more study of men is not needed. What is emerging in recent decades in several disciplines, however, is the need to better understand boys and men for who they are. What needs to be heard is what males say spirituality and religiosity means to them. What is needed is a focus on their experiences and not just their behavior with a consciousness of what it means to be a boy or a man in our culture.

Boyd, Muesse, and Longwood (1996) have focused on college men's spirituality. Kirkley (1996) has asked the question: Is it manly to be Christian? Bill Shipper and Merle Longwood are preparing a study of the spiritual lives of American college men. Their current project is to research the impact of discernment groups or spirituality groups on college men by looking at those groups on different college campuses. Their expectation is that the religious missions of institutions have different effects on men's religious and spiritual development. What emerged from their study (funded by PTEV) of spirituality groups is that self-understanding is promoted when men tell their stories in confidential safe places. Enhanced self-understanding was reflected in deeper and satisfying relationships within the groups ("I am closer to the groups members than to my friends") and enhanced relationships with significant others outside the groups. Members developed a greater sense of spirituality and connection to God, the universe, and others. There was a more sophisticated understanding of what vocation meant to the participants, although it appeared in the later years of group participation. There was evidence of improved life skills of listening, sharing, and reflection. Although not all had decided on their true callings, their vocational priorities had been refined in the process.

If there is one overriding recommended best practice that has come out of this grant program and the pilot projects, it is that college men's groups—more specifically men's spirituality groups—are well worth attempting on any campus even

---

[22] Rhoda Reddock and Patricia Mohammed in the Centre for Gender and Development studies, University of the West Indies, have become keenly interested in the importance of creating safe reflection spaces for young men as part of their development and will soon offer important insights to help in the understanding of this on a deeper level.

though they may take different forms on different campuses. With over 10 years of success involving 150–200 college men and 20 mentors each year and several studies of their success, St. John's has spawned other versions of mens' spirituality groups on campuses funded by the Lilly grant. During the grant period, the University of Portland, Siena College, and Wagner College found their own versions to be successful in different ways.

Keith Daniel, the chaplain at Duke University, is also deeply interested in this approach to the topic, which is closely related to the many years of his own work in a men's group and his attempt to identify the formation process for African-American men. He suggests reading Bass's (2001) *Receiving the Day* and Eldrege's *Wild at Heart* (2001) and is writing on the masculine journey and the male heart. One might say that if attention is not paid to a positive ritual dimension of college life, male students will create their own rituals that might not be aligned with institutional values. The national drink-a-case-of-beer day and hazing are two sad examples. Daniel has summarized what is at stake here: "What we are about is unlocking men's hearts" (K. Daniel, personal communication, August 2007).

Unlocking the Hearts of Boys and College Men would perhaps be the best name for a program to create the conditions for college men to do deeper reflection and to work on the social conventions that prohibit them from finding their passions. The environments that are safe havens from the video games and the peer and academic pressures that reinforce insensitivity can be created on campuses; these can be places where boys and men can get in touch with where their hearts are and listen for the "still small voice." This may be the most compelling metaphor for the program described in these pages.

Where Does the Work Go from Here?
More Men's Groups and Expanding the High School Youth Track

Given the success of the social norm masculinity research and research on college men's spirituality groups described above, we decided to end the grant with a deeper look at 10 campuses on these scales. These data are now being collected and will form the basis for a case we seek to make for why men's groups should be considered seriously for implementation on many campuses. Longwood, Shipper, and a team of researchers (Steve Hoover, Tim Baker, and me) from the Minnesota State Colleges are in the process of surveying college men on most of the Lilly Grant campuses. The data will be analyzed to see if the patterns described above hold true.

Meanwhile, Jeff Kaster, project leader of the Youth Track Initiative at St. John's, is leading an effort with additional generous funding from the Lilly Endowment. Already, it is clear to him: "We have only scratched the surface of many complex realities that have an impact on vocational discernment in high school youth; we need to be much more intentional about exploring the theology of baptism and vocation and its impact on our understanding of gender, gender roles, power and privilege; we must become more aware of the cultural issues that influence male participation in youth ministry, but more importantly we need to challenge cultural gender norms in light of the gospel; and we need to listen to the diversity of voices of the young church. We should listen to what they think, believe, and feel about vocation, youth ministry, and gender issues" (Jeff Kaster—in his end of grant report, Spring 2010).

Listening to the voices of high school youth will be essential to understanding the issues raised in this book. It will be essential in crafting a curricular response that is faithful to the gospel.

And so the program described in these pages will live on and will do so in many different forms. Some of the projects described are being continued at campuses because they were successful at making changes in campus culture to create better learning environments for college men. The Luther College program is a good example of this. Others will live on in the present volume and in research, presentations, web seminars and publications that are to come (Kellom, Groth, Daniel, Marks, & Johnston, 2010). In general, the Lilly Grant program was an extraordinarily successful experience for all involved, and it is with gratitude to the Lilly Endowment and all who participated and will continue the work that we end this chapter of the story of our efforts to find best practices for engaging more college men.

References

Astin, A., & Astin, H. (2003). Spirituality in higher education, a national study of college students' search for meaning and purpose. Higher Education Research Institute (HERI), http://www.gseis.ucla.edu/heri/spirituality.html.

Bass, D. (2001). *Receiving the day: Christian practices for opening the gift of time*. San Francisco: Jossey-Bass.

Boyd, S., Muesse, M., & Longwood, M. (Eds.). (1996). *Redeeming men: Religion and masculinities*. Louisville: Westminster John Knox Press.

Brannon, R., & Pleck, J.H. (1978). Male roles and the male experience. *Journal of Social Issues 34*, 1–4.

Chickering, A., Dalton, J., & Stamm, L. (2006). *Encouraging authenticity and spirituality in higher education*. San Francisco: Jossey-Bass.

CIRP (2010). Cooperative Institutional Research Program, Higher Education Research Institute (HERI) at the University of California, Los Angeles. http://www.heri.ucla.edu/cirpoverview

Eldredge, J. (2001). *Wild at heart: Discovering the secret of a man's soul*. Nashville: Thomas Nelson.

Fowler, J. (1995). *Stages of faith: The psychology of human development*. San Francisco: HarperOne.

Groth, M. (2010). *Being and working with college males*. Unpublished manuscript.

Hesse, H. (2002). *Siddhartha*. New York: Penguin Books.

Kellom, G., Groth, M., Daniel, K., Marks, B., & Johnston, S. (2010, March 27). Panel Presentation: Best practices for college males' engagement in the common good: Pilot projects from fourteen colleges and universities. Presented at the American Men's Studies Association AMSA annual meeting, Atlanta.

Kilmartin, C. (2000). *The masculine self* (2nd ed.). New York: McGraw-Hill.

Kimmel, M. (2009). *Guyland. The perilous world where boys become men.* New York: Harper and Row.

Kirkley, E. (2007. Is it manly to be Christian? The debate in Victorian and modern America. In S.M. Boyd, M. Muesse, & M. Longwood (Eds.), *Redeeming men: Religion and masculinities* (pp. 80–88). Louisville: Westminster John Knox Press.

Levant, R., & Richmond, K. (2007). A review of research on masculinity ideologies using the Male Role Norms Inventory. *The Journal of Men's Studies, 15*(2), 130-146.

Narayan, R. (2006). *The Ramayana: A shortened prose version of the Indian epic.* New York: Penguin Books.

O'Neil, J., Helms, B., Gable, R., David, L., & Wrightsman, L. (1986). Gender role conflict scale: College men's fear of femininity. *Sex Roles, 14*(5-6), 335–350.

Parks, S. (2000). *Big questions, worthy dreams: Mentoring young adults in their search for meaning, purpose, and faith.* San Francisco: Jossey-Bass.

Real, T. (1997). *I don't want to talk about it.* New York: Scribner.

Sax, L. (2008). *The gender gap in college: Maximizing the developmental potential of women and men.* San Francisco: Jossey-Bass.

Stamm, L. (2006). The dynamics of spirituality and the religious experience. In A. Chickering, J. Dalton, & L. Stamm (Eds.), *Encouraging authenticity and spirituality in higher education* (pp. 37–65). San Francisco: Jossey-Bass.

Participating Schools and Contact Personnel

- Augustana College: Professor Robert Haak, who turned it over to Rebecca A. Poock, Community Engagement Coordinator
- Davidson College: Tim Beach-Verhey, PTEV Program Director
- Duke University: Reverend Keith Daniel, Campus Ministry Office
- Georgetown College: Roger Ward, Coordinator of the Meetinghouse Project, who turned it over to Bryan Langlands of Campus Ministry
- Gustavus Adolphus College: Chris Johnson, Director of the Center for Vocational Reflection.
- Hastings College: Professor Daniel Deffenbaugh, Department of Religion, and Ronald Chesbrough, Vice President for Student Affairs
- Hope College: Professor David S. Cunningham
- Luther College: Stuart Johnston, Licensed Mental Health Counselor
- Morehouse College: Professor Bryant T. Marks, Psychology Department
- Saint John's University: Gar Kellom, Director, the Center for Men's Leadership and Service
- Siena College: Professor Merle Longwood, Religion Department
- University of Portland: Josh Noem, Assistant Director for Faith Formation in the Office of Campus Ministry
- Wabash College: Charles Blaich, who turned it over to Anne Bost and Sonia Nino, research fellows at the Center for Inquiry in the Liberal Arts
- Wagner College: Professor Miles Groth, Psychology Department

Further Reading

Allen, K., & Kellom, G. (2001a). The role of spirituality in student affairs and staff development. In M. Jablonski (Ed.), *Student spirituality and student affairs practice* (pp. 47–56). New Directions for Student Services, #95, San Francisco: Jossey-Bass.

Allen, K., & Kellom, G. (2001b). Learning to connect, spirituality and leadership. In V. Miller & M. Ryan (Eds.), *Transforming campus life: Reflections on spirituality and religious pluralism* (pp. 161–172). New York: Peter Lang.

Beaudoin, T. (2000). *Virtual faith.* New York: John Wiley & Sons.

Berry, W. (1999). *The memory of old Jack* (2nd ed.). Washington, DC: Counterpoint.

Bissinger, H. (2004). *Friday night lights* (2nd ed.). Cambridge: DaCapo Press.

Boyd, S., Muesse, M., & Longwood, M. (Eds.). (1996). *Redeeming men: Religion and masculinities.* Louisville: Westminster John Knox Press.

Chickering, A., Dalton, J., & L. Stamm, L. (Eds.). (2006). *Encouraging authenticity and spirituality in higher education.* San Francisco: Jossey-Bass.

Colton, L. (2001). *Counting coup* (2nd ed.). New York: Warner Books.

DeBoer, K. (2004). *Gender and competition.* Monterey: Coaches Choice.

Englar-Carlson, M., & Stevens, M. (Eds.). (2006). *In the room with men.* Washington, DC: American Psychological Association.

Guinness, O. (2003). *The call* (2nd ed.). Nashville: Thomas Nelson.

Huang, C., & Lynch, J. (Eds.). (1995). *Mentoring: The Tao of giving and receiving wisdom.* New York: HarperCollins.

Iversen, J. (2005). *21.* New York: Simon Pulse.

Just, W. (2005). *An unfinished season* (2nd ed.). New York: Houghton Mifflin.

Longwood, M. (2007). Forging the male spirit: The spiritual lives of college men. Paper presented at American Men's Studies Association meeting, Kansas City, March 30–April 1.

Maclean, N. (2001). *A river runs through it and other stories* (2nd ed.). Chicago: University of Chicago Press.

Mahan, B. (2002). *Forgetting ourselves on purpose.* San Francisco: Jossey-Bass.

Marx, J. (2003). *Season of life.* New York: Simon & Schuster.

Moehringer, J. (2005). *The tender bar.* New York: Hyperion.

Pellegrini, R., & Sarbin, T. (Eds.). (2002). *Between fathers and sons.* Binghamton, NY: Haworth Clinical Practice Press.

Pollack, W. (1999). *Real boys* (2nd ed.). New York: Henry Holt.

Rindo, R. (1995). *Secrets men keep.* Minneapolis: New Rivers Press.

Schwehn, M., & Bass, D. (Eds.). (2006). *Leading lives that matter.* Grand Rapids, MI: William B. Eerdmans.

Taylor, C., & Taylor-Ide, D. (Eds.). (2002). *Just and lasting change. When communities own their futures.* Baltimore: Johns Hopkins University Press.

Tolstoy, L. (1981). *The death of Ivan Ilyich.* New York: Bantam Books.

Wiltshire, S. (1998). *Athena's disguises.* Louisville: Westminster John Knox Press.

APPENDICES

Appendix A
PTEV Programs That Attract Substantially Higher Numbers of One Gender or the Other

Those That Attract More Women

Missions/service learning (9)
Retreats (9)
Discussion groups (5)
Ministries/ministry preparation (5):
- Youth (1)
- Lay preparation (1)
- Ministerial mini-grants (1)
- Liturgical music preparation (1)
- Women's ministry and leadership program participation (1)

Internships (4):
- Congregational (2)
- Summer (2)

Vocational exploration/spiritual formation (3)
Leadership development (3)
Summer programs (2)
Reflection/exploration programs (2)
Mentoring (2)
Seminary preparation (2)

Other—Academic
- Scholars programs
- Liberal-arts-oriented programs
- Women's studies program through PTEV
- Institution's curricular program (which includes scholarships)
- Nursing, physical therapy, and occupational therapy programs

Other
- College conference
- *Enneagram System*[23] workshops
- Paid leadership roles in residence hall ministry
- PTEV-program-sponsored intentional Christian community (in a house in the campus student community)

---

[23] The Enneagram System is a model of human personality that uses an enneagram, or nine-sided star polygon, as a template. Source: http://www.enneagraminstitute.com/intro.asp

- Career services week
- Worship attendance
- Speakers

Those That Attract More Men

Ministry (5)
- Ministry student formation
- Ministry discernment
- Programs related to consecrated/priestly ministry groups
- Programs specifically about ministerial vocations
- Congregational ministry opportunities

Activities (4)
- Science-oriented programs
- Intermural sport and obviously single-gender sports, such as men's soccer
- Hands-on activities
- Campus ministry mountain camping event

Seminary/divinity school preparation (3)

Internships (2)

Other
- Small leadership/discussion group
- Fellowship of Christian Athletes
- Courses

Those That Attract Similar Numbers of Men and Women in Proportion to Enrollment

Internships (2)
Divinity school/seminary preparation (2)
National Orthodox Christian Fellowship programs
Required general education course for new students
Summer ministry grants
Pre-theology programs
Presidential honors program
Vocational retreat participation

Appendix B
Lessons Learned from PTEV Programs Working to Address Gender Imbalance

Making Men Comfortable with Theological Exploration of Vocation

- Men want to "do" together, not "be" together.
- Men are less willing than women to be with people they don't know—recruiting cohorts and allowing them to remain together is more effective than reaching out to individuals.
- Gain support and involvement of those faculty and staff respected by men, who teach in more heavily male departments, such as athletic coaches
- Help men understand how their maleness can be an asset to various programs. They are not used to seeing it as a factor.
- Gender-balanced leadership in programs helps students identify with a same-gender role model. It's even more helpful if the male role model is identified with traditionally masculine activities, such as football.
- Use a "ministry of presence"; be engaged in the activities that interest male students.
- The most successful outreach comes when the person doing the outreach is well-integrated into the campus life as a whole and makes connections that can grow toward helping guide people toward exploring vocations.
- Work with departments that have a heavy concentration of men, focus on activities that men enjoy, and let reflection happen around these activities.
- Targeted outreach is usually most successful, such as a personal invitation, especially if it comes from a male.
- Programs that rely on faculty nominations will help with balance, although this results in more competitiveness among women.

Incentives

- Giving men incentives (restaurant gift certificates) to recruit their male friends can be effective.
- Don't underestimate the appeal of offering free food with the activity, especially for students who live off campus.

Countering Outside Influences

- Parents can be a barrier to male participation in service and reflection activities. They have different expectations of sons and of daughters. Addressing this up front, during the parent component of orientation, can help.

Appendix C
Responses to Participant Surveys

		First Survey			Second Survey		Both Surveys	
Institution	#P	#R	RR (%)		#R	RR (%)	#R	RR (%)
Augustana College	17	2	11.8		0	0.0	0	0.0
Duke University	20	7	35.0		4	20.0	3	15.0
Georgetown College	10	3	30.0		2	20.0	2	20.0
Gustavus Adolphus College	11	1	9.1		2	18.2	0	0.0
Hastings College	13	8	61.5		8	61.5	6	46.2
Hope College	331	64	19.3		87	26.3	33	10.0
Luther College	76	13	17.1		7	9.2	4	5.3
Siena College	20	6	30.0		10	50.0	6	30.0
St. John's University	22	7	31.8		3	13.6	2	9.1
University of Portland	27	15	55.6		11	40.7	8	29.6
Wabash College	4	2	50.0		1	25.0	1	25.0
Wagner College	4	1	25.0		1	25.0	1	25.0
Totals	**555**	**129**	**23.2**		**136**	**24.5**	**66**	**11.9**

#P = Number of participants   #R = Number of responses   RR = Response rate

INDEX

Academic Impressions 21
Adam, Where Are You? Why Black Men Don't Go to Church 68
adventure travel 170-182
African American Male Identity and Spirituality 64
African-American men 62, 63, 64, 66, 71, 72, 275, 280
alumni 98-105
American Men's Studies Association 11, 14, 22, 275, 282
Annual Conference on the College Male 11, 88, 89, 228
Antwone Fisher 229, 232
application rates 252-254
armored boy 137
athletes 85-97 athletics 158, 268, 271, 276
attendance rates 252-263
Augustana College 16, 17, 89, 98-104, 270
Avatar 274

baptism 261-263
Barr, Cameron 185
Beach-Verhey, Tim 15
Beaudin, William, Fr. 208
Beleaguered Rulers: The Public Obligation of the Professional, 159
Bible, The Holy 71
Big Questions, Worthy Dreams 103
Black maleness 63
Blaich, Charles 14, 15, 48, 253, 274
Bonhoeffer, Dietrich 229
Booher, Kristin 184
Born to Run 273
Bost, Anne 15, **158-169**
Brod, Harry 21
Brooks, Catherine **24-39**
Brooks Research 16, 17
Brouwer, Wayne 57
Bruketta, Thomas **195-207**
Buddhism 110-117, 121, 125-128, 131, 133
Burshteyn, Dmitry 210
Butts, Calvin 63

C. Charles Jackson Foundation 141
Called to Serve 98

calling 61-73, 86, 217, 224-225
Center for Inquiry in the Liberal Arts 46
Center for Men's Leadership and Service (CMLS) (Saint John's University) 10, 14, 16, 17, 21, 22, 91, 107
Center for Vocational Reflection (CVR) (Augustana College) 98, 99, 100, 102, 103, 104, 134, 136
Charles in Charge 262
Chesbrough, Ronald D. **74-83**
Chodorow, Nancy 79
Christian Reformed Church 39
church 254, 257, 258, 262, 263 attendance 67
Clayton, Obie 277
Cleary, Corbin J. 107, **108-110**, 267
coaches 86-88, 94, 95
College Men's Initiative 228, 230
College of Saint Benedict 10, 11, 108, 129
College Senior Survey 162
College Students and Service: A Mixed Methods Exploration of Motivations, Choices, and Learning Outcomes 76
Common Fire 155
Conference on the College Male 11, 17, 19-22, 48
Corrie, Elizabeth 251, 253, 256, 261
Council of Christian Colleges and Universities 40
CrossRoads Project (Hope College) 42-45, 48, 49, 59
Cunningham, David S. 14, 15, **39-60**

Dalai Lama 110, 111, 114, 121-123, 273
Daloz, Laurent A. Parks 135, 136, 137, **146-157**, 273
Daniel, Keith 15, **227-230**, 280
Davidson College 8, 15, **183-193**, 270
Deep M-Pact (project) **134-145**, 146, **149-155**
Deffenbaugh, Daniel G. 16, **74-83**
Dharma 116, 117, 126, 127
disclosure 271, 272
Doerr, Roger 75, 76, 82
Duke University 8, 15, 19, **227-235**, 270, 280
Durnin, Mike 86
Dwyer, Daniel, Fr. 210

Edie, Fred P. 18, 251, 253, 261, 263
Ehrmann, Joe 86, 89
emerging adulthood (Arnett) 50
engagement 39-59
enrollment 8, 10, 24-33, 43, 75, 195
Evangelical Lutheran Church in America 85, 134
expository writing 58

facilitation 65, 69, 70
Faculty Seminar 50, 51, 54, 57
fathers 63, 66, 70, 259, 261
field trips 43, 48, 53
Fight Club 94
Firmin, Michael W. 21, **236-249**
five wells (Morehouse) 64
Food 4 Thought (program) 75, 82
Franciscans 212-216
Franke, Terry 271
Franklin, Robert Michael 11, 64, 275
fraternities 98-105
Fraternity Alumni Network (FAN) 98-105
Fund for Theological Education 13, 17, 24
Furman University 8

gender disparity, in college 8, 11, 19, 24, 40
gender theory 12, 19
Georgetown College 8, 15, **170-182**, 270
Gilligan, Carol 79, 80
Gilmore, David 147, 149
Glover, Kyle 217, 222, **223-224**
Good Will Hunting 94
Grennes, Matthew 158
Grimm, Jamie **195-207**
Grimm, Jordan 85, **94-96**
Groth, Miles 16, **217**, **224-226**
Gustavus Adolphus College 16, 17, **134-145**, **146-157**, 270
Guyland 271

Haak, Robert 16
Hager, Andrew **217-222**
Hande, Katherine 18
Hastings College 16, **74-83**, 270
Heisler, Edward 21, **236-249**
Heller, Juliann 251
Higher Education Research Institute 162

Hilding, Benjamin **134-145**
Hope College 8, 14-15, **39-60**, 270
Horn, David 251, 252
Huddleston, Jesse 227, **230-235**
hyper-masculine 63, 73

I Don't Want to Talk About It 278
Iliad 152
India 107-113, 120, 122, 124-133
initiation, male 149, 150, 155, 156
Integrated Postsecondary Education Data System 25
internships 32
Involving College Males (project) 170
Involving More Men in Vocational Discernment Activities: Identifying and Implementing Best Practices (Lilly) 170

Jackson, Samuel 64
Jock, William 217, **222-223**
Jodock, Darrell 135
Johnson, Christopher 16, **134-145**
Johnston, Stuart (Stu) 13, 15, **85-87**, 88, 89, 93, 94, **96-97**
Jones, Marquan **61-73**
Journal of Men's Studies, The 22, 277
Justad, Mark 14

Kaster, Jeffrey 17-19, **251-264**
Katz, Jackson 276
Kaufman, Michael 21
Kellom, Gar **8-23**, 24, 34, 91, **107-108**, 110, 129, 130, 227, **266-282**
Kennedy-Farrell, Megan 251, 253, 258
Kilmartin, Chris 10, 275
Kimmel, Michael 21, 271
King, Martin Luther 63
Knowledge Community for Men 22
Kohlberg 79, 80

Langlands, Bryan 15, **170-182**
Larson-Taylor, Barbara 149
leadership 9-17, 21, 22, 41, 46
League of Extraordinary Gentlemen, The (LXG) **195-207**, 268 core values 197, 198, 201 evaluation 202 format 199 history 195 logo 197, 199 mentor reports 202 pre- and

INDEX

posttesting 204 structure 197 student perspective 201
Lee, Spike 64
leisure time 78
Leitch, Ashleigh 107, 108, **124-129**
Lilly Endowment 8, 9, 15, 16, 18, 19, 20, 24, 33, 34, 39, 41, 55, 61, 74, 75, 88, 89, 93, 107, 108, 134, 141, 170, 173, 175, 181, 183, 184, 185, 193, 208, 217, 224, 251, 252, 257, 266, 270, 271, 272, 280, 281
Liss, Walter, Br. 210
Lives to Offer 251, 254, 255
Long, Kyle 151
Longwood, W. Merle 14, 16, 20, **208-216**
Lord of the Rings 273, 274
Lovelace, Mark 95
Luther Athletes Serving Others (LASO) 89-93
Luther College 8, 13, 15, **85-97**, 270, 281

Mable, Phyllis 273
Male Initiative 183, 184
man up 63
manhood 147-149, 152-154, 218, 219, 220, 222, 226, 230, 231, 232, 234
Manquisition 201
Mansgiving 201
Marks, Bryant T. 13, 16, **61-73**
Martin, Karen **183-193**
masculinity 20, 21, 85-87, 89, 93, 96, 271, 275-277, 278, 280 false 87 misperceived 277 strategic 87
May, Kevin 107
Mays, Benjamin E. 68
Mellody, Michael 185
Mellon Foundation 11
men's colleges 10, 11, 14
men's health 21, 22
Men's Leadership Team (MLT) 140-142
Men's Leadership Through College (course) 76
men's movement 149
Men's Spirituality Program (University of Portland) 196, 197
Men's Studies Press, The 10
mentoring 134-145, 150, 218, 220, 221, 224, 270, 272 intergenerational 136-138, 144, 154 mentoring community 134-138, 140, 143, 145

Mercer, Joyce Ann 251, 254
micro-grants **170-182**, 270
ministry preparation 32
Mohammed, Patricia 279
monastic life 110-123, 125, 127
monomyth (Campbell) 156
Montaño, Jesus 55, 56
Morehouse College 11, 13, 14, 16, **61-73** mission statement 64 Morehouse Male Initiative Seminar 61-73 Morehouse Man 11, 275
Moss, Otis, Jr. 63
Muesse, Mark 210
Myhre, Jennifer 92

National Association of Student Personnel Administrators 22
National Basketball Association (NBA) 188
National Center for Victims of Crime 236
National Collegiate Athletic Association 92
National Survey of Student Engagement 41
Native American literature 56
Nelson, Jessica 107, 108, **124-129**
Nepal 107-111, 122, 124, 129-133
Ninon, Sonia 15, **158-169**
Noddings, N. 79
Noem, Josh 16, **195-207**

O Brother Where Art Thou 274
O'Neil scale 277-278
Obama, Barack Hussein 68
Odyssey 152
Ogden, Samuel 211
Ondell, Todd 94, 95, 96
Osborne, Mark 107

partnerships (Faculty-Student-Expert) 14
pastoral leadership 9
PathWays (program) 8, 229-230
Peacebuilders 251-253, 258, 259
Phillips, Gary 14
pilot projects 9, 15, 17, 18, 20 pilot schools 14, 15, 17, 19
Placher, William 11
Plunge to Poverty 170, 171, 178, 180
Poock, Rebecca A. **98-105**
postsecular academy 52
prayer 67

Index

Pross, Christoph 185
puer aeternus 137, 151

race, and PTEV 25, 28, 30
Raverty, Aaron 110
Receiving the Day 280
Reddock, Rhoda 279
Reformed Church in America 39
religious altruism 112, 114, 125, 127
Research and Theory Team 13, 14, 20
Ries, Jack 109
road trips 270 Road Trip Nation 184, 185, 270
Road Trip project (Davidson college) 184-193
Roehling, Pat 46
Rooy, John Van 107, 108, **131-132**

Sachs, Jeffrey 131
Saladin, Brett 266
Satcher, David 64
Sax, Linda 276
Schipper, William, Fr. 208
Season of Life 85, 86, 91
Seifert, Charles 210
Seminar, Academic Impressions Web 21
Senior Seminar 43, 55
service learning 9
sexism 236, 239, 240, 241, 243, 244, 246, 247, 248
sexual ethics 54
sexual orientation 255, 261
Shipper, William C., Fr. 210
Siddhartha 274
Siena College 14, 16, 20, 208, 209, 210, 211, 212, 213, 214, 215, 216, 270, 272, 280
Simon, Carol 54
Simon, Caroline 45
Smith, Katherine Hande 251, 253
spirituality 9-23, 64, 67-71, 223-225, 251, 253, 254, 256, 257, 259, 270, 272, 275-282 spirituality groups 208-216
St. John's University **10-23**, 39, 88, 91, **107-133**, 196, 208-216, 217, 224, 227, 228, 251-253, 256, 266-277, 280. *See also* Center for Men's Leadership and Service
Star Wars 273, 274
Stewart, Coran **170-182**

Stewart, Joanne 51
Storslee, Mark 231
Student Athlete Advisory Committee (SAAC) 88
student leaders 267
suicide 13, 148
Sullivan, Louis 64
Summer Seminar 49, 51, 53, 56
Surface, Jacob 158

testimonials 65, 70, 73
The Audacity of Hope 68
The Mentor's Guide 101
The Road Less Traveled 68
The Scandal of the Evangelical Mind 52
Theological Exploration of Vocation (PTEV) 8-17, 24-34, 39-43, 45-46, 48, 59, 74, 94, 134, **158-169**, 183, 185, 227, 274, 275, 277, 279 PTEV Programs that attract substantially higher numbers 286, 288 lessons learned 288
Theological Programs for High School Youth (Lilly) 18, 19
think-tank 10, 18, 19, 251, 253-255, 263
Thomas, Alvin 107, 108, **110-124**
Thurman, Howard 63, 229
Tibet 110-112, 115, 120-133 Tibetan Buddhism 110, 121, 131
Torigian, Alec 109
Total Leadership 76
Tough Guise 276

University of Portland 16, **195-207**

violence 255, 261-263 against women 236-241, 244-248 antiviolence groups 236, 238, 240, 244-246 gender equality 236-248 knowledge and empathy 239 male privilege 244, 246
Visions for Black Men 68
vocation 8-10, 12, 16, 18, 19, 21, 24, 98, 101, 104, 105, **158-169** attitudes toward 35-37 discernment **8-23**, 41, 43-45, 59, 61, 72, 85, 86, 93, 94, 107, 108, 110, 111, 113, 118, 121, 124, 125, 129, 146, 150, 154, 170, 179, 181, 229, 232, 251, 254-256, 261, 263 language of 43, 45, 59

293

INDEX

Vocation and Values Program (Hastings) 74-76, 82-83
Volunteer Tibet 111, 115, 120
volunteering and volunteerism 9, 109, 110, 230, 233, 234, 253, 256, 257
vulnerable expression 61-63, 66-73

Wabash College 11, 14, 15, **158-169**, 252, 253, 263, 270, 274 Gentlemen's Rule 158
Wabash Study 41, 45-48, 50, 51, 59, 146, 151
Wagner College 16, 17, **217-226**, 270, 272, 280 Men's Center 217, 224 Men's Project 217, 218, 220, 223-225
Wallace, Michael 107, 108, **129-131**
Ward, Roger 15
Wehr, Peter 85, 87, **88-93**
Wiginton, Melissa 13, 17
Wild at Heart 280
Wollenhaupt, Grant 266
Wrestling with Manhood 276

Young, Jennifer 58
Youth Ministry 251-257, 259, 261, 263
Youth Track 16, 18, 19, 251, 270, 280